Antique Trader®

Kitchen Collectibles

PRICE GUIDE

Edited by **Kyle Husfloen**

Published by

700 East State Street • Iola, WI 54990-0001
715-445-2214 • 888-457-2873
www.krausebooks.com

Our toll-free number to place an order or obtain a free catalog is (800) 258-0929.

ON THE COVER: Left: a Clawson & Clark No. 1 Upright Coffee Mill, **$1,050**; center: a Master egg beater patent-dated 1909, **$1,500**; right: Ceramic two-piece teapot-style juice reamer with colorful flowers, made in Japan, **$60-$70**; upper right: Rice Crispy Chef chalkware string holder, **$145**.

Library of Congress Control Number: 2007924545

ISBN-13: 978-0-89689-567-6
ISBN-10: 0-89689-567-X

Designed by Wendy Wendt
Edited by Kyle Husfloen

Printed in China

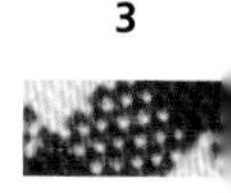

Table of Contents

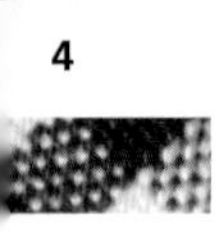

Collecting From Our Kitchens

Most of us probably have many fond memories of time spent in our Mom's or grandmother's kitchen while growing up. Of course, we've all heard that "The Kitchen is the Heart of the Home," and in many ways it was and is. The sights, the sounds and the scents of the kitchen can stir up many a happy memory.

I've been fortunate to have had the chance to "experience" during my lifetime a diversity of kitchens, from simple farm house kitchens harking back to the early decades of the 20th century, to remodeled streamlined wonderlands of today. Each can have its special appeal. For me, the old-time kitchen seems to have the greatest attraction, though. I can recall visits to a small country kitchen over 50 years ago…well worn but cozy with the old wood burning range, oilcloth-covered kitchen table and simple café curtains. Like "vintage" kitchens from

My mom standing proudly in her brand new kitchen in early 1956. Note the built-in dishwasher in the foreground, a real status symbol back then. The "Mod" hanging fixture above the table did pull up and down and, yes, the vinyl and tubular steel chairs were bright yellow to match the yellow Formica top on the kitchen table.

generations before, this room had seen the hustle and bustle of the day-to-day life of a hardworking farm family of eight. I can also recall with happy memories the "state of the art" kitchen in the new home my folks built in 1955. It's a bit hard for me to realize that the furniture, appliances, dishes and utensils that were my mother's pride and joy are now "hot" collectibles.

These are just a couple of the numerous kitchens I can recall with happy memories and so I'm pleased to present here a guide to collecting the vast array of "kitchen collectibles" that are so popular with collectors today.

In order to present the topic in an organized manner, I have chosen to divide this book into two main sections: The Vintage Kitchen – 1850-1920, and The Modern Kitchen – 1920-1980. These dates are somewhat arbitrary since you will find some items included here that pre-date 1850 and a few that may post-date 1980. However, I based this plan on the fact that during the early 20th century the American kitchen saw a rapid evolution brought about by technology. By the 1920s electricity was becoming more widespread around the country and electrical appliances were becoming an essential part of the "modern" kitchen of that day. The storage and preparation of foodstuffs became easier and more efficient and gradually the Victorian era quaintness gave way to a "streamlined" modern look.

Today I think folks who collect the dishes, utensils and appliances of the past are generally divided into two groups...those who prefer the "primitive" charm of items commonly in use before around 1920 and those who focus on the plethora of objects produced since then. Whether you enjoy the "antique" look or select objects used in kitchens of the 1930s, 1940s, 1950s or 1960s, there certainly are plenty of fun items to choose from. Additionally, it's nice to know that there are neat pieces to fit every budget, from a 1930s wooden-handled utensil for under $10 to a rare early American hand-carved burl wood bowl worth over $1,000.

I hope you'll enjoy looking through this comprehensive guide to the Great American Kitchen. You'll find over 2,300 individual listings highlighted by nearly 1,400 full-color photos, all organized for easy reference. I'm including a detailed "Table of Contents" to help guide you through this adventure and I hope these pages will stir up many a happy memory for you too.

Kyle Husfloen, Editor

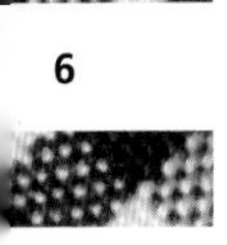

Special Contributors

This price guide would note have been possible without the expert input of a number of contributors, people with special knowledge of specific subcategories of kitchen collectibles. I would like to acknowledge these folks here.

A special "thank you" is extended to my Contributing Editor, Francee Boches of Cheshire Cat Antiques. She did major work in updating pricing information on a number of categories and also supplied a wonderful selection of new color images included here.

Her knowledge of this huge collecting field was invaluable.

Francee Boches
Cheshire Cat Antiques
162 Pinecrest Dr.
Miami Springs, FL 33166-5249
(305) 884- 0335

The many other contributors are listed alphabetically below along with their specialties:

Ellen Bercovici
360 – 11th Ave. So.
Naples, FL 34102 - Egg Times, Pie Birds, String Holders

Bobbie Zucker Bryson
634 Cypress Hills Dr.
Bluffton, SC 29909-6110
e-mail: Napkindoll@aol.com - Napkin Dolls, Reamers, Tea Serving Accessories

Ruth Capper
1167 Teal Road SW
Dellroy, OH 44620 - Cookie Cutters

Kerra Davis
1770 Mershon Road
Merhson, GA 31551
(912) 647-2886 - Hallmark Cookie Cutters

Joan M. George
67 Stevens Ave.
Oldbridge, NJ 08856
e-mail: drjgeorge@nac.net - Egg Cups

Gail Peck
Country Crock Antiques
2121 Pearl St.
Fremont, NE 68025
(420) 7231-5721 - Red Wing Pottery

LuAnn Riggs
1781 Lindberg Dr.
Columbia, MO 65201
e-mail: artichokeannies@bessi.net - Cow Creamers

Steve Stone
12795 W. Alameda Pkwy.
Lakewood, CO 80225
e-mail: Sylvanlvr@aol.com - Blue & White Pottery

Don Thornton
Thornton House
P.O. Box 57
Moss Beach, CA 94038-0057 - Egg Beaters

Bruce and Vicki Waasdorp
P.O. Box 434
Clarence, NY 14031
(716) 759-2361
Web: www.antiques-stoneware.com - Stoneware Pottery

Mike White
40 Dalewood Dr.
Lexington, VA 24450
e-mail: mwhite@ntelos.net - Coffee Mills

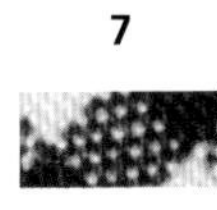

Collecting Guidelines for Kitchen Collectibles

by Francee Boches

The kitchen has always been the heart of the home and one of its most important rooms. Until the mid-20th century, the women of the house spent most of their day in the kitchen either preparing meals for the family or preserving food for later use. Therefore, items found in the kitchen were strictly functional and little thought was given to their decorative appeal. Before electrical appliances, all the chopping, mixing, peeling, and tasks were done by hand. In the 1930s the manufacture of mass-produced colored glass made pieces affordable and glass companies began to tempt homemakers with everyday objects that were attractive as well as practical. These allowed the women to add a flare to the kitchen. This trend continued and even expanded in the 1950s and '60s as glass companies in the United States saw the increased potential for kitchen glassware.

Collecting of kitchen collectibles has become very popular in the last 30 years. Not only do these items have nostalgic appeal but they also represent some very creative designs that one can use and enjoy everyday. There has been a resurgence of interest in kitchen decoration and appreciation for the artistry and novelty of kitchen items used by our grandmothers, great-grandmothers and their mothers. This interest has been encouraged by home decorating gurus as well as the ability to find these treasures at local antiques shows, flea markets, and even in Grandma's cupboards.

Small Turned Wood Painted Jar

Kitchen antiques from the 18th and 19th centuries are mostly metal kitchen tools or pottery or wooden items – many unique primitives. During the second half of the 19th century and into the early 20th century a much wider range of manufactured tools and accessories were widely available. Then, by the 1930s, in the era of the Great Depression, women were introduced to brightly colored and decorated glassware for the kitchen. Colored glass became affordable at the local Five & Dime and homemakers could afford to have a set of green glass mixing bowls or pretty milk glass spice shakers for their kitchen. Suddenly the kitchen became a room one could decorate and make a pretty space rather than just a practical work area.

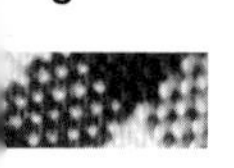

This approach to the kitchen as an expression of the taste of the woman of the house drove the marketing of practical but decorative glassware which continued after World War II when the returning service men and their wives were all setting up new households.

There are many types of kitchen items to collect so many people tend to specialize in a particular category. One popular area of collecting is kitchen utensils including items like griddle cake tuners or spatulas, egg beaters, pot lifters, egg separators, cooking spoons, ladles, mashers, rolling pins, ice cream scoops, etc. Also popular are the more intricate and sometimes fanciful designs of mechanical tools like nutmeg graters, apple peelers and corers, cherry pitters, and more. Early kitchens were full of pots and pans, mostly made of iron that could be used in the fireplace or on a wood-burning stove. There were also pottery and wooden bowls for mixing and making bread. Examples of all these early pieces have survived and can be located with diligent searching. These handcrafted pieces are very desirable especially as the "Country Kitchen" look has become popular. Many of these items, like toasters, also help trace the history of American industrial expansion and the evolution of home cooking.

Other collectors enjoy the kitchen glass of the 20th century, collecting either by type or piece (e.g. bowls, reamers, grease jars, spice jars, canisters) or by color (transparent green, opaque blue, milk glass, Jadite green). Another big area of collecting

Cat with Fireplace Condiment Set

is salt and pepper shakers as these include all types of materials and themes. They also come in a wide range of prices so can fit all collecting budgets. One can collect by type, such as glass or ceramic pieces, but probably the most popular way of collecting kitchen shakers is by category such as figural animals, cats, cartoon characters, vegetables, humorous, state souvenirs, and many, many others. Anything that was used in the kitchen has a collecting niche including egg timers, napkin ladies, match holders, and so much more.

Collecting Kitchen Tools

The key to collecting vintage kitchen tools is to find items in as close to original condition as possible. Wooden tools or wood-handled tools should be free of any cracks or chips and the paint should be complete with only the fading you find pleasing. The metal parts of tools should be free of any pitting or gouges or rust. Also look for pleasing and unusual designs. For example a griddlecake turner with holes forming a star shape on the flipper blade is more appealing and valuable than one with no design or a few random holes. In the same way a

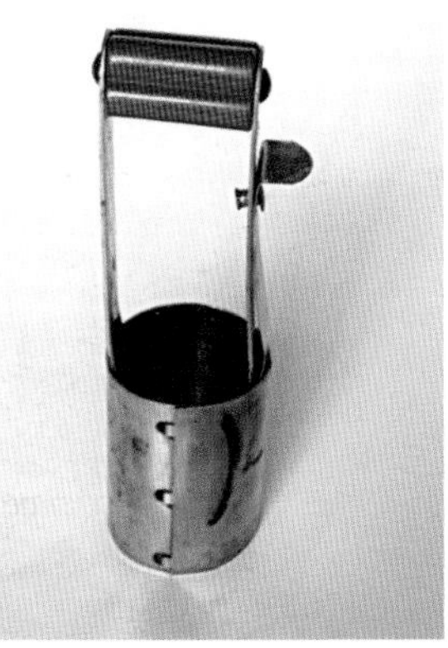

Apple Corer with Bakelite Handle

wooden handled potato masher with bright red paint and stripes of cream and black is rarer and more desirable than one whose handle is just painted red. Bakelite-handled tools should also be free of blemishes and are more valuable if the color of the Bakelite has not darkened or gotten cloudy with age. Most desirable of the Bakelite tools are ones where the handles are made up of more than one color of Bakelite or have interesting carving or shape. Many tool collectors have display items in excellent condition and purchase some of lesser condition and value pieces for everyday use.

For 18th and 19th Century iron tools and mechanical devices some wear is acceptable especially for rare or unusual forms. Remember that these were heavily used items and will always show some signs of age. Look for unusual mechanisms that set the tool apart whether or not it is a more efficient design. A lot of imagination went into inventing and patenting some of these early tools and it's that bit of history that adds to the value. For cast-iron cooking pans and pots remember also to consider scale as well as design. Especially large pieces and miniatures will catch the collector's interest quickly.

Collecting Kitchen Glass

Kitchen glass collectors usually are

Fire King Tulips Pattern Mixing Bowl

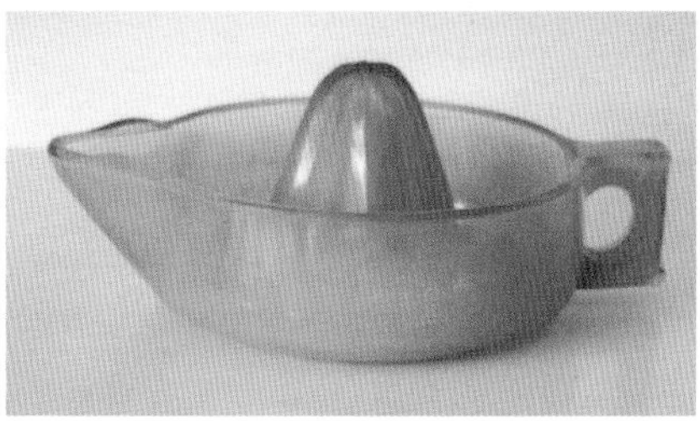

Butterscotch Glass Reamer

divided into those with an interest in 1930s glass and those enamored of 1950s – 1970s glass. Here trends change depending on the colors in vogue in home decoration and the impact of well-known home decoration gurus. The most highly collected color in 1930s glassware is transparent green which is sometimes referred to as green Vaseline glass since it will fluoresce under black light. There is such a wide range of pieces made by several glass companies that collectors can spend years putting together a collection of enormous variety. For other kitchen glass lovers, the rare colors are more fun but they are harder to find and will be more expensive once found. Many collectors look for specific types of kitchen utensils like reamers or measuring cups and revel in the number of colors and shapes they can find. Fire-King, a line of glass made by Anchor Hocking Glass starting in the 1950s, has become a collectible category on its own. This line combines great colors like Jade-ite and turquoise and fanciful enamel decorations on milk glass (e.g. Tulips, Modern Tulips, Kitchen Aides) featured on practical pieces you can use everyday. Moreover, these pieces coordinate with the glass dinnerware the company made at the same time. For kitchen glass even more than other kitchen items, condition is the major factor in value and desirability. The glass should be free of any chips or cracks or cloudiness due to water staining. Scratches from mixing spoons or other utensils also greatly diminish the value of the piece. The rarity of the color for that particular item is the next most important factor. A Sunkist reamer may be very affordable in milk glass but the same reamer in caramel brown will cost you a pretty penny. Finally, value is also dependent on how many other collectors are excited about the piece. Often a new collector is wise to find colors or forms that they find appealing but are not the "in" category at the moment. Sadly, due to the increased popularity of kitchen glass in recent years a number of reproductions are being made in China and the USA in forms and colors very similar to older items. Therefore, it is highly recommended that collectors starting out in popular colors like Jade-ite study reference books to see what was originally made and attend Depression glass and antiques shows and buy from experienced dealers to avoid being taken in by current fantasy or reproduction items.

Finally, one of the joys of searching for kitchen collectibles is that there were so many items made and more will be appear in the future. The choice of what to collect is vast. New collecting areas, that start at very affordable prices, are constantly developing. Currently collectors are discovering items from the 1970s through the 1990s such as Pyrex glass bowls, Corning ware pots and pans, kitschy plastic ware, and electrical appliances. As U.S. manufacturers of glass kitchenware, tools and appliances fade away in the face of foreign competition, American-made kitchen collectibles will become even more cherished by collectors since they represent the lost art of making household goods that are uniquely American in design and construction.

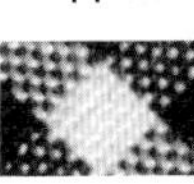

PART I: THE VINTAGE KITCHEN - 1850-1920

Chapter 1

Coffee Mills

Coffee mills, commonly called grinders, are perfectly collectible for many people. They are appealing to the eye and are frequently coveted by interior decorators and today's coffee-consuming homeowners. Compact, intricate, unique, ornate, and rooted in early Americana, coffee mills are intriguing to everyone and are rich and colorful.

Coffee milling devices have been available for hundreds of years. The Greeks and Romans used rotating millstones for grinding coffee and grain. Turkish coffee mills with their familiar cylindrical brass shells appeared in the 15th century, and perhaps a century or two later came the earliest spice and coffee mills in Europe. Primitive mills were handmade in this country by blacksmiths and carpenters in the late 1700s and the first half of the 19th century. These were followed by a host of commercially produced mills, which included wood-backed side mills and numerous kinds of box mills, many with machined dovetails or finger joints. Characterized by the birth of upright cast-iron coffee mills, so beautiful with their magnificent colors and fly wheels, the period of coffee mill proliferation began around 1870. The next 50 years saw a staggering number of large and small manufacturers struggling to corner the popular home market for box and canister-type coffee mills. After that, the advent of electricity and other major advances in coffee grinding and packaging technology hastened the decline in popularity of small coffee mills.

Value-added features to look for when purchasing old coffee grinders include:

- *good working order and no missing, broken, or obviously replaced parts*
- *original paint*
- *attractive identifying markings, label or brass emblem*
- *uncommon mill, rarely seen, or appealing unique characteristics*
- *high quality restoration, if not original.*

—Mike White

Box Mills

Box mill, advertising mill w/colorful litho printing made for Hoffmann's Old Time Coffee, based on Arcade's Telephone Mill (ILLUS., top next column)................ **$1,650**

Advertising Coffee Mill

Parker National Box Mill

Box mill, iron cover w/gear opening & crank & sunken hopper, on wooden box w/pull-out drawer in front, Parker National (ILLUS.).. **$100**

Logan & Strobridge Brighton No. 1180 Box Mill

Box mill, iron crank & side handle on wooden box w/pull-out drawer in front, 1 lb. capacity, Logan & Strobridge Brighton No. 1180 (ILLUS.) **$150**

Decorative Moravian Box Mill

Box mill, raised brass hopper & crank, Moravian base & inlaid drawer, signed by maker (ILLUS.) **$200**

Norton Painted Tin Box Mill

Box mill, raised iron hopper & crank on tin canister w/picture of woman painted on front, drawer in back, patented Norton (ILLUS.) **$650**

Arcade Favorite No. 357 Box Mill

Box mill, raised iron hopper w/patented partial cover design & crank on wooden box w/pull-out front drawer, Arcade Favorite No. 357 (ILLUS.) **$100**

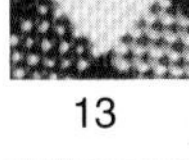

Rare Metal Mill with Sliding Door

Box mill, rare metal model w/sliding door on front by Parker, Brown's 1860 patent (ILLUS.) **$1,700**

Peck, Stow & Wilcox Box Mill

Box mill, w/decorative iron top & open hopper, Peck, Stow & Wilcox (ILLUS.)............. **$350**

Box mill, w/iron top & cover, No. 1100 Quick Grinder by Landers, Frary & Clark (ILLUS., top next column) **$250**

Box mill, w/raised hopper, patented partial cover design, Arcade (ILLUS., middle next column)... **$130**

Box mill, w/raised tin hopper, Parker Eagle No. 314 (ILLUS., bottom next column) **$120**

No. 1100 Quick Grinder

Arcade Box Mill with Raised Hopper

Parker Eagle No. 314 Coffee Mill

Arcade No. 777 Box-style Coffee Mill

Box mill, wooden, w/decorative iron top & pivoting lid embossed "IXL, Arcade Mfg. Co.," side crank, Home Coffee Mill No. 777, 11" h. (ILLUS.) **$700**

Primitive Coffee Mills

Early Blacksmith's Mill

Blacksmith's mill, iron & steel, 9" hopper, mounted on post, ca. 1790 (ILLUS.) **$950**

Box mill, w/brass hopper & Moravian base, crank on back, Belgium (ILLUS., top next column) **$400**

Wall canister mill, wooden, 5 x 10" rectangular hopper, metal inserts used as grinding blades, ca. early 1800s, France (ILLUS., middle of next column)................. **$900**

Primitive Belgian Box Mill

Wooden French Wall Canister Mill

Side Mills

Sunflower Design Coffee Mill

Side mill, bronzed cast iron, hanging model, sunflower design, No. A-17, 7" h. (ILLUS.) **$375**

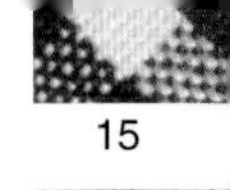

Parker No. 370 Coffee Mill

Side mill, cast iron w/wood backing board, decorative, Parker No. 370; smaller sizes No. 350 & 360 were also made (ILLUS.) ... **$250**

Kenrick Patented Side Mill

Side mill, iron, sliding cover, Kenrick patented, England (ILLUS.)............................ **$110**

Peck Smith Mfg. Side Coffee Mill

Side mill, tin hopper on wood backing, brass emblem reads "Peck Smith Mfg." (ILLUS.).. **$100**

Sun Mfg. Co. No. 94 Side Mill

Side mill, w/tin hopper & lid, Sun Mfg. Co. No. 94, ca. early 1900s (ILLUS.)................ **$150**

Peck, Stow & Wilcox Coffee Mill

Side mill, w/wood backing, brass emblem embossed w/the script logo "PS&W" for Peck, Stow & Wilcox, American (ILLUS.).... **$200**

Upright Mills

Rare Large Enterprise Floor Model Mill

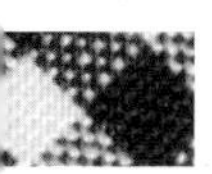

Upright mill, cast iron, Enterprise No. 218 floor model w/double 35" wheels & large brass hopper w/spread-winged eagle finial, original painted base & tin handled decorated bing, 50-70% original paint, late 19th c., 35" w., 70" h. (ILLUS., previous page) **$3,393**

L.F. & C. Universal Coffee Mill

Upright mill, cast iron, L.F. & C. New Britain, Conn. Universal, overall green paint w/gold highlights, hand crank w/wooden grip, slide-out base drawer, mounted on wooden board, all-original & like new, late 19th c., 11 1/2" h. (ILLUS.) **$320**

Enterprise No. 3 Upright Mill

Upright mill, cast iron, w/11" wheels, pivoting cover on hopper, all original, Enterprise No. 3 (ILLUS.) **$1,400**

Star No. 7 by Troemner

Upright mill, cast iron, w/15" wheels, all original, Star No. 7 by Troemner (ILLUS.) **$1,600**

Charles Parker No. 3000 Coffee Mill

Upright mill, cast iron, w/sliding hopper cover & flower decals, 10 3/4" wheels, Charles Parker No. 3000 (ILLUS.) **$2,200**

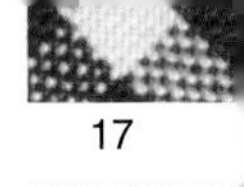

Miniature Upright Coffee Mill

Upright two-wheel mill, cast iron, miniature model for children, two 2"-h. wheels, Arcade No. 7, rare, overall about 2 1/2" h. (ILLUS.) **$350**

Coles No. 4 Upright Coffee Mill

Upright two-wheel mill, cast iron, pivoting lid on hopper, two 12"-h. wheels, Coles No. 4 (ILLUS.) **$950**

Upright two-wheel mill, cast iron, single wheel, cup, patented Clawson & Clark No. 1 model (ILLUS., top next column) **$1,000**

Clawson & Clark No. 1 Upright Mill

Enterprise No. 7 Upright Coffee Mill

Upright two-wheel mill, cast iron, w/17" wheels, pivoting cover on hopper, original red paint, decals & pin striping, 1898 patent date marked on grinding burrs, Enterprise #7 (ILLUS.) **$1,500**

Enterprise No. 4 Upright Coffee Mill

Upright two-wheel mill, cast iron, w/nickel-plated brass hopper, 10 3/4" wheels, Enterprise No. 4 (ILLUS.) **$2,000**

Wall Canister Mills

Arcade's Crystal No. 3 Coffee Mill

Wall canister mill, Arcade's Crystal No. 3, the most popular coffee mill ever produced, the glass to catch the ground coffee is marked "Arcade Mfg. Co., 3" (ILLUS.) **$475**

Brighton Queen No. 150

Wall canister mill, decorative, w/embossing on glass canister, Brighton Queen No. 150 by Logan & Strobridge, 16" h. (ILLUS.).. **$900**

Peugeot Freres Porcelain Coffee Mill

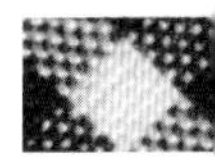

Wall canister mill, porcelain, colorful graphics, made by Peugeot Freres, France, ca. 1936, one in a set of ten (ILLUS., previous page) **$450**

Steel Wall Canister Coffee Mill

Wall canister mill, steel, w/oval window & tin cup, Bronson-Walton Oplex No. 10 (ILLUS.) **$350**

Wall canister mill, wood, glass & metal, w/blue paper label that reads "X-Ray Coffee Mill No. 1, Manufactured by Arcade Mfg. Co.," detachable cast-iron catch cup (ILLUS., top next column) **$250**

"X-Ray Coffee Mill No. 1"

One-of-a-Kind Wall Mill

Wall-mounted canister mill, cast iron, decorative design based on Ami Clark's 1833 patent, w/adjusting thumbscrew in back & two-sided grinding burr, only known example (ILLUS.)......................... **$2,500**

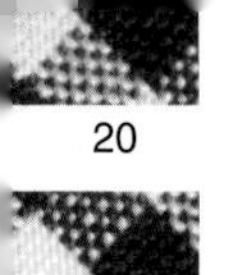

Children's Ceramic Wall Canister Mill

Wall-mounted canister mill, ceramic, children's model, glass measure, "Cafe" on front, Europe, about 6" h. (ILLUS.)............. **$420**

Red Iron Clamp-on Wall Mill

Wall-mounted canister mill, iron, clamp-on type, w/pivoting lid, red, rare National Specialty No. 0 (ILLUS.) **$310**

Douwe-Egberts Koffie Wall Mill

Wall-mounted canister mill, ceramic w/glass measure, marked on front "Douwe-Egberts Koffie," Europe (ILLUS.).......... **$140**

L.F. & C. Universal No. 24 Wall Mill

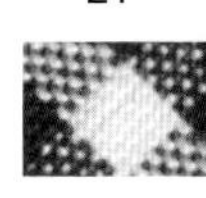

Wall-mounted canister mill, iron & glass, w/2-qt. jar, L.F. & C. Universal No. 24 (ILLUS., previous page) **$190**

Bronson-Walton Holland Beauty Wall Mill

Wall-mounted canister mill, litho-printed tin, decorated w/picture of woman in period clothing, Bronson-Walton Holland Beauty (ILLUS.)... **$510**

Rare Hollis Telephone Wall Mill

Wall-mounted canister mill, wood, w/side crank, rare patented Hollis Telephone model (ILLUS.)....................................... **$1,100**

Miscellaneous Mills

Child's Box-type Coffee Mill

Child's box mill, A.C. Williams Daisy No. 867, 2 1/2 x 2 1/2" base, same size as Arcade's Little Tot, but metal castings are different (ILLUS.).. **$150**

Universal Coffee Mill

Shelf clamp-on, cast iron, clamp-on type, original label marked "Universal #010 Coffee Mill" Pat'd Feb. 14, 1905 (ILLUS.) **$95**

Clamp-on Enterprise No. 0

Shelf clamp-on, cast iron, Enterprise No. 0, 12" h. (ILLUS.) **$175**

Parker No. 3 Planters' Mill

Wall-mounted corn & coffee grinder, cast iron, 17" wheel, Parker No. 3 Planters' Mill (ILLUS.) **$650**

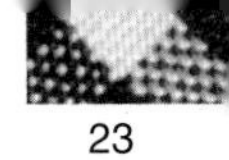

Chapter 2

Cookie Cutters

Advertising-type, tin, w/advertising reading "Garland Stoves and Ranges - The World's Best," 2 3/4 x 3 3/4" **$175**

Cottolene Shortening Cookie Cutter

Advertising-type, tin, w/fold down handle, "Cottolene Shortening," given by companies in the early 1900s (ILLUS. left with Rabbit cookie cutter) **$35-40**

Five Varied Tin Cookie Cutters

Bird tin, handmade, common (ILLUS. bottom left w/four other varied cookie cutters) **$45**

Cavalryman, tin, a cavalryman on horseback against a solid flat back w/tiny vent hole, minor dents & rust, 19th c., 8 3/4 x 10" (ILLUS., top next column) **$489**

Circle with handle, used for several purposes such as apple corer, funnel, donut cutter or cookie cutter, early 1900s (ILLUS., middle next column)................ **$50-75**

Large Tin Cavalryman Cookie Cutter

Circle with Handle Cookie Cutter

Four animals, tin, in the shape of four different animals, marked "DAVIS BAKING POWDER," set of 4 (ILLUS., top next page).. **$45**

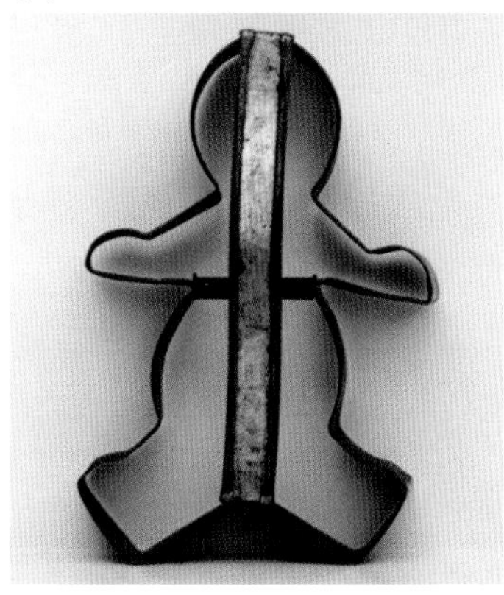

Gingerbread Man Cookie Cutter

Gingerbread man, tin, outline style w/strap handle, late (ILLUS.) **$18**

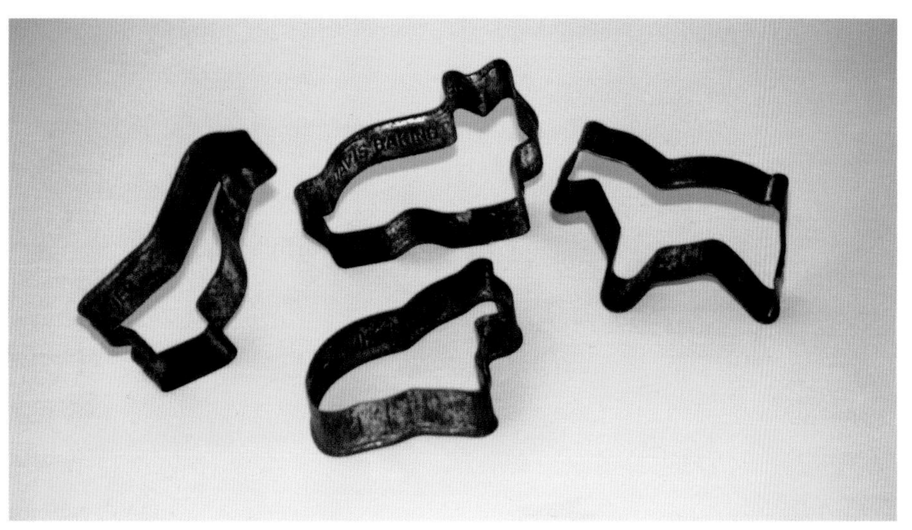

Set of Four Animal-shaped Tin Cookie Cutters

Gingerbread Man w/Heart Cookie Cutter

Gingerbread man with heart, tin, flat back, signed B. Cukla, Hammer Song, Boonsboro, Maryland (ILLUS.) **$25-30**

Gingerbread woman with rounded dress, heavy tin, large, edges & corners turned in, no signature **$25-35**

Heart, tin, a large size w/a backplate pierced w/two holes, applied back handle, 8 1/4" l. **$50**

Heart in crimped circle, tin, common (ILLUS. top w/four other varied cookie cutters, page 23) **$45**

Hearts, early tin w/strap handle, double overlapping hearts, 2 1/2 x 4" **$225**

Horse, tin, handmade late 1800s, common (ILLUS. center w/four other varied cookie cutters, page 23) **$135**

Lion, tin, light-weight stylized design of a lion, manufactured, also found as a rabbit, doll-like girl, etc., on a rectangular background, handled, for cookies or cakes, each **$15**

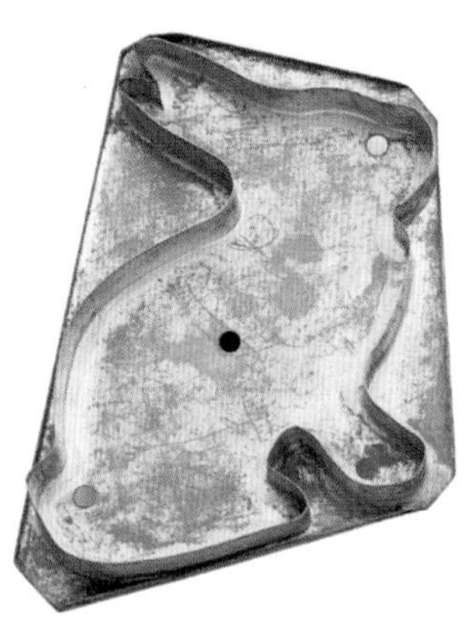

Large Tin Rabbit Cookie Cutter

Rabbit, tin, a seated rabbit on a solid sheet backing w/a small vent hole, late 19th - early 20th c., 10 1/2" l. (ILLUS.) **$201**

Rabbit, tin, embossed "Formay," standard self handle, sold on West Coast, Swift & Co., 3 x 8 1/8" (ILLUS. right with Cottolene Shortening cookie cutter, page 24) **$25-50**

Rabbit running, tin, stylized design w/backplate pierced w/two holes, applied back handle, 7 1/4" l. **$50**

Reindeer, tin, hand-made design of a reindeer, tin cut closely to edge of design, no handle, for cookies or cakes, 5 x 6" **$125**

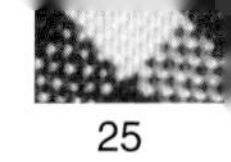

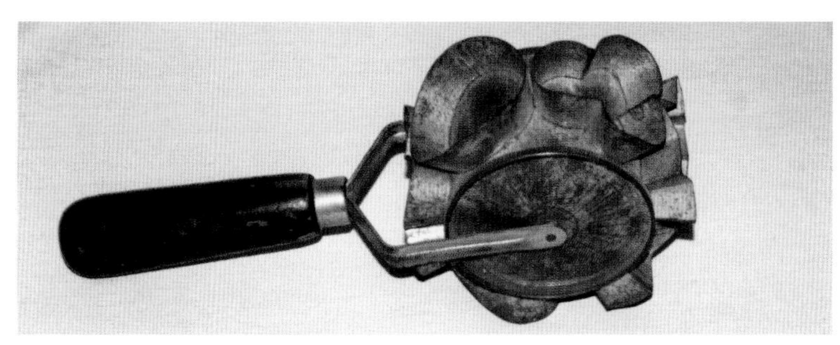

Tin & Wood Roller-type Cookie Cutter

Reindeer, tin, manufactured, common (ILLUS. left w/four other varied cookie cutters, page 23) **$25**

Roller-type, tin & wood, roller cutter w/six designs, black-painted wooden handle, 9" l. (ILLUS., top of page)............................. **$65**

Rooster Cookie Cutter

Rooster, heavy plated tin w/back, cutter edge 3/4" deep, handmade (ILLUS.) **$95**

Santa Claus, tin, stylized figure w/a rectangular backplate w/hole, marked "Cake Art Germany," 4 1/2 x 11 1/2" (soldered seam loose).. **$150**

Snowman, galvanized metal, flat back handle w/edges turned under, no signature on cutter, Baxter Oberlin, Angola, Indiana **$20-30**

Soldier on horseback, figural, soldier wearing plumed helmet, 9" l., 10" h. (some rust & a loose seam) **$935**

Antique Tin Stag Cookie Cutter

Stag, tinned sheet iron, large antlered stag, two holes in backplate, 19th c., 6 1/8 x 6 1/2" (ILLUS.) **$176**

Tulip, tin, handmade, common (ILLUS. bottom right w/four other varied cookie cutters, page 23)... **$75**

Miniature Cutters & Container

Varied designs, miniature, eleven various tin designs in 3 1/2" d. round tin container, the set (ILLUS.)....................................... **$95**

Chapter 3

Crockery & Dishes

Wildflower Batter Jar & Pail

Rare Early Stoneware Anchovy Jar

Anchovy jar, stoneware, wide cylindrical body w/angled shoulder to a wide molded mouth, blue-trimmed impressed swimming fish & balloon design all around the shoulder, attributed to Old Bridge, New Jersey potter, in-the-making dark clay color, rare, ca. 1810, 1 qt., 6 1/2" h. (ILLUS.)... **$743**

Apple tray, tole, rectangular w/low flared sides & flaring rounded ends, interior sides decorated w/white bands w/feathered tulips & leaves in red, yellow & olive green, the bottom w/a crystalized band, slate blue border & a worn center w/traces of yellow, worn exterior japanning, early 19th c., 7 3/4" x 12 5/8", 2 3/4" h. **$660**

Batter jar, cov., blue & white pottery, stenciled Wildflower patt., Brush-McCoy Pottery Co., small, 6" d., 5 3/4" h. (ILLUS. right with Wildflower batter pail, top of page).. **$350**

Cowden & Wilcox Early Batter Jug

Batter jug, stoneware, wide ovoid body tapering to a short, wide cylindrical neck, short angled shoulder spout, shoulder loops for holding the wire bail handle w/turned wood grip, cobalt blue brushed drooping flower below the impressed mark of Cowden & Wilcox, Harrisburg, Pennsylvania, on the back, brushed plume accents

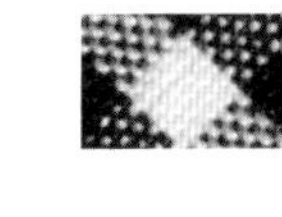

at spout & shoulder loops, design fry on blue, large, long stack mark in the back design, surface wear at base & bail handle, use staining, ca. 1850, 1 gal., 9" h. (ILLUS.) .. **$880**

Batter pail, blue & white pottery, bail handle, stenciled Wildflower patt., Brush-McCoy Pottery Co., 4 7/8" h. (ILLUS. left with batter jar, top previous page).............. **$375**

Bean crock, "Heinz," cov., ceramic, electric variety, panel on front reads "Heinz - Oven - Baked - Beans"............................... **$116**

Bean pot, cov., Red Wing pottery, white & brown glaze, advertising, "Christmas Greetings from Christle's Cash Store, Brillion, Wis.," rare **$145**

Bean pot, cov., Red Wing pottery, white & brown glaze, advertising "Geo. C. Radloff, Farmersburg, Iowa"............................. **$115**

Advertising Beater Jar

Beater jar, blue & white pottery, cylindrical w/molded rim, two blue bands & advertising, "Stop And Shop at Wagner's Cash Grocery, Kingsley, Iowa," 4 3/4" h. (ILLUS.)...................................... **$325**

Beater jar, Red Wing pottery, cylindrical, Sponge Band line....................................... **$325**

Bowl, 8" d., Red Wing pottery, spongeware paneled, advertising "Swanson & Nelson, Chisago City" [sic], very rare.............. **$250**

Bowl, Red Wing pottery, Sponge Band line, South Dakota advertising in bottom, No. 7.. **$285**

Blue & White Banded Yellowware Bowl

Bowl, yellowware, 8" d., rim decorated w/blue band between two thin white bands, body decorated w/blue band between two thin white bands, all above impressed vertical ridges, common (ILLUS.) **$45-50**

Bowl, turned burl, low turned foot below the rounded flaring sides w/a turned rim, good figure & dark patina, 19th c., 9" d., 2 1/2" h.. **$1,380**

Bowl, yellowware, miniature, 4 1/2" d., 2" h., flat rim, body decorated w/wide blue band between two thin white bands, rare (ILLUS. right with other yellowware banded small bowl, bottom of page)............ **$45**

Two Miniature Yellowware Banded Bowls

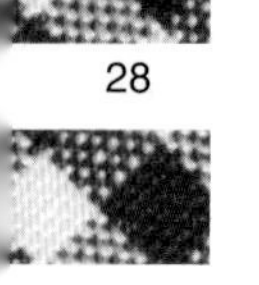

Fine Large Oblong Painted Wood Bowl

Shaker-carved Black Walnut Long Bowl

Bowl, yellowware, 4 1/2" d., 2 3/4" h., rim decorated w/blue band between two tin white bands, body decorated w/blue band between two thin white bands (ILLUS. left with other miniature yellowware bowl, bottom previous page) **$45**

Bowl, hand-hewn walnut, unusual shallow leaf shape, mellow brown finish, 8 3/8 x 21", 4 1/2" h. (minor rim chip) **$86**

Bowl, carved & painted wood, a flat rectangular bottom & very wide flaring sides & an oval rim, the exterior w/original old blue paint, 19th c., 14 x 25 1/4", 5 1/4" h. (ILLUS. inverted, top of page) **$1,380**

Nice Large Blue-Painted Wooden Bowl

Bowl, turned & painted wood, wide flaring rounded sides w/an indented rim band, natural interior & light blue-painted exterior, 18 1/2" d., 5 1/2" h. (ILLUS.) **$173**

Bowl, cov., mahogany w/old red, pumpkin orange & black painted line decoration, small turned foot below the wide half-round bowl w/a fitted domed cover w/button finial, found in Indiana, 19th c., 7 3/4" d., 5 3/4" h. **$550**

Bowl, carved black walnut, rectangular trencher style, gently curved base, carved end handholds, Shaker-made, Enfield, Connecticut, 19th c., age crack, 15 5/8 x 28 1/2", 6" h. (ILLUS., second from top of page) **$441**

Bowl, hand-turned w/turned foot, widely flaring fairly shallow form, dark brown finish, raised rim band, 23 1/4" d., 6 3/8" h. (age split) **$201**

Bowl, turned ash burl, very wide & deep sides w/incised decorative line below the rim, good nut brown color & tight figure, large size, 19th c., 18 1/2" d., 6 1/2" h. (short rim age crack) **$3,080**

Bowl, 7" d., blue & white pottery, embossed Beaded Rose patt., A.E. Hull Pottery Co. **$150**

Bowl, 7" d., Red Wing pottery, deep rounded & ribbed sides, white-glazed & decorated w/pale pink & blue bands (ILLUS., next page) **$75-125**

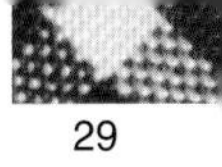

White-glazed Bowl with Pink & Blue Bands

Bowl, 7" d., Red Wing pottery, Dunlap, brown & white glaze, advertising "Columbia Metal Products Co., Chicago, Ill." **$45**

Large Early Turned Elm Bowl

Bowl, turned elm, wide shallow rounded sides w/flat rim, good patina, 19th c., 20 1/2" d., 7" h. (ILLUS.) **$1,265**

Large Natural Turned Wood Bowl

Bowl, turned wood, deep wide rounded sides w/a molded rim band, unpainted, two early zigzag staples holding a crack together runs around the diameter, 19th c., 23 3/4" d., 7" h. (ILLUS.) **$120**

Large Gray Line (Sponge Band) Bowl

Bowl, 9" d., Red Wing pottery, Gray Line (Sponge Band) ware, deep rounded & ribbed sides w/a narrow sponged orange band flanked by thin blue bands (ILLUS.) **$175-225**

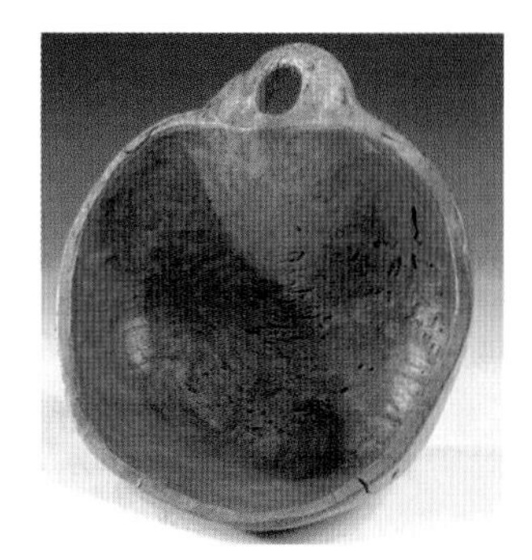

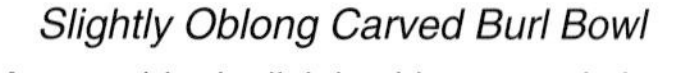

Slightly Oblong Carved Burl Bowl

Bowl, carved burl, slightly oblong rounded form w/an integral rim handle w/finger ring hole, 19th c., 9 1/2" l. (ILLUS.) **$632**

Fine Carved Burl Bowl

Bowl, carved burl, wide well-rounded form w/tight small mottled grain, rich patina, 19th c., 14" d. (ILLUS.) **$1,207**

Large & Well-turned Burl Walnut Bowl

Bowl, turned walnut burl, round w/a small flat bottom w/wide rounded sides & a thick molded rim, 19th c., 18 1/2" d. (ILLUS.) **$1,673**

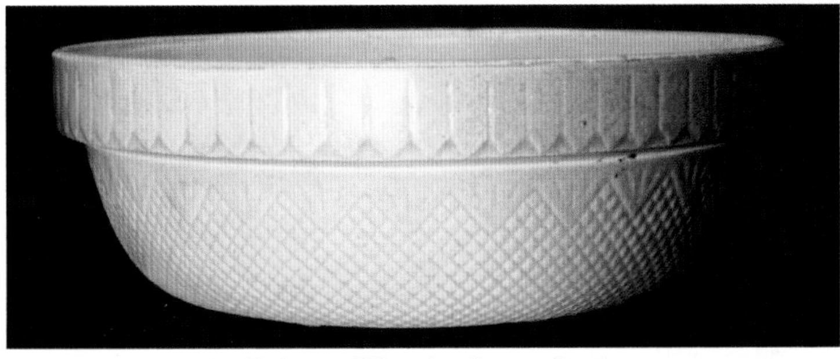

Embossed Venetian Pattern Bowl

Bowl, 7" d., 2 1/2" h., blue & white pottery, embossed Venetian patt., same as Reverse Pyramids w/Reverse Picket Fence but w/honeycomb at bottom, Roseville Pottery (ILLUS., above)................................ **$50**

Stenciled Wildflower Bowl

Bowls, blue & white pottery nesting-type, stenciled Wildflower patt., Brush-McCoy Pottery Co., 4" to 14" d., depending on size (ILLUS. of 10" d. size).................. **$150-450**

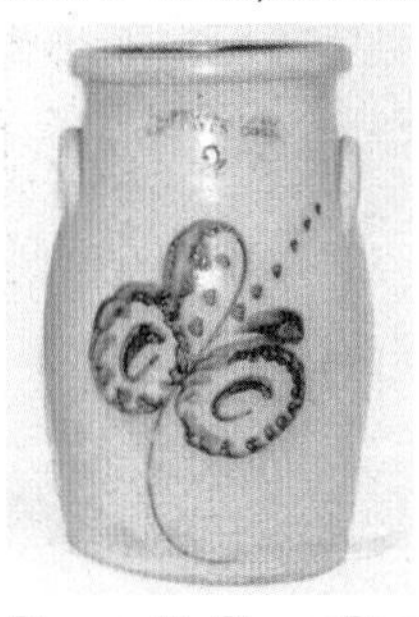

Small Churn with Clover Decoration

Butter churn, stoneware, swelled cylindrical body tapering to a thick molded mouth flanked by eared handles, cobalt blue slip-quilled large three-leaf clover design below the blue-tinted impressed mark of S. L. Pewtress & Co., Fairhaven, Connecticut & a size number, design fry, uncommon small size, ca. 1880, 2 gal., 12" h. (ILLUS.).. **$358**

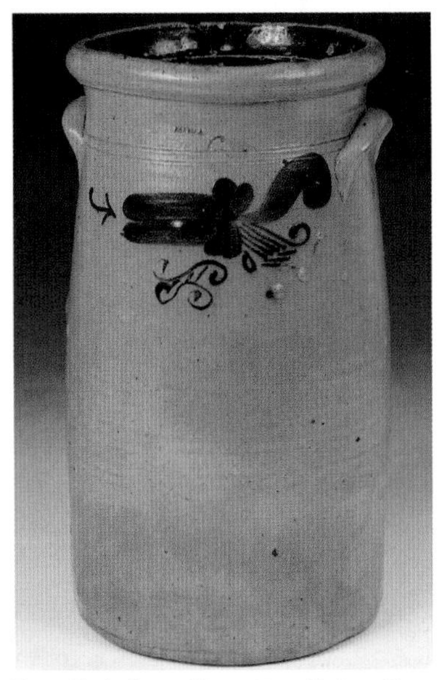

Rare Early Iowa Stoneware Butter Churn

Butter churn, stoneware, tall slightly tapering cylindrical body w/a flared molded rim & eared handles, cobalt blue brushed long stylized floral design at the top below the impressed mark “Cedar Falls, Iowa - 6,” probably by Martin White, ca. 1865, crack on reverse w/minor losses, 6 gal., 17 1/4” h. (ILLUS.) **$2,875**

Butter churn, stoneware, tall slightly ovoid body w/molded rim & eared handles, cobalt blue large slip-quilled bull’s-eye flower design, impressed mark of New York Stoneware Co., Fort Edward, New York, ca. 1880, 5 gal., 17 1/2" h. **$330**

Butter crock, cov., blue & white pottery, embossed Butterfly patt., Nelson McCoy Sanitary Stoneware Co., 10 lb. size, 9 1/2" d., 6" h. **$275**

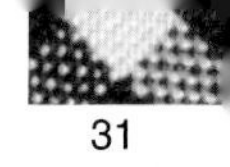

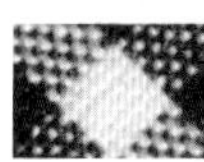

Eagle Butter and Salt Crocks

Cows & Columns Butter Crock

Butter crock, cov., blue & white pottery, embossed Cows and Columns patt., found in five sizes from 2 lbs. to 10 lbs., Brush-McCoy Pottery Co., ranges (ILLUS.) .... **$425-650+**

Butter crock, cov., blue & white pottery, embossed Eagle patt., A.E. Hull Pottery Co., 6" d., 6" h. (ILLUS. right, top of page) **$700**

Butter crock, cov., blue & white pottery, embossed Grape and Leaves Low patt., Robinson Clay Products, 6 1/2" d., 3" h. **$250**

Butter crock, cov., blue & white pottery, embossed Lovebird patt., A.E. Hull Pottery Co., 6" d., 4 34" h. (ILLUS., top next column) **$650**

Butter crock, Red Wing pottery, blue sponge glaze, no markings **$325**

Butter crock, Red Wing pottery, white glaze, 4" wing mark, “20 lbs” stamped above wing, very rare **$1,100**

Lovebird Butter Crock

Nice Covered Cake Crock with Flowers

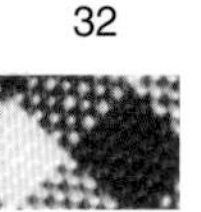

Cake crock, cov., stoneware, eared handles, large cobalt blue brushed flower & leaves band around the sides, flat cover w/brushed blue leaves, unsigned, couple of rim chips, extensive knob chipping on cover, ca. 1850, 2 gal., 11" d., 7" h. (ILLUS., previous page) **$688**

Candy pan, copper, shallow round flat-bottomed pan w/angled open brass rim handles, folded rim, 19th c., 20" d., 7" h. (ILLUS. right with brass frying pan, page 35) **$2,300**

Embossed GrapeWare Canister

Canister, blue & white pottery, embossed GrapeWare patt., "Pepper," no cover, 3 3/8" h. (ILLUS.) **$400**

Stenciled Floral Pattern Canister

Canister, cov., blue & white pottery, stenciled Floral patt., "Coffee," probably A.E. Hull Pottery Co., 5 7/8" h. (ILLUS.) **$275**

Churn, w/pottery lid & wooden dasher, Red Wing pottery, white glaze, 4" wing mark, blue oval pottery stamp below wing, 5 gal. **$450**

Churn, w/pottery lid, Red Wing pottery, white glaze, 4" wing mark, blue oval pottery stamp above wing, 6 gal. **$595**

Churn w/wooden lid & dasher, Red Wing pottery, swelled cylindrical body, Union Stoneware Co., large wing mark, 3 gal. **$325**

Coffeepot, cov., punched tin, tall pigeon-breasted body on a flaring footring, small domed hinged cover, strap handle, finely worked design of tulips in a flowerpot w/a heart, three bands of wavy intersecting lines & "Samuel and Lida Leidy," handle stamped "M.U.," attributed to M. Uebele of Berks County, Pennsylvania, first half 19th c., 10 3/4" H. (few areas of resoldering, spout w/minor damage).................... **$4,125**

Early Tin Lighthouse-shape Coffeepot

Coffeepot, cov., tin, lighthouse-style, flared tall tapering cylindrical ringed body w/a domed cover, a flattened rectangular serpentine spout, large strap handle w/hand grip, early, cover finial missing, some rust, 11 1/2" h. (ILLUS.) **$200-500**

Coffeepot, cov., tole, tall slighting tapering cylindrical body w/flaring base band, hinged low domed cover, strap handle, angled gooseneck spout, worn dark japanned background w/bold fruit & floral designs in unusual blue, red, yellow, olive green & tan w/white circular backgrounds, early 19th c., 10 3/4" h. (wear w/minor resoldering) **$963**

Coffeepot, cov., tole, tall tapering cylindrical body w/a long domed hinged cover, long angled straight spout & C-form strap handle, original red ground w/ornate stylized floral designs in yellow, green & unusual black & white, yellow flourishes on the cover, some wear, America, first half 19th c., 8" h. (ILLUS., next page)............ **$5,463**

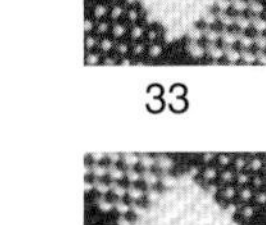

Outstanding Early Tole Coffeepot

Cooking or preserving kettle, cov., blue & white pottery, bail handle, embossed Peacock patt., Brush-McCoy Pottery Co., 5 qt. **$1,100**

Early Cream Pot with Script Name

Cream pot, stoneware, ovoid body w/a wide cylindrical neck & flat rim flanked by eared handles, double stamped "2" above a cobalt blue script "Butter" on one side & "Dolly" on the other side, probably New York state, ca. 1840, professional restoration to a hairline, 2 gal., 10 1/2" h. (ILLUS.) **$798**

Cream Pot with Bold Blue Flowers

Cream pot, stoneware, ovoid form w/a molded rim & eared handles, slip-quilled large cobalt blue blossoms on leafy stems below the number "3," impressed mark of T. Harrington, Lyons, New York, washed in blue, ca. 1850, 3 gal., 12" h. (ILLUS.) **$2,200**

Rare Anchovies Storage Crock

Crock, blue & white pottery, anchovies storage-type, swelled cylindrical form, three blue bands around top & bottom, stenciled on the side "A. Rensch & Co. - Anchois (sic) Mustard [over a fish] - Toledo, O.," impressed on the bottom "Burley, Winter & Co. - Crooksville, O.," 10 1/2" h. (ILLUS.) **$575**

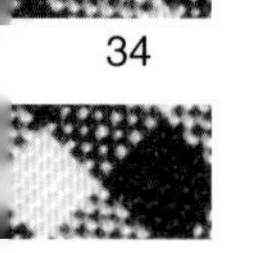

Unsigned Flower-decorated Small Crock

Crock, stoneware, flat-bottomed wide ovoid body tapering to a flattened molded wide mouth, light cobalt blue large brushed tulip above leaves design, unsigned but probably Pennsylvania origin, minor glaze burn or cinnamon clay color occurred in the making, minor surface wear & use staining on the back, ca. 1850, 1 pt., 5 1/4" h. (ILLUS.) **$688**

Crock, w/molded rim, Red Wing pottery, white-glazed, large "2" over double birch leaves & oval marks, Red Wing Union Stoneware, 2 gal., 9 3/4" d. **$85**

Unique Crock with a Camel Scene

Crock, stoneware, wide cylindrical form w/molded rim & eared handles, cobalt-blue slip-quilled decoration of a standing camel w/palm trees & a pyramid in the distance, impressed mark of Wm. A. Macquoid & Co., Little Wst. 12th St., New York, New York, small rim chip on front, tight full-length hairline on back, ca. 1870, 1 1/2 gal., 10" h. (ILLUS.) **$12,650**

Crock, stoneware, cylindrical w/molded rim & eared handles, cobalt blue slip-quilled fat bird w/head up perched on a small leafy sprig, impressed mark "Ottman Bros. & Co. - Fort Edward, NY - 3," professional restoration to full-length hairline on front, ca. 1870, 3 gal., 10" h. **$209**

Advertising Crock with Large Hen

Crock, stoneware, advertising-type, cylindrical w/molded rim & eared handles, slip-quilled cobalt blue large hen pecking at corn, impressed advertising for Cornells & Mumford, Providence, Rhode Island, above a "2", unsigned Norton of Bennington pieces, ca. 1865, 2 gal., 9 1/2" h. (ILLUS.) **$3,300**

Bennington Crock with Slender Bird

Crock, stoneware, cylindrical w/molded rim & eared handle, dark cobalt blue slip-quilled slender bird w/crest perched on a leafy sprig design below the impressed mark "E. & L. P. Norton - Bennington, VT - 3," small stone ping in the design w/minor stain, stabilized long hairline from rim

on the back, ca. 1880, 3 gal., 10 1/2" h. (ILLUS.) **$633**

Fruit jar, cov., Red Wing pottery, white glaze, blue or black stamp, "Stone - Mason Fruit Jar - Union Stoneware Co. - Red Wing, Minn.," very rare, 1 gal. **$1,100**

Fruit Jar with Screw-on Lid

Fruit jar, Red Wing pottery, screw-on metal lid, cylindrical w/tapering shoulder, white-glazed, black stamp reads "Stone - Mason Fruit Jar - Union Stoneware Co. - Red Wing, Minn.," 2 qt. (ILLUS.) **$275**

A Brass Frying Pan & Copper Candy Pan

Frying pan, brass, round shallow pan w/a slender long iron handle ending in a long turned wood grip, mid-19th c., pan 11" d. (ILLUS. left with copper candy pan) **$633**

Early Pease-type Turned Wood Jar

Jar, cov., turned wood, squatty bulbous body w/incised rings tapering to a domed cover w/large button handle, varnish finish, attributed to Pease of Ohio, splits reinforced w/glue & a pegged hole in bottom, 19th c., 7" h. (ILLUS.) **$259**

Small Turned Wood Painted Jar

Jar, cov., turned wood, thick round foot supporting the squatty bulbous ring-turned body w/a fitted cover w/a tall ring-turned knop finial, old mustard yellow paint, 19th c., base 3" d., 3 3/4" h. (ILLUS.) **$575**

Jar, cov., burl, wide urn-shaped turned body on a wide disk foot, fitted domed cover w/raised button finial, good patina & good figure, traces of dark red color, 19th c., 6" h. **$7,700**

Jar, cov., slightly tapering cylindrical shape w/base & rim molding, deep cranberry red stain, stamped label "Berea Souvenir 1909," attributed to Pease of Ohio, 5 1/8" d., 6 5/8" h. (minor edge wear) **$330**

Jar, cov., turned hardwood, squatty bulbous body on a narrow flared round foot, fitted low domed cover w/urn-shaped finial, old varnish finish w/good patina, attributed to Pease of Ohio, 19th c., 6 1/2" d. 6 3/4" h. (age crack) **$660**

Jar, cov., turned wood, barrel-shaped w/ring-turned base & rim band, fitted slightly domed cover w/small button knob, overall fan-shaped vinegar sponge decoration in red over mustard yellow, good color, 19th c., 8 3/4" d., 9" h. (glued repair, damage on cover flange & age crack) **$1,210**

Heinz's Raspberry Jelly Crock

Jelly crock, "Heinz's Raspberry Jelly," cov., stoneware, cylindrical, w/colorful label featuring illustration of various fruits & banners reading "Heinz's Raspberry Jelly" & "Standard Quality," lid w/wire closure, 5 1/2" d., 9" h. (ILLUS., previous page) **$288**

Milk crock, blue & white pottery, embossed Apricot patt., A.E. Hull Pottery Co., 10" d., 5" h. **$225**

Lovebird Pattern Milk Crock

Milk crock, blue & white pottery, embossed Lovebird patt., w/bail handle, A.E. Hull Pottery Co., 9" d., 5 1/2" h. (ILLUS.) **$500**

Stoneware Milk Pan with Plume Decor

Milk pan, stoneware, deep slightly flaring cylindrical sides w/a molded rim & pinched spout, decorated w/five small brushed cobalt blue plumes around the sides & three dashes under the spout, unsigned, size designation tooled just below the spout, X-shaped hairline at the base w/a grease stain, ca. 1850, 1 1/2 gal., 11 1/2" d., 6" h. (ILLUS.) **$330**

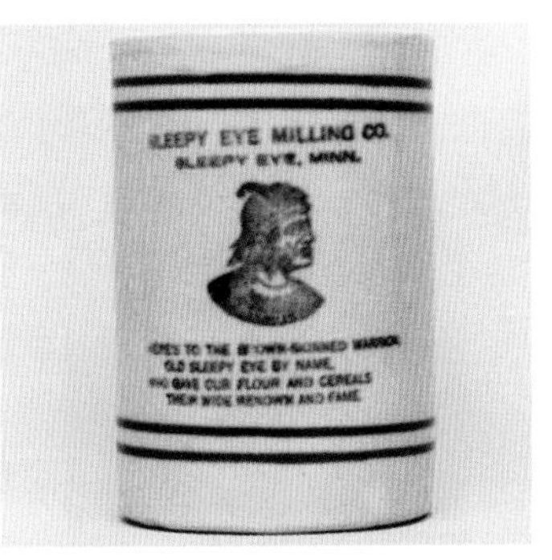

Rare Sleepy Eye Advertising Verse Mug

Mug, Red Wing pottery, Sleepy Eye verse-type, cylindrical white glazed form w/double blue bands flanking Sleepy Eye advertising, a bust of Chief Sleepy Eye & a verse (ILLUS.) **$2,500-2,800**

Red Wing Packing Jar with Cover & Seal

Packing jar, cov., Red Wing pottery, cylindrical w/rounded shoulder & cylindrical neck w/original ball-lock sealing mechanism & wire bail handle w/wooden grip, white glaze, a script "3" above the 4" red wing & oval Red Wing Union Stoneware marks, 3 gal. (ILLUS.) **$275-325**

Blue Chain Link Pattern Pitcher

Pitcher, 5" h., pottery, molded Chain Link patt., solid dark blue glaze (ILLUS.) **$45**

Brown-glazed Stoneware Pitcher

Pitcher, 8 1/2" h., stoneware, footed bulbous body tapering to a tall neck w/molded rim & deeply molded spout, strap handle, unsigned, overall dark brown alkaline glaze, some very minor surface chipping at the back rim, ca. 1870, 1/2 gal. (ILLUS.) **$303**

Pitcher, 10" h., stoneware, ovoid body tapering to a wide cylindrical neck w/pinched spout, impressed 3/4 capacity mark below the spout & above a cobalt blue brushed cluster of cherries decoration, unsigned but probably from New Jersey or Pennsylvania, glaze burn & mottled clay color, ca. 1850 (ILLUS., top next column)... **$990**

Pitcher, blue & white pottery, Diffused Blue, plain smooth shape, found in 1/4, 1/2, 5/8- & 1-gallon size, smallest is rarest, depending on the size **$150-225**

Tall Stoneware Pitcher with Cherries

Avenue of Trees Pitcher

Pitcher, 8" h., blue & white pottery, embossed Avenue of Trees patt. (ILLUS.)...... **$325**

Beaded Swirl Pattern Pitcher

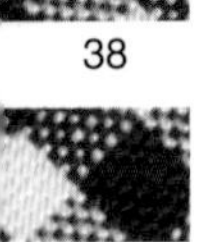

Pitcher, 6 1/2" h., blue & white pottery, embossed Beaded Swirl patt., A.E. Hull Pottery Co. (ILLUS., previous page)................ **$950**

Embossed Cherry Band Pitcher

Pitcher, 9 1/2" h., blue & white pottery, embossed Cherry Band patt., Red Wing Pottery Co., 8 pt., available in numerous sizes, the smallest being the most valuable, often seen w/printed advertising, which adds $300 minimum to the value, without advertising (ILLUS.) **$225-400**

Large-sized Cow Pitcher

Pitcher, blue & white pottery, embossed Cow patt., A.E. Hull Pottery Co., five sizes, rarest 5 3/4" h. to 9" h. (ILLUS. of 9" size)... **$250-600**

Pitcher, 7 1/2" h., 6 1/4" d., blue & white pottery, embossed Dainty Fruit patt., A.E. Hull Pottery Co.. **$550**

Pitcher, 9" h., blue & white pottery, embossed Dutch Boy and Girl Kissing patt., Brush-McCoy Pottery Co. or J.W. McCoy Pottery Co. (ILLUS., top next column) **$250**

Dutch Boy and Girl Kissing Pitcher

Printed Nautilus Pattern Pitcher

Pitcher, 8 1/2" h., blue & white pottery, stenciled Nautilus patt., A.E. Hull Pottery Co. (ILLUS.).. **$300**

Blue Stupid Pattern Pitcher

Pitcher, 8" h., 6" d., blue & white pottery, Stupid patt., Diffused Blue bands (ILLUS., previous page)... **$450**

Preserve jar, stoneware, advertising-type, gently swelled cylindrical form tapering to a molded rim, cobalt blue brushed double plain bands & a squiggle band around the top & a single plain band around the base, the whole center of the side stenciled in cobalt blue w/inscription reading "From Ood's Hardpan Crockery - Lockhaven, PA," the oversized "C" & "Y" in "Crockery" flanking the center part of the inscription, a stenciled size number flanked by leafy scrolls below the inscription, unknown maker, excellent condition, ca. 1870, 2 gal., 11 1/2" h.......... **$1,705**

Preserve Jar with Blue Inscription

Preserve jar, cov., stoneware, cylindrical body tapering to a flaring flat neck & inset cover w/disk finial, large cobalt blue slip-quilled "2 Quarts" in script below a round blue-trimmed tooled & impressed circle mark for a Cortland, New York factory, ca. 1860, 2 qt., 7 1/2" h. (ILLUS.) **$303**

Rare Fish-decorated Preserve Jar

Preserve jar, stoneware, tapering cylindrical form w/molded rim & eared handles, slip-quilled cobalt blue swimming fish, impressed mark of H.M. Whitman, Havana, New York, trimmed in blue, w/original hand-wrought iron lid, ca. 1860, 1 gal., 9" h. (ILLUS.) **$7,425**

Preserve jar, stoneware, cylindrical tapering slightly to an upright rim & eared handles, finely incised design of large double pod-like flowers on leafy stems washed w/cobalt blue, impressed mark of J.M. Mott & Co., Ithaca, New York, washed w/blue, minor staining, ca. 1855, 2 gal., 11" h. **$3,630**

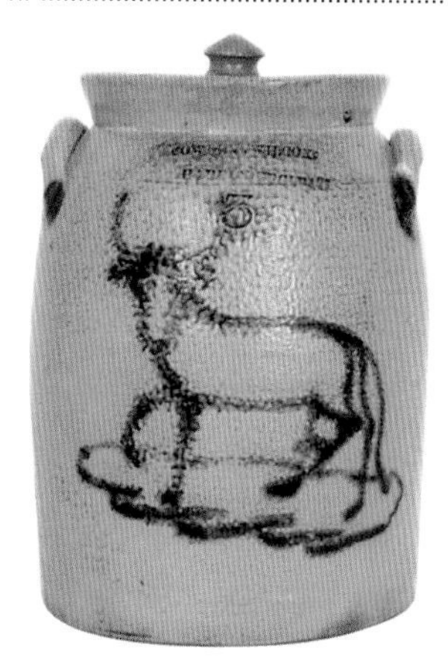

Preserve Jar with Rare Long Horn Cow

Preserve jar, cov., stoneware, tapering cylindrical form w/eared handles & short flared rim w/inset cover, slip-quilled cobalt blue scene of a Texas Long Horn steer, impressed mark of Cowden & Wilcox, Harrisburg, Pennsylvania, & a "3," overglazed in the making, ca. 1870, 3 gal., 12 1/2" h. (ILLUS.)........................ **$14,300**

Howard Raspberry Preserves Crock

Preserves crock, "Howard Raspberry Preserves," stoneware, cylindrical, small wire ring handles at sides, w/colorful la-

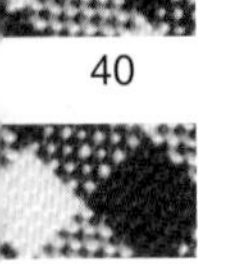

bel featuring illustration of various fruits & banners reading "Howard Brand Raspberry Preserves," 4 1/2" d., 5" h. (ILLUS.) **$288**

Refrigerator jar, stacking-type, Red Wing pottery, short form w/a molded rim, white-glazed w/narrow blue bands & "Red Wing Refrigerator Jar" on the side, 5 1/2" d. **$225**

Stenciled Wildflower Roaster

Roaster, cov., blue & white pottery, stenciled Wildflower patt., Brush-McCoy Pottery Co., 12" d., 8 1/2" h. (ILLUS.)............. **$450**

Advertising Hanging Salt Box

Salt box, cov., blue & white pottery, Diffused Blue patt., Western Stoneware advertising-type, "You Need Salt, We Need You - The Hodgin Store, Whittier, Iowa," 4 1/4" h. (ILLUS.) **$600**

Salt box, cov., blue & white pottery, embossed Apple Blossom patt., Burley-Winter Pottery Co., 6" d., 4" h. **$400**

Embossed Daisy on Snowflake Salt Box

Salt box, cov., blue & white pottery, embossed Daisy on Snowflake patt. (ILLUS.) **$250-275**

Salt box, cov., hanging-type, blue & white pottery embossed Eagle patt., A.E. Hull Pottery Co., 6" d., 4" h. (ILLUS. left w/Eagle butter crock, page 31) **$250**

Spice jar, cov., blue & white pottery, stenciled Snowflake patt., various spices, A.E. Hull Pottery Co., each **$150-225**

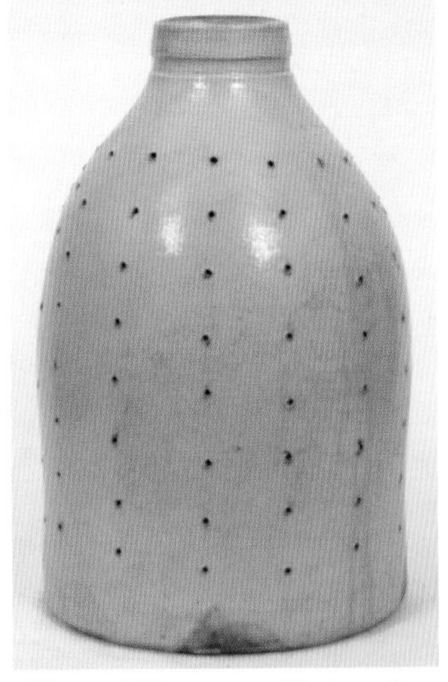

Unusual Stoneware Strainer-Jug

Strainer-jug, stoneware, cylindrical body tapering to a short wide molded mouth, no handle, pierced overall w/strips of small holes down the sides, possibly an oyster strainer, unmarked, stack marks at base, some minor use staining, ca. 1870, 2 gal., 13 1/2" h. (ILLUS.). **$358**

Tea caddy, cov., tole, cylindrical w/a flattened shoulder centered by a short neck w/fitted cap cover, dark brown japanned ground decorated w/a band of red, yellow & green fruit, 19th c., 4 1/8" h. (some wear, mainly on the cover) **$523**

Tea caddy, cov., tole, footed casket-form, rectangular w/flaring curved sides & a flat-sided stepped & domed cover w/embossed pull finial, on small paw feet, golden japanning w/yellow bands, white stripes & black leopard spots, painted heart escutcheon, early 19th c., 3 1/4 x 4 1/2", 4 3/8" h. (minor wear, two short seam splits) **$1,100**

Scarce Chrysolite Tea Steeper

Tea steeper, cov., Graniteware, Chrysolite & White Swirl (dark green & white) patt., cylindrical w/rim spout & black strap side handle, domed cover w/knob finial, late 19th - early 20th c., 4 1/4" d., 5" h. (ILLUS.) **$450**

Blue & White Tea Steeper with Tin Lid

Tea steeper, cov., Graniteware, Blue & White Swirl patt., cylindrical w/rim spout, strap side handle, domed tin cover w/wooden knob finial, 5" d., 5" h. (ILLUS.) **$250**

Large Blue & White Swirl Teakettle

Teakettle, cov., Graniteware, Blue & White Swirl patt., wide flat bottom & domed body w/a domed cover w/knob finial, wire bail swing handle w/turned wood grip, serpentine spout, late 19th - early 20th c., 10" d., 7" h. (ILLUS.) **$300**

Miniature Solid Blue Teakettle

Teakettle, cov., Graniteware, Solid Blue, miniature, wide flat bottom & domed body w/domed cover & knob finial, serpentine spout, overhead swing strap handle, late 19th - early 20th c., 3" d., 2 1/2" h. (ILLUS.)...................................... **$400**

Columbian Graniteware Teakettle

Teakettle, cov., Graniteware, Blue & White Swirl patt., wide flat bottom & domed body w/domed cover & knob finial, wire swing bail handle w/turned wood grip, serpentine spout, Columbian Ware, late 19th - early 20th c., 10 1/2" d., 7" h. (ILLUS.) **$650**

Cobalt Blue & White Swirl Teakettle

Teakettle, cov., Graniteware, Cobalt Blue & White Swirl patt., wide flat bottom w/high

domed body, domed cover w/knob finial, serpentine spout, coiled iron swing bail handle, late 19th - early 20th c., 7 1/4" d., 7 1/4" h. (ILLUS.) **$800**

Blue & White Pottery Teapot

Teapot, cov., blue & white pottery, Swirl patt., spherical body w/row of relief-molded knobs around the shoulder, inset cover w/knob finial, swan's-neck spout, shoulder loop brackets for wire bail handle w/turned wood grip, blue 6" d., 6" h. (ILLUS.)... **$800+**

Graniteware Agate Ware Child's Teapot

Teapot, cov., child's, Graniteware, Agate Ware, ovoid body on disk foot, tapering to domed lid w/finial, C-form handle, serpentine spout, decorated w/simple line decoration in blue, 3 1/2" h. (ILLUS.)........... **$35**

Diamond Ware Blue & White Teapot

Teapot, cov., Graniteware, Blue Diamond Ware (Iris Blue & White Swirl patt.), bulbous body tapering to a domed cover w/button finial, serpentine spout, C-form handle, late 19th - early 20th c., 5 1/2" d., 6" h. (ILLUS.)... **$700**

Teapot, cov., Graniteware, Grey Mottled patt., spherical w/low domed cover & wooden knob finial, serpentine spout, C-form handle, late 19th - early 20th c., 3 1/2" d., 5" h. (ILLUS. right with other miniature Grey Mottled teapot, page 43) ... **$200**

Toleware Teapot

Teapot, cov., tole,oval form w/angled front spout & shaped hinged lid, strap handle, decorative finial, back & front decorated w/two-part rose w/leaves, the lid w/blue/green leaf design, 5 3/4" h. (ILLUS.) **$1,840**

Rare Early American Tole Teapot

Teapot, cov., tole, tall oval body w/a slightly domed top fitted w/a hinged strap cover, straight angled spout, C-form strap handle, black ground, decorated on the sides w/a large deep red circle painted w/white leaf sprigs, the circle beneath an arched wreath of red & orange blossoms & shaded green leaves, probably Pennsylvania, ca. 1830, 6" h. (ILLUS.)........................... **$5,019**

Toy White Agate Ware Teapot

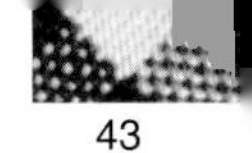

Teapot, cov., toy-sized, Graniteware, Agate Ware, overall white, domed cover, strap handle, long serpentine spout, probably made in Germany or Austria, ca. 1890, 5" l., 3" h. (ILLUS., previous page) **$75**

Grey Graniteware Miniature Teapots

Teapot, cov., Graniteware, Grey Mottled patt., spherical w/low domed cover & wooden knob finial, straight spout, C-form handle, late 19th - early 20th c., 3 1/2" d., 5" h. (ILLUS. left with other miniature Grey Mottled teapot) **$200**

Bulbous Solid Blue Teapot

Teapot, cov., Graniteware, Solid Blue, bulbous body w/hinged domed cover w/button finial, serpentine spout, C-form strap handle, late 19th - early 20th c., 4 1/2" d., 5 1/4" h. (ILLUS.) **$80**

Chapter 4

Kitchen Furniture

Early Dough Box on Legs

Dough box on legs, pine, a rectangular top w/breadboard ends above the deep box w/canted dovetailed sides, raised on a base w/a canted apron & four simple turned canted legs, nice old color, some minor repairs, probably late 19th c., 21 x 42", 25" h. (ILLUS.) **$489**

Nice Country American Cherry Dry Sink

Dry sink, cherry, the hinged rectangular top opening to a well above a pair of paneled cupboard doors w/brass H-hinges & latches, simple bracket feet, sink missing liner & replaced w/plywood panel, mid-19th c., 20 x 36 3/4", 33 3/4" h. (ILLUS.) **$690**

Dry sink, painted & decorated poplar, the long arched splashback above a long well above a case w/a pair of large paneled cupboard doors above simple bracket feet, old dark brown graining over an amber-colored ground, evidence of earlier red, interior w/two shelves painted light green, wear, door latch missing, 19th c., 17 3/4 x 45", 36" h. (ILLUS., top next column) **$575**

Painted & Decorated Poplar Dry Sink

Fine Painted Pine Hutch-type Dry Sink

Dry sink, painted pine, hutch-style, a raised back w/a long narrow shelf raised on shaped brackets above the long well, the case w/a pair of paneled doors opening to a shelf, old mustard green over the original blue, some scrapes, original cast-iron door latch w/porcelain knob, mid-19th c., 18 1/2 x 43", 40 1/2" h. (ILLUS.) **$1,495**

Dry sink, painted pine & poplar, a long rectangular shallow well w/a half-round backsplash toward one end, the base w/two large paneled doors opening to two shelves, gently serpentine apron & low bracket feet, old worn blue over earlier red paint, mid-19th c., 19 1/2 x 45", 32" h. (restorations, backboards renailed, few door pegs replaced).............. **$1,430**

Dry sink, painted pine & poplar, a narrow rectangular shelf atop the raised backboard flanked by shaped sides on the long well above a pair of drawers w/turned wood knobs over a pair of paneled cupboard doors opening to two shelves, simple bracket feet, old yellow paint over earlier colors, signed in pencil

Rare Dated Ohio Dry Sink

in one drawer "Thos. Underwood, Clark Co. Ohio, August 10, 1881," 18 x 42", 41" h. (ILLUS.) **$4,025**

Early New England Painted Dry Sink

Dry sink, painted pine, the deep rectangular top well above a mid-molding above a single flat door, original old grey paint, originally built-in so no back, New England, 19th c., 17 x 28 1/2", 26 1/2" h. (ILLUS.) **$1,783**

Dry sink, painted pine, the open rectangular top well above a case w/a single raised panel door w/H-hinges & a metal latch, simple delicate bracket feet, old red wash, first half 19th c., from Maine, replaced hardware, 18 x 37", 33" h. (ILLUS., top next column) **$900**

Old Painted Pine Maine Dry Sink

Dry sink, painted walnut, hutch back-style, the raised back w/a low arched long crestrail above a narrow shelf over the long zinc-lined well w/curved sides, the case fitted w/two large double-paneled doors w/turned wood knobs & a very small drawer at the top corner of one end, simple bracket feet, old brown over mustard yellow paint, wear & chips to base, mid-19th c., 22 x 70 1/4" l., 47" h. (ILLUS., top next page) **$2,875**

Simple Pine Dry Sink

Dry sink, pine, a serpentine back rail above a rectangular well on one side & a rectangular work top above a single drawer at the other, a single paneled door in the base w/a cast-iron latch w/porcelain knob, serpentine apron & bracket feet raised on casters, second half 19th c., 28 1/2" w., 30 1/2" h. (ILLUS.) **$345**

Rare Large & Long Hutch-style Dry Sink

Two-door Country Pine Dry Sink

Dry sink, pine, the open rectangular top w/slightly angled sides above the case w/a pair of paneled cupboard doors opening to a shelf, flat base on low bracket feet & low arch-cut ends, honey brown patina, second half 19th c., 20 1/2 x 46 1/2", 35 1/2" h. (ILLUS.) **$575**

Early Dry Sink with Nice Old Finish

Dry sink, stained hardwood, the rectangular top well w/dovetailed construction above a case w/a pair of tall paneled cupboard doors opening to a shelf, low arched apron & simple bracket feet, nice weathered old finish, open crack in one side, mid-19th c., 16 1/2 x 38 1/2", 41" h. (ILLUS.) **$460**

Early Tennessee Jackson Press Cupboard

Jelly (a.k.a. Jackson press) cupboard, Classical style, cherry, the low arched back crest above a rectangular top above a pair of drawers w/early pressed glass knobs projecting over a pair of wide paneled cupboard doors flanked by freestanding columns, a reeded central stile between the doors, double-knob-turned feet, signed under one drawer & dated 1835, Tennessee, 23 x 44", 46" h. (ILLUS.) **$4,025**

Fine Painted Country Jelly Cupboard

Jelly cupboard, painted & decorated country-style, rectangular top w/a deep flaring cornice above a single tall & wide four-panel door w/turned wood knob opening to three shelves, flat base raised on heavy ring- and knob-turned legs, original lock, remnants of early red paint under grain painting, probably from Pennsylvania or Ohio, mid-19th c., 21 x 40", 61 1/2" h. (ILLUS.) **$3,738**

One-piece Painted Jelly Cupboard

Jelly cupboard, painted pine, the rectangular top w/a molded cornice above a single tall beaded board door w/old brass ring pull opening to four shelves & flanked by wide front sides, low shaped bracket feet, old pale green paint, back half of top w/earlier grey, chips on base, rear foot replaced, 19th c., 19 1/2 x 42", 4' 5" h. (ILLUS.).. **$518**

Painted Pine Jelly Cupboard

Jelly cupboard, painted poplar, the rectangular top w/a narrow cornice above a single large door w/six glass panes above two lower panels, opening to four shelves, molded base on small disk feet, old red paint, interior w/later blue paint, reconstruction, 19th c., 17 x 43 1/2", 5' 5 1/4" h. (ILLUS.) **$1,035**

Simple Pine Jelly Cupboard

Jelly cupboard, pine, the rectangular top above a large single two-panel cupboard door opening to three shelves, low scalloped apron & bracket feet, refinished,

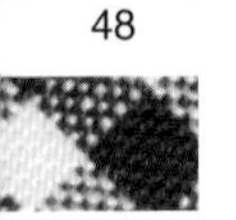

some reshaping of aprons, latch replaced, first half 19th c., 16 1/2 x 45", 4' h. (ILLUS.) **$805**

Shaker-attributed Jelly Cupboard

Jelly cupboard, poplar, the rectangular top w/a low three-quarters gallery above two long narrow drawers w/small wood knobs above a pair of tall paneled cupboard doors opening to three shelves w/wooden knobs, original red wash, attributed to the Mt. Lebanon Shaker community, one back leg replaced, 20 1/4 x 49", 5' 1/4" h. (ILLUS.) **$1,953**

Tall Cherry & Walnut Cupboard

Jelly cupboard, walnut & cherry, the thick rectangular top above a single tall two-panel cupboard door w/wooden thumb latch & small steel lock escutcheon, opening to four later shelves, flat apron on curved bracket feet, old finish, pegs removed from interior, one rear foot w/break, cornice replaced, 19th c., 12 1/2 x 33", 5' 7" h. (ILLUS.) **$1,035**

Early Eight-tin Pie Safe

Pie safe, ash or chestnut, mortise-and-tenon construction, rectangular top w/a molded cornice above two frame-and-panel doors, each door w/four hand-punched tins w/circular & floral decoration, vertical tongue-and-groove backboards w/cut nails, found in Blountville, Tennessee, later red paint on front & molding, sides w/old peeling brown paint, tins w/scattered rust, 17 1/2 x 52", 73 1/2" h. (ILLUS.) **$2,090**

Pie safe, country-style, pine, rectangular top w/molded cornice above a case w/center two-panel cupboard door flanked by compartments missing their original punched tin or screen wire covering, the lower case w/another two-panel central door flanked by plain side panels, square stile legs, old worn finish, Newberry or Kershaw County, South Carolina, mid-19th c., 19 x 53 1/2", 5' 8 1/4" h. (ILLUS., next page)................................ **$1,115**

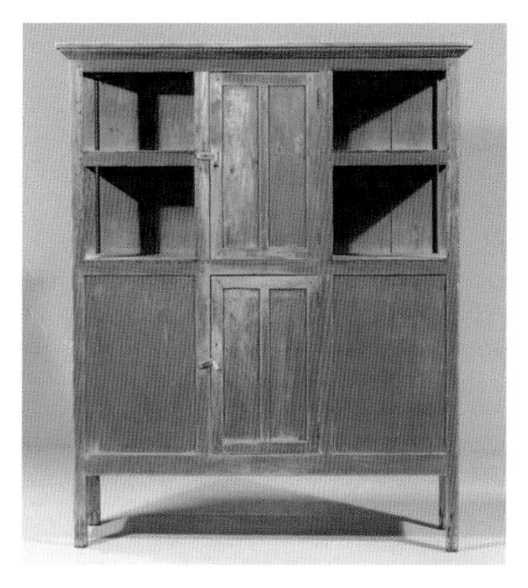

Early Southern Pie Safe

Tennessee Six-tin Pie Safe

Pie safe, hardwood, the rectangular top w/a shaped back panel above two tall paneled doors, each w/three punched tins w/heart & circle decoration, doors w/pegged construction, square tapering stile legs, horizontal backboards w/original cut nails, Carter County, Tennessee, old brown paint w/losses, tins w/scattered rust, 16 x 40", 59" h. (ILLUS.) **$1,320**

Hardwood Country Pie Safe

Pie safe, hardwood, rectangular top above a pair of drawers w/wooden knobs over a pair of three-panel doors fitted w/replaced punched-tin panels decorated w/circle, star & quatrefoil designs, three matching tins in each side, flat apron, square stile legs, late 19th c. (ILLUS.) **$310**

Painted Double-door Pie Safe

Pie safe, hardwood w/old brown paint, the rectangular top above two dovetailed drawers above two doors each w/a large four-section tin, each tin section w/diamond-shaped central medallion w/stars, punched-tin side panels, turned feet, hor-

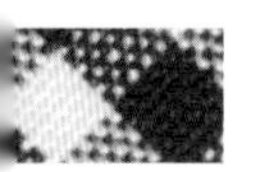

izontal backboards w/cut nails, Cocke County, Tennessee, scrapes, scuffs & losses to painted surface, 18 1/2 x 54 1/4", 42" h. (ILLUS.) **$2,750**

Late Oak & Hardwood Pie Safe

Pie safe, oak & hardwoods, a thin rectangular top above a pair of tall doors fitted w/replaced pierced-tin panels w/a star design above a narrow long bottom drawer w/a stamped leafy scroll design, straight stile legs, late 19th c. (ILLUS.) **$350**

Old Painted Pine Pie Safe

Pie safe, painted pine, single-board rectangular top w/old breadboard ends added above a pair of tall two-panel doors inset w/two pierced-tin panels decorated w/flower designs, two matching tins in each side, flat apron on angled bracket feet, old brown paint, backboards replaced, 19th c., 16 1/2 x 42", 4' 1 5/8" h. (ILLUS.).. **$748**

Nice Painted Pie Safe

Pie safe, painted poplar & chestnut, the long rectangular top above a single long drawer w/wooden knobs over a pair of doors each set w/two punched-tin panels decorated w/a pinwheel & quarter-round design, two matching tin panels in each side, flat apron, square stile legs, original reddish brown paint, 19th c., 17 1/2 x 42", 44 3/4" h. (ILLUS.) **$2,013**

Walnut & Cherry Pie Safe

Pie safe, walnut & cherry, mortise-&-tenon construction, the rectangular top above two dovetailed drawers w/cut-nail construction above two doors each fitted

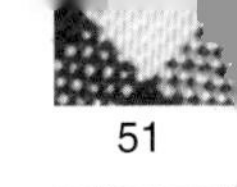

w/four punched-tin panels, each panel w/designs of urns & grapes & star corners, punched-tin panels in sides, turned legs, original brass hinges, vertical backboards w/cut nails, attributed to Rich family shop, Wythe County, Virginia, 1830-80, old refinishing, drawer bottoms w/chips, traces of old blue paint, top w/stains & small separations, 17 x 50", 4' 3" h. (ILLUS.) **$6,600**

Pie Safe from Tennessee

Pie safe, walnut & poplar, rectangular top above a row of three dovetailed drawers above two doors each w/two large punched-tin panels w/circular centers flanked by two candlesticks w/tulips in upper corners, chamfered horizontal backboards, turned feet, Sullivan County, Tennessee, refinished, several patches, minor surface flaws & scratches, 18 1/2 x 55 1/4", 47" h. (ILLUS.) **$9,350**

Pie safe, walnut, the rectangular top above a pair of deep drawers w/replaced oval brasses above a pair of tall doors each w/three replaced pierced-tin panels, old matching tin panels in the sides, flat apron raised on baluster- and ring-turned legs w/knob feet, mouse hole & chips on drawer front & openings, refinished, 19th c., 18 1/2 x 42", 4' 6 1/2" h. (ILLUS., top next column).. **$575**

Pie safe, walnut, the rectangular top over two drawers w/nailed construction above a pair of doors, each w/two punched-tin panels w/eagle designs, Scott County, Virginia, probably mid-19th c., old refinishing w/scratches & losses, replaced glass pulls, 18 x 43", 45" h. (ILLUS., bottom next column) **$2,420**

Old Walnut Pie Safe

Walnut Pie Safe from Virginia

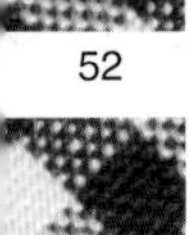

Chapter 5

Kitchen Utensils

Egg Beaters

Eggbeaters are pure Americana! No other invention (although apple parers come close) represent America at its best from the mid-19th century to the 1930s or '40s. Eggbeaters tell the unbeatable story of America—the story of demand for a product, competition, success, retreat, failure, faith, and revival.

The mechanical (rotary) eggbeater is an American invention, and ranks up there with motherhood and apple pie, or at least up there where it counts—in the kitchen. American ingenuity produced more than 1,000 patents related to beating eggs, most before the 20th century.

To put it in perspective, try to imagine 1,000 plus ways to beat an egg. Here's a clue, and it's all due to Yankee tinkering: There are rotary cranks, archimedes (up and down) models, hand-helds, squeeze power, and rope and water power—and others. If you ever wanted a different way to beat an egg it was (and is) available.

Today, eggbeaters are a very popular Americana kitchen collectible—a piece of America still available to the collector, although he/she may have to scramble to find the rare ones.

But, beaters are out there, from the mainstay A & J to the cast-iron Dover to the rarer Express and Monroe. There is always an intriguing mix, ranging in price from less than under $10.00 to the hundreds of dollars.

—Don Thornton

Items are listed alphabetically by manufacturer

A & J USA Ecko Egg Beaters

A & J, Ecko, wood handle, rotary w/apron marked "A&J USA Ecko," on a two-cup measuring cup marked "A&J" (ILLUS.) **$35**

A & J, metal, rotary crank, marked "A&J Pat. Oct. 9, 1923 Made in U.S.A.," 8 1/4" to 10" **$10**

A & J, archimedes "up & down" style, marked "Patd Oct. 15 07 Other Pat Pend'g," 9 1/4" **$100**

A & J, archimedes "up & down" style, marked "A & J Pat'd Oct. 15 07 Other Pats Pending," 12 1/2" **$25**

Androck, Bakelite handle, metal rotary, marked "Androck," 11" (ILLUS. with large group of Androck beaters, bottom of page) **$30**

Androck, metal rotary, wood handle, marked "Androck," 11" (ILLUS. with large group of Androck beaters, bottom of page) **$15**

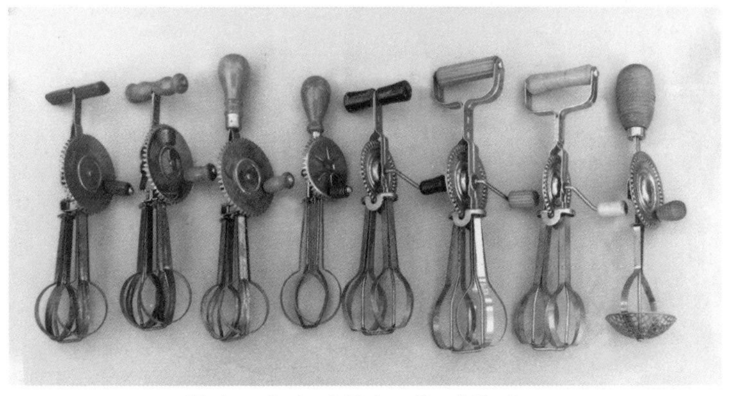

Various Androck Rotary Crank Beaters

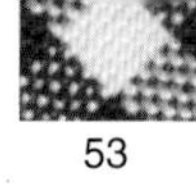
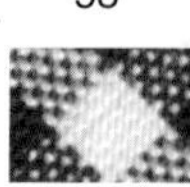

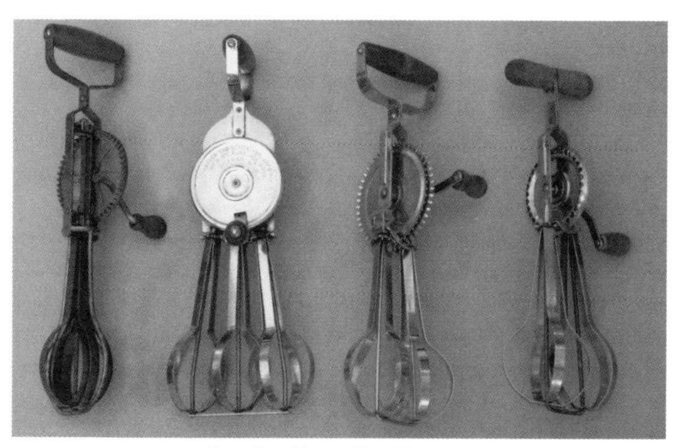

Aurelius Bros. Egg Beaters

Androck, plastic handle, rotary, marked "Another Androck Product," 12 1/2" (ILLUS. with the large group of Androck beaters, bottom previous page) **$15**

Aurelius Bros., wood handle, rotary marked "Ideal Mille Lacs Mfg. by Aurelius," 10 3/4" h. (ILLUS. right, top of page) **$50**

Aurelius Bros., wood handle, rotary, rare triple dasher, rotary marked "Master Egg Beater Mfd. By Aurelius Bros., Braham, Minn. Pat. Appld. For," 11 1/2" h. (ILLUS. left center, top of page) **$300**

Aurelius Bros., wood handle, rotary w/double gearing, marked "Aurelius Bros., Braham, Minn. Pat. Nov. 9, 1926," 11 1/2" h. (ILLUS. left, top of page) **$45**

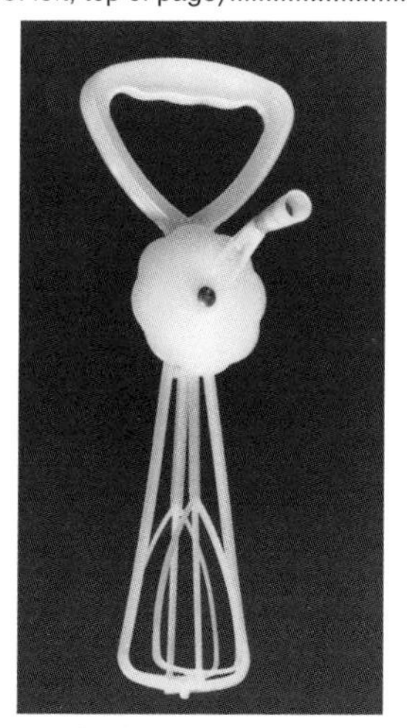

Blisscraft of Hollywood Egg Beater

Blisscraft of Hollywood, plastic, rotary, marked "Blisscraft of Hollywood Pat. USA Pend.," scarce, 12" h. (ILLUS.) **$75**

Cyclone, cast iron, rotary marked "Cyclone Pat. 6-25 and 7-16 1901," 11 1/2" h. (ILLUS. center two, top next page) **$50**

Cyclone, cast iron, rotary marked "Cyclone Pat 6-25-1901 Reissue 8-26-1902," 13 1/2" h. (ILLUS. far left & right, top next page) **$75**

Patented "Dover" Egg Beater

Dover, cast-iron w/tin dashers, cut-out letters "D-O-V-E-R" spelled out on the rotary wheel, also marked "Patented Feb. 9, 1904 - New Style" (ILLUS.) **$175**

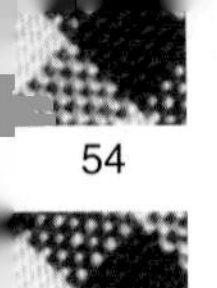

Cylcone Egg Beaters

Dover, cast-iron w/tin dashers & stand, marked "Dover Egg Beater - Patd May 6th 1873 Apr. 3d 1888 Nov. 24th 1891"..... **$200**

Dover, cast iron, rotary tumbler model (smaller dashers to fit in glass or tumbler), marked "Dover Egg Beater Pat'd Made in Boston U.S.A.," 9" **$75**

Dover, cast iron, nickel-plated, D-handle, rotary marked "Genuine Dover, Dover Stamping Co.," 11 1/4" h............................. **$50**

Dover, cast iron, rotary marked "Dover Egg Beater Patd May 6th 1873 Apr 3d 1888 Nov. 24th 1891 Made in Boston U.S.A. Dover Egg Beater Co.," 11 1/4" h. **$40**

Dover, cast iron, rotary marked "Dover Egg Beater Pat. May 31 1870," 12 1/2" h........... **$75**

Dream Cream, rotary turbine marked "The Dream Cream Trade Mark Whip Manufactured by A.D. Foyer & Company Chicago," 10" h... **$25**

Express, cast iron, rotary w/fly swatter dasher, marked "Pat. Oct. 25, 1887" only, rare, 11 1/2" h. (ILLUS., next column)........ **$950**

F. Ashley, archemides, "up & down" style, marked "F. Ashley Patent Appl For," 15" **$400**

Family, cast iron, "Family. Egg. Beater. Pat Sep 26, 1876," 10" **$800**

Hand-held, plastic handle, marked "Patent No. 2906510" **$5**

Express Egg Beater w/Fly Swatter

Hand-held, all-wire, unmarked, 13" h. **$35**

Henderson Corp., steel, "Minute Maid Henderson Corp. Pat Pend Seattle U.S.A.," 11 1/2" **$250**

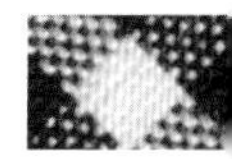

Holt-Lyon Egg Beaters

Holt-Lyon Side-Handle Egg Beaters

Holt-Lyon, cast iron, side-handle, marked "H-L Co.," 8 1/2" h. (ILLUS. right)............... **$150**

Holt-Lyon, cast iron, side-handle, marked "Holt's Egg Beater & Cream Whip Pat. Aug. 22-'98 Apr. 3-00," 8 1/2" h. (ILLUS. left).. **$150**

Holt-Lyon, cast-iron propeller, marked "Lyon Egg Beater Albany N.Y. Pat. Sep 7 '97," 10" h. (ILLUS., top of page)............... **$150**

Jaquette Bros., scissors-type, cast iron, marked "Jaquette Bros No. 1," 7 1/2" l. **$900**

Jaquette Bros., scissors-type, cast iron, marked "Jaquette Bros No. 2," 8 3/4" l. **$500**

Jiffy Cream Whip, tin top w/slightly green glass jar, marked "Jiffy Cream Whip - Patented Dec. 12, 1922 - Kohler Die & Sp'lty Co. DeKalb, Ill U.S.A."...................... **$150**

Knovex, metal, "Konvex Mfg. Co. Dayton, Ohio Patented Aug. 23, 1927 & July 24, 1928" marked on wheel, great pivotal action of bowl-shaped beater w/holes at base.. **$425**

Ladd, metal rotary, marked "No. 0 Ladd Beater Pat'd July 7, 1908 Feb. 2 1915 United Royalties Corp.," 9 3/4" h. (ILLUS. with grouping of Ladd beaters, top next page)... **$15**

Ladd, wood handle, metal rotary, marked "No. 00 Ladd beater Patd Oct. 18, 1921 United Royalties Corp.," 11" l. (ILLUS. with grouping of Ladd beaters, top next page)... **$12**

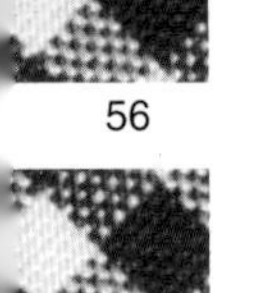

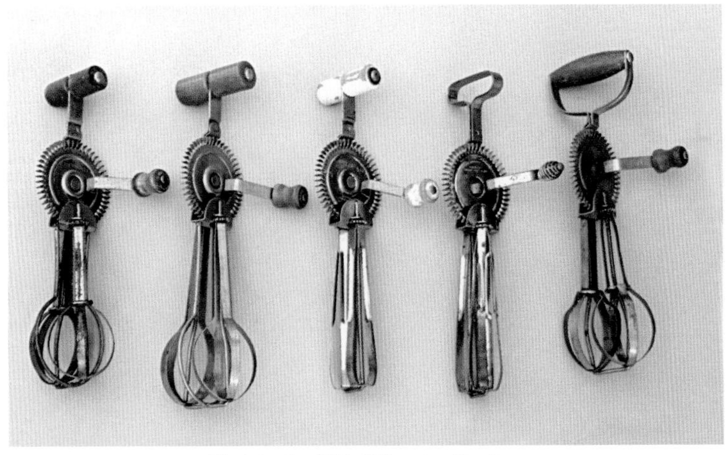

Various Ladd Ball Bearing Beaters

Ladd, metal rotary, marked "No. 1 Ladd Beater July 7, 1908, Oct, 1921," 11 1/2" h. (ILLUS. with grouping of Ladd beaters, top of page) **$15**

Ladd, tumbler model, metal rotary, marked "No. 5 Ladd Ball Bearing Beater Oct. 18 1921," 11 1/2" h. (ILLUS., top of page) **$35**

Ladd, beater held in two-part apron marked "Ladd No. 2," embossed on pedestal jar "Ladd Mixer No. 2," 13 1/2" h. (ILLUS. with grouping of Ladd beaters, top of page) **$200**

Rare Patented Master Egg Beater

Master, cast iron w/nickel plate, "Master Pat. Aug. 24-09," 10 3/4" (ILLUS.) **$1,500**

Merry Whirl, metal w/vertical wooden handle, marked "Merry Whirl - Pat. 11-28-16 Other Pat. Pend." **$20**

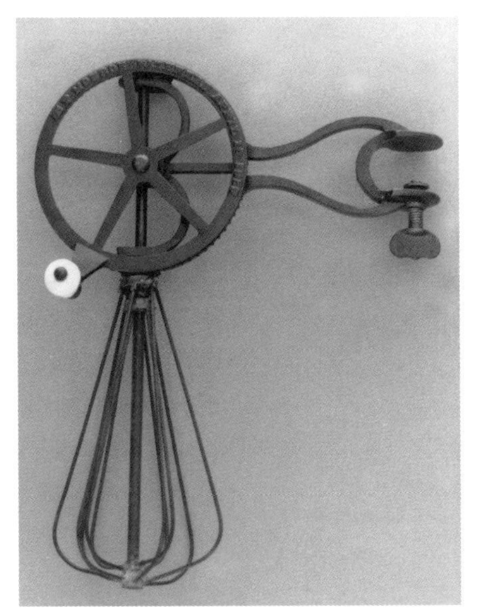

Monroe Rotary Egg Beater

Monroe, cast-iron rotary, shelf mount, marked "EP Monroe patented April 19 1859," 10 1/2" h. (ILLUS.) **$2,000**

New Keystone Beater, cast-iron top w/wire dashers & glass base, marked "New Keystone Beater No. 20 - North Bros. Pat Dec 15 '85" **$350**

P-D-&-Co., cast-iron rotary w/spring dasher bottom w/the word "E - A - S- Y" cut-out on spokes of main gear wheel & marked "Pat Sept. 28 26," 9 3/4" h. **$500**

Peerless, cast-iron w/tin dashers, marked "Peerless Egg Beater - Patent Applied For" **$1,000**

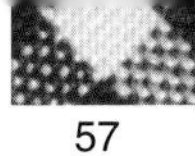

Perfection, cast iron, "Perfection Pat'd Feb. 22, 1898 Albany N.Y.," 10 1/4" **$350**

Hutchinson Iron & Glass Egg Beater

S & S Hutchinson, cast-iron wheel mechanism on a footed glass bowl base, pierced wheel with "S-S" marked "S&S Hutchson, New York, Pat. Appl. For," clear glass bowl base embossed "S&S Trade Mark Reg. U.S. Pat. Off. 852 Vernon Ave. Long Island City, N.Y.," 9 1/2" h. (ILLUS.) **$375**

S & S Hutchinson, cast-iron & glass rotary (w/Hutchinson cut-out in wheel) marked "Hutchinson New York Pat. apld For," footed clear glass bowl base embossed on apron "130 Worth St. New York J. Hutchinson S&S Trade Mark," 9 1/2" h. **$400**

S & S Hutchinson Rotary Egg Beater

S & S Hutchinson, heavy tin rotary marked "S&S Hutchinson No. 2 New York Pat. Sept. 2, 1913," w/heavy tin apron on ribbed glass jar embossed "National Indicator Co. No. 2 S&S Trade Mark Long Island City," 9 1/2" h. (ILLUS.) **$450**

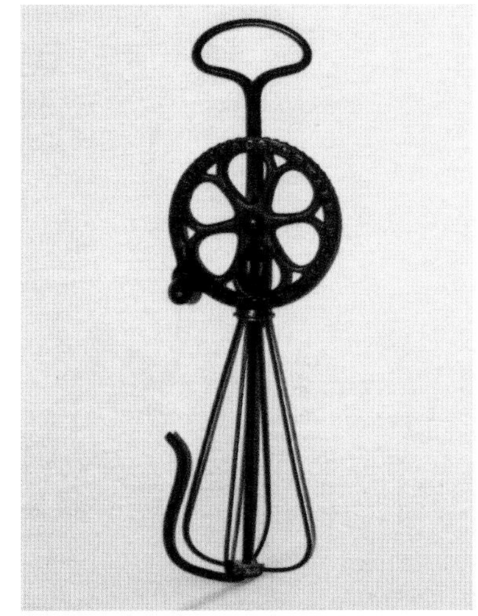

Rare R.P. Scott & Co. Eggbeater

Scott, cast iron, rim of wheel marked "R.P. Scott & Co. Newark N.J. Patented," 10 1/2" l. (ILLUS.) **$1,250**

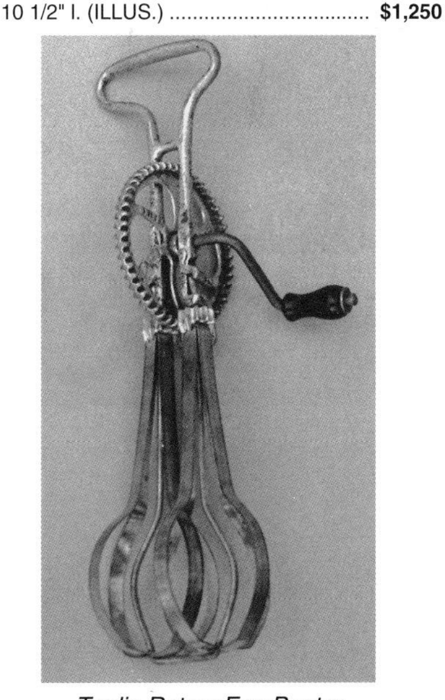

Taplin Rotary Egg Beater

Taplin, cast-iron rotary, marked "The Taplin Mfg. Co. New Britian Conn, U.S.A

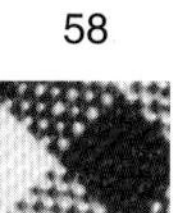

Light Running Pat. Nov. 24 '08," 12 1/2" h. (ILLUS.) $45

The World Beater, water-powered, painted tin top w/decal reading "The World Beater Mfrd by the World Novelty Co. Elgin, Ill." $125

Triumph, cast-iron w/tin dashers, marked "Triumph Sept 26, 1876" $750

Up-To-Date, metal, "Up-To-Date" egg/cream whip works on the Archimedian up & down action, patented April 10, 1906 .... $275

Miscellaneous

Apple corer - segmentor, cast iron & steel, a circle w/12 segmentors, cores & segments when apple is pushed through it, marked "Apple Cutter, Rollman Mfg. Co., Mr. Joy," 4 1/2" d. $35

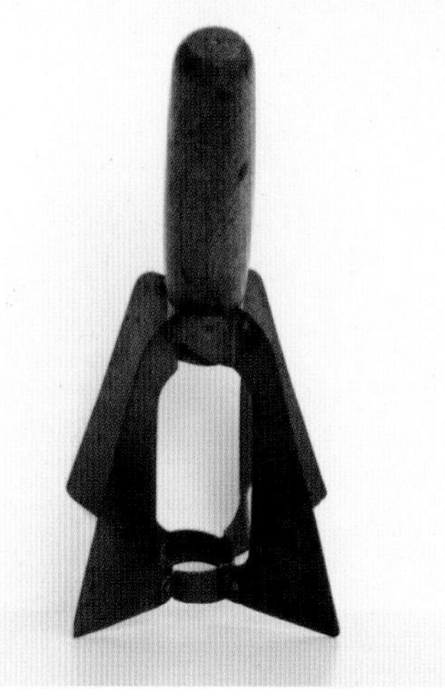

Tin & Wood Apple Corer/Segmentor

Apple corer - segmentor, tin apple corer w/four-section segmentor, wood handle, manufactured, no markings (ILLUS.) $55

Apple peeler, cast iron, "Baldwin".................. $125

Apple peeler, cast iron, "F.W. Hudson Improved - Pat. Dec. 2, 1862"........................ $150

Apple peeler, cast iron, marked only "Reading, PA" on turntable $200

Apple peeler, cast iron, "Nonpareil Parer, Patented May 6, 1858 J.L. Haven & Co. Cin. O".. $1,000 +

Apple peeler, cast iron, "Pat June 9, 1872 Mfd by G. Bergner Washington, MO," no segmenter $1,500

Apple peeler, cast iron, "Patd Oct. 5, 1880," unmarked Peck, Stow & Wilcox................ $275

Apple peeler, cast iron, "The Favorite L.A. Sayre Newark, N.J.".................................. $250

Apple peeler, cast iron, "White Mountain Apple Made by Goodell Co. Antrim, N.H. USA" $35

Rare Wiggin Apple Peeler

Apple peeler, cast iron, "Wiggin Pat. Aug. 4, 1868" (ILLUS.) $1,000

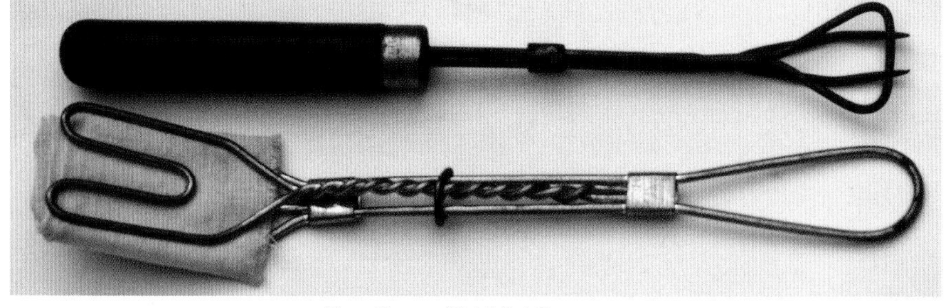

Two Bacon (Griddle) Greasers

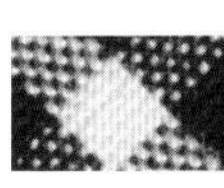

Bacon (griddle) greaser, black wood handle, marked "SANITARY GREASER HOLDER, OBLOSSER MFG. CO., FEB 5, 1910" (ILLUS. top w/other griddle greaser, bottom previous page) **$25**

Bacon (griddle) greaser, close-wrapped bottom fingers, "'FAIRY' griddle greaser PAT Dec. 1903" (ILLUS. bottom w/other griddle greaser, bottom previous page) **$35**

Twisted Wire Basket

Basket, wire w/twisted wire center handle, 7" at widest diameter (ILLUS.) **$85**

Unusual Wrought-iron Bird Spit

Bird spit for fireplace, wrought iron, three flattened arched legs w/penny feet sup-

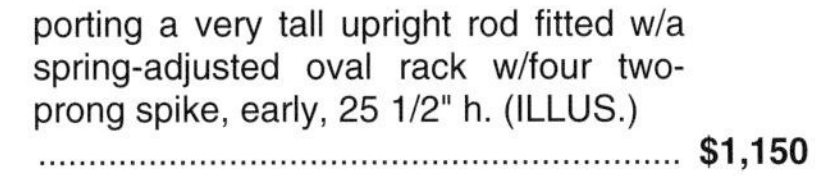

porting a very tall upright rod fitted w/a spring-adjusted oval rack w/four two-prong spike, early, 25 1/2" h. (ILLUS.) **$1,150**

Rolling Tin Biscuit Cutter

Biscuit cutter, tin, rolls three biscuits at a time, Pat. Sept. 12, 1893 (ILLUS.) **$65**

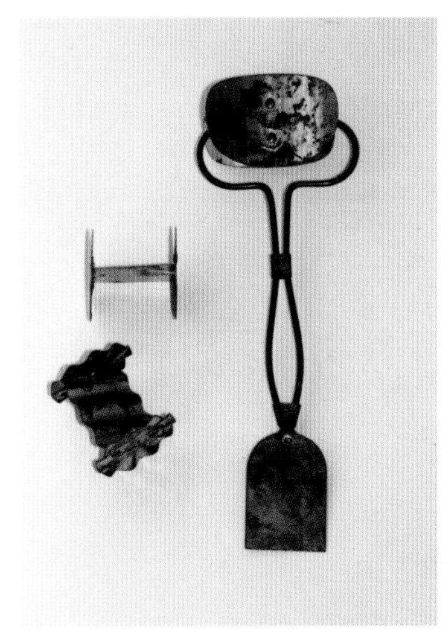

Biscuit Cutter with Interchangeable Discs

Biscuit cutter, w/three interchangeable discs, marked "Patented Felds MFG Co. INC; Jamestown, NY," complete, available (ILLUS.)...................................... **$100-125**

Early Decoraitve Pierced Brass Brazier

Brazier, brass, two-part, a high domed cover ornately pierced w/delicate lattice swags, leaf bands & a lower Greek key band & topped by a tall turned finial, the stepped & widely flaring base w/a pierced Greek key apron & raised on tall flat legs w/paw feet, probably Europe, 19th c., 30" d., 32" h. (ILLUS.) **$1,495**

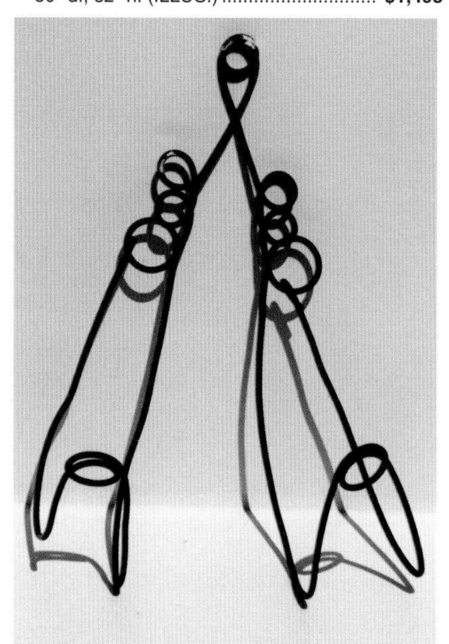

Wire Broom Holder

Broom holder, wire, ca. 1890 (ILLUS.) **$65**

Early Painted Stave Bucket

Bucket, cov., slightly tapering cylindrical form w/stave construction wrapped by three lapped bands, red-painted ground w/flat fitted black cover & black bands, red bentwood swing handle, painted in white on the side "C.R. Tartar," illegible lettering on handle, cover w/mark of "N. & J. Howe & Co. Fitzwilliam, N.Y.," 19th c., wear, bands loose, loss on handle peg, 13" d., 16" h. (ILLUS.) **$353**

Butter churn, cast-iron gear on tin top w/fruit jar base, "Schmidt Bros. Lancaster, PA" **$400**

Butter churn, Dazey Churn No. 80, "Patented Feb. 14, 11 / Dazey Churn & Mfg. Co. St. Louis, MO. Made in USA" **$200**

Butter churn, table model, all-tin, marked only "FRIES" **$85**

Butter churn, table model, cast iron frame w/tin container, "1 Gal. - Patented 130B Dazey Churn & Mfg. Co. St. Louis MO" cast in top of frame **$650**

Butter churn, table model, cast iron & tin top w/glass jar, "Dazey No. 20 - Patented Feb 14, 22 - Dazey Churn & Mg. Co., St. Louis, MO Made in U.S.A." **$250**

"The Home Butter Maker" Churn

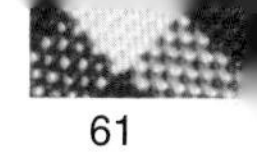
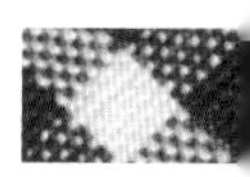

Butter churn, table model, tin & cast-iron top w/unmarked glass jar, "The Home Butter Maker, Kohler Die & Specialty Co. Dekalb, Ill USA" (ILLUS., previous page) **$125**

Old Oak Stave Butter Churn

Butter churn, lid & dasher, oak, stave construction w/five riveted steel bands, carved bottom, broom-handled dasher, 19th c., 19 1/2" h. (ILLUS.) **$288**

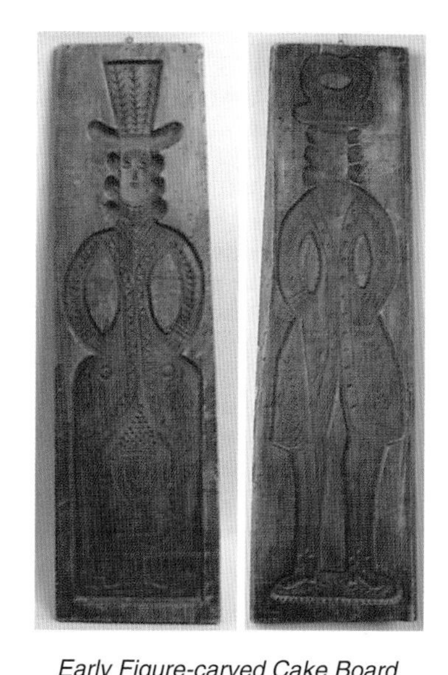

Early Figure-carved Cake Board

Cake board, double-sided, rectangular, one side carved w/a full-length figure of a man in 18th c. costume, the other side carved w/a matching figure of a woman, some worm holes, early, 10" w., 33" l. (ILLUS. of both sides) **$575**

Cake mold, copper turk's turban design w/swirled ribbing, late 19th c., 8 1/2" d., 3 3/4" h. (ILLUS. right with lobed food mold, page 87) **$575**

Cake turner, tin, horseshoe-shaped w/star marked "M.C.W. Cake Turner, Pat. Apr. 2. 07," wire handle flips it (ILLUS., bottom of page) **$115**

Horseshoe & Star Cake Turner

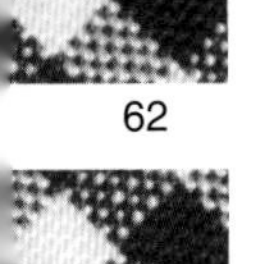

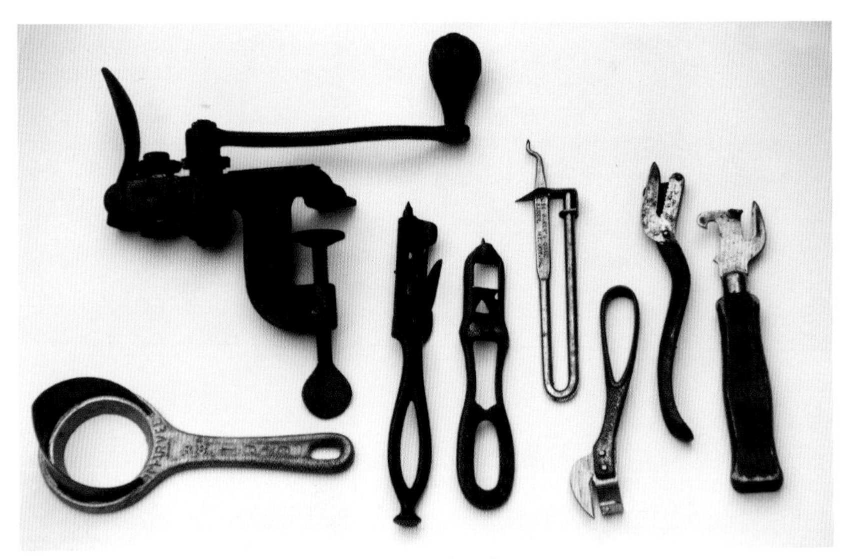

Various Vintage Can Openers

Can opener, aluminum w/steel blade, marked "Marvel" (ILLUS. bottom left w/other can openers, top of page) **$65**

Can opener, cast iron, adjustable clamp-on style, "Blue Streak" (ILLUS. top left w/other can openers, top of page) **$85**

Can opener, cast iron, adjustable, marked "World's Best, Dillsburg, Pa." (ILLUS. fifth from right w/other can openers, top of page) **$40**

Can opener, cast iron, adjustable, unmarked (ILLUS. sixth from right w/other can openers, top of page) **$60**

Can opener, cast iron, "Delmonico, Pat Feb 11 1898" (ILLUS. second from right w/other can openers, top of page) **$30**

Can opener, cast iron, marked "OK Pat 90 EWR," 7" l. **$45**

Can opener, cast iron, mounted on board, Williams's Patent of Jan 8, 1878, rare (ILLUS., bottom of page)........................... **$275**

Can opener, cast iron, Never Slip model, marked "Pat May 17, 92" (ILLUS. third from right w/other can openers, top of page)... **$25**

Can opener, cast iron & steel, marked "World's Best, Pittsburgh, PA" **$45**

Williams's Patent Can Opener

Can opener, cast iron, swings open, "Universal Dazey Americana New Britain, Conn. USA Patent Applied For" **$100**

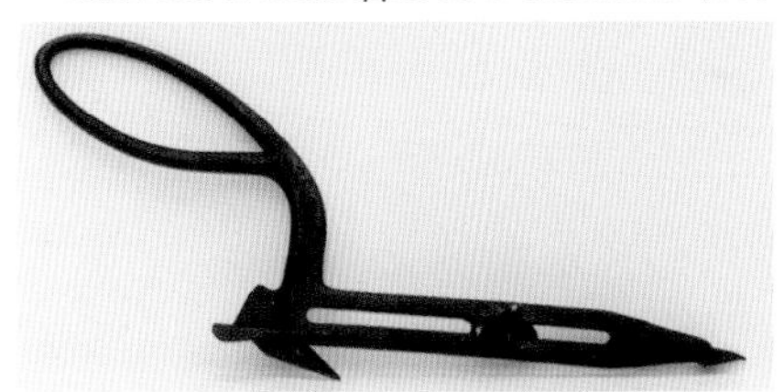

Gun-Style Can Opener

Can opener, cast-iron, gun-like structure w/three ways of penetrating can (ILLUS.) .. **$115**

Can opener, cast-iron w/steel blade, figural bull's head, 7" l. **$25**

Can opener, cast-iron w/steel blade, marked "Pat Apl. 2 90," 5" l. **$25**

Melco Kut-Rite Can Opener

Can opener, metal, Kut-Rite, Melco Mfg. Co., St. Louis, Missouri (ILLUS.) **$125**

Can opener, steel, marked "Use Baker's Coal, F.H. Baker, Mt. Joy, Pa." (ILLUS. fourth from right w/other can openers, top previous page) **$35**

Can opener, steel w/wooden handle, marked "Sure Cut," patent-dated "7-19-94" **$15**

Can opener, wooden handle, marked cap lifter & can opener (ILLUS. far right w/other can openers, top previous page) **$5**

Candle mold, twelve-tube, a round flat base w/flared rim supporting the slender cylindrical tubes topped by a matching round top centered by a cylindrical cap w/conical top fitted w/a small wire bail handle, 19th c., 9" d., overall 13 1/2" h. (ILLUS., top next column) **$575**

Candy kettle, copper, a large half-round form w/a heavy rolled rim & heavy riveted iron loop rim handles, early 20th c., 20" d. (ILLUS., middle next column) **$259**

Canister, cov., tole, cylindrical w/a hinged fitted cover w/small wire bail handle, dark japanned ground decorated w/stylized red, yellow & green flowers, some wear, 19th c., 4 1/2" d., 3 1/2" h. (ILLUS. center with tole document box & match holder, bottom this column).................................... **$288**

Fine 12-Tube Cylindrical Candle Mold

Large Old Copper Candy Kettle

Three Pieces of Early Decorative Tole

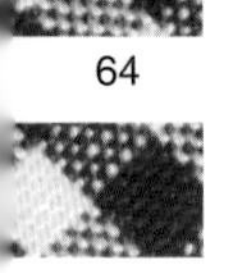

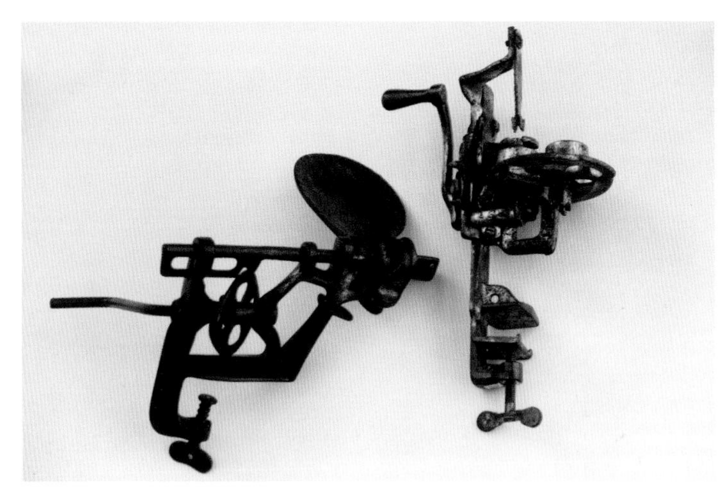

New Standard Cherry Pitters

Cherry pitter, cast iron, mechanical, marked "NEW STANDARD CORP. MT. JOY, PA., PATS. PEND," common (ILLUS. right w/New Standard Cherry Stoner model, top of page) **$145**

Cherry pitter, cast iron, mechanical, "wobble" wheel, marked "NEW STANDARD CHERRY STONER N.S. HDWE WKS," common (ILLUS. left w/other New Standard cherry pitter, top of page)..................... **$95**

Cherry pitter, cast iron, clamp-on style, push action pits two cherries at one time, marked "New Standard Cherry Stoner, Duplex No. 35 Mt. Joy PA U.S.A." **$85**

Cherry pitter, cast iron, "Enterprise Cherry Stoner Pat Appl'd For No 12," 13".............. **$125**

Cherry pitter, cast iron, standing on four legs, "Electric Cherry Seeder".................... **$125**

Cherry pitter, cast iron, standing on three legs, "Pat'd Nov 17, 1863"......................... **$200**

Cherry pitter, cast iron, "The Boss Raisin Seeder, Pat. Pdg.," 11 3/4" **$150**

Cherry pitter, cast iron, "The Rapid Mfd By Ed Parker Co Springfield Ohio Pat Pend" **$1,000**

Cherry pitter, cast iron w/three legs, marked "Pat'd Nov. 17, 1863" (ILLUS., top next column)... **$145**

Cherry pitter, nickel-plated cast iron, "New Standard Corp. Mt. Joy, PA. Pat. Pend. No. 50" in all caps **$35**

Cherry pitter, tin, a flat tray base centered by a narrow upright rectangular compartment below the flaring feeding bin, the upper section w/moveable plungers, spring-loaded mechanism for pitting eight cherries at a time, 19th c., 10" w., 13" h. (ILLUS., bottom next column) **$288**

Cast-Iron Patented Cherry Pitter

Unusual Old Tin Cherry Pitter

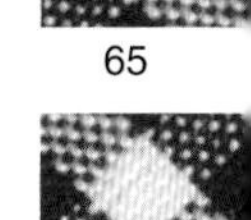

Single Cherry Pitter

Cherry pitter, tin, single pitter, no markings (ILLUS.) **$30**

Cherry pitter, tin, spring-action, pits eight cherries at once, marked "Marshall Mfg. Co. Cherry Pitter, Omaha, Neb. Pat. Jan. 4 1916" **$250**

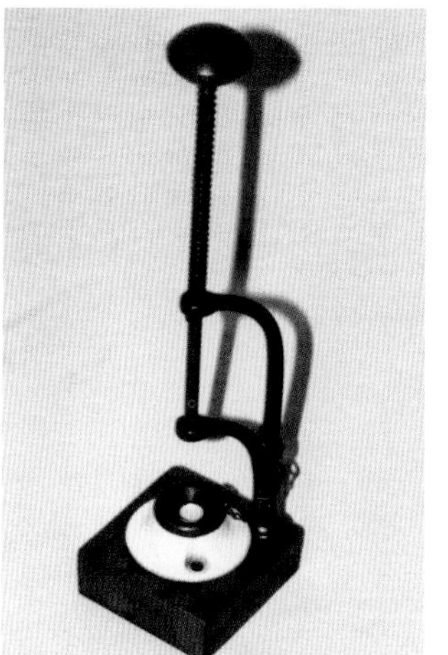

Wood, Porcelain & Iron Cherry Pitter

Cherry pitter, wood, porcelain & cast iron, crack-type, unmarked, 10 1/2" (ILLUS.) **$125**

Chocolate grater, tin spring-loaded box which sits on tin grating cylinder & slides back & forth (similar to the Edgar nutmeg grater), marked "The Edgar" Pat. Nov. 10, 1896 (ILLUS., top next column) **$85-125**

Chopper, cast iron handle w/two metal blades, handle marked "Pat'd. May 2, 93 No. 20 Croton, NY" (ILLUS., middle next column) **$45**

Tin Spring-Loaded Chocolate Grater

Two-Bladed Metal Chopper

Chopper with Rotating Blade

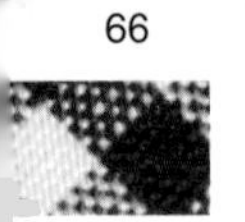

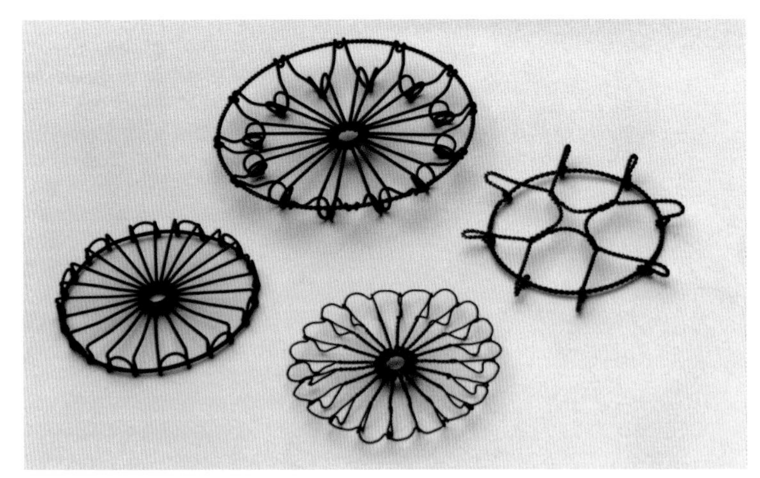
Various Coffeepot or Teapot Stands

Chopper, wood handle w/pivoted rotating triangular blade featuring coarse, fine & smooth sides, wooden handle (ILLUS., previous page) **$65**

Coffee roaster, cast iron, hinged "cannon ball" shape sits in a three-legged rim, wire bail handle, marked "Wood's Patent, Roys and Wilcox Co., Harrington's Import, Berlin Ct. Pat'd 5 17 1859," two sizes **$585**

Coffeepot or teapot stand, wrapped wire in a star pattern, hard to find (ILLUS. top w/three other stands, top of page) **$85**

Coffeepot or teapot stand, wrapped wire, typical radiating design, common (ILLUS. left w/three other stands, top of page).......... **$35**

Coffeepot or teapot stand, wrapped wire w/diamond center, hard to find (ILLUS. right w/three other stands, top of page) **$45**

Coffeepot or teapot stand, wrapped wire w/scalloped sides, common (ILLUS. bottom w/three other stands, top of page) **$55**

Combination funnel/apple corer/grater/cookie cutter, marked "PAT. APPD FOR," hard to find (ILLUS. center top w/other combination utensils, bottom of page)... **$225**

Combination kettle bail carrier/meat tenderizer/trivet/pudding dish carrier/pie remover/stove lid lifter, cast iron, marked "THAYERS PAT MAY 24, 1881" (ILLUS. top left w/other combination utensils, bottom of page) **$85**

Four Early Combination Kitchen Utensils

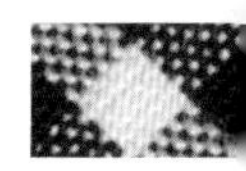

Nice Early Wood & Metal Cranberry Scoop

Combination spatula/meat tenderizer, iron w/wood handle, marked "PATENT JULY 11, 1916," hard to find (ILLUS. right w/other combination utensils, bottom previous page) **$135**

Combination trivet/fish scaler/bottle opener/can opener/hammer & tack pull, cast iron, marked "SIX IN ONE MFG BY PARK NOVELTY CO. BALTO MD," has been reproduced (ILLUS. bottom left w/other combination utensils, bottom of previous page) **$75**

Cookie board, rectangular flat board w/small rectangular integral handle at one end, chip-carved in the center w/a large compass star framed by geometric carved corners, good patina, 19th c., 6 3/4" w., overall 12 3/4" l. **$468**

Unusual Patented Iron Cork Extractor

Cork extractor, cast iron, a tall arched body decorated w/ornate delicate scrolls, a hinged turned wood handle, large hand-grips at the sides of the bottom, adjustable extracting mechanism on the front, marked "Champion," patent-dated in 1898, 9" h. (ILLUS.) **$316**

Cranberry scoop, wooden curved-bottom box w/a galvanized metal back & 22 long pointed wooden teeth, galvanized metal side straps, the flat top w/a rectangular wood frame enclosing a galvanized metal panel, low open top end brackets joined by front & back round grip bars, late 19th - early 20th c., 21" l., 10" h. (ILLUS., top of page) **$200-250**

Early Toleware Dipper

Dipper, tole, cylindrical bowl w/tapering strap handle, the bowl decorated w/red & mustard decorative band on black ground, the handle w/mustard & red leaf decoration, bowl 3 1/2" d., 2 1/4" h., 8" w/handle (ILLUS.) **$480**

Dish drainer, tin & wire, wire dish rack fits into rectangular tilted pan (ILLUS., top next page) **$50**

Document box, cov., tole, rectangular w/domed hinged cover w/brass bail handle, original yellow, red & black paint w/fruit, foliage & flourishes, tin hasp, some wear, first half 19th c., 4 3/4 x 8 3/4", 5 1/4" h. **$1,121**

Document box, cov., tole, rectangular w/low domed cover & wire pail handle, (ILLUS. bottom with tole canister & match holder, page 63) **$460**

Document box, cov., tole, rectangular w/domed hinged cover w/wire ring handle & tin hasp, original painted decoration of red & white roses w/green & yellow foliage on three sides & yellow decoration on the cover, japanned ground, wear, mainly on cover, damage to hasp, first half 19th c., 4 3/4 x 9 3/4", 6 1/4" h. **$805**

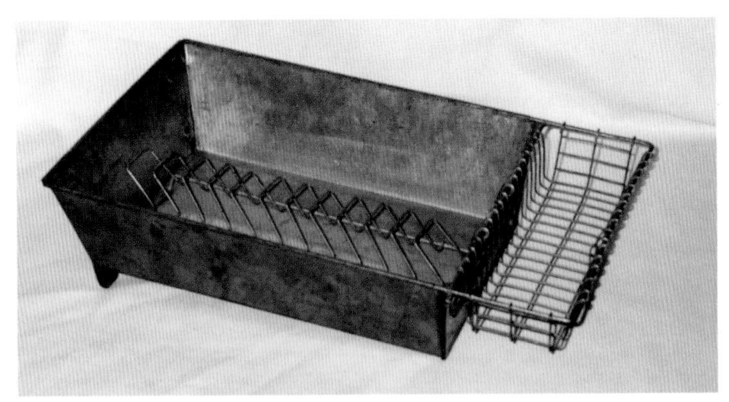

Metal Dish Drainer with Rack & Pan

Black-decorated Tole Document Box

Document box, cov., tole, rectangular w/hinged domed cover w/wire loop handle, original painting w/black ground decorated on the front w/a yellow band trimmed w/large red berries & green leaves, overall yellow swags & petal devices, artist-initials "d/c" on a white band, minor wear, America, 19th c., 4 3/4 x 8 3/4", 5 1/2" h. (ILLUS.) **$1,495**

Wrought-Iron Dough Scraper

Dough scraper, wrought iron w/multi-faceted knob, mid-1800s (ILLUS.) **$200**

Egg carrier, wire, round w/loops of wire forming bottom below six rings to hold eggs, looped wire center handle, ca. 1890 .... **$125**

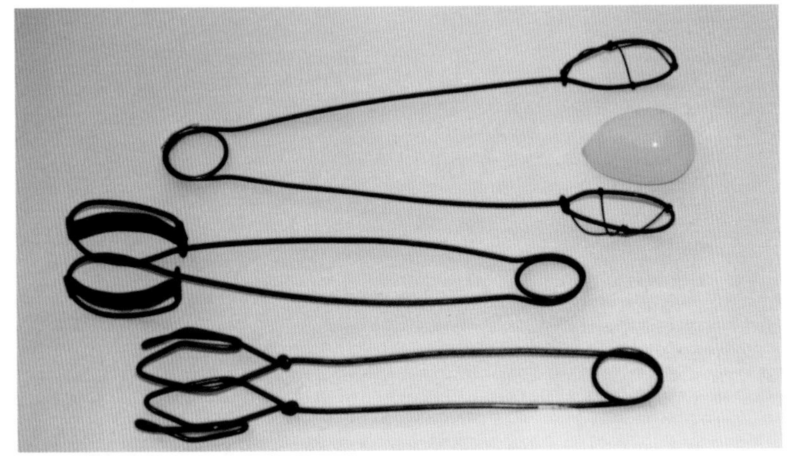

Three Wire Egg Lifters

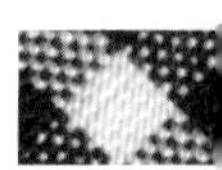

Reliable Mfg. Co., Los Angeles Egg Scale

Egg lifter, heavy twisted wire in diamond-shaped bowl, hard to find (ILLUS. bottom w/other wire egg lifters, bottom previous page) **$40**

Egg lifter, thin wire in egg-shaped bowl (ILLUS. top w/other wire egg lifters, bottom previous page) **$35**

Egg lifter, tin, marked on straps "PAT DEC 16 1913," common (ILLUS. center w/other wire egg lifters, bottom previous page) **$25**

Egg scale, metal, platform-style, "Reliable Mfg Co./Los Angeles Calif," 8 3/4" (ILLUS., top of page) **$75-85**

Egg scale, tin & aluminum, marked "Acme Egg Grading Scale Pat. June 24, 1924 - The Specialty Mfg. Co. St. Paul, Minnesota," 9 3/4" h. **$30**

Egg scale, tin, marked "H.L. Piper Montreal," four egg holes **$100**

Egg Baking Powder Egg Separator

Egg separator, tin, advertising-type, border stamped "Egg Baking Powder - Something to Crow About" (ILLUS.) **$45-55**

Egg separator, tin, advertising-type, "Compliments of Mothers Oats" **$30**

Egg separator, tin, advertising-type, "Use Big Jo Flour - Best in The World" **$15**

Unusual Early Brass Fireplace Reflector

Fireplace reflector, hand-wrought brass & iron, a large half-round shield form w/an arched band of buttons around the high domed répoussé center decorated w/stylized shell & leafy scroll designs, a wide bottom band w/raised buttons, all raised on three twisted iron legs joined by a bowed lower stretcher base & ending in slender scrolled feet, dark toning & some surface rust, probably 18th c., 21" w., 24" h. (ILLUS.) **$345**

Fireplace roaster, hand-wrought iron, a long flat tapering handle ending in a heart-shaped loop, the round rotating roasting rack divided into four quadrants, each w/three tight scrolls, raised on arched feet, America, late 18th c., overall 28" l., rack 12" d., 3 1/2" h. **$1,150**

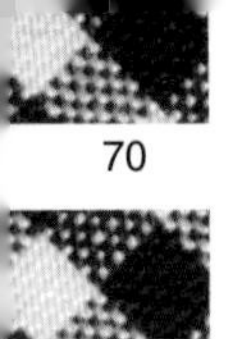

Tin Marked Fish Scaler

Unusual Early Iron Fireplace Trivet

Fireplace trivet, wrought iron, rectangular form w/long flat side bars raised on scroll-tipped legs, eight crossbars, the back w/a curved upright strap handles w/heart-shaped top w/a hanging hole, early, 9 x 13" (ILLUS.) **$201**

Fish scaler, tin, three grating sides, long cylindrical handle marked "FISH SCALER," rare (ILLUS., top of page) **$65**

Flour sifter, tin, child's, Hunter Flour sifter, marked " Hunter's Toy - Sifter - Pat. May 16, 71 - Apr. 7, 74 - Buy A Big One," 2 1/4" h., rare (ILLUS. center with two other flour sifters, bottom of page)............. **$225**

Flour sifter, tin, cylindrical shape, marked "GEM SIFTER MANUF BY JL CLARK, MANU. CO ROCKFORD, ILL.," common (ILLUS. bottom w/three other wood & tin flour sifters, top of next page) **$45**

Flour sifter, tin, divided w/lids on both ends, marked "Bromwells Multiple"........................ **$28**

Three Varied Tin Flour Sifters

Four Various Wood & Tin Flour Sifters

New Shaker Flour Sifter

Flour sifter, tin, mesh screen in bottom, shake handle from side to side for action, marked "The New Shaker Sifter, Center Drive, Prevents Tipping, Pat. Applied For," two-cup size (ILLUS.) **$35**

Flour sifter, tin, paper label for Hunter's Flour sifter (ILLUS. left with two other flour sifters, bottom of previous page)........ **$55+**

Flour sifter, tin w/brass disc on handle, tapering cylindrical shape, marked "LIC'D BY NATL MFG. CO," hard to find (ILLUS. right w/three other wood & tin flour sifters, top of page) **$75**

Flour sifter, tin w/cast-iron legs, stenciled on side " The GEM Flour & Saucer Sifter - Patd. Dec. 26 1865," rare (ILLUS. right with two other flour sifters, bottom of previous page) .... **$250+**

Flour sifter, tin w/wire handle, advertising-type, "Snow King Powder - 30 Years of Success," 3 1/2" d. plus handle **$50**

Flour sifter, tin & wood, "Duplex Sifter 5 cup, Pat. Nov. 1917 & 1922, Mfg. by Ullrich Tinware Co." **$30**

Flour sifter, wood, stenciled "Blood's Sifter Pat Sept 17, 1861" **$375**

Flour sifter, wood w/bottom screens, rectangular, marked "Bloods Improved Sifter" (ILLUS. top w/three other wood and tin flour sifters, top of page) **$295**

Flour sifter, wood & wire, cylindrical shape, w/concentric wire w/wooden grip, marked "JONES FLOUR & MEAL SIFTER, AP'L 17, 66," hard to find, 2 pcs. (ILLUS. left w/three other wood & tin flour sifters, top of page) **$125**

Flour sifter, wooden, elevated frame w/revolving brush inside, stamped "W. Foyes Flour Sifter, Patented Sept 12, 1865" **$325**

Flour sifter, wire mesh bowl encompassed by three wire legs w/removable insert of rotating center blade, stamped "Boon, Mills & Co., Pat'd. Jan. 17, 1870," 9" d. **$285**

Flour sifter/scoop, tin w/half round wire mesh scoop & removable screwed-on long handle, marked "Pillsbury's Flour Universal Scoop with Flour Attachment" **$110**

Flour sifter/scoop, tin & wire mesh, half round scoop w/removable screwed-on long handle, marked "Pillsbury's Flour Universal Scoop with Flour Attachment" **$110**

Flue Cover with Pretty Victorian Girl

Flue cover, lithographed paper in frame, a round colorful bust portrait of a pretty late-Victorian girl wearing a large bonnet w/deep reddish plumes & poppy blossom & tied w/matching sash, thin brass frame w/a pierced hanging mount at the top, minor water stain at bottom, ca. 1900, 14 1/2" d. (ILLUS.) **$259**

Four Varied Wire Fly Swatters

Fly swatter, wire handle & circular wire mesh w/three protrusions to keep fly from smashing against wall, hard to find (ILLUS. left w/three other fly swatters) **$40**

Fly swatter, wire handle & rectangular screen, common (ILLUS. second from left w/three other fly swatters) **$15**

Fly swatter, wooden handle & fine wires in fan shape, marked on brass "PAT'D JAN 8, 1895," common (ILLUS. second from right w/three other fly swatters) **$75**

Fly swatter, wooden handle & wire ovoid screen w/cloth border, common (ILLUS. right w/three other fly swatters) **$30**

Victorian Mechanical Food Charger

Food charger, mechanical, a large wheel-operated cast-iron mechanism w/an arm fitting into a deep cylindrical copper container, all mounted on a rectangular board base, second half 19th c., 16" l. (ILLUS.) **$258**

Iron Single Blade Food Chopper

Food chopper, hand-wrought iron, single blade, wood handle, ca. 1850 (ILLUS.)........ **$30**

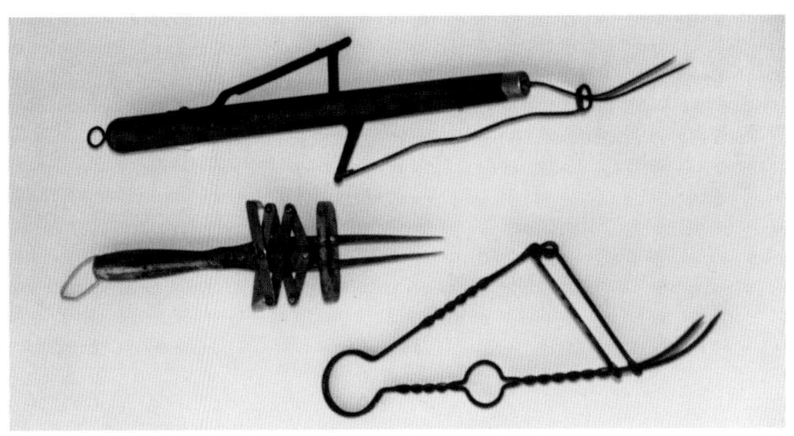

Three Varied Fork Ejectors

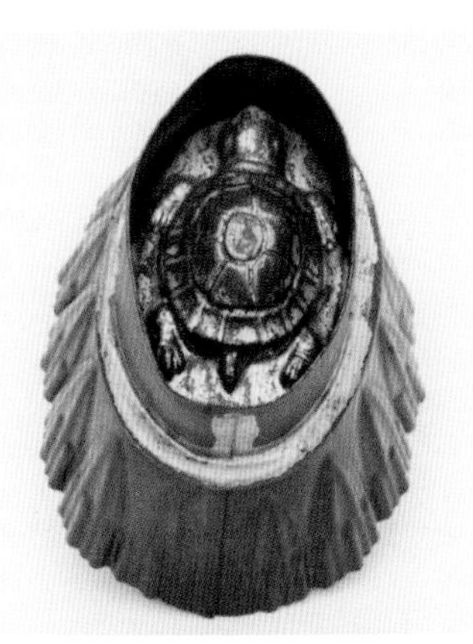

Turtle-design Tin Food Mold

Goblet with "Make-Do" Base

Food mold, tin, oval, molded with turtle on top, deep fluted sides, 4 1/4" l., 3 1/4" h. (ILLUS.) **$225**

Fork ejector, metal, squeeze to eject item on fork, common (ILLUS. center w/other fork ejectors, top of page) **$25**

Fork ejector, twisted wire, squeeze to eject item on fork, common (ILLUS. bottom w/other fork ejectors, top of page)................ **$35**

Fork ejector, wood handle, projection at top is pushed to eject item on fork, hard to find (ILLUS. top w/other fork ejectors, top of page).. **$65**

Goblet, glass top w/replaced old tin "make-do" base, make-do's becoming very collectible (ILLUS., top next column) **$125**

Grater, tin, hand-punched, common (ILLUS. left w/other tin grater, bottom next column) **$45**

Grater, tin, manufactured, common (ILLUS. right w/other tin grater, bottom next column).. **$20**

Two Early Tin Graters

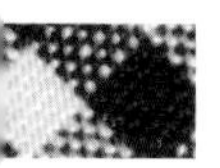

Griddle - pancake iron, cast iron, divided into three or more round areas each w/a lift-lid, marked "Pat. Jan 25 1881, S Mfg. Co., New York" **$175**

Pressed Copper & Brass Ice Bucket

Ice bucket, cov., cylindrical shape, w/brass riveted side handles, lid handle & foot-ring, the lower body pressed w/hammered design, complete w/liner, 12 x 15" (ILLUS.) **$201**

Ice cream freezer, tin w/advertising, "Champion Triple Action - Brooklyn, NY," 8" d., 13" h.. **$200**

Jar lid reformer, cast-aluminum w/wooden handle, round, marked "Miller Pattern Co. Toledo, Ohio," 3" d. **$45**

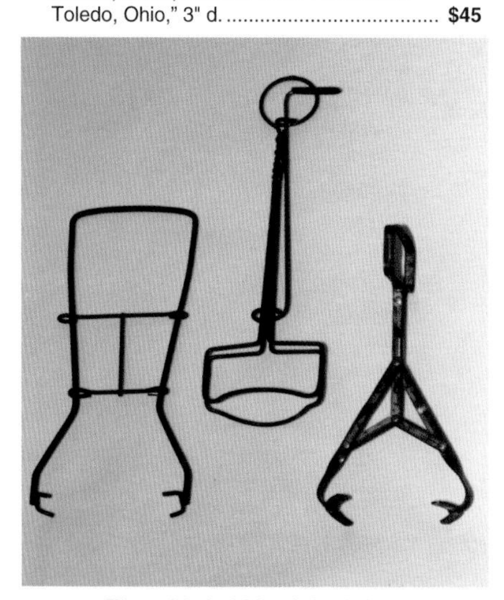

Three Varied Metal Jar Lifters

Jar lifter, flat steel hinged framework w/two incurved claws at the bottom (ILLUS. right with two other jar lifters) **$25**

Jar Lifter with Wooden Handle

Jar lifter, steel w/turned wood handle, marked "Pat Pend," 8 1/2" h. (ILLUS.) **$30**

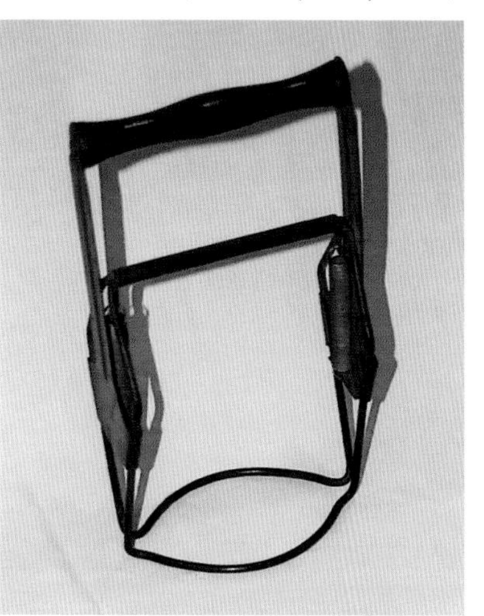

Tin & Wood Jar Lifter

Jar lifter, tin w/red wood handle, spring-operated, marked "Pat. Pend," 8 1/2" l. (ILLUS.) **$25-35**

Jar lifter, wire, high arched & squared wire handle continuing to down to two claws (ILLUS. left with two other jar lifters, previous column).. **$25**

Jar lifter, wire, long wire handle w/spring operation for the rectangular grippers (ILLUS. center with two other jar lifters, previous column)... **$30**

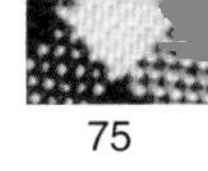

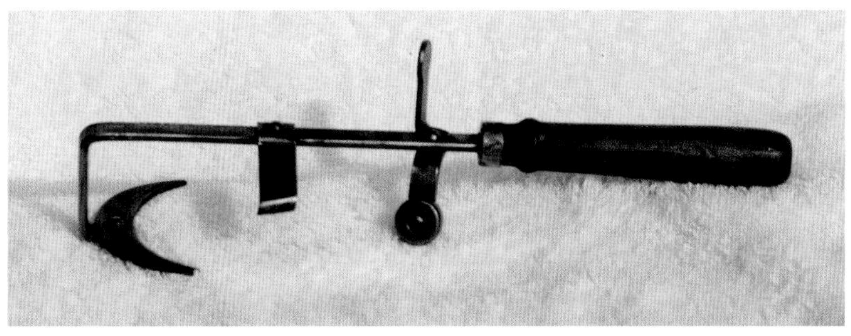

Marked W. Fabrick Jar Sealer

Patented Iron Jar Opener

Jar opener, cast iron, very unusual screw clamp mechanism, marked "Pat June 18, 1888," 8 3/4" l. (ILLUS.) **$150**

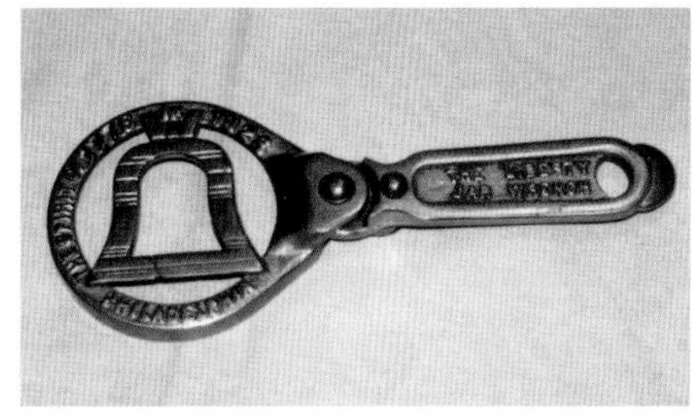

Marked 1926 Liberty Jar Opener

Jar opener, cast iron w/nickel plate, opener w/outline of bell in center & "The Spirit of 1776 in 1926 Philadelphia" around rim, handle marked "The Liberty Jar Wrench," 7" (ILLUS.) **$75**

Jar opener, steel w/tin strap, scissors-type, marked "Pat Feb 11, 1902," 7 3/4" l. **$10**

Jar opener, tin, "The Turney Mfg. Co. Detroit, Mich Pat Oct 31, 1905" **$30**

Jar opener, wood & steel w/spring-operated mechanism, marked "Ken Standard Corp. Evansville, Ind Jar Wrench Pat Pend," 6" d. **$50**

Jar opener, wood, tin & wire, marked "Off-On Jar Cap Remover - Detroit, Michigan - Patented In Canada, Patent Pending in USA," 4" d. **$75**

Jar sealer, metal w/wooden handle, marked "W. Fabrick, Elgin, Ill." (ILLUS., top of page) **$65**

Unusual Early Copper Covered Kettle

Kettle, a deep cylindrical form w/a slightly rounded bottom, the slightly domed hinged cover pierced w/overall decorative holes, iron side rim handle for holding wooden extension, early 19th c., 19" l. (ILLUS.).. **$104**

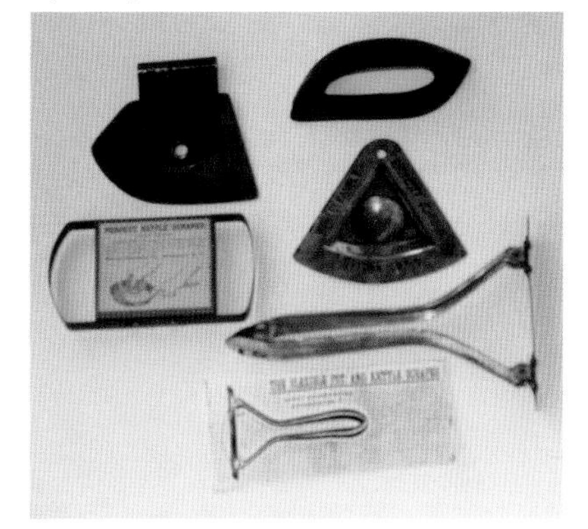

Various Kettle & Pot Scrapers

Kettle scraper, wood & steel, rectangular wooden body w/flexible steel bands at each end, paper label reading "PERFECT KETTLE SCRAPER" followed by short paragraph & illustration of pan & scraper, hard to find (ILLUS. center left w/other scrapers) **$75**

Kettle Stand with Cabriole Legs

Kettle stand, brass, the rectangular top w/a slightly bowed front above a conforming scroll-cut front apron w/front cabriole legs, iron rod back legs, a cast brass handle flanking the top, 19th c., 11 3/4 x 18 3/4", 12" h. (ILLUS.) **$201**

Pierced Brass & Iron Kettle Stand

Kettle stand, D-form cast brass top w/ornate pierced scroll & floral medallions around the skirt, raised on three wrought-iron cabriole legs ending in large penny feet, a decorative rosette missing on front, 19th c., 10 1/2 x 13", 13 1/2" h. (ILLUS.) **$460**

Knife sharpener, steel, combination can opener, marked "Lightning Sharpener," 5 1/2" l. **$30**

Kraut cutter, a long flat rectangular board inset w/an angled metal cutting blade, the heart-shaped top w/a small hanging hole, well scrubbed & used surface, 7" w., 21 1/2" l. (ILLUS., top next column) **$345**

Kraut cutter, pine w/good patina & traces of old red, rectangular board w/screwed-on side rail, angled blade, a heart-shaped cut-out crest w/hanging hole, 19th c., 7 3/4" w., 19" l. (wear, some old splits) **$110**

Kraut Cutter with Heart-shaped Top

Kraut cutter, two-tier style, hickory or ash w/old brown surface, steel blade & brass fittings in the top level, the two levels supported between pierced scroll-cut sides, 19th c., 7 x 13", 7 1/4" h. (age splits, one scallop missing) **$86**

Kraut cutter, walnut, rectangular board w/screwed side rails, angled blade, round crest w/hanging hole, old patina, 7 1/2 x 24 1/2" **$83**

Sammis Patented Lemon Reamer

Lemon reamer, cast iron, marked "EM Sammis - Pat Sept 21, 1876," 14" l. (ILLUS.) **$500**

Lemon reamer, cast iron, marked "Pat Nov 21, 1885," 9 1/2" l. **$25**

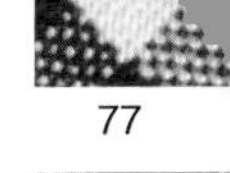
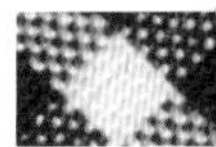

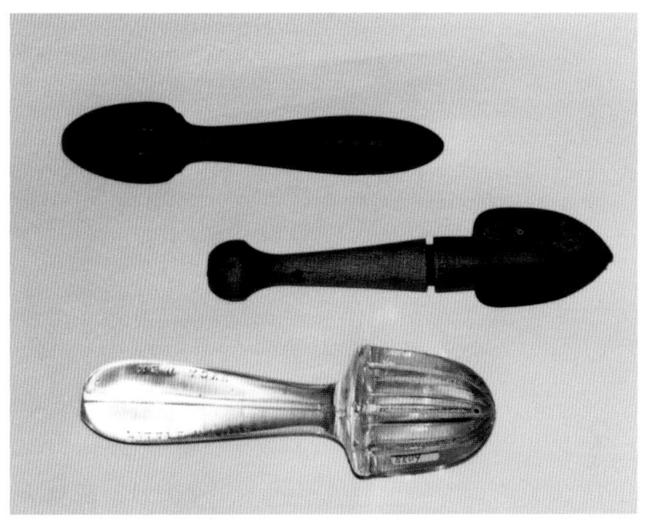

Old Wood & Glass Lemon Reamers

Lemon reamer, glass, molded form, marked "LITTLEHANDY LEMON SQUEEZER, SILVER & CO., NEW YORK," common (ILLUS. bottom w/two other lemon reamers, top of page)............... **$75**

Lemon reamer, tin & wood, pointed tin blades, sometimes w/serrated edges, wooden handle w/groove to prevent juice from running, hard to find (ILLUS. center w/two other lemon reamers, top of page)... **$125**

Lemon reamer, wood, conical grooved body (ILLUS. top w/two other lemon reamers, top of page)................................... **$75**

Upright Iron Lemon Squeezer/Slicer

Lemon squeezer/slicer, cast iron, combination cutter & squeezer on wood base w/crank action of handle forcing juice from lemon, inserts often missing, approx. 13" h. (ILLUS.) **$200-225**

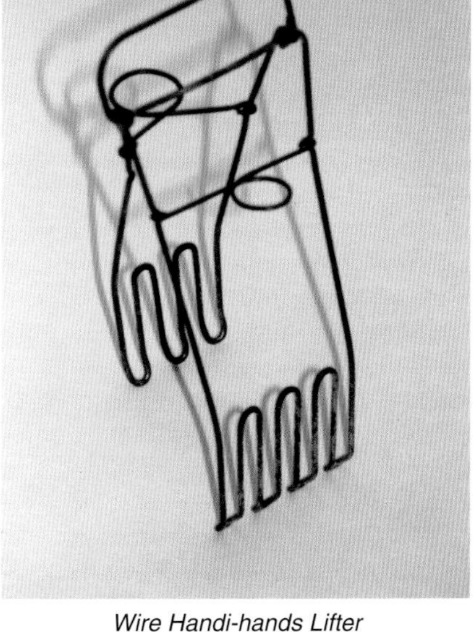

Wire Handi-hands Lifter

Lifter, handi-hands-style, wire, two hinged hand-like sections used to lift items from kettles, etc. (ILLUS.) **$65**

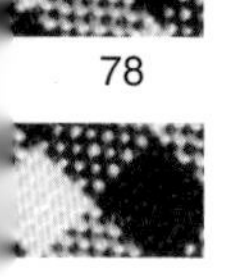

Tin Collapsable Lunch Pail

Lunch pail, tin & wire, collapsible-type, four sections, marked "Pat. Feb. 26 1884" (ILLUS.) **$95-125**

Match holder, tole, hanging-type, rounded scalloped crest w/hanging hole, w/starburst & flourishes on the pocket in shades of blue, yellow & red on a black ground, 19th c., 7 1/2" h. (minor wear)....... **$660**

Match holder, tole, hanging-type, the tall cut-out back plate w/an arched & fanned top rim & centered by a hanging hole framed by a diamond-shaped arrangement of dark red & yellow leaves, the squared bottom fitted w/a narrow projecting open match holder decorated w/a smoky white band & a yellow & red fruit flanked by green leaves, slight wear, 19th c., 7 1/2" h. (ILLUS. top with tole canister & document box, page 63)...................... **$2,128**

Match safe, tole, original japanned ground & paint w/a tulip on a white band on the front & swags on the cut-out & crimped crest, wear, 19th c., 7 1/2" h. **$575**

DeLaval Cream Separator Match & Toothpick Holder

Match & toothpick holder, "DeLaval Cream Separators," tin litho, form of a cream separator, panel at bottom reads "The DeLaval Separator Co." w/list of cities where it operated, in original cardboard box, box is 4 x 6 1/2", 1 1/4" h. (ILLUS. w/box) **$550**

Mayonnaise mixer, cast iron & glass, "Universal Mayonnaise Mixer and Cream Whipper Made by Landers, Frary & Clark, New Britain, Conn. USA"................. **$450**

Mayonnaise mixer, tin & glass, "Wesson Oil Mayonnaise Maker," 8 1/2".................... **$35**

Measuring cup, tin, one-cup w/measuring lines, marked "Rumford" **$30**

Measuring spoons, tin, 1/4 tsp. or 15 drops, 1/2 tsp. or 30 drops & 1 tsp. or 60 drops, marked "Original," the set (ILLUS. right with two other sets of spoons, bottom of page).. **$50**

Measuring spoons, tin, a tsp. or 60 drops, 1 dessert or 120 drops & 1 tbs. or 230 drops, marked "UNIVERSAL," rare, the set (ILLUS. left with two other sets of spoons, bottom of page) **$85**

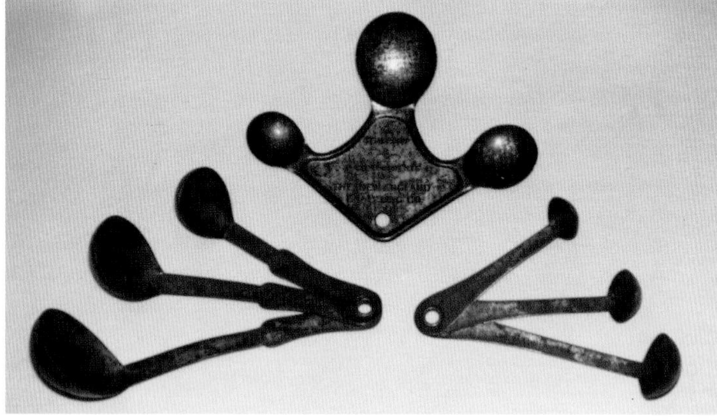

Three Sets of Metal Measuring Spoon Sets

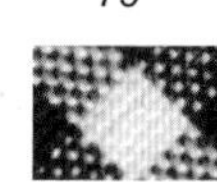

Measuring spoons, tin, combination, 1/4 tsp., 1/2 tsp., & 1 tsp., marked "COMPLIMENTS OF THE NEW ENGLAND ENAMELING CO.," rare, the set (ILLUS. center with two other sets of spoons, bottom previous page) **$125**

Meat tenderizer, cast iron, handled w/five toothed rows in a rectangular frame, marked "Pat. Appd. For".............................. **$45**

Meat tenderizer, cast iron, handled, w/five toothed rows in rectangular frame, marked "Pat. Applied For" **$55**

Mortar & pestle, carved & painted birch, mortar w/a wide band around the base w/an ovoid body, old red paint, good patina, split, overall 8 1/4" h. **$230**

Mortar & pestle, turned burl w/flame graining, a thick ringed foot below the wide cylindrical bowl, pestle of darker wood, probably lignum vitae, 19th c., overall 7" h., the set (age splits) **$374**

Muffin pan, tin, 12-cup size, plain (ILLUS. top, left, with various pans & molds, top page 82)... **$12**

English Tin Acme Nut Grater

Nut grater, tin, half-round w/hanging hole at top, stamped "Acme Nut Grater Rd 114671," English (ILLUS.)........................... **$40**

Iron Perfection Nut Cracker

Nutcracker, cast iron, clamp-style for attaching to table edge, clamp-form cracker, marked "Perfection Nut Cracker - Made in Waco, Texas - Patented 1914," 6 x 6 1/2" (ILLUS.).................................. **$55-65**

Early Cast-iron Dog Nutcracker

Nutcracker, cast iron, model of a large standing dog on a rectangular platform base, hinged long tail operates the nut-cracking jaws, traces of gold paint, late 19th c., 4 1/2 x 7 1/4", 5" h. (ILLUS.) **$294**

Rare Francis Nutmeg Grater

Nutmeg grater, cast iron, marked "Francis Grater Pat'd," rare (ILLUS.)................... **$1,000+**

Nutmeg grater, cast iron, tin & wire, patented by Church in 1886, 7" l. (ILLUS., top next page).. **$375**

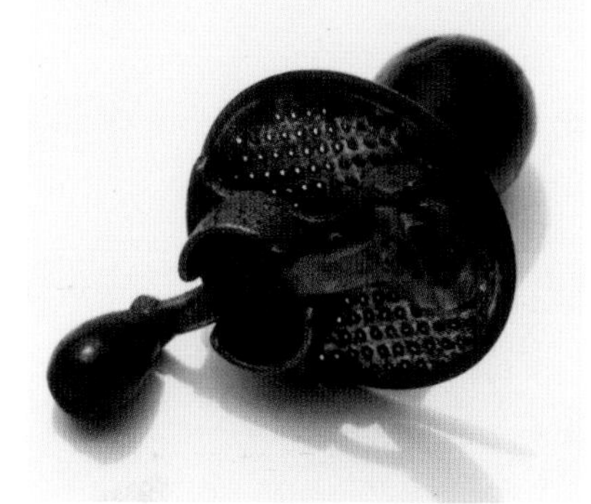

"The Gem" Nutmeg Grater

Nutmeg grater, cast iron, tin & wood, "The Gem" (ILLUS.)... **$75-85**

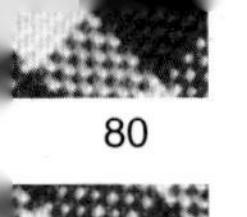

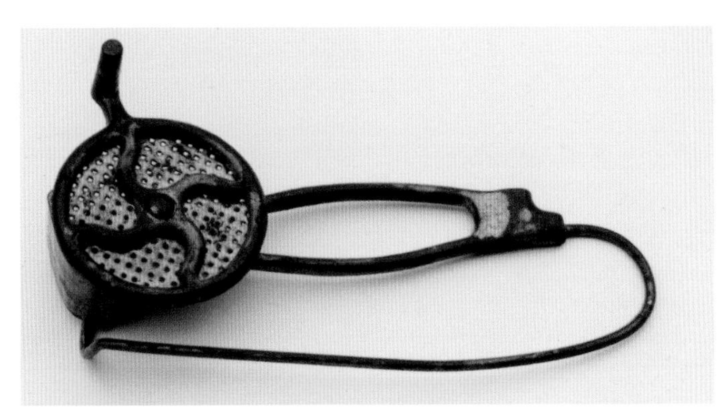

Church Nutmeg Grater

Two Early Tin Nutmeg Graters

Nutmeg grater, tin, circular disk w/wooden knob & low strap handle, rare (ILLUS. top with coffin-style grater) **$550**

Nutmeg grater, tin, coffin-style w/long square box to hold nutmeg, wire crank handle, marked "KREAMER" (ILLUS. bottom with rare circular grater) **$35**

Nutmeg grater, tin, marked "H. Carsley, Patented Nov. 20, 1855, Lynn, Mass," rare (ILLUS., top next column) **$975**

Nutmeg grater, tin, triangular w/wood plunger, stamped "Patented Oct. 13th 1857," remnants of blue japanning (ILLUS., bottom next column) **$550**

Rare Carsley Nutmeg Grater

Triangular Nutmeg Grater with Plunger

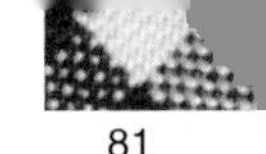

Tin Nutmeg Grater with Plunger

Nutmeg grater, tin w/wood plunger, known by patentee Hughes, sometimes stamped Pat. Feb. 27, 1877, 3 3/4" h. (ILLUS.) **$425**

Nutmeg grater, tin & wood, marked "Dec 25, 1877," 6 1/2" l. **$125**

Nutmeg grater, wooden, nicely turned base handle below squared grater box w/side crank handle & cylindrical top fitted w/a brass cap marked "Patent Apr 2 1867," paper label reads "Champion Grater Co. Boston" **$475**

"Common Sense" Nutmeg Grater

Nutmeg grater, wood handle w/tin perforated disk, marked "Common Sense," patented 7/23/1867 by Whitney & Davis of Maine, 5" l. (ILLUS.) **$495**

Rare Sterling Nutmeg Grater

Nutmeg grater, sterling silver oval cylindrical case w/engine-turned design & hinged cover holding the grater, touch marks for Thomas Hall, Exeter, England, 1855-56, 1 1/4" w., 3" l. (ILLUS.) **$275**

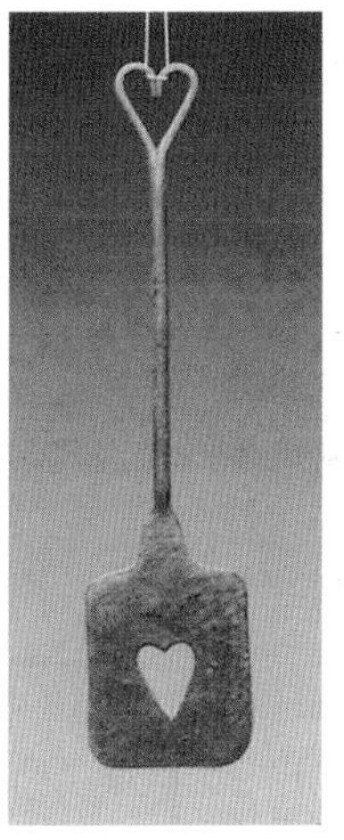

Fine Early Wrought-iron Oven Peel

Oven peel, hand-wrought iron, the flat rectangular blade w/a small heart cut-out, long rounded bar handle ending in a heart-shaped loop, some rusting & pitting, early, blade 4 1/2" w., overall 19" l. (ILLUS.).. **$518**

Group of Various Pans & Molds

Pan, roll, tin w/twelve molds, marked "KREAMER" (ILLUS. middle row, left, with group of pans & molds, top of page)..... **$20**

Pan, tin, w/six molds, marked "KREAMER" (ILLUS. middle row, right, with various pans & molds, top of page) **$25**

Pan, tin, w/six molds, possibly used for pancakes (ILLUS. bottom with various pans & molds, top of page)................................... **$40**

Pan scraper, metal, ball of linked wire w/twisted wire handle (ILLUS. left w/two other pan scrapers, bottom of page)............ **$35**

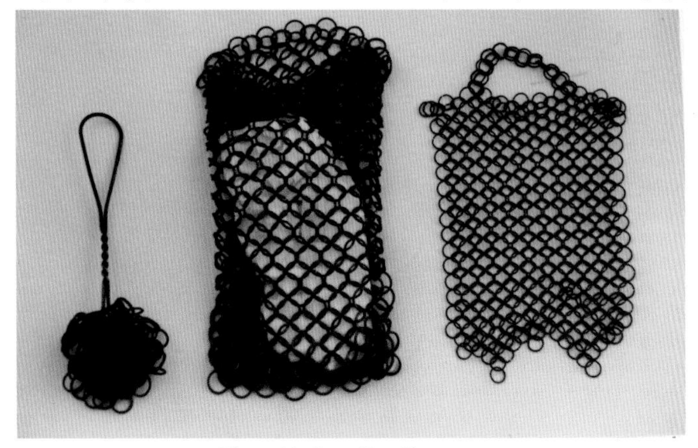

Three Various Pan Scrapers

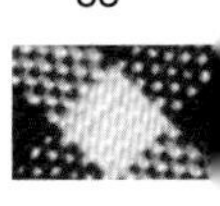

Pan scraper, metal, rectangular, linked wire pocket form for holding bar of soap, hard to find (ILLUS. center w/two other pan scrapers, bottom previous page).................. **$65**

Pan scraper, metal, rectangular, single layer of linked wire w/small linked wire handle, patented Oct. 10, 1871, hard to find (ILLUS. right w/two other pan scrapers, bottom previous page) **$45**

Pan/mold, tin, w/three small rectangular molds (ILLUS. top row, right, with various pans & molds, top of previous page)............ **$15**

Rollman Mfg. Co. Peach Stoner

Peach stoner, cast iron, "Rollman Mfg. Co. Pat Pend Mount Joy PA U.S.A.," 8 3/4" (ILLUS.).. **$250**

Rare Early Copper Peanut Boiler

Peanut boiler, cov., deep rectangular double-lined base w/a body band below a rounded shoulder fitted w/a slender cylindrical spout, a four-sided tapering domed cover w/a brass ball finial, 19th c., 13 1/2 x 18", 21" h. (ILLUS.) **$2,530**

Pie crimper, brass w/a design on the handle, 6" l. **$75**

Pie crimper, brass wheel w/wooden handle (ILLUS. bottom w/three other pie crimpers, bottom of page)..................................... **$45**

Pie crimper, cast-iron wheel w/wooden handle, ca. 1820 (ILLUS. top w/three other pie crimpers, bottom of page).................. **$95**

Group of Four Varied Pie Crimpers

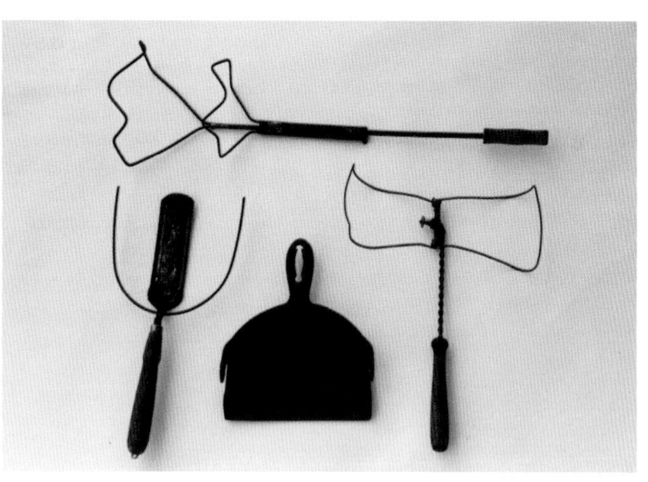

Four Pie Lifters of Various Types

Pie crimper, tin wheel & handle, handmade, possibly 10th anniversary piece, 9" l., rare (ILLUS. second from top w/three other pie crimpers, bottom previous page) **$250**

Pie crimper, wood chip-carved wheel & handle, long end is set on table as crimper is rolled along edge of pie crust, rare (ILLUS. second from bottom w/three other pie crimpers, bottom previous page)...... **$125**

Pie lifter, cast iron, marked "PAT'D MARCH 16 1880," rare (ILLUS. bottom row, center, with three other pie lifters, top of page) **$95**

Pie lifter, twisted wire, mechanical, swivels in oven to allow pie to turn & bake evenly, marked "PAT'D SE 27 '87," rare (ILLUS. top with three other pie lifters, top of page)... **$185**

Pie lifter, wire handle w/wood insert, two hinged wings on opposite end which act to grab pan (ILLUS., bottom of page) **$95**

Pie lifter, wire in the form of a semicircle around a thin tin spatula w/wood handle (ILLUS. bottom row, left, with three other pie lifters, top of page) **$75**

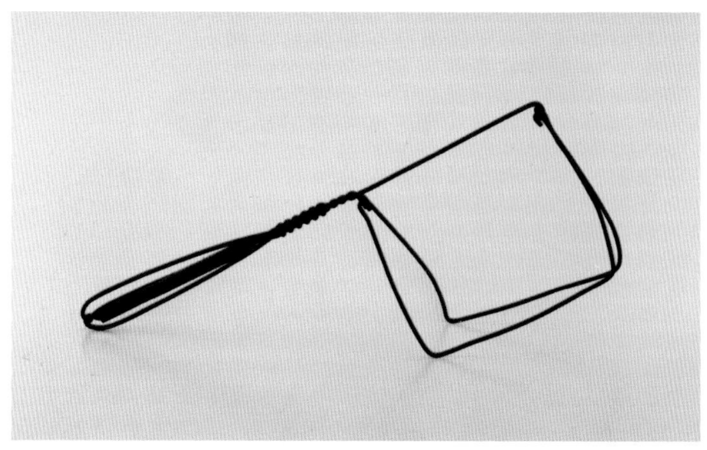

Wing-style Wire Pie Lifter

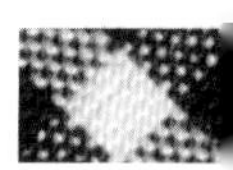

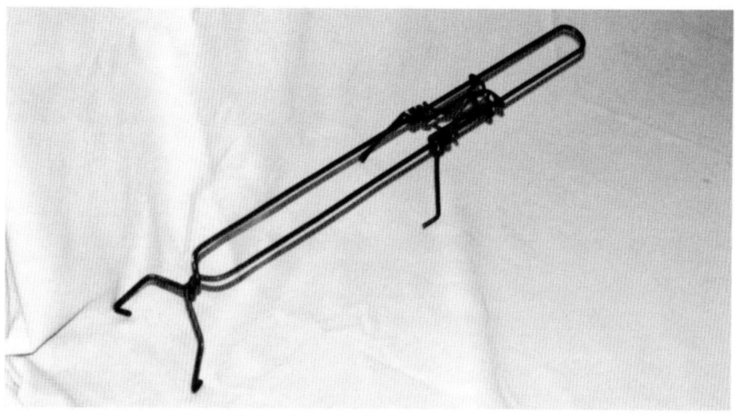

Long Handled Wire Pie Lifter

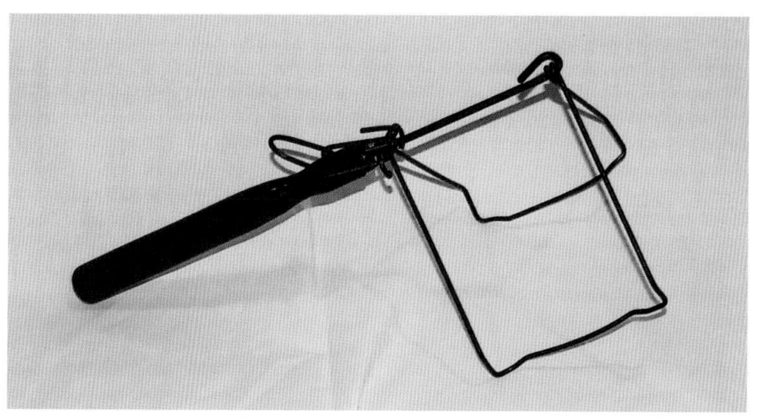

Unusual Wire & Wood Pie Lifter

Pie lifter, wire, long spring-action loop handle, unmarked, 19" (ILLUS., top of page) **$50**

Pie lifter, wire w/a red wood handle, paper label reads "Manufactured by W.M. Streets Wickenburg, Arizona," 14 3/4" l. **$30**

Pie lifter, wire w/long turned black wood handle, an unusual wire lever top opening the wire grips, 12 1/2" l. (ILLUS., second from top) **$75**

Pie lifter, wire & wood, two wire arms operate like butterfly wings for lifting pie from oven, 20" l. (ILLUS. bottom row, right, with three other pie lifters, top previous page) **$50**

Pie pan, tin, advertising, marked "Baked By Wassel," apple design in center (ILLUS., next column) **$40**

Wassell Advertising Tin Pie Pan

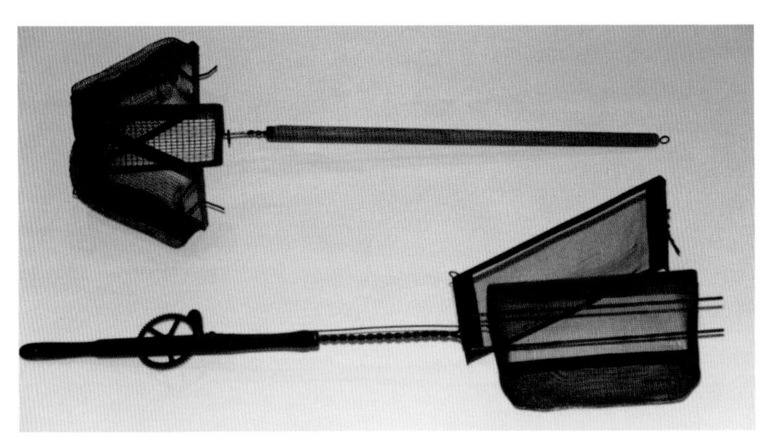

Two Early Popcorn Poppers

Tin Pie Pan with Star design

Pie pan, tin, pierced star design holes in bottom, used to make crisper crusts (ILLUS.) **$55**

Primitive Wooden Hanging Plate Rack

Plate rack, wall-mounted, pine frame w/flat shaped end boards w/heart-shaped tops, joined across the top w/three bars form a rack & across the bottom w/two bars, fitted w/a wooden openwork rack for 18 plate slots, one end w/an attached round wire soap holder, 7 1/2 x 21 1/2", 18" h. (ILLUS.) **$431**

Popcorn popper, double-sided mesh basket for popcorn or chestnuts, long wooden handle, hard to find (ILLUS. top w/other popcorn popper, top of page) **$85**

Popcorn popper, mesh basket, mechanical wooden handle w/crank to turn that moves basket back & forth, rare (ILLUS. bottom w/other popcorn popper, top of page) **$385**

Pot & kettle scraper, tin, advertising type, triangular, reading "ENDICOTT JOHNSON SHOES FOR THE WHOLE FAMILY" (ILLUS. right center w/other scrapers, bottom of page 75) **$35**

Pot & kettle scraper, tin, flat surface attached to bracketed handle, unattached label reading "THE FLEXIBLE POT AND KETTLE SCRAPER" followed by short paragraph & illustration of scraper (ILLUS. bottom w/other scrapers, bottom of page 75) **$35**

Pot & kettle scraper, tin, flat surface w/swivelling handle, marked "PERFECT SCRAPER, PAT MAY 21, 89" (ILLUS. top left w/other scrapers, bottom of page 75).... **$110**

Pot scraper, cast iron, ovoid shape w/cutout handle, marked "C.D. KENNY CO TEAS, COFFEES, SUGAR POT SCRAPER," hard to find (ILLUS. top right w/other scrapers, bottom of page 75) **$175**

Pot scraper, graniteware, advertising-type, marked "Penn Stoves" **$150**

Pot scraper, graniteware, advertising-type, marked "Red Wing Flour" **$650**

Pot scraper, graniteware, advertising-type, "Sharples Cream Separator" **$250**

Pot scraper, grey graniteware, in the shape of a loaf of bread, advertising-type, marked "American Maid Bread" **$250**

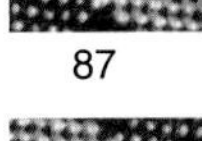

Triangular Pot Scraper

Pot scraper, tin, triangular shape w/thumb print center, usually w/advertising, marked around rim "Engman-Matthews - South Bend Ind. - The Range Eternal," used to scrape debris from corners of pots & pans (ILLUS.) **$65**

Potato baker, tin, advertising, four potato holder, marked "COMSTOCK POTATO BAKER," rare (ILLUS. right with two other potato bakers, below) **$145**

Three Early Tin Potato Bakers

Potato baker, tin, advertising, six potato holder (potatoes were placed on protrusions, preventing them from exploding & rolling around in oven), marked "RUMFORD" (ILLUS. left with two other potato bakers) **$110**

Potato baker, tin, advertising, ten potato holder, marked "Thayer & - Sherwood - COAL - AND - PRODUCE - Both Phones - LIVONIA, N.Y.," rare (ILLUS. center with two other potato bakers) **$165**

Spring-action Potato Masher

Potato masher, double-spring-action type w/two heavy wire wavy sections, one over the other, turned wooden handle (ILLUS.) **$45**

Two Early Copper Molds

Pudding mold, copper molded domed shape w/lobed sides centered at the top by a six-point star, 19th c., 10" d., 5 1/2" h. (ILLUS. left with turk's turban cake mold) **$604**

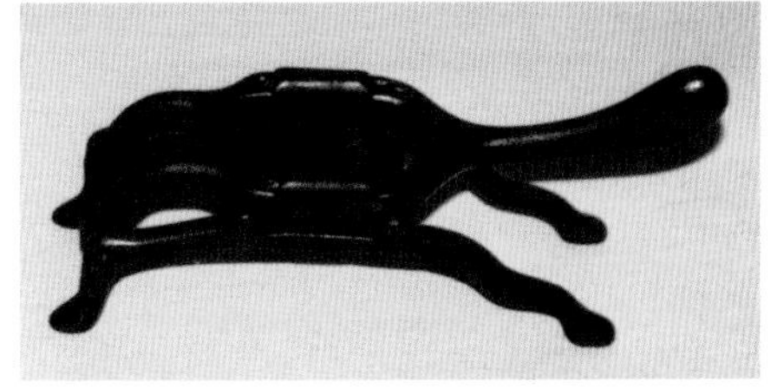

Cast-Iron Patented Raisin Seeder

Raisin seeder, cast iron, four leg base, "Pat'd May 7, 95," 6" (ILLUS.) **$500**

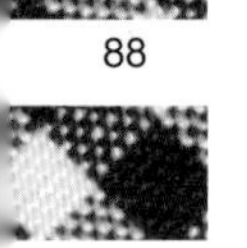

Group of Five Varied Raisin Seeders

Raisin seeder, cast iron, marked "Enterprise Mfg. Co. Philadelphia, PA USA - Pat. Apr. 2, Aug. 20, 95 - Pat Apl'd For - Wet The Raisins - No. 36" **$45**

Raisin seeder, cast iron, marked "Magic Factory Antrum NH - Patd Feb 13th 1894" **$1,250**

Raisin seeder, wire w/cast-iron body, known as "Headless Horseman," marked "PAT'D MAY 7, 95" (ILLUS. bottom w/four other raisin seeders, top of page).... **$450**

Raisin seeder, wire w/cast-iron body & table clamp, marked "FISKE, PAT AUG 16 1870," hard to find (ILLUS. right w/four other raisin seeders, top of page) **$495**

Raisin seeder, wire w/cast-iron body & table clamp, marked "THE EZY PAT MAR 21 1895" (ILLUS. center w/four other raisin seeders, top of page) **$300**

Raisin seeder, wire w/wooden handle, marked "COLUMBIAN MAY 2, 1893," hard to find (ILLUS. center left w/four other raisin seeders, top of page) **$375**

Raisin seeder, wire w/wooden handle, marked "EVERETT" (ILLUS. top left w/four other raisin seeders, top of page) **$50**

Rolling pin, amber blown glass, hollow w/closed handles, 19th c., 13 3/4" l. **$275**

Three Sizes of Wildflower Rolling Pins

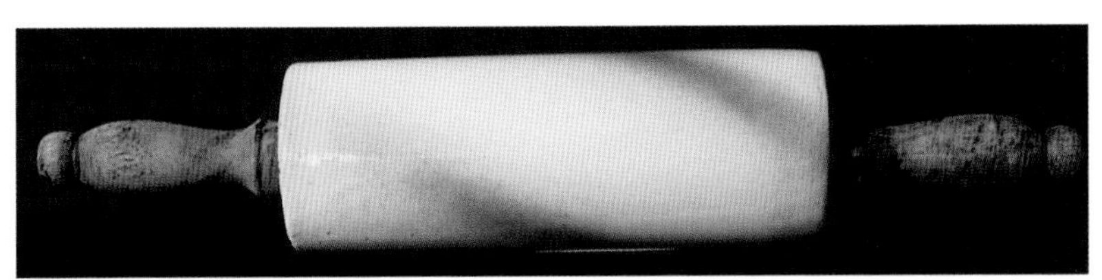

Blue Swirl Pattern Rolling Pin

Rolling pin, blue & white pottery, stenciled Wildflower patt., Brush-McCoy Pottery Co., small, 3" d., 8" l. (ILLUS. center with two other Wildflower rolling pins, bottom previous page) **$600**

Rolling pin, blue & white pottery, stenciled Wildflower patt., large baker's type, Brush-McCoy Pottery Co., stoneware roller, 3 1/2" d., 14 1/2" l. (ILLUS. bottom with two other Wildflower rolling pins, bottom previous page) **$800**

Rolling pin, blue & white pottery, stenciled Wildflower patt., Brush-McCoy Pottery Co., medium size, stoneware roller, 4" d., 12" l. (ILLUS. top with two other Wildflower rolling pins, bottom previous page) .. **$500**

Rolling pin, blue & white pottery, turned wooden handles, Swirl patt., 8" l. (ILLUS., top of page) **$1,250**

Rolling pin, china, blue on white Blue Onion patt., wooden handles, Germany, 19th c. **$125-150**

Rolling pin, china, white roller w/green handles (ILLUS. top left with three other rolling pins, top next column) **$30**

Rolling pin, peacock blue blown glass, hollow w/closed handles, rare, 19th c., 14" l. (ILLUS., middle next column)..................... **$400**

Rolling pin, salt-glazed stoneware, trimmed w/orange bands, Red Wing Union Stoneware, early 20th c. **$125-185**

Rolling pin, stoneware, Monmouth-Western Stoneware, advertising-type, white-glazed body decorated w/rust red bands & printed flour advertising, turned wood handles, (ILLUS., bottom of page) **$700-800**

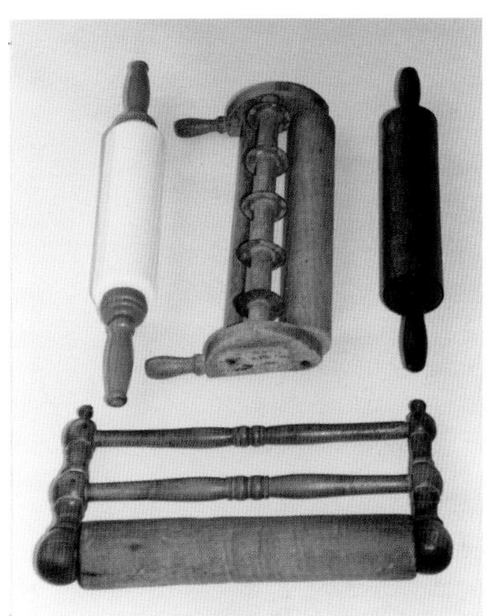

Four Various Rolling Pins

Early Peacock Blue Blown Glass Rolling Pin

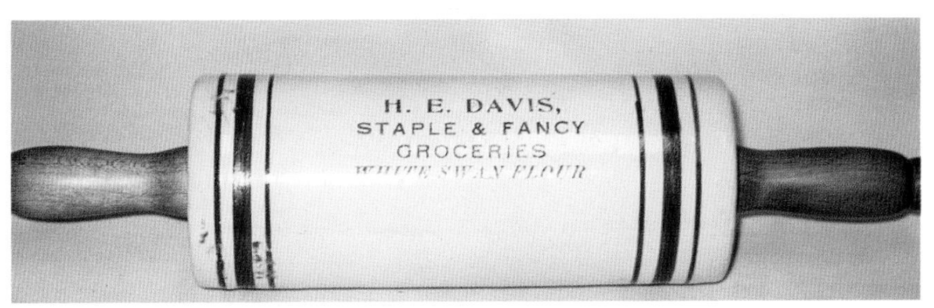

Rare Rust-decorated Advertising Rolling Pin

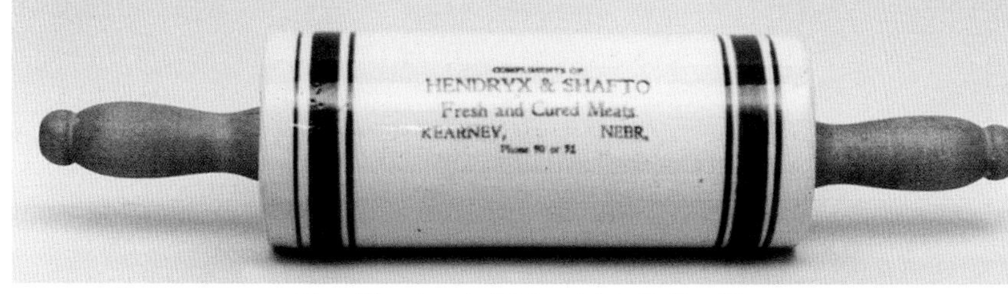

Rare Blue-banded Advertising Rolling Pin

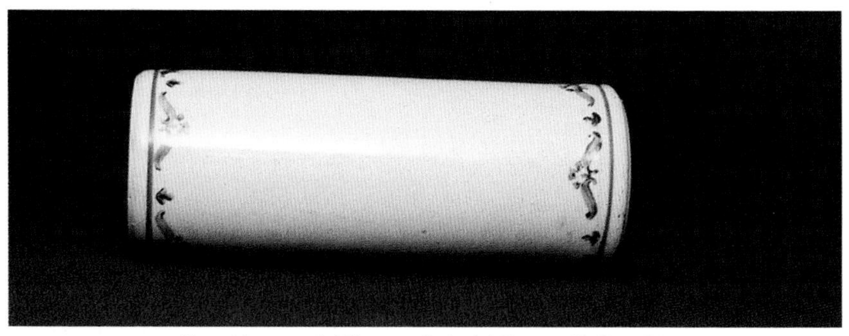

Rare Monmouth-Western Colonial Pattern Rolling Pin

Rolling pin, stoneware, Monmouth-Western Stoneware, advertising-type, white-glazed & decorated w/dark blue end bands & printed Nebraska advertising in the center, turned wood handles, (ILLUS., top of page) **$800-1,000**

Rolling pin, stoneware, Monmouth-Western Stoneware, Colonial patt., cylindrical w/printed blue swag bands at each end, no handles, early 20th c. (ILLUS., second from top) **$1,000-1,200**

Rolling pin, stoneware w/wooden handle, white w/three rust-colored bands at each end, 8" l. **$250**

Rolling pin, stoneware, white w/brown bands, advertising, marked "Bryant & Yeldell Clayton, Illinois," 8" l. plus handles **$550**

Rolling pin, tin w/wood handles (ILLUS. top right with three other rolling pins, page 89) **$300**

Rolling pin, wood, handmade, w/two scroll-cut handles (ILLUS. bottom with three other rolling pins, page 89) **$250**

Rolling pin, wood, w/slicing wheels, marked on paper label "manufactured by the Southern Pin CO, Nough TN, Patented July (?)," rare (ILLUS. top center with three other rolling pins, page 89) **$275**

Rolling pin, wooden, hand-turned w/some decorative carving, 19th c. **$85-200**

Rolling pin, wooden, turned wood handles, the cylinder carved w/20 springerle designs in rows of blocks, early, overall 17" l. (ILLUS., bottom of page) **$250-350**

Rolling pin, yellowware pottery w/wooden handles, 8" l. **$550**

Wooden Springerle Rolling Pin

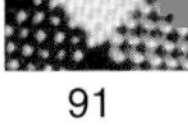
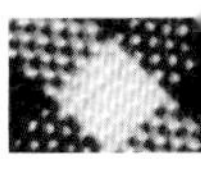

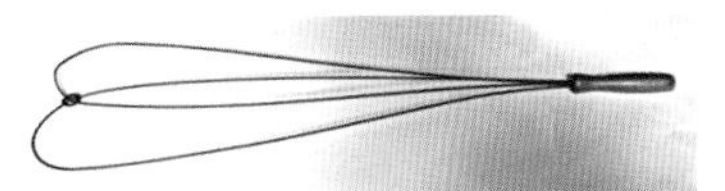

Wire Rug Beater with Green-painted Wooden Handle

Rug beater, looped wire w/two overlapping loops connected w/a round metal ring, green-painted wooden handle, late 19th - early 20th c., 9 1/2" w., 32" l. (ILLUS.) **$20-30**

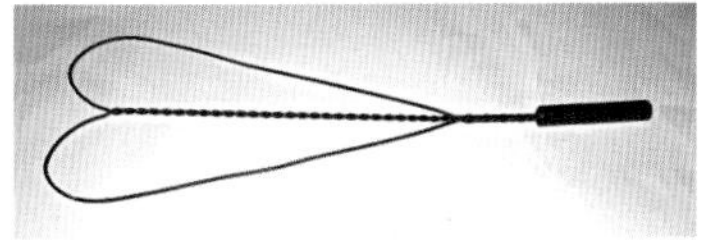

Heart-Shaped Early Wire Rug Beater

Rug beater, wire w/a heart shape & a twisted wire down center, wooden handle w/most of the original red paint worn off, late 19th - early 20th c., 9" w., 27" l. (ILLUS.) **$25-35**

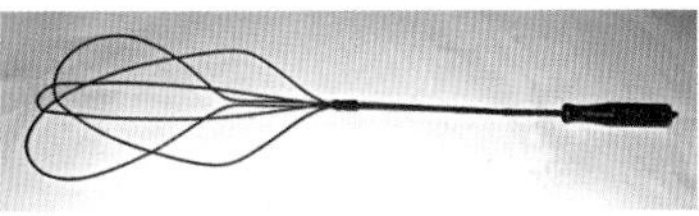

Wire Rug Beater with Complex Woven Design

Rug beater, wire w/complex woven design forming three loops of different widths & angles, turned maple handle, late 19th - early 20th c., 9" w., 29" l. (ILLUS.) **$30-40**

Early Painted Hanging Scouring Box

Scouring box, wall-type, painted, the upright backboard w/sharply tapering curved sides w/a hanging hole at the top, a blocked projection at the center back, shaped narrow sides above the dovetailed open bottom box compartment, original old reddish brown paint, 19th c., 2 3/4 x 8 3/4", 16 3/4" h. (ILLUS.) **$900**

Six-in-one tool, cast iron, multi-purpose tool used as a trivet, dish carrier, pie lifter, stove top lifter, a tenderizer & a pouring aid, marked "Thayer Pat May 24,81" **$85**

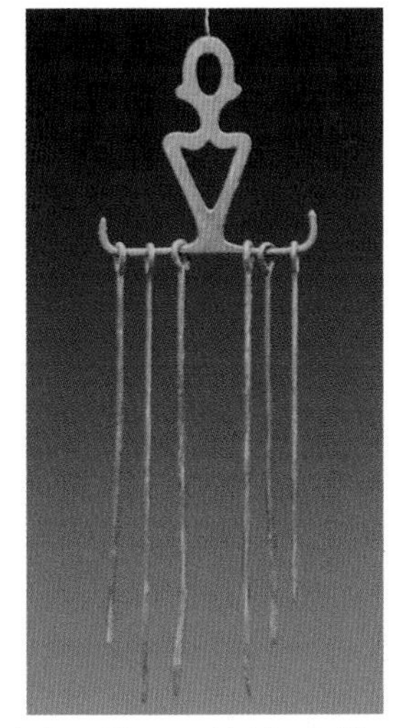

Early Iron Skewer Holder & Skewers

Skewer holder & skewers, hand-wrought iron, the holder w/the flattened top composed of an oval loop above a triangular loop ending in two slender projecting arms w/upturned ends, each arm suspending three long slender skewers, early, skewers 7 1/2" to 9 1/2" l., holder 4 1/4 x 4 1/4", the set (ILLUS.)................... **$330**

Skillet, cast iron, "Griswold No 4" **$26**

Skillet, cast iron, large emblem, no heat ring, Griswold #2.. **$350**

Skillet, cast iron, large emblem w/smoke ring, Griswold #14...................................... **$200**

Skillet, cast iron & red enamel, Griswold #5 .... **$40**

Early Domed Tin Spatter Lid

Spatter lid, domed tin w/finely pierced holes & wood finial, comes in two sizes, "Pat Jan 3 1899" (ILLUS.).................................... **$55**

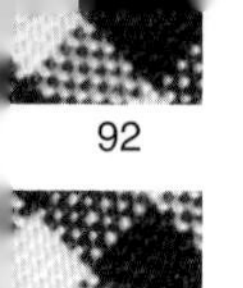

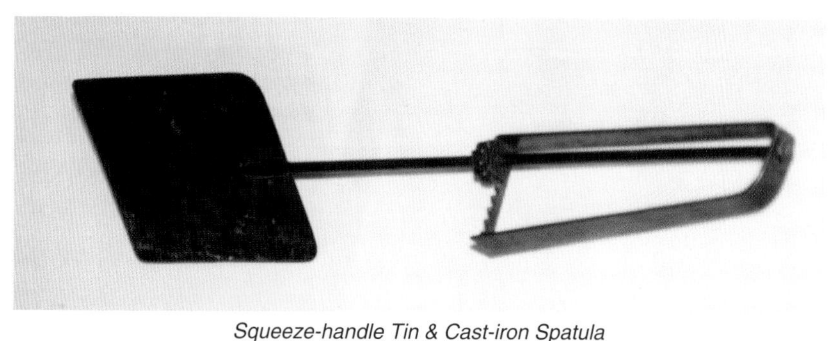

Squeeze-handle Tin & Cast-iron Spatula

Spatula, tin & cast iron, mechanical, squeezing handle flips end (ILLUS.) **$75**

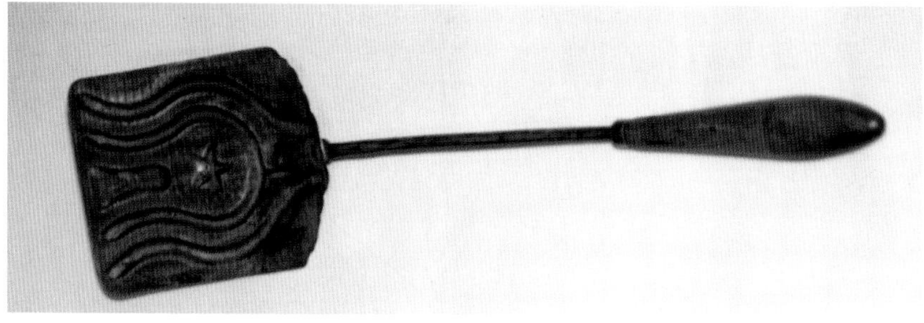

Spatula with Decorated Tin Blade & Wooden Handle

Spatula, tin w/wood handle, decorated w/tulip & star design, hard to find (ILLUS.) **$35**

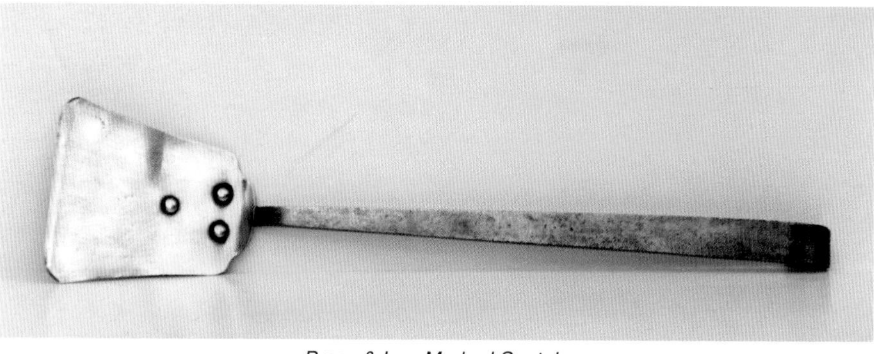

Brass & Iron Marked Spatula

Spatula, wrought-iron handle w/brass spatula blade, marked "F. B. S. Canton, Ohio, Pat. Jan. 26, 1886" (ILLUS) **$75**

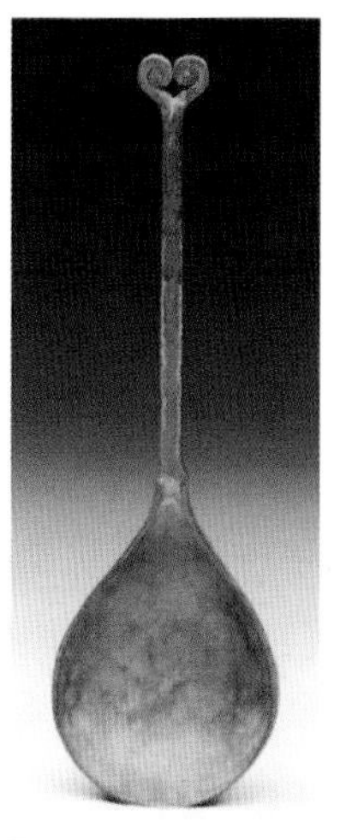

Nice Early Wrought-iron Spoon

Spoon, hand-wrought iron, deep tapering oblong bowl w/a long squared handle w/a tight ram horn curved end, very early, 7 1/4" l. (ILLUS.) **$403**

Spoon, tin, measuring type, w/bottle opener in handle (ILLUS. bottom left with three other tin spoons) **$15**

Spoon, tin, ripple egg beater type, marked "PAT AUG 6 1872," rare (ILLUS. bottom right with three other tin spoons) **$125**

Group of Four Old Tin Spoons

Spoon, tin, single-slotted w/bottle opener in handle, marked "GRANDMA'S LOPSIDED MIXING SPOON" (ILLUS. bottom center with three other tin spoons) **$25**

Spoon, tin, whipping type, four slots, marked "App'd for," rare (ILLUS. top with three other tin spoons) **$25**

Oval Tin Spoon Holder

Spoon holder, tin, oval shape w/seven holes & ridge around edge, w/hook, to be placed on side of kettle for drippings from spoon, unmarked (ILLUS.) **$35**

Spoon rack, hanging-type, butternut or walnut w/old faint bluish green graining on a black ground, red bird's claw decoration, three racks mounted on a vertical board w/incurved sides between each rack, arched & pierce-cut crest & triangular cut-out scallops along the bottom edge, 19th c., 10" w., 20" h. (nailed splits, one scallop repaired) **$288**

Spoon rack, painted pine, a narrow shelf w/narrow scroll-cut apron & fifteen cut-outs for spoons mortised into narrow scalloped end supports, rosehead nails, old black paint, early, 5 x 13", 13 1/4" h. (some regluing at joints, age splits & chip on top edge)... **$413**

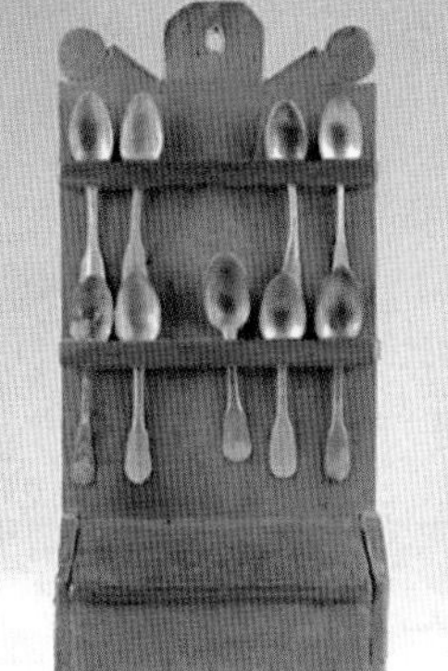

Rare Early Spoon Rack & Spoons

Spoon rack-wall box, cherry & pine, the tall wide backboard w/an angle-carved crest centered by an arched tab w/a hanging hole, two rows of spoon racks holding twelve spoons above a slant-lidded rectangular box at the bottom, together

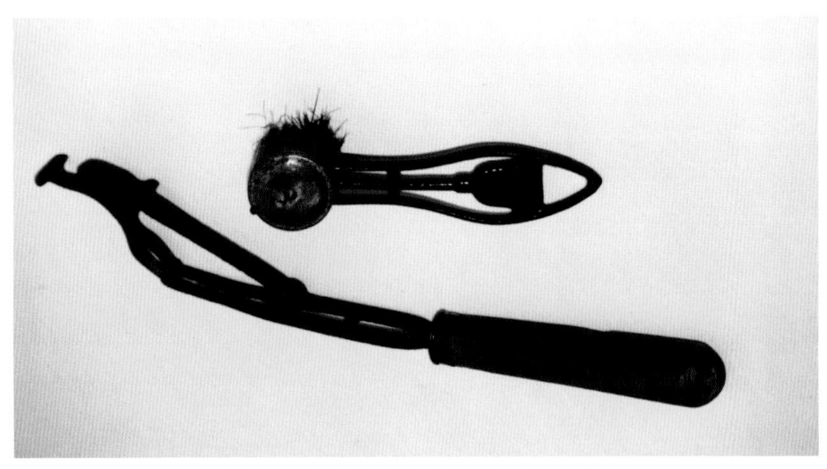

Stove Blackening Brush & Stove Lid Lifter

w/eight pewter spoons & one other spoon, New England, 18th c., 6 x 12", 25" h. (ILLUS..) **$1,898**

Stove blackening brush, tin w/cast-iron handle, marked "Pat. Aug 6 '95" (ILLUS. top w/stove lid lifter, top of page) **$30**

Stove lid lifter, cast iron w/wooden handle, mechanical, hard to find (ILLUS. bottom w/stove blackening brush, top of page) **$35**

Old Painted Sugar Bucket

Sugar bucket, cov., stave construction w/three finger lappets w/copper tacks, swing bentwood hickory bail handle, old mustard yellow paint, 19th c., minor wear & edge chips, 13 3/4" h. (ILLUS.)............... **$460**

Sugar bucket, cov., stave construction w/three finger lappets w/copper tacks, old bluish grey paint over earlier colors, bottom painted green, arched bentwood swing handle, 19th c., 21" h. (old chips on the lid) **$489**

Sugar maple mold, tin, w/six molds (ILLUS. middle row, center, with various pans & molds, top of page 82) **$25**

Sugar nippers, hand-wrought iron, scissor-form w/slender gently arched handles & hinged heavy incurved tips ending in small curved blades, stamped star & scallop design & inscribed "J. Nibb," 19th c., 9 1/4" l. **$358**

Tea strainer, tin, advertising-type, marked "All Allen's Teas & Coffees Strictly Guaranteed"... **$25**

Tea strainer, tin, advertising-type, marked "Daniel Webster Flour - Better Than The Best"... **$20**

Tea strainer, tin, advertising-type, marked "Royal Crest Dairy" **$25**

Tea strainer, tin, advertising-type, marked "Use Big Jo Flour - The Best In The World" **$30**

Small Marked Brass Teakettle

Teakettle, cov., brass, deep cylindrical sides w/domed top w/low domed cover & knob finial, long angled spout, overhead strap bail swing handle, marked "Toronto Fletcher Co. Ltd.," early 20th c., 6" l., 3 3/8" h. (ILLUS.) **$30**

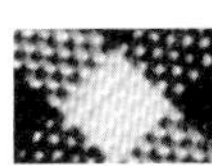

Three Gorham Victorian Teakettles

Early 19th Century Brass Teakettle

Teakettle, cov., brass, flat-bottomed bulbous body w/a short cylindrical neck, angled snake spout, upright shape strap swing bail handle, ringed domed cover w/knob finial, early 19th c., 9 1/2" h. (ILLUS.) **$604**

Brass Teakettle with Glass Handle

Teakettle, cov., brass, wide squatty bulbous body raised on four small knob feet, serpentine spout, fixed upright scrolls in handle joined by a baluster-form blue opaline glass hand grip, probably Europe, late 19th c., 10" l. (ILLUS.).................. **$51**

Two Early Copper Teakettles

Teakettle, cov., copper, bulbous ovoid body w/a flat bottom, wide short cylindrical neck w/a fitted domed cover w/brass knob finial, angled snake-form spout, overhead swing strap bail handle, possibly European, early 19th c., 10 liter size, body 11 1/2" h., w/handle 15 1/2" h. (ILLUS. left with smaller teakettle).. **$1,150**

American Dovetailed Copper Teakettle

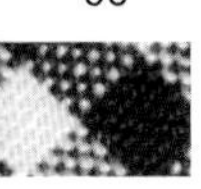

Teakettle, cov., copper, flat-bottomed dovetailed body w/a wide base & tapering sides to a short cylindrical neck w/a fitted low domed cover w/baluster-form finial, angular snake spout, overhead brass strap swing bail handle, stamped number "6," American-made, 19th c., overall 13" l. (ILLUS., previous page) **$1,208**

Teakettle, cov., copper, flat-bottomed spherical body w/an overall hand-hammered design, flat dished cover w/knob finial, serpentine spout, fixed uprights joined by a turned black wood grip forming the handle, mark of the Gorham Mfg. Co., Providence, Rhode Island, date code for 1883, 7 1/2" h. (ILLUS. left with other Gorham teakettles, top of previous page) **$200-400**

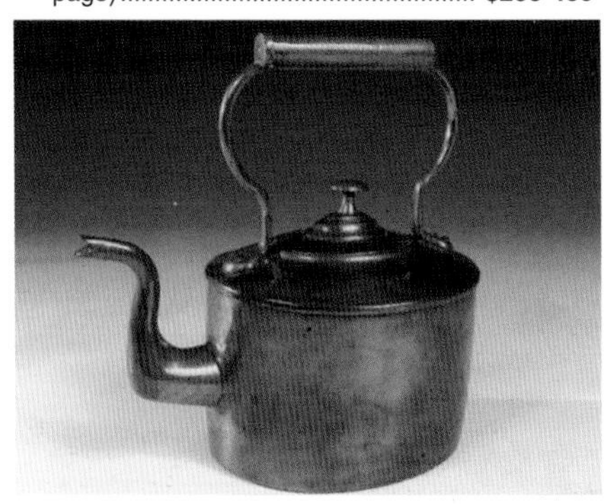

Tall Oval Copper Teakettle

Teakettle, cov., copper, oval cylindrical body w/deep sides below the wide angled shoulder, ringed domed cover w/mushroom finial, angular snake spout, fixed tall brass curved supports joined by a bar handle, tin-lined, 19th c., 11" h. (ILLUS.)..... **$201**

Revere Ware Copper Teakettle

Teakettle, cov., copper, Revere Ware, domed beehive body w/applied black Bakelite handle and bird whistle spout, marked on bottom "Revere Solid Copper - Rome, N.Y.," 7 1/4 x 7 1/2" (ILLUS.) **$100**

Teakettle, cov., copper, wide flat bottom & slightly tapering cylindrical sides w/a wide rounded shoulder centering a short neck w/a fitted domed cover w/knob finial, angular snake-form spout, tall fixed brass scrolled uprights joined by a copper bar forming handle, early 19th c., 11" d., 12 1/4" h. (ILLUS. right with liter teakettle, previous page)........................... **$805**

Early Squatty Tin Teakettle

Teakettle, cov., tin, wide slightly tapering squatty domed form, straight angled spout, strap handle (ILLUS.)........................ **$50**

Teakettle on stand, cov., copper, flat-bottomed spherical hand-hammered body applied w/polished silver designs of flowering stalks, butterflies & storks in the Japanesque taste, flat dished cover w/knob finial, serpentine spout, fixed uprights joined by a turned black wood handle, mark of Gorham Mfg. Co., Providence, Rhode Island, date code for 1883, 7 1/2" h. (ILLUS. right with other Gorham teakettles, top previous page)................. **$2,350**

Teakettle on stand, cov., copper, kettle w/wide squatty bulbous hand-hammered body applied w/dark silver figures of butterflies, birds & flowering branches in the Japanesque taste, a short neck w/a fitted domed & ribbed cover w/button finial, serpentine spout, fixed short copper scrolls joined by a high arched wooden handle, raised on a stand w/forked uprights above a platform w/a burner & raised on four canted legs, mark of Gorham Mfg. Co., Providence, Rhode Island, date code for 1883, 11" h. (ILLUS. center with other Gorham teakettles, top previous page) **$1,293**

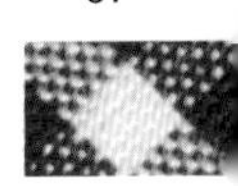

Three Graduated Scottish Copper Teakettles

Teakettles, cov., copper, wide slightly flaring cylindrical body w/wide rounded shoulder centering a flat mouth, ringed domed cover w/acorn finial, angled spout, fixed overhead brass handles w/cylindrical copper grip, Scotland, ca. 1900, graduated sizes 11" h., 13" h. & 14" h., the set (ILLUS., top of page) **$403**

Copper Teapot on Iron Legs

Teapot, cov., copper, bulbous nearly spherical body w/an angled shoulder to a short cylindrical neck w/a fitted domed cover w/scroll finial, tapering cylindrical side handle fitted w/a baluster-turned black wood handle w/pointed terminal, body raised on three straight riveted wrought-iron legs, probably Europe, 19th c., wear, spout pressed in, 8" h. (ILLUS.) **$125**

Toaster, wire w/wood handle, bread was placed between decorative wire, rare (ILLUS. center with two other toasters, bottom of page) **$65**

Toaster, wire w/wood handle, bread was placed between decorative wire, rare (ILLUS. top with two other toasters, bottom of page) **$65**

Toaster, wire w/wood handle, mechanical, lever was pulled to open wire circles to insert bread (ILLUS. bottom with two other toasters, bottom of page) **$45**

Early Wrought-iron Toasting Rack

Toasting rack, fireplace-type, hand-wrought iron, the revolving rack composed of two open squares enclosing scrolled hearts, revolving on a three-legged bar base w/a long curved handle w/a hanging hole in the diamond point end, late 18th - early 19th c., overall 16" l. (ILLUS.)... **$575**

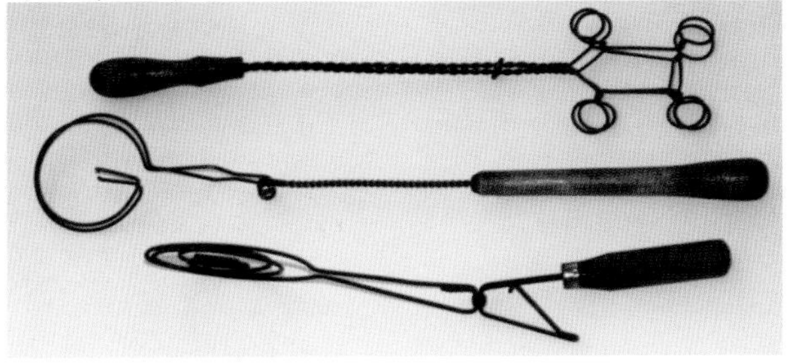

Group of Three Wire Toasters

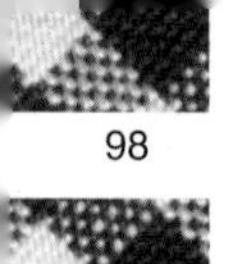

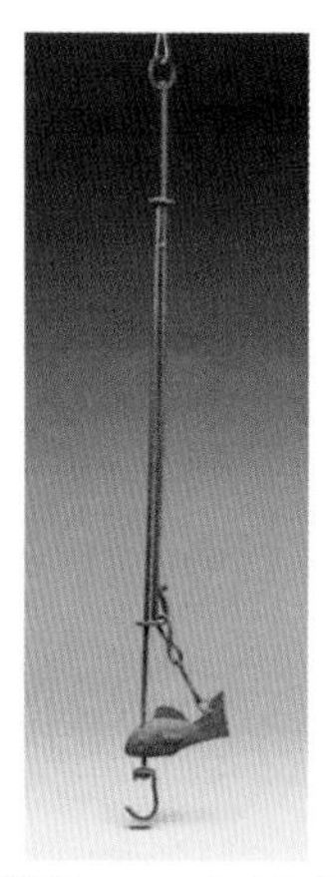

Unusual Old Trammel with Figural Fish

Trammel, fireplace-type, hand-wrought iron, two long narrow rods linked w/chain w/a 7" l. figural fish-form adjustment w/a round loop handle & several hooks for hanging, unusual form, adjusts from 41" to 70" (ILLUS.) **$805**

Large Early Hand-wrought Iron Trivet

Trivet, hand-wrought iron, a flat rectangular plate w/angled back corners, raised on three iron bar legs joined by a T-form stretcher, a long twisted iron handle w/loop end projecting from the back edge, early 19th c., 12 3/4 x 30", 8 3/4" h. (ILLUS.) **$288**

Trivet, wire, rounded starburst design of stamped wire w/double-loop ends & triangles, used as a coffeepot or teapot stand **$45**

Trivet, hand-wrought, model of a coiled snake, on three short scroll legs, incised underside, found in Pennsylvania, 19th c., minor surface corrosion, 4 3/4 x 10 1/2", 3 1/4" h............................ **$978**

Cast-iron Advertising Trivet

Trivet, cast-iron, advertises "C D Kenny Teas, Coffees, Sugars, 60 Stores," 5" l. (ILLUS.).. **$145**

Wafer iron, cast iron, traditional scissor-form w/a pair of hinged round disks on long handles ending in a loop catch, one disk intaglio-cast w/a spread-winged American eagle & shield w/a banner in its beak reading "E Pluribus Unum," Pennsylvania, ca. 1800, overall 29 1/4" l. **$1,610**

Wafer iron, hand-wrought iron, hinged scissor-form w/long slender handles ending in a pair of rectangular plates each incised w/a rectangular zigzag border enclosing a monogram "E.R.D." & heart on one & initials "I.D." & a heart on the other, dated 1763, Pennsylvania, overall 32 1/2" l. **$978**

Canvas & Iron Folding Water Bucket

Water bucket, folding-type, canvas over a steel frame, stenciled base marked "Planet Co.," wire bail handle, late 19th c., 9 3/4" h. (ILLUS.) **$58**

PART II: THE MODERN KITCHEN - 1920-1980

Chapter 6

Crockery & Dishes

Cow Creamers

Bennington Pottery Cow Creamer

Bennington pottery, platform-type, Rockingham glaze, rare, missing lid, chip on one horn, tail repair, expect damage as this creamer is a rare find in any condition, 5 x 7" (ILLUS.) **$450-550**

Bisque Cow Creamer

Bisque porcelain, highly textured bisque body, black spots, pink bow, w/yellow bell at neck, all glazed, "Japan" paper label, 4 1/4 x 5 3/4" (ILLUS.) **$20-24**

Black Ceramic Cow Creamer

Ceramic, black high-gloss glaze over red clay pottery, highly detailed, cold-painted features, maker unknown, 5 x 5 1/2" (ILLUS.) **$39-44**

Blue Painted Japanese Cow Creamer

Ceramic, blue painted flowers on both sides, molded green bell around neck, flowers in various colors, ink stamped "Japan" on bottom, 5 1/4 x 7 3/4" (ILLUS) **$32-35**

Blue Polka-dotted Cow Creamer

Ceramic, blue polka-dots on white glazed pottery, molded bell at neck, eyes accented w/long lashes, unmarked, maker unknown, 5 1/2 x 5 3/4" (ILLUS.) **$49-55**

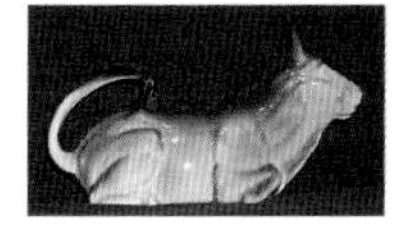

Brahma Cow Creamer

Ceramic, Brahma, laying down, black at top, graduating to reddish brown over cream pottery, highly glazed, unglazed bottom, very unusual, maker unknown, 3 3/4 x 8 3/4" (ILLUS.) **$39-45**

Brown & White Cow Creamer

Ceramic, brown markings on white glazed ceramic, h.p. eyes, tail curls down & connects to back hind leg forming handle, unmarked, 4 x 7" (ILLUS.) **$21-24**

Common Cow Creamer

Ceramic, brown markings over highly glazed white ceramic, ink stamped number "B544" underneath, common, 3 1/2 x 5 3/4" (ILLUS.) **$22-26**

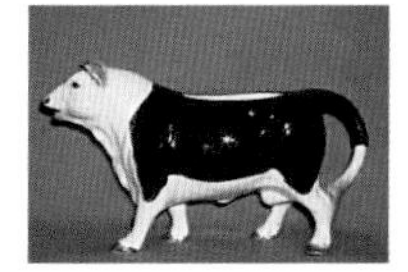

Brown & White Bull Creamer

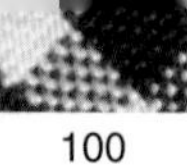

Ceramic, bull, brown & white, grey hooves & facial shading, tail curls under to form handle, ink stamped "K393," maker unknown, 4 1/2 x 7 3/4" (ILLUS., previous page) **$29-35**

Grouping of Bull Creamers

Ceramic, bull creamers, also found w/matching salt & pepper shakers, stamped "Made in Japan," also "Occupied Japan," 3 x 3", each (ILLUS.) **$19-24**

Ceramic, bull creamers, also found w/matching salt & pepper shakers, stamped "Made in Japan," also "Occupied Japan," larger sizes, each **$24-35**

Cow Creamer Bust

Ceramic, bust-form, brown markings on white w/pink ears, cheeks & mouth, bulging eyes, yellow horns & bell at neck, commonly found in various other animal shapes, h.p. marked "Japan," 4 x 4" (ILLUS.) **$24-28**

Artmark Originals Cow Creamer

Ceramic, bust-form, dark brown w/lighter brown paint-dripping effects, gold highlights on tips of horns, lashes & bell, bottom red & gold foil paper label, h.p., "Artmark Originals, Japan," 3 1/2 x 5 3/4" (ILLUS.) **$25-29**

Smiling Cow Creamer

Ceramic, bust-form, golden ringlets & horns at crown, molded blue bell about the neck, black markings, highly detailed smiling features, ink stamped "M6149 Japan," original price 49 cents, 4 x 4 1/4" (ILLUS.) **$49-55**

Comical Cow Creamer

Ceramic, comical, pink on white, ink stamped "Japan" on bottom, original ink stamp price of 19 cents on bottom of hoof, 4 x 5" (ILLUS.) **$19-24**

Dark Brown Walking Cow Creamer

Ceramic, dark brown over red clay, highly glazed, w/gold accents about the feet & eyes, light brown drippings of paint at opening, missing paper label, Japan, 4 1/2 x 5 1/2" (ILLUS.) **$19-23**

Cow Creamer with Shamrocks

Ceramic, dark green shamrocks on white glaze, tail curls underneath to form handle, marked "Cream" on front side, unmarked, 5 x 8" (ILLUS.) **$40-45**

Blue Floral Cow Creamer

Ceramic, dark & light blue flowers on white glaze, w/blue nose & ears, tail curled up over back to form handle, "Cream" stamped on one side, bottom ink stamp "E-3801," 4 1/4 x 7" (ILLUS.) **$39-46**

Flat-Bottomed Cow Creamer

Ceramic, flat bottom, turquoise spots on cream glazed pottery w/brown accents,

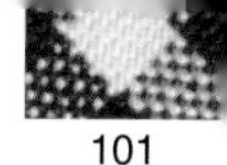

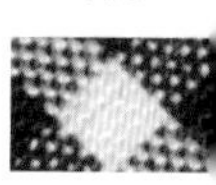

molded bell at neck, rouge painted jaw area, unmarked, unglazed bottom, 5 1/2 x 7" (ILLUS.) **$65-69**

Handpainted Cow Creamer

Ceramic, h.p. floral on white, molded bell at neck, many found with "Souvenir" label from places visited, Japan, 3 1/4 x 5 1/4" (ILLUS.) **$14-19**

Holly Ross Cow Creamer

Ceramic, h.p. flower on one side, bud on reverse, facial features, hooves & ribbon in gold, w/gold under glaze bottom marks, artist signed "Holly Ross, LaAnna, PA. Made in the Poconos," 5 x 7 1/2" (ILLUS.) **$39-45**

Otagiri Cow Creamer

Ceramic, h.p., w/gold foil label "M O C Japan, Otagiri 1981," embossed underneath, foil label on side, "Handpainted," still being produced, common, by Otagiri, 3 x 5 1/2" (ILLUS.) **$12-15**

Black Cow Creamer

Ceramic, highly-glazed black over red clay, cold-painted features in pink, blue & gold, pottery bell w/painted flower attached by metal chain, original lid w/tip of tail ornamental to top, unmarked, 5 1/2 x 6" (ILLUS.) **$34-39**

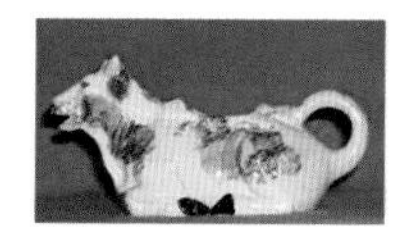

Sponged Design Cow Creamer

Ceramic, laying down, legs tucked underneath, dark green sponging over brown, yellow & cream glazed pottery, "Made in Japan" bottom ink stamp, rare sponged design, 3 1/2 x 7 1/4" (ILLUS.) **$95-100**

Brown & White Cow Creamer

Ceramic, light brown over white, sometimes mistaken as the popular "Elsie" creamer, h.p. dark green garland at neck & bow on tail, black hooves, eyes shut w/fine lashes, unmarked, 6 x 6" (ILLUS.) **$25-29**

Tan & White Japanese Cow Creamer

Ceramic, light tan over white, high glaze, large black painted eyes & hooves, bottom ink stamp "B588," "Japan," 3 3/4 x 5 3/4" (ILLUS.) **$14-19**

Calico Cow Creamer

Ceramic, lying down, dark blue on white, "Milk" stamped on one side, bottom ink stamp "Calico Burleigh Staffordshire England," new, still in production, 3 x 7 1/4" (ILLUS.) **$35-39**

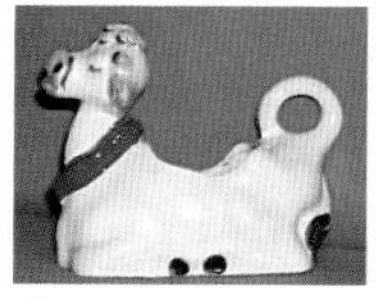

Cow Creamer with Eyes Shut

Ceramic, lying down, eyes shut, yellow crown, pink nose, highlighted in brown on

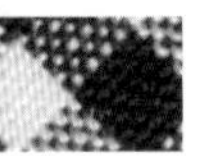

white glazed pottery, tail curled up to form handle loop over rear, impressed branding iron marking "R" within a "G" on back side, unglazed pottery bottom, maker unknown, 5 x 6 1/2" (ILLUS.) **$42-45**

Black & White Lustre Cow Creamer

Ceramic, lying down, feet tucked under, lustreware w/black spots & gold accented horns, red ink stamp "Made in Japan," 4 x 6" (ILLUS.).. **$27-32**

Handpainted Japanese Cow Creamer

Ceramic, lying down, red dotted flowers on white w/dark green tail, hooves & crest, pink nose & ribbon, bottom marking "Hand Painted Japan," 1950-60, 4 x 6 1/2" (ILLUS.).................................. **$24-29**

Miniature Japanese Cow Creamer

Ceramic, miniature, h.p. flower on each side, stamped "Japan" on front hooves, 2 1/4 x 3 1/2" (ILLUS.)............................ **$16-20**

Orange & White Cow Creamer

Ceramic, orange spots on both sides over white, black tail & facial features, unmarked, 1960 (ILLUS.)........................... **$19-24**

Petite Cow Creamer

Ceramic, petite, decorated w/flowers on white glaze, molded bell at neck, unmarked, Japan, 4 1/2 x 4 3/4" (ILLUS.).. **$16-19**

Mottled Pink Cow Creamer

Ceramic, pink mottled high glaze, grey base, horns & tail, black ink stamp "Made in Japan" w/flower in middle, very unusual, 4 1/2 x 6 1/4" (ILLUS.)....................... **$49-55**

Gold Accented Cow Creamer Pitcher

Ceramic, pitcher, black high gloss w/22 kt. gold detailed accents, bottom stamped in gold "Pearl China Co., hand decorated, 22 kt. Gold, U.S.A.," impressed "#635," larger than usual cow creamer, 6 1/2 x 6 1/2" (ILLUS.) **$29-35**

Kenmar Purple Cow Creamer

Ceramic, purple glazed, small tin bell attached at neck w/fine wire, gold foil label marked "Kenmar, Japan," various colors, common, mint w/bell, 4 1/2 x 6 1/2" (ILLUS.) **$25-29**

Cow Creamer w/Pink Flowers

Ceramic, reddish brown on cream, pink flowers at base, unmarked, w/flat bottom base, 1950-60, 3 3/4 x 5 1/2" (ILLUS.) .. **$19-25**

Common Japanese Cow Creamer

Ceramic, reddish brown over cream, Japanese, mass-produced before, during & after the war, found in many sizes, colors & various markings, common, 3 1/2 x 5 1/4" (ILLUS.) **$25-28**

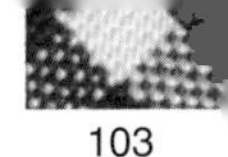
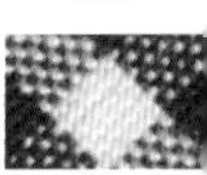

Brown Cow Creamer & Sugar Set

Ceramic, set: cow creamer & cov. sugar; brown markings over white, large prominent eyes, molded bells at neck, standing cow creamer, lying down sugar w/lid, tail curls up to form handle on lid of sugar, unmarked, 1950, creamer 5 1/4 x 5 1/2" h., sugar 4 3/4 x 6", the set (ILLUS.) **$42-49**

Purple Cow Creamer & Sugar Set

Ceramic, set: cow creamer & cov. sugar; purple accents on white, sugar has satin ribbon on head, sold by Norcrest China Co., unmarked, "Japan," common, also found w/matching salt & pepper shakers, creamer 6 x 4 3/4" h., sugar 3 x 4 3/4", the complete set (ILLUS.) **$29-35**

Cow Creamer & Sugar

Ceramic, set: cow creamer, cov. sugar, salt & pepper; grey & black markings on white, highly glazed, removable salt & pepper heads, warehouse find, "Japan" stamped, mint in box, 5 x 5", the set (ILLUS. of part w/creamer on right) **$39-44**

Handpainted Creamer & Sugar Set

Ceramic, set: creamer & cov. sugar; purple over white glaze, large pink flared nostrils, yellow horns, hooves & tails, tails curl up over backs to form handles, ink stamp "52/270" under glaze, foil gold & black paper stickers "Made in Japan," marked "Thames, Handpainted," found w/matching salt & pepper, complete, mint, creamer 5 x 5 1/2", sugar 4 1/2 x 6", the set (ILLUS.) **$45-49**

Creamer from Purple Cow Set

Ceramic, set: creamer & matching cov. sugar; purple over white glaze, yellow horns & molded bell at neck, "Japan" paper label, 1950-60, both 4 1/2 x 4 1/2", the set (ILLUS. of creamer only) **$29-32**

Blue Tulip Decorated Cow Creamer

Ceramic, sitting, blue tulips on white glaze, bottom ink stamp "Japan" under glaze, 1950-60, common, 3 3/4 x 4" (ILLUS.) . **$14-19**

Kent Ceramic Cow Creamer

Ceramic, sitting, brown w/white spots, gold molded bell around neck, tail curled up connecting at back of neck to form handle, bottom impressed stamp "Kent," 5 1/4 x 6" (ILLUS.) **$24-29**

Sitting Bust Cow Creamer

Ceramic, sitting bust, reddish brown, bottom ink stamp "Made in Japan," 3 1/2 x 3 3/4" (ILLUS.) **$29-35**

Sitting Cow Creamer w/Flowers

Ceramic, sitting, flowers on both sides over deep yellow chrome, enhanced gold highlights around features, no bottom markings, 4 3/4 x 6 1/2" (ILLUS., previous page) **$39-45**

Sitting Cow Creamer

Ceramic, sitting, mottled brown on white pottery, yellow tail forming handle, found w/many other color variations, top of head is both opening & pouring vessel, unmarked (ILLUS.) **$14-19**

Japanese Ceramic Cow Creamer

Ceramic, small, blue, w/molded green bell around neck, "Made in Japan" ink stamp underneath, 3 1/2 x 5" (ILLUS.) **$30-35**

Nashville Souvenir Cow Creamer

Ceramic, souvenir-type from Nashville, Tennessee, Music City, U.S.A., usually gold in color, found w/all states printed on side, paper label "Made in Japan," common, 3 1/2 x 5" (ILLUS.)......................... **$14-19**

Early 1940s Cow Creamer

Ceramic, two large black spots on cream w/black hooves, unmarked, early 1940s, formerly used as a planter, also found in brown on cream, 5 1/2 x 7" (ILLUS.)...... **$39-45**

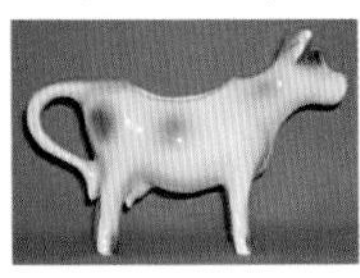

Simple Brown-spotted Cow Creamer

Ceramic, very simple in form & markings w/five light spots about body, horns & hooves highlighted in brown, paper label missing, 4 1/4 x 5 3/4" (ILLUS.) **$24-29**

Cow Creamer w/Pink & Grey Transfers

Ceramic, w/pink & grey flower transfer on both sides & gold hooves, found in various floral designs, unmarked, 5 1/2 x 7" (ILLUS.)... **$39-45**

Seated Brown-spotted Czech Creamer

Czechoslovakian pottery, sitting, orange spots on white porcelain, black tail, circle black ink stamp "Made in Czechoslovakia," 4 3/4 x 5 3/4" (ILLUS.).................... **$75-78**

Czechoslovakian Cow Creamer

Czechoslovakian pottery, sitting, orange w/black ears & tail, dime size circle black ink stamp "Made in Czechoslovakia," minor paint wear, 4 3/4 x 5 3/4" (ILLUS.)... **$59-65**

Delft Faience Cow Creamer

Delft faience, exceptional blue coloring, windmill scene on front side, unmarked, 4 1/4 x 6 1/2" (ILLUS.) **$124-130**

Delft Pottery Cow Creamer

Delft pottery, handpainted, light blue w/darker blue accents, signed by the artist, lidded opening, unusual that tail

doesn't form handle, bottom marking under glaze "Made in Holland," mint, 3 3/4 x 6" (ILLUS.) **$129-135**

Delft pottery, painted & lightly glazed porcelain, cow dressed in assorted men's clothing, either sitting or standing, rare & very desirable **$165-179**

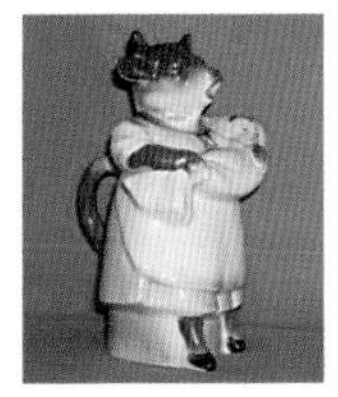

Standing Cow Creamer w/Infant

German china, standing in upright position, reddish brown cow wearing a white & blue dress, holding an infant in a blanket, bottom circular ink stamp "Made in Germany," rare, 3 3/4" w., 5 3/4" h. (ILLUS.) **$400-475**

German Porcelain Cow Creamer

German porcelain, brown markings over white, black highlights on tail, hooves & horns, unmarked, 4 1/2 x 5 1/2" (ILLUS.) **$48-52**

Brown & Cream German Cow Creamer

German porcelain, brown on cream porcelain, black accented tail, horns & hooves, red ink stamped "Germany," 3 1/2 x 5" (ILLUS.) **$55-59**

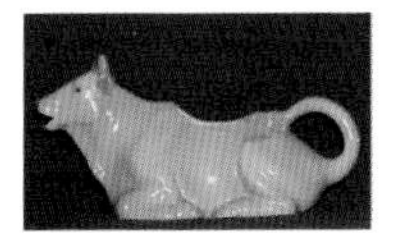

German Green Reclining Cow Creamer

German porcelain, lying, w/tail curled up to form handle, impressed "Germany 1391" on back side, unusual light green color, mint, 3 1/2 x 7 1/2" (ILLUS.) **$114-120**

Miniature German Cow Creamer

German porcelain, miniature, grey/black on fine white porcelain, impressed on back "Germany," 2 5/8 x 3 5/8" (ILLUS.) **$45-55**

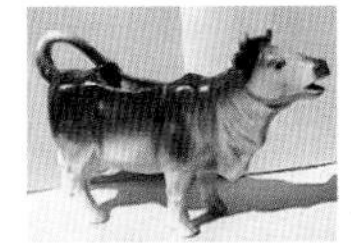

German Porcelain Standing Creamer

German porcelain, reddish brown graduating to white on softly glazed fine porcelain, extremely detailed features, impressed on reverse side "Germany 8610," 7 1/2" h., 4 3/4" l. (ILLUS.) **$75-82**

Goebel China Cow Creamer

Goebel china, brown markings on cream glazed ceramic, tin gold bell on string, tail curls under to form handle, unmarked, opening 2 1/4", 3 3/4 x 5 3/4" (ILLUS.) .. **$32-36**

Brown-spotted Goebel Cow Creamer

Goebel china, brown markings on white, original tin bell on cord, full "Bee" blue ink stamp, "Germany," 5 x 7 1/2" (ILLUS.) .. **$74-79**

Ironstone China Cow Creamer

Ironstone china, lying, w/legs tucked under, burgundy floral transfer on both sides, backstamp reads "Charlotte Royal Crownford Ironstone England," commonly found mold w/markings of different companies in various colors, marked "Made in England," 3 1/2 x 7" (ILLUS.) .. **$39-45**

Black Platform-Style Cow Creamer

Jackfield pottery, high-gloss black glaze over red clay w/gold trim, on platform w/lid, Shropshire, England, 4 1/2 x 6 1/4" (ILLUS.) **$139-145**

Jackfield Cow Creamer

Jackfield pottery, platform base, high-gloss black glaze over red clay, gold details, w/original lid, Shropshire, England, 5 x 7 1/4" (ILLUS.) **$195-225**

Limoges Porcelain Cow Creamer

Limoges porcelain, solid white, highly glazed, stamped in green ink inside top opening "Limoges, France," common mold, used for some souvenir items, 4 1/2 x 6 1/2" (ILLUS.) **$25-29**

Rare Occupied Japan Cow Creamer

Occupied Japan china, lying down, legs folded underneath, irregular spots, graduating colors of greens & brown on cream, ink stamped "Made in Occupied Japan," rare, mint, 5 1/4 x 7" (ILLUS.) ... **$69-75**

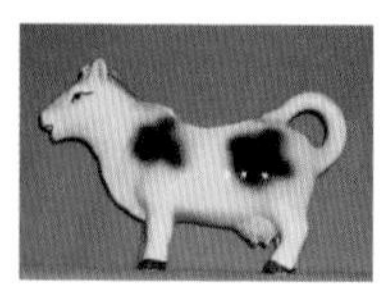

Occupied Japan Cow Creamer

Occupied Japan china, various dark brown markings, white background, glazed, tail curls up to form handle, found w/many different Japan stamps, common, prices depend on bottom markings, largest size 5 x 8" (ILLUS.) **$35-39**

Japanese Cow Creamer w/Lacy Collar

Porcelain, grey on white w/gold accents, very delicate & lacy collar around neck w/bell attached, eyes shut, red ink stamp "Japan" on hoof, 3 3/4 x 4 1/2" (ILLUS.) **$21-24**

German Porcelain Cow Creamer

Porcelain, white, tail & horns missing black cold-paint due to wear, "Germany" impressed on back underneath, 4 3/4 x 7" (ILLUS.) **$64-69**

Brown Pottery Cow Creamer

Pottery, medium brown sponged markings, blue molded bell at neck, unmarked, 1970-80, 4 1/2 x 6" (ILLUS.) **$12-17**

Pottery Cow Creamer

Pottery, pink accents on cream, green dots around neck forming a bow, lock handle tail, unmarked, 3 1/2 x 5" (ILLUS.) **$14-19**

Fine Early Staffordshire Cow Creamer

Staffordshire pottery, cov., platform-type, sponged dark brown & orange over white pottery, milkmaid seated on green base, facing forward, ca. 1810-20, 6 1/2" l. (ILLUS.) **$1,200-1,400**

Purple Sponged Cow Creamer

Staffordshire pottery, cov., sponged purple lustre over cream glazed pottery, orange backstamp "Old Staffordshire Ware, England," 1910-20, small chip on ear, 6 1/2" l. (ILLUS.) **$165-179**

Staffordshire pottery, cov., standing, sponged in manganese & yellow, milkmaid seated performing her task at oblong platform base, facing left, ca. 1780, repair, 6 3/4" l. **$1,400-1,800**

Later Staffordshire Cow Creamer

Staffordshire pottery, pink floral transfer on white, w/yellow bell at neck, unmarked, England, 20th c., 5 x 8" (ILLUS.) **$80-95**

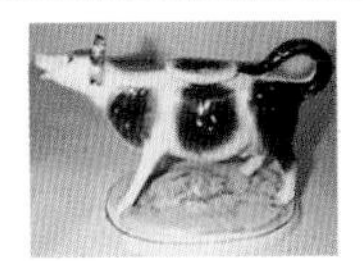

Old Staffordshire Spotted Cow Creamer

Staffordshire pottery, platform-type, reddish brown spots over white, embossed green flower on platform, w/original lid, early, dates from 1870, minor paint loss to be expected, 4 1/2 x 6 1/2" (ILLUS.) **$225-250**

Staffordshire solid agate, cov., body, two legs & suckling calf w/brown & ochre striations, the group modeled standing on a domed rectangular plain creamware base, the cover applied w/a creamware flower-form knop, ca. 1775, 8" l. (restoration to front of base, cover, calf's legs, horns & tail, tiny glaze chips) **$2,875**

English Sterling Silver Cow Creamer

Sterling silver, cov., ornate flowers around lid w/fly perched on top, marks "RC" w/"M" in a shield, lion w/raised paw facing left, leopard's head, letter "e," English, ca. 1960, still being produced, expect to pay more for earlier versions, 5.2 oz., 4 x 6" (ILLUS.)....................... **$500-700**

White Lusterware Cow Creamer

White lustreware china, w/gold horns & tail, opening highlighted in gold, unmarked, mint, 4 3/4 x 6 1/2" (ILLUS.)..... **$74-79**

Yellowware pottery, cov., standing on a platform, lid w/little or no repair, similar to the Bennington cow creamer, very rare **$1,500-2,000**

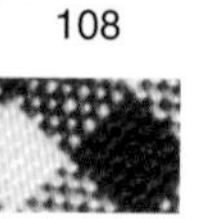

Egg Cups

Ceramic egg cups were a common breakfast table accessory beginning about the mid-19th century and were used for serving soft-boiled eggs. Ceramics egg "hoops" or "rings" were used for many years before the cup-form became common. Egg cups continue to be produced today, and modern novelty and souvenir types are especially collectible.

The descriptions and values listed here were provided by collector Dr. Joan M. George, who notes that values for older egg cups are based on their marks, rarity and recent sales results.

Bucket-style, blue monogram "EIIR," for Queen Elizabeth II, England, 1950s **$22**

Bucket-style, commemorates death of Princess Diana, England, 1997 .... **$35**

Bucket-style, souvenir of Portsmouth, England w/picture of the HMS Victory, England, 1996 .... **$8**

English Gollywog Egg Cup

Bucket-type, colored design of a Gollywog pointing to a stove, Robertsons & Sons, England, ca. 1960s (ILLUS.) **$35**

Bjorn Wiinblad Designed Egg Cup

Bucket-type, colorful stylized modernistic design, Bjorn Wiinblad, Rosenthal, Germany, 1985 (ILLUS.) **$45**

Double, decorated w/a chick & a green stripe, Roseville Pottery, ca. 1919............ **$250**

Double, Garland patt., dark red flower on a grey ground, Stangl Pottery, ca. 1960s....... **$20**

Double, Luckenbach Line, pennant w/logo, unmarked, American-made......................... **$50**

Double, Mexicana patt. by Homer Laughlin, ca. 1930s **$40**

Singapore Bird Pattern Egg Cup

Double, Singapore Bird patt., Oriental-style design of birds & flowering branches on a celadon green ground, Adams, England, ca. 1950s (ILLUS.)....................... **$25**

Double, souvenir of Caesar's Palace, Las Vegas, Nevada, brown design, 1993.......... **$18**

Hoop-style, green transfer-printed design of people & houses, Staffordshire, England, 19th c. **$65**

Hoop-style, white decorated w/green garland band & gilt scrolls, Haviland, Limoges, France, 1990s **$85**

W.H. Goss Crest Egg Cup

Single, banner w/crest marked "Ye Ancient Port of Seaford," W.H. Goss, England, 1930s (ILLUS., previous page) **$20**

French Bart Simpson Egg Cup

Single, Bart Simpson bust, yellow w/blue base, France, 1997, large (ILLUS.)............. **$25**

Single, Bayeux Tapestry, white ground w/a picture showing a portion of the tapestry, Limoges, France, 1998 .... **$15**

French Bellhop Egg Cup

Single, bellhop wearing blue hat & coat, cigarette in his mouth, France, ca. 1920 (ILLUS.) **$70**

Rare Betty Boop Egg Cup

Single, Betty Boop head, red dress, grey lustre hair, Germany, ca. 1930s (ILLUS.) **$300**

Minton Blue Delft Pattern Egg Cup

Single, blue floral Delft patt., gold band trim, Minton, England, 1990s (ILLUS.)................ **$55**

Single, Booth's "Pompadour" patt., multicolored flowers, Silicon China, England, ca. 1920s **$30**

Figural Bugs Bunny Egg Cup

Single, Bugs Bunny head, grey & white, part of a set including Tweety Bird, Tasmanian Devil & Sylvester the Cat, unmarked, large size, 1980s, each (ILLUS.) **$25**

Handled Quaker Oats Man Egg Cup

Single, bust of the Quaker Oats Man, handled, tall, England, 1920s (ILLUS.) **$65**

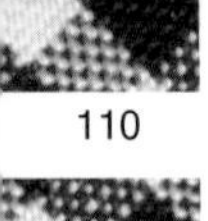

Single, CAAC insignia of star & wings, small, current, China **$12**

Single, color copy of the Mona Lisa on a white cup, unmarked, France, 1998........... **$10**

New York-Brooklyn Bridge Egg Cup

Single, color scene of bridge w/"New York & Brooklyn Bridge," Germany, early 20th c. (ILLUS.)... **$35**

Souvenir Cup with Dutch Children

Single, color scene of Dutch children around the sides, printed in gold at the top "Souvenir Holland," unmarked, 1930s (ILLUS.)... **$32**

Early Goebel Boy's Head Egg Cup

Single, comical boy's head, painted features, high collar below chin, Goebel, Germany, ca. 1930s (ILLUS.) **$140**

Goebel Girl's Head Egg Cup

Single, comical girl's head, painted features, ruffled collar & pink hair band, Goebel, Germany, ca. 1930s (ILLUS.)...... **$140**

Single, commemorates the wedding of Princess Grace & Prince Rainier of Monaco, France, 1956... **$95**

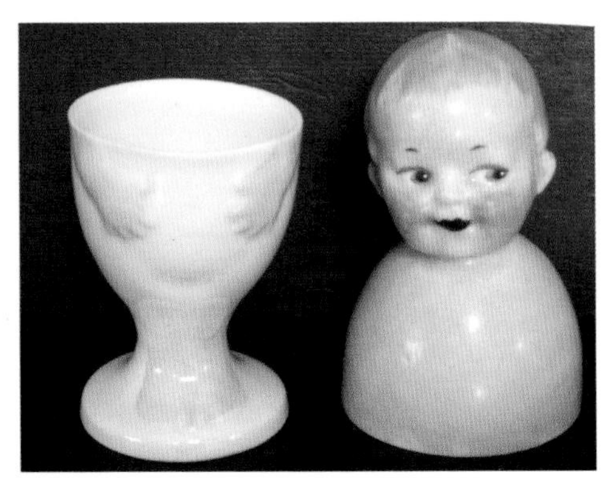

Rare Baby Doll Figural Egg Cup

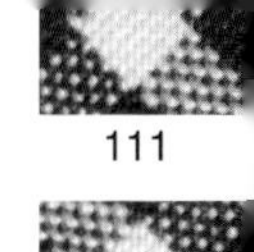

Charles & Diana Divorce Egg Cup

Single, commemorating the divorce of Prince Charles & Princess Diana, Coronet Pottery, England, 1996 (ILLUS.) **$30**

Single, cov., baby doll head & shoulders painted in natural colors form the top, the footed base shows the hands & feet, unmarked, probably American-made, ca. 1930s, rare (ILLUS. of base, bottom previous page).. **$150**

Single, cov., full-figure English Beefeater guard, England, 1999................................. **$15**

Goebel Daffodil Egg Cup from Series

Single, daffodil blossom, one of an annual series of flowers, birds & animals by Goebel of Germany, 1982 (ILLUS.) **$25**

Single, dark blue jasper ware w/white coat-of-arms of the Dominion of Canada, England, ca. 1950...................................... **$40**

Single, decorated by hand w/blue scroll arches trimmed w/gold, Davenport, England, 1887 .... **$85**

Single, deeply scalloped rim, Blue Orchid patt., Meissen, Germany, 1988 (ILLUS., top next column)... **$95**

Single, faience, h.p. w/colorful blue & yellow florals & scrolls, France, ca. 1920s (ILLUS., middle next column)...................... **$45**

Single, figural Swee'pea, from Popeye cartoons, KFS Vandor Imports, Japan, 1980, large size... **$55**

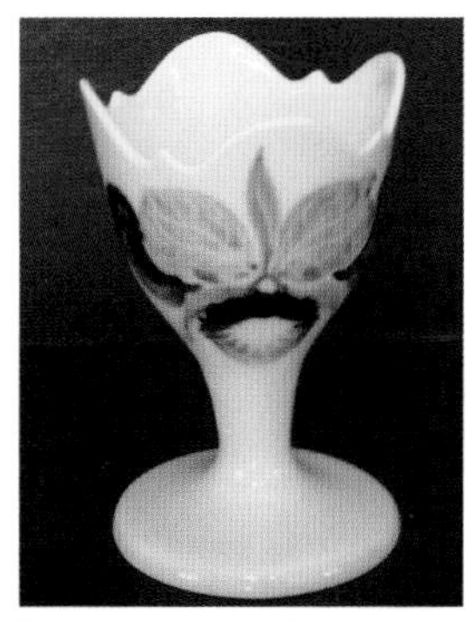

Meissen Blue Orchid Egg Cup

French Faience Egg Cup

Single, figural ugly man's face in grey clay, large nose & blue & white eyes, England, 1999.. **$15**

Single, flow blue Watteau patt., two figures in landscape having a picnic, Doulton, Ltd., England, ca. 1900 .... **$85**

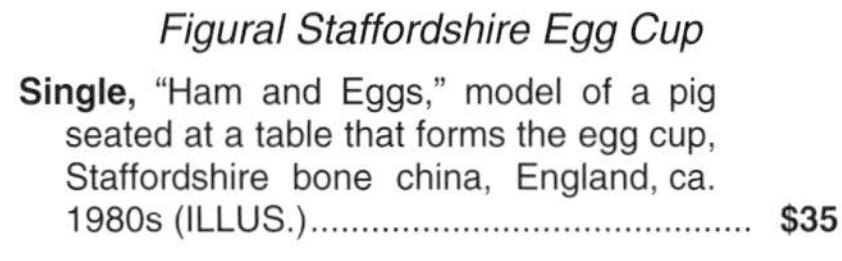

Figural Staffordshire Egg Cup

Single, "Ham and Eggs," model of a pig seated at a table that forms the egg cup, Staffordshire bone china, England, ca. 1980s (ILLUS.).. **$35**

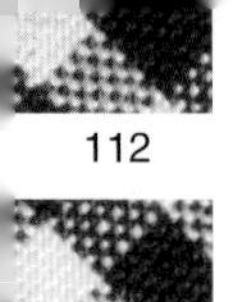

Early Mintons Floral Egg Cup

Single, hand-decorated w/a colorful floral & geometric border band above floral garlands, Mintons, England, ca. 1890s (ILLUS.) **$50**

Single, hand-decorated w/a face, Desimone, Italy, ca. 1980s **$40**

Harrod's Bear Egg Cup

Single, Harrod's bear mascot, standing wearing trademark green Harrod's sweater, tall, England, 1999 (ILLUS.) **$35**

Single, Humpty Dumpty body in blue, sitting on a wall titled "Humpty Dumpty Egg Cup," egg would form the head, unmarked, ca. 1920s **$45**

Jemima Puddleduck Egg Cup

Single, Jemima Puddleduck standing beside a bush-form cup, one from a set of Beatrix Potter characters, Enesco, 1999, each (ILLUS.) **$35**

Single, King Edward VII coronation commemorative, portrait wearing crown, England, 1901 .... **$85**

Single, King George V of England coronation commemorative, England, 1911 .... **$65**

Royal Albert, England Egg Cup

Single, Lady Carlyle patt., decorated w/large clusters of flowers below a scalloped pink rim band, Royal Albert, England, ca. 1950s (ILLUS.) **$35**

Longwy Pottery Egg Cup

Single, large bright pink blossoms & branches on a light blue ground w/dark blue foot & rim, Longwy, France, ca. 1920s (ILLUS., previous page) **$60**

Hutschenreuther "March" Egg Cup

Single, lightly scalloped rim, colorful design of exotic bird & flowering branches, one of a series representing the months, marked "MARZ - Hutschenreuther," Germany, 1980s (ILLUS.) **$25**

Single, Marilyn Monroe picture transfer-printed on hollow cup, England, 2002......... **$15**

Rare Early Minnie Mouse Egg Cup

Single, Minnie Mouse, pointed nose & large ears, wearing orange skirt & blue blouse on a green base, Japan, ca. 1930s (ILLUS.) **$55**

Modern Cow-form Egg Cup

Single, model of a cow, round, painted black & white over green grass, Knobler, U.S., 1987 (ILLUS.)..................................... **$15**

English Lion-form Egg Cup

Single, model of a lion supporting the cup on its back, tan lustre glaze, Royal Fenton, Staffordshire, England, ca. 1930s (ILLUS.).. **$25**

Single, model of a peacock, colorful bird supporting the cup on its back, Sarreguemines, France, ca. 1930s **$50**

Unusual Train Egg Cup - Whistle

Single, model of a train engine w/whistle at end, marked "Foreign" in a circle on the base, Germany, ca. 1920s (ILLUS.) **$175**

Figural Noah's Ark Egg Cup

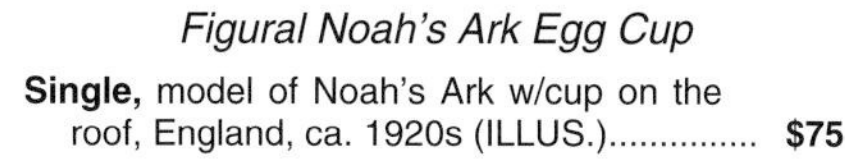

Single, model of Noah's Ark w/cup on the roof, England, ca. 1920s (ILLUS.)............... **$75**

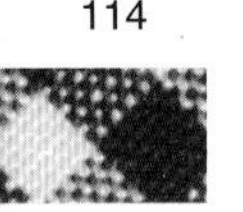

Single, Muppets, either Statler, Waldorf, Sam or Zoot, American-made, 1981, each **$50**

Royal Doulton Nanking Egg Cup

Single, Nanking patt., band of stylized colorful flowers & blue ribbons, Royal Doulton, England, ca. 1930s (ILLUS.) **$28**

Single, Niagara Falls picture titled "Niagara Falls Prospect Point Canada," Japan, 1930s **$28**

Royal Doulton Egg Cup in Orange

Single, orange rim band of stylized floral panels above floral sprigs, gold rim band, Royal Doulton, England, ca. 1930s (ILLUS.) **$35**

Mintons Egg Cup

Single, overall dark blue branching design on exterior & interior, gold rim stripes, Mintons, England, ca. 1910 (ILLUS.) **$50**

Torquay Pottery Egg Cup

Single, painted sea gull & "Torquay" on a dark blue ground, Torquay, England, 1985 (ILLUS.) **$35**

Royal Delft Floral-Painted Egg Cup

Single, painted w/small stylized blue flower sprigs, Royal Delft, Germany, 1967 (ILLUS.) **$55**

Single, picture of Queen Elizabeth of England as a child, England, 1937 .... **$90**

Early Tower of London Egg Cup

Single, pink lustre ground around a white reserve w/a black transfer-printed scene

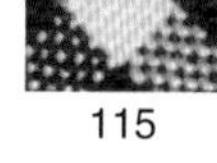
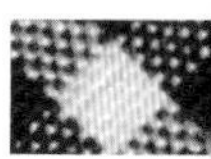

of the Tower of London, Germany, early 20th c. (ILLUS.) **$25**

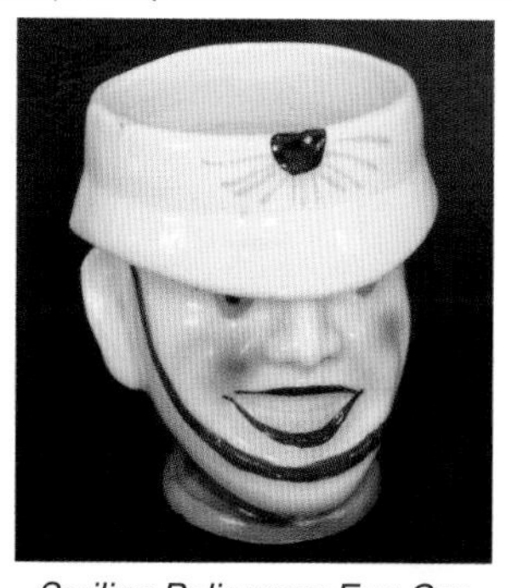

Smiling Policeman Egg Cup

Single, policeman, smiling & wearing a helmet w/a chin strap, unmarked, ca. 1930 (ILLUS.) **$40**

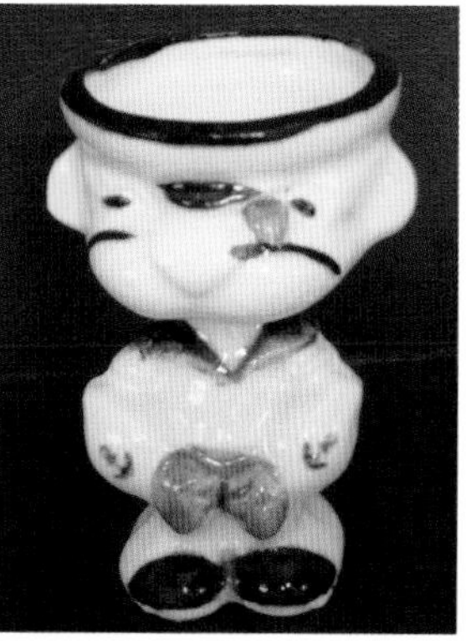

Early Figural Popeye Egg Cup

Single, Popeye full-figure, standing wearing a white suit w/blue trim & anchors, Japan, 1930s (ILLUS.) **$125**

Single, Prince Charles, "Spitting Image," Luck & Flaw, England, 1980s **$55**

Single, Prince William birth commemorative, family portrait, Coronet, England, 1982 .... **$30**

Single, Queen Elizabeth II 70th birthday commemorative, England, 1996 .... **$25**

Single, Queen Elizabeth II Golden Jubilee commemorative w/portrait & royal crest, England, 2002 .... **$25**

Single, Queen Mary of England coronation commemorative, mate to George V cup, England, 1911 .... **$50**

Single, Rhodes, Greece, white w/picture, 2000 .... **$6**

Single, rim band in blue & gold w/tiny red blossoms, Wedgwood, England, 1990s (ILLUS., top next column) **$25**

Single, Royal Copenhagen "Flora Danica" patt., hand-painted, Denmark, current **$475**

Modern Wedgwood Egg Cup

Single, Royal Doulton example decorated w/roses & gold garlands, England, 1927 .... **$50**

Chintz "Welbech" Pattern Egg Cup

Single, Royal Winton Chintz "Welbech" patt., England, 1999 (ILLUS.) **$35**

Single, "Running Legs," white cup attached to legs w/yellow shoes, Carlton Ware, England, 1970s **$40**

Single, scalloped bottom, black transfer-printed scene of "Porta Nigra, Tier," oldest city in Germany, Germany, 1998 .... **$15**

Rare Disney Snow White Egg Cup

Single, Snow White, standing beside cup marked w/her name, Walt Disney Enterprises, part of a set, Japan, 1937 (ILLUS.) **$225**

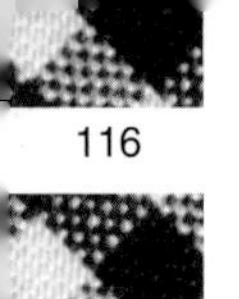

The Drunk Figural Egg Cup

Single, The Drunk, silly face of a man w/half-closed eyes & tongue hanging out, unmarked, ca. 1930s (ILLUS.) **$75**

Single, Union Pacific Railroad "Winged Streamline" design, Scammell China, 1930s **$65**

Egg Cup Decorated with Chickens

Single, upper section decorated in color w/scenes of chickens, yellow foot, gold rim bands, unmarked, 1930s (ILLUS.) **$35**

Single, white ground w/a flag in an oval, titled "Nova Scotia," Canada, 2001 .... **$7**

Winston Churchill-VE Day Egg Cup

Single, Winston Churchill portrait against the Union Jack, commemorates 50th Anniversary of VE Day, Norwich Bone China, England, 1995 (ILLUS.) **$55**

Shy Lady Egg Cup by Goebel

Single, woman w/center-parted brown hair pulled into a bun, shy smile & side-glancing eyes, yellow bow at neck, Goebel, Germany, ca. 1930s (ILLUS.) **$140**

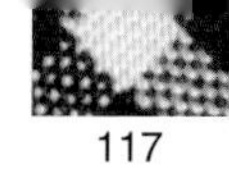

Chapter 7

Kitchen Accessories

Cookie Cutters - General

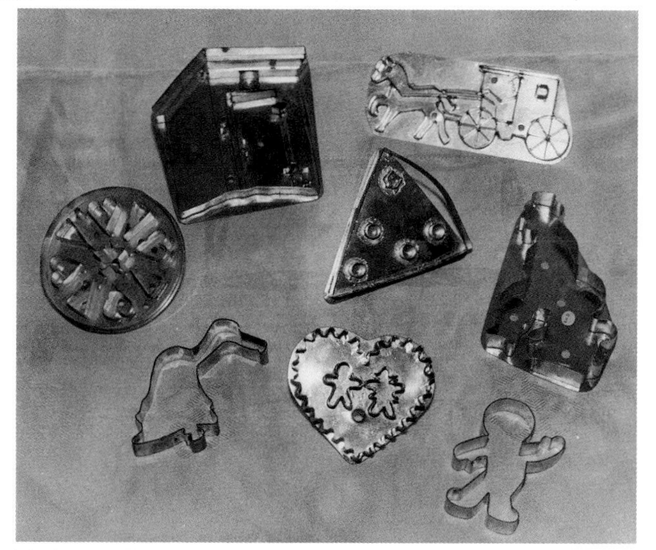

Amish Horse & Buggy, Buzzard, Cathedral Window & Other Cookier Cutters

Amish horse & buggy, by Eugene Valasek, Canton, Ohio (ILLUS. top row, right, with Buzzard, Cathedral Window & other cutter cutters)........ **$25-30**

Beelzebub and Various Other Early Cookie Cutters

Beelzebub, tin, replica of an antique cutter, made to look old (ILLUS. bottom row, left, with Bird, Circle, Gingerbread Girl, Gingerbread Woman & Six-Sided cookie cutters)........ **$20-25**

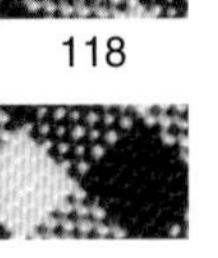

Bird, tin, outline of bird, narrow (ILLUS. top row, right, with Beezlebub, Circle, Gingerbread Girl, Gingerbread Woman with legs & Six-Sided cookie cutters, bottom previous page) **$10-20**

Buzzard, by Little Fox Factory, Bucyrus, Ohio (ILLUS. center row, left, with Amish Buggy, Cathedral Window & other cookie cutters, top previous page)........................... **$5**

Cathedral window, by Eugene Valasek, Canton, Ohio (ILLUS. cemter row, left, with Amish Buggy, Buzzard & other cookie cutters, top previous page)................ **$25-30**

Circle, crinkled edges, early 1900s (ILLUS. bottom row, center, with Beezlebub, Bird, Gingerbread Girl, Gingerbread Woman with legs & Six-Sided cookie cutters, bottom previous page) **$30-35**

Gingerbread boy waving, outline-style, by Little Fox Factory, Bucyrus, Ohio (ILLUS. bottom row, right, with Amish Buggy, Buzzard & other cookie cutters, top previous page) **$5**

Gingerbread Boy & Girl Cookie Cutters

Gingerbread boy with buttons, tin, w/handles, signed E. Valasek, 1979, Canton, Ohio (ILLUS. right with Gingerbread Girl with Skirt) **$15-20**

Gingerbread girl, heavy tin, no signature (ILLUS. top row, left, with Beezlebub, Bird, Circle, Gingerbread Woman with legs & Six-Sided cookie cutters, bottom previous page) **$25-30**

Gingerbread girl, with skirt, tin, w/handles, signed Gene Valasek, 1980, Canton, Ohio (ILLUS. left with Gingerbread Boy with Buttons) **$25-30**

Gingerbread woman with legs, galvanized metal, flat back handle w/edges turned under, no signature on cutter, Baxter Oberlin, Angola, Indiana (ILLUS. top row, center with Beezlebub, Bird, Circle, Gingerbread Girl & Six-Sided cookie cutters, bottom previous page) **$25-35**

Hansel & Gretel set: Hansel, Gretel, witch, tree, gingerbread house; first boxed set, plastic, w/recipes & story of Hansel & Gretel, Educational Products, 1947, front of box features Mr. Meiro, owner of E.P. Co., wife & two daughters, set of six cutters in original box (ILLUS., bottom of page) **$150**

Heart, w/Gingerbread tiny boy & girl inside, has a crinkled edge handle w/edge folded to outside, signed inside of heart B. Cukla©, Hammer Song, Boonsboro, Maryland (ILLUS. bottom row, center, with Amish Buggy, Buzzard & other cookie cutters, top previous page)................. **$25-35**

Outhouse, by Eugene Valasek, Canton, Ohio (ILLUS. top row, left, with Amish Buggy, Buzzard & other cookie cutters, top previous page) **$30-40**

Six-Sided, replica of a cutter a roving tinsmith would have made in the late 1800s or early 1900s (ILLUS. bottom row, right, with Beezlebub, Bird, Circle, Gingerbread Girl & Gingerbread Woman with legs cookie cutters, bottom previous page).. **$20-30**

Swiss cheese slice, small "Ohio" in upper left hand corner, by Stan Baker, Dover, Ohio (ILLUS. middle row, center, with Amish Buggy, Buzzard & other cookie cutters, top previous page) **$25-30**

Woman on pot, replica of a cutter in the Historical Society Collection at Lewiston, Pennsylvania, by Bob Jones, Allen Park, Michigan (ILLUS. middle row, right, with Amish Buggy, Buzzard & other cookie cutters, top previous page) **$30-50**

Hansel & Gretel Set of Cookie Cutters

Cookie Cutters - Hallmark - General

Fire Chief badge, soft vinyl, yellow, 1978, 4 1/2" **$3-5**

Fozzie Bear, hard plastic, brown, white & lavender, signed H.A., 1980, 4 1/2" **$10-12**

Gingerbread boy or girl, either hard plastic or soft vinyl, brown, 1977 .... **$7-12**

Good luck, hard plastic, yellow & red, this cutter is mint in package but cellophane packages don't inflate value, 1979, 2 3/4" **$3**

Goofy in Space Helmet Cookie Cutter

Goofy in space helmet, soft vinyl, blue, 1979, signed WDP, 3 1/2" (ILLUS.) **$10-15**

Ice cream cone, soft vinyl, orange, 1980, 5" **$4-7**

Joan Walsh Anglund Doll Cookie Cutter

Joan Walsh Anglund, reissued in pink, signed Wolfpit Enterprises, Inc., 1980, 4 1/2" (ILLUS.) **$7-10**

Joan Walsh Anglund, soft vinyl, orange, signed Wolfpit Enterprises, Inc., 1978, 4 1/2" **$10-12**

Peanuts characters, first Peanuts set featuring Linus, Lucy, Snoopy & Charlie Brown, hard plastic w/curved handles, colors varied but for the set to be complete each cutter must be a different color - blue, orange, red, green or white, signed United Features Syndicate, 1971, all about 4 3/4", set of 4 .... **$45-65**

Raggedy Ann & Andy Cookie Cutters

Raggedy Ann & Andy, hard plastic, one red, one blue, signed BM for Bobbs Merrill, the company that held the copyright at the time, originally sold for 75¢, 1972, 4 3/4", pr. (ILLUS.) **$12-25**

Cookie Cutters - Hallmark - Holiday

Christmas, angel w/lute, soft vinyl, blue, 1979, 4" **$4-6**

Christmas, candy cane, soft vinyl, red, 1979, 3" **$3-5**

Four Christmas Motif Cookie Cutters

Christmas, Christmas motifs, snowman, angel, tree, Santa, hard plastic, red or green, 4 1/4", 1973, set of 4 (ILLUS.) **$45-60**

Christmas, gingerbread man, soft vinyl, brown, 1981, 2 1/4" **$4-6**

Christmas, holly leaves, soft vinyl, green, 1979, 2 1/2" **$2-5**

Christmas, "JOY" ornament, soft vinyl, red, 1979, 2 3/4" **$3-6**

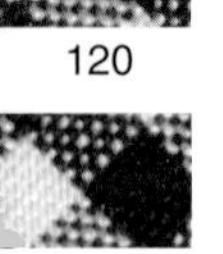

Christmas, kneeling angel, soft vinyl, yellow, 1982, 2 1/2" **$1-3**

Linus & Snoopy Cookie Cutters

Christmas, Peanuts characters Charlie Brown, Linus, Snoopy & Lucy, hard plastic, various colors, white, red, blue & green, to be complete set each cutter must be a different color, signed United Features Syndicate, 1972, 3 1/2" to 4 1/2", set of 4 (ILLUS. of Linus & Snoopy) .... **$50+**

Christmas, printed "HOHOHO," soft vinyl, green, 1984, 3 3/4" **$2-3**

Colored Reindeer Cutter from 1979

Christmas, reindeer, hard plastic, brown, red, white & green, painted, hard to find, 1979, 4 1/2" (ILLUS.) **$15-20**

Christmas, rocking horse, hard plastic, white, gold, red, green & brown, dated 1981, 4" .... **$25+**

Christmas, Santa, hard plastic, white, red, black & gold, 1982, 4 1/2" **$8-10**

Santa Head Cookie Cutters

Christmas, Santa head, hard plastic, red or green, 1974, 5" (ILLUS.) **$40**

Christmas, Santa sleigh, hard plastic, brown, red, white & green, 1979, 3"....... **$10-12**

Christmas, Santa w/candy cane, soft vinyl, red, 1981, 4 1/4" **$4**

Christmas, Santa w/sack on back, soft vinyl, red, 1979, 4"....................................... **$5-8**

Christmas, snowflake, soft vinyl, white, 1980, 2 1/2"... **$3-5**

Snowman Head Cookie Cutters

Christmas, snowman head, hard plastic, red or green, 1974, 5 1/4" (ILLUS.)............. **$45**

Christmas, snowman w/bird, soft vinyl, white, 1981, 4 1/2" **$5**

Christmas, snowman w/broom, soft, white, 1979, 2 1/2"... **$2-5**

Christmas, star, hard plastic, red or green, 1977, 2 1/2"... **$5-7**

Christmas, Teddy bear, soft vinyl, tan, 1983, 2 1/4".. **$2**

Christmas, toy soldier, 1983, soft vinyl, red, 4 1/4".. **$5**

Christmas, tree, hard plastic, green, gold, red & white, 1980, 4 1/2" **$12**

Christmas, wreath, soft vinyl, green, 1980, 3 1/4"... **$3-5**

Easter, Barnaby Bunny, hard plastic or soft vinyl, yellow, blue or pink, 1978, 5".......... **$7-10**

Easter, bunny, hard plastic, white, blue, yellow & pink, 1982, 4 3/4" **$10-12**

Easter, bunny head, soft vinyl, blue, 1980, 4".. **$4-6**

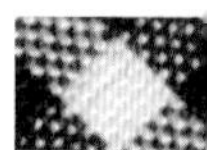

Duck with Daisy & Flower Cookie Cutters

Easter, bunny w/basket, hard plastic, white, pink, blue, yellow & brown, 1979, 4 1/4" **$10-12**

Chickery Chick Easter Cookie Cutter

Easter, Chickery Chick, hard plastic or soft vinyl, yellow, blue or pink, 1978, 5" (ILLUS.) **$12-22**

Easter, duck, soft vinyl, yellow, 1982, 4"........ **$2-4**

Easter, duck w/daisy, hard plastic, white, yellow, green, orange & brown, 1979, 4 1/4" (ILLUS. left with flower cookie cutter, top of page).. **$7-9**

Easter, Easter motifs, egg, rabbit, boy & girl, hard plastic, varied colors, lime green, blue, yellow & pink, to be a complete set must be one of each color, originally sold for $1.50, 1974, 3 3/4" to 4 1/2", set of 4 (ILLUS., top next column) **$35-50**

Easter, egg decorated w/flowers, hard plastic, lavender, 1984, 2 3/4" **$1-4**

Set of Easter Motif Cookie Cutters

Easter, egg, hard plastic, blue, white, green & lavender, 1981, 4 1/4" **$6-8**

Easter, flower, hard plastic, white, green, orange & pink, 1980, 4 1/4" (ILLUS. right with duck & daisy cookie cutter)............. **$10-12**

Easter, lamb, soft vinyl, white, 1980, 4" **$2-5**

Easter, smiling egg, soft vinyl, blue, 1981, 4".. **$2-4**

Easter, tulip, soft vinyl, blue, 1982, 4"............ **$2-4**

Fall, acorn, hard plastic or soft vinyl, brown or golden, 1976, 4".................................... **$3-6**

Fall, apple, soft vinyl, red, 1981, 3 1/2" **$2-3**

Fall, football helmet, soft vinyl, red, 1978, 4" .. **$3-6**

Fall, football player, soft vinyl, gold, 1983, 4 1/2"... **$1-2**

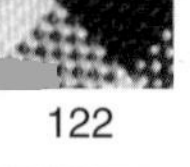

Fall, football, soft vinyl, brown, 1978, 4 1/2" ... **$5-7**
Fall, leaf, hard plastic or soft vinyl, brown or yellow, 1976, 4" ... **$10**
Fall, maple leaf, soft vinyl, rust, 1981, 3 3/4" .. **$1-2**
Fall, owl, soft vinyl, gold, 1980, 3 3/4" ... **$3-5**
Fall, scarecrow, soft vinyl, orange, 1984, 4 3/4" ... **$2-5**
Fall, squirrel, soft vinyl, orange, 1980, 4 1/4" .. **$2-4**
Fall, tee-shirt, soft vinyl, blue, 1984, 3 1/2" **$1-2**
Halloween, bat, soft vinyl, black, 1982, 2 1/2" ... **$1-3**
Halloween, "BOO" ghost, soft vinyl, white, 1981, 3 1/4" ... **$5-7**
Halloween, cat w/tail up over back, soft vinyl, black, 1979, 4 1/4" ... **$6-7**
Halloween, crouching cat, hard plastic or soft vinyl, black or orange, 1976, 2 3/4" ... **$10-15**
Halloween, ghost, hard plastic or soft vinyl, white or orange, 1976, 3 1/2" ... **$5-7**
Halloween, Halloween motifs, owl, witch head, pumpkin & cat head, hard plastic, orange, 1973, 3 1/2", set of 4 ... **$50-60**
Halloween, Jack-o'-lantern, hard plastic, orange, 1976, 3" ... **$10-12**
Halloween, scarecrow, hard plastic, yellow, green, orange & black, 1979, 4 1/4" ... **$15-20**
Halloween, skull, soft vinyl, white, 1980, 4 1/4" ... **$2-4**

Snoopy on Pumpkin Cookie Cutter

Halloween, Snoopy on pumpkin, hard plastic, orange, signed United Features Syndicate, has sold for over $100, original price 75¢, 1974, 6 1/2" (ILLUS.) ... **$50-60**
Halloween, spider, hard plastic, black, orange, gold, green, yellow & white, 1981, 3 1/2" ... **$10-12**
Halloween, super bat, hard plastic, purple, black, white & red, 1980, 3" ... **$15**
Halloween, vampire, hard plastic, blue, black, yellow, red & white, 1979, 4 1/4" (ILLUS., top next column) ... **$10-12**
Halloween, witch, side view, hard plastic or soft vinyl, orange, 1976, 3 1/2" ... **$4-6**
Halloween, witch, soft vinyl, purple, 1983, 4 1/4" ... **$1-3**

Vampire Cookie Cutter

Halloween, witch standing wearing pointed hat, soft vinyl, orange, 1979, 4" ... **$4-6**
St. Patrick's Day, ... **$6**
St. Patrick's Day, beer mug, soft vinyl, green, 1985, 4 1/4" ... **$1-3**
St. Patrick's Day, hat w/shamrocks, hard plastic, greens & gold, hats a' plenty for the luck of the Irish, 1981, 4 1/2" ... **$10**

Kermit & Shamrock Cookie Cutter

St. Patrick's Day, Kermit the Frog w/shamrock, soft vinyl, lime green, signed "H.A.," 1982, 3 1/2" (ILLUS.) ... **$4-7**
St. Patrick's Day, Leprechaun, hard plastic, greens, tan, brown & black, painted, 1979, 5" ... **$10-15**
St. Patrick's Day, Leprechaun, soft vinyl, translucent green, 1981, 4 1/4" ... **$1-4**
St. Patrick's Day, puppy w/shamrock, soft vinyl, green, 1984, 3 3/4" ... **$2-4**
St. Patrick's Day, round derby, soft vinyl, green, hats a' plenty for the luck of the Irish, 1980, 3" ... **$4-6**
St. Patrick's Day, shamrock, soft vinyl, green, 1980, large, 3 1/4" ... **$4-6**

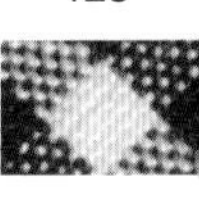

St. Patrick's Day, small shamrock, hard plastic, green, 1977, 2 3/4" **$6**

Thanksgiving, cornucopia, soft vinyl, gold, 1978, 3" **$2-3**

Thanksgiving, Pilgrim bird, soft vinyl, brown, 1980, 4 1/4" **$2-4**

Thanksgiving, Pilgrim boy or girl, 1976, hard plastic, orange, tan or brown, 1976, miniature, 2 3/4", each **$10-15**

Thanksgiving, Pilgrim boy's head, soft vinyl, orange, 1978, 4 1/2" **$2-4**

Thanksgiving, printed "GOBBLE," soft vinyl, orange, 1984, 2" **$1-2**

Turkey from Thanksgiving Set

Thanksgiving, Thanksgiving motifs, Pilgrim boy & girl, leaf & turkey, hard plastic, various colors, red, green, orange & tan, to be complete set each cutter must be a different color, turkey will sell for $20,1974, 3 1/2" to 5 1/4", set of 4 (ILLUS. of turkey) **$25-40**

Thanksgiving, turkey, hard plastic, orange, tan or brown, 1976, 2 3/4" **$5-7**

Valentine's Day, charmer girl, soft vinyl, red, 1984, 3 3/4" **$3-6**

Cupid Holding Heart Cookie Cutter

Valentine's Day, Cupid holding small red heart, hard plastic, flesh, white, yellow & brown, 1979, 3 1/2" (ILLUS.) **$10**

Valentine's Day, Cupid, soft vinyl, pink, 1981, 4 1/4" **$4-6**

Valentine's Day, dove, hard plastic, pinks, gold & white, all of the Hallmark cutters of this type are called "painted" by collectors, 3 1/4" **$10**

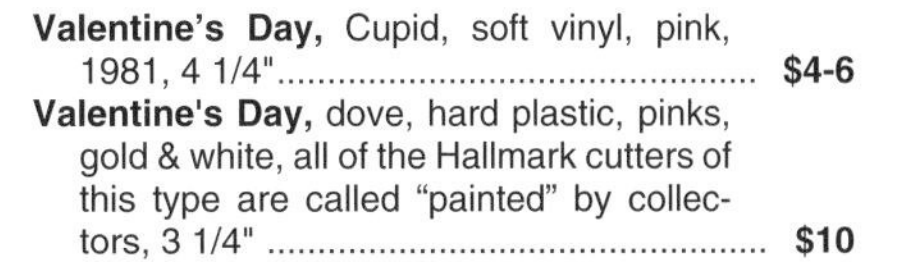

Heart & Cupid Cookie Cutters

Valentine's Day, heart & Cupid set, hard plastic, red, 1974, heart 3 1/4", Cupid 3 3/4", pr. (ILLUS. of both) **$25-30**

Valentine's Day, hearts, hard plastic, solid red, pink, lavender or yellow, hearts said "Love Ya" or "Hi Cutie," 1977, 2 3/4" **$2-3**

Valentine's Day, Hug Bug heart, soft vinyl, red, 1980, 3" **$3-7**

Kermit with "Be Mine" Heart Cutter

Valentine's Day, Kermit the Frog, hard plastic, greens, red, gold, white & black, w/a cheery smile & a "Be Mine" heart, Hallmark loved to use Jim Henson's muppets & Kermit was one of their favorite characters, signed "H.A.," 1981, 4 1/2" (ILLUS.) **$8-10**

Valentine's Day, koala bear, soft vinyl, red, 1981, 3 1/2" **$2-5**

Valentine's Day, Mickey Mouse heart, soft vinyl, red, signed WDP, 1980 .... **$12-15**

Valentine's Day, printed "LOVE," hard plastic, red, pink, lavender & yellow, 1977, 2 1/4" **$4-7**

Valentine's Day, script "Love," hard plastic, white, pink, red & gold, 1981, 3" **$6**

Valentine's Day, smiling heart, soft vinyl, red, 1982, 3" **$3-6**

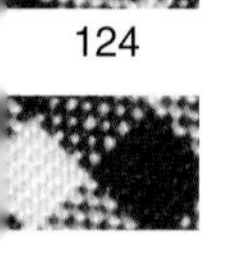

Chapter 8

Egg Timers

A little glass tube filled with sand and attached to a figural base measuring between 3" and 5" in height was once a commonplace kitchen item. Although egg timers were originally used to time a 3-minute egg, some were used to limit the length of a telephone call as a cost saving measure.

Many beautiful timers were produced in Germany in the 1920s and later in Japan, reaching their heyday in the 1940s. These small egg timers were commonly made in a variety of shapes in bisque, china, chalkware, cast iron, tin, brass, wood or plastic.

Egg timers had long been considered an essential kitchen tool until, in the 1920s and 1930s, a German pottery company, W. Goebel, introduced figural egg timers. Goebel crafted miniature china figurines with attached glass vials. After the Great Depression, Japanese companies introduced less detailed timers. The Goebel figural egg timers are set apart by their trademark, delicate painting and distinctive clothes. It is best to purchase egg timers with their original tube, but the condition of the figure is most important in setting prices.

Angel, ceramic, wearing blue robe & gold wings, w/verse "May the meals that I...," unmarked **$45-65**

Goebel Baker Egg Timer

Baker, ceramic, Goebel (ILLUS.) **$50**

Bear, ceramic, howling, USA **$50-75**

Bear, ceramic, wearing chef's outfit, marked "Japan" **$65-85**

Bellhop, ceramic, Oriental, kneeling, marked "Germany" **$65-85**

Bellhop, ceramic, Oriental, wearing red outfit, marked "Germany" **$65-85**

Bellhop, ceramic, talking on telephone, marked "Japan," 3" h. **$45**

Bellhop, ceramic, wearing green uniform, marked "Japan," 4 1/2" h. **$70**

Bellhop, ceramic, wearing white uniform w/buttons down leg seam, marked "Germany" **$65-85**

Bellhop, composition, holding bouquet of flowers, marked "Germany" **$85-115**

Bird, ceramic, red bird sitting by yellow post, marked "Germany" **$50**

Bird, ceramic, sitting on nest, wearing white bonnet w/green ribbon, Josef Originals sticker **$45**

Bird & Egg Near Stump Egg Timer

Bird, ceramic, standing next to stump w/egg at base, shades of brown w/green grassy base & leaves on stump, Japan (ILLUS.) **$50**

Birdhouse, wood, hanging-type, white w/red perch & roof................................. **$10-15**

Birds, ceramic, double-type, yellow, modeled by Reinhold Unger, Goebel, Germany, 1934 .... **$85-100**

Black Baby Egg Timer

Black baby, ceramic, sitting w/left arm holding timer (ILLUS.)...................................... **$125**

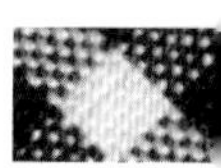

Boy on Chamber Pot Egg Timer

Black boy, holding timer in right hand & sitting on chamber pot, marked "Foreign" (ILLUS.) **$85-110**

Black chef, ceramic, sitting w/arm up holding timer, variety of sizes, Germany **$65-95**

Black chef, ceramic, standing, marked "Llangollen" **$95**

Black Chef with Fish Egg Timer

Black chef, ceramic, standing w/large fish, timer in fish's mouth, Germany, 4 3/4" h. (ILLUS.) **$125**

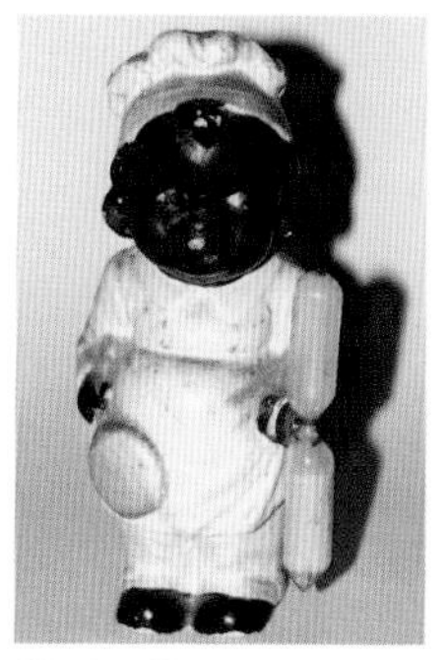

Black Chef w/Frying Pan Egg Timer

Black chef with frying pan, composition, Japan (ILLUS.) **$95**

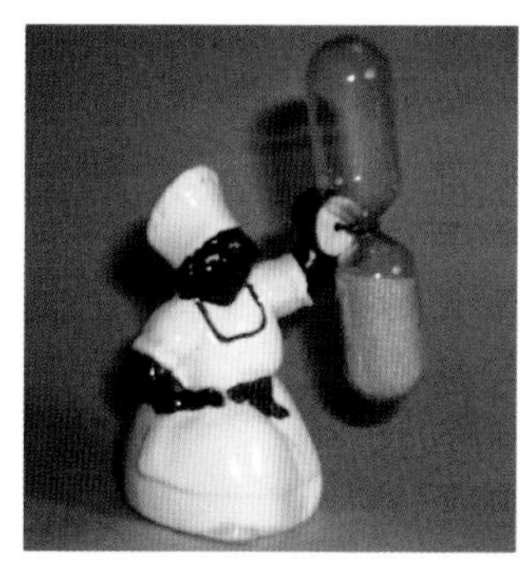

Lady Chef Egg Timer

Black lady chef, ceramic, sitting, Germany (ILLUS.) **$95**

Bo-Peep Egg Timer

Bo-Peep, ceramic, "Bo-Peep" on base, Japan (ILLUS.) **$95**

Boy, ceramic, holding blackbird, unmarked **$65-85**

Boy, ceramic, holding rifle, marked "Germany" **$50**

Boy, ceramic, playing guitar, marked "Germany," 3 1/2" h. **$50**

Boy, ceramic, skiing pose, marked "Germany," 3" h. **$50**

Swiss Boy Egg Timer

Boy, composition, wearing Swiss outfit, marked "Germany" (ILLUS., previous page) **$65-75**

Wooden Boy Egg Timer

Boy, wood, w/red cap, standing & holding a glass tube in each hand, unmarked, 4 1/2" h. (ILLUS.) **$65-75**

Boy Chef Egg Timer

Boy chef, ceramic, sitting w/raised arm, Germany (ILLUS.) **$65**

Goebel Egg Timer with Boy & Girl

Boy & girl, ceramic, flanking timer on oblong base, boy w/white pants, dark blue coat & yellow cap, girl in red dress w/white apron & large dark blue hat, Goebel, Germany (ILLUS.) **$95**

Buccaneer Egg Timer

Buccaneer, ceramic, hanging-type, w/white polka-dotted red scarf, Germany (ILLUS.) **$100-150**

Butler, ceramic, wearing white outfit w/black jacket, Germany **$65-85**

Cat, ceramic, black cat w/white-tipped tail sitting by fireplace, "Ireland" painted on front, marked "Manorware, England" **$25-35**

Cat, ceramic, white & black cat, marked "Germany" **$65-85**

Wooden Cat Egg Timer

Cat, wooden, black cat w/yellow eyes & red collar on domed yellow base, timer lifts out of back (ILLUS.) **$35**

Cat, ceramic, standing by base of grandfather clock, Germany, 4 1/2" h. **$35**

Chef, ceramic, female, kneeling, Germany **$50-75**

Chef, ceramic, holding blue spoon, marked "Germany" **$50**

Chef, ceramic, holding egg, Germany **$45-65**

Chef, ceramic, holding fish, Japan **$95-125**

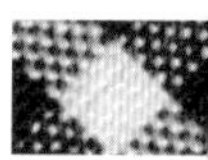

Chef, ceramic, holding knife, Japan **$45-65**
Chef, ceramic, holding plate, Japan **$45-65**
Chef, ceramic, holding spoon, Japan **$45-65**
Chef, ceramic plate w/hole to hold timer, which removes to change, Japan................ **$50**
Chef, ceramic, w/removable timer............. **$65-85**
Chef, ceramic, w/towel drapped over arm, Japan **$45-65**
Chef, ceramic, white w/black shoes & hair, marked "Germany"................................ **$45-65**
Chef, ceramic, winking, white w/black shoes & trim, turning figure on its head activates sand, 4" h. **$65**
Chef, composition board, black chef holding platter of chicken, w/pot holder hooks......... **$50**
Chef, composition, w/cake, Germany............. **$85**
Chef, metal, w/platter & knife **$50-75**

Egg Timer with Chef Holding Egg

Chef, porcelain, white & blue, holding reddish orange egg, supporting timer, Germany (ILLUS.).. **$50**
Chef, wood, Little Black Sambo, wearing red & white checked apron, The Pohlson Galleries **$85-100**
Chef, wood, "Time Your Egg"......................... **$20**
Chefs, ceramic, man & woman, Goebel, Germany, 4" h. **$100**
Chick, ceramic, white, yellow & purple chick, marked "Japan"................................ **$35**
Chicken, ceramic, multicolored, marked "Germany" **$75-95**
Chicken, ceramic, white & red, flat back, marked "Japan"..................................... **$45-65**
Chicken, ceramic, white w/black wings & tail feathers, marked "Germany" **$50**
Chicken, ceramic, white w/brown wings & tail, marked "Germany" **$75-95**
Chicken, on nest, green plastic, England, 2 1/2" h. **$20**
Chicken, wings hold tube, ceramic, Germany, 2 3/4" h. **$65**
Chimney sweep, ceramic, Goebel, Germany (ILLUS., top next column)...................... **$50**
Chimney sweep, ceramic, wearing black outfit w/top hat, carrying ladder, Germany **$50**

Goebel Chimney Sweep Egg Timer

Clockman Planter

Clock, ceramic, clock face, w/man's plaid suit & tie below, w/planter in back, Japan (ILLUS.).. **$25**

Clown Egg Timer

Clown, ceramic, Germany (ILLUS.)................ **$95**
Clown, ceramic, w/ball on head, marked "Japan"... **$45-65**

Clown on phone, ceramic, standing, full-figured, Japan **$65**

Colonial lady with bonnet, ceramic, variety of dresses & colors, Germany, 3 3/4" h., each **$50**

Colonial man, ceramic, yellow & white, Japan **$50**

Colonial man in knickers, ruffled shirt, ceramic, Japan, 4 3/4" h. **$75**

Dog, ceramic, black Poodle, sitting, Germany **$75**

Dog, ceramic, Dachshund, red w/hole in back for timer, label on back reads "Shorty Timer" **$65**

Green Dog Egg Timer

Dog, ceramic, green, looking at his tail (ILLUS.) **$75**

Lustreware Dog

Dog, ceramic, lustre ware, white w/brown ears & tail, Japan (ILLUS.) **$65**

Dog, ceramic, Pekingese, standing brown & white dog, marked "Germany" **$65**

Dog Egg Timer

Dog, ceramic, sitting, white w/brown tail & ears, timer in head, Germany (ILLUS.) **$75**

Dog, ceramic, white & brown dog w/red collar sitting by post, marked "Germany" **$65-85**

Dog, ceramic, white dog w/brown ears, tail & paws, blue collar, marked "Japan" **$45-75**

Dog, ceramic, white w/brown ears, tail & paws, marked "Germany" **$65-85**

Scottie Egg Timer

Dog, chalkware, white Scottie (ILLUS.) **$45-65**

Dog, lustre, white & yellow, holding red flower, marked "Germany" **$95**

Dogs, ceramic, Scotties, brown, standing facing each other holding timer in paws, marked "Germany" **$95**

Duck, wood, hanging-type, duck sitting on green egg w/three egg timer glasses, marked "Germany" **$35**

Dutch boy, ceramic, standing by green post, Japan, tall **$35**

Dutch boy, ceramic, wearing orange scarf, Japan $45-65

Dutch boy, ceramic, white w/red scarf around neck, kneeling, Japan $35

Dutch boy, ceramic, yellow pants, brown shoes, hat, scarf, Japan $35

Dutch Boy Egg Timer

Dutch boy, composition, blue pants & hat, red shirt, white tie w/blue polka dots, Germany (ILLUS.) $50

Goebel Dutch Boy & Girl Egg Timer

Dutch boy & girl, ceramic, double-type, timer marked w/3-, 4- & 5-minute intervals, Goebel, Germany, 1953 (ILLUS.) $75

Dutch couple by windmill, ceramic, Japan $65

Dutch girl, ceramic, all white w/blue trim at waist & neckline, kneeling $50-75

Dutch girl, ceramic, talking on telephone, Japan $45

Dutch girl, ceramic, w/orange scarf at neck, Germany $50

Dutch girl, ceramic, w/red heart on apron, Germany $50

Dutch girl, ceramic, white w/blue apron & trim, Germany (ILLUS., top next column) ... $50

Dutch Girl Egg Timer

Yellow Dutch Girl Egg Timer

Dutch girl, ceramic, yellow (ILLUS.) $35

Dutch girl, composition, wearing blue dress & yellow apron, walking, Germany......... $65-85

Dutchman, ceramic, holding pipe, Japan $50

Elephant, ceramic, white, sitting w/timer in upraised trunk, marked "Germany" $50

Elf by Well Egg Timer

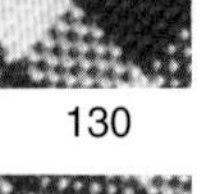

Elf by well, ceramic, Manorware, England (ILLUS., previous page) **$25**

English Bobby Egg Timer

English Bobby, ceramic, Germany (ILLUS.) ... **$75**

Lustreware Fish Egg Timer

Fish, ceramic, lustre ware, burgundy, yellow & green, Germany (ILLUS.) **$85**

Fisherman Egg Timer

Fisherman, ceramic, standing, wearing brown jacket & hat, tall black boots, carrying a large white fish on his shoulders, timer attached to mouth of fish, Germany (ILLUS.)... **$85**

Friar Tuck, ceramic, double-type, modeled by Helmut White, timer marked w/3-, 4- & 5-minute intervals, Goebel, Germany, 1956... **$65**

Friar Tuck, ceramic, single, Goebel, Germany, 4" h.. **$50**

Frog, ceramic, multicolored frog sitting on egg, marked "Japan".................................. **$65**

Fruit, wood, double-headed....................... **$10-15**

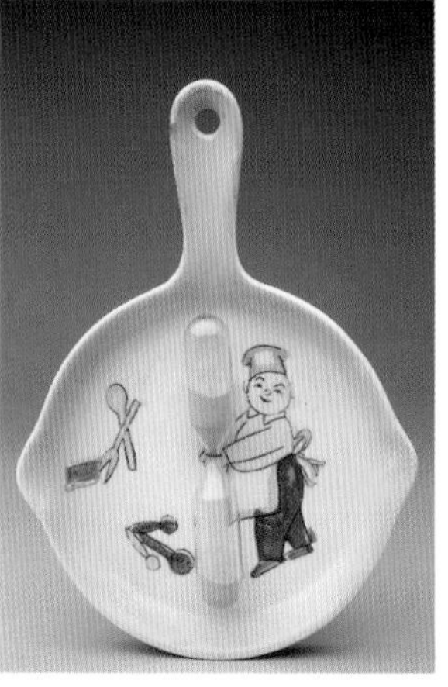

Frying Pan Egg Timer

Frying pan, ceramic, hanging-type, w/picture of chef & cooking utensils, Japan (ILLUS.) **$20-35**

Garden boy, ceramic, holding shovel & wearing hat, Germany........................... **$75-95**

Geisha woman, ceramic, marked "Germany".. **$85-95**

Genie Egg Timer

Genie, w/recipe holder in back (ILLUS.) ... **$75-95**

Girl, ceramic, holding ball at shoulder, marked "Germany"..................................... **$50**

Girl, ceramic, holding cup, marked "Germany"... **$65**

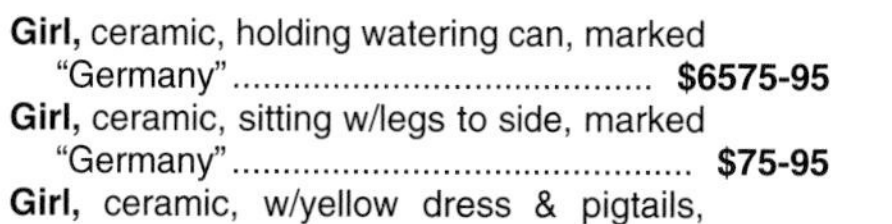

Girl, ceramic, holding watering can, marked "Germany" **$6575-95**

Girl, ceramic, sitting w/legs to side, marked "Germany" **$75-95**

Girl, ceramic, w/yellow dress & pigtails, marked "Germany" **$75-95**

Golliwog Egg Timer

Golliwog, bisque, England, 4 1/2" h., minimum value (ILLUS.) **$150**

Grandfather clock, composition, Manorware, England **$35**

Happy the Dwarf, ceramic, from "Snow White & the Seven Dwarfs," Maw Co., England **$75**

Honey bear, ceramic, brown & white, w/timer in mouth made to resemble milk bottle, Cardinal China Co., No. 1152 ..... **$65-85**

House, ceramic, handpainted w/clock face on front, Japan **$35**

Huckleberry Finn, ceramic, sitting in front of post, Japan **$100**

Humpty Dumpty, ceramic, wearing hat & bow tie, turn onto head to activate sand, marked "California Cleminsons" **$35**

Indian Egg Timer

Indian, ceramic, kneeling, white, wearing headdress w/red, blue & green feathers, holding timer in one hand, marked "Germany," rare (ILLUS.) **$100-150**

Indian, plastic, "Indian Josephine," hanging-type, w/inscription on front "For boilum eggs...," 4 1/2 x 5 1/2" **$15-20**

Kitchen Maid, ceramic, w/measuring spoons **$95**

Lady mouse, ceramic, wearing green dress w/yellow apron & bonnet, Josef Originals sticker **$15-25**

Lady on phone, ceramic, Japan **$35-50**

Leprechaun, brass, w/green clover at base **$25-35**

Leprechaun, glazed chalkware, sitting by tree stump, marked "Manorware," England **$35**

Lighthouse, glazed chalkware, white & blue, Manorware, England **$35**

Lighthouse, lustre, yellow & orange, Germany **$35**

Little Boy Egg Timer

Little boy, ceramic, standing wearing black shorts & shoes & large red bow tie, Germany (ILLUS.) **$95**

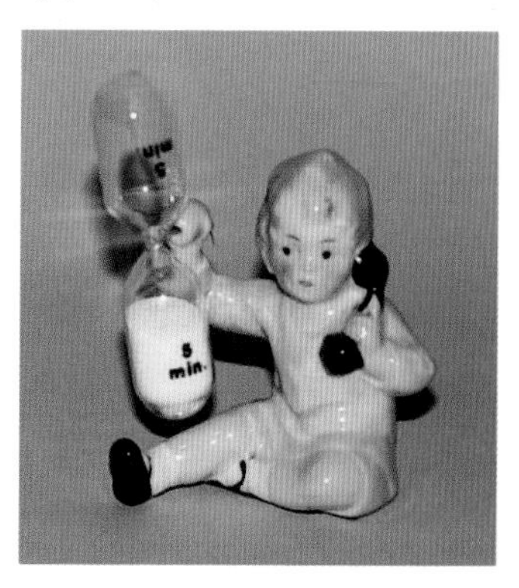

Little Girl On Phone Egg Timer

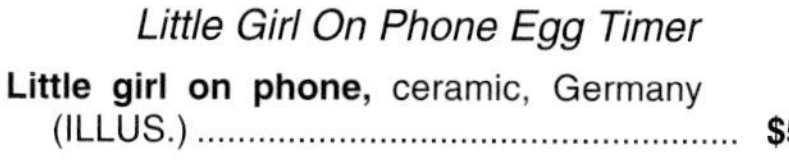

Little girl on phone, ceramic, Germany (ILLUS.) **$50**

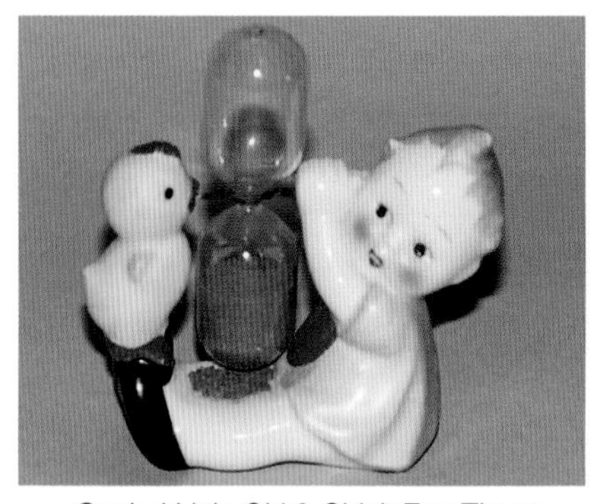

Goebel Little Girl & Chick Egg Timer

Little girl with chick on her toes, ceramic, Goebel, Germany (ILLUS.) **$125**

Maid, ceramic, on telephone, marked "Japan" **$35-45**

Maid, ceramic, wearing green dress w/red collar & white apron, marked "Japan" **$45-65**

Maid, wood, hanging-type, maid holding pie **$20-25**

Mammy, painted wood, flat cut-out form w/holder for egg timer at the front, one arm extends to hold potholders **$85**

Mammy, tin lithographed, mammy cooking on gas stove, w/pot holder hooks, unmarked, 7 3/4" h. **$125**

Man, ceramic, Colonial, wearing black tailcoat, Japan **$65-85**

Man, wood, double-headed man w/pipe..... **$10-15**

Man, wood, hanging-type, man under umbrella w/basket of eggs, Germany.......... **$20-35**

Men, wood, playing checkers, "Three minutes!" on base **$25-45**

Minuteman, ceramic, holding rifle & leaning against stone wall, "Kitchen Independence" on front base, marked "Enesco" & "Japan" **$35**

Mother Rabbit Egg Timer

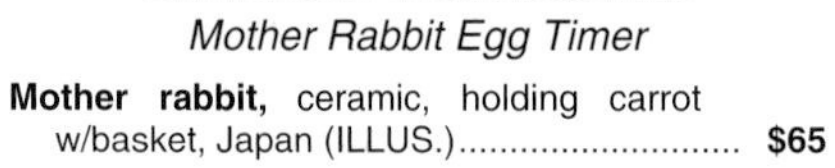

Mother rabbit, ceramic, holding carrot w/basket, Japan (ILLUS.) **$65**

Mouse Chef Egg Timer

Mouse, ceramic, sitting & holding timer, brown w/white apron marked "Chef" in red letters, Josef Originals (ILLUS.) **$35**

Mouse, chalkware, yellow & green, Josef Originals, Japan, 1970s, 3 1/4" h. **$15-25**

Mr. Pickwick, ceramic, double-type, green, Germany, 4" h. .... **$165+**

Mrs. Claus Egg Timer

Mrs. Claus, ceramic, in yellow dress w/green collar, cuffs & hem, w/red bag full of gifts & black bag w/timer (ILLUS.) **$85**

Newspaper boy, ceramic, Japan, 3 1/4" h. **$50**

Oliver Twist, ceramic, wearing red pants & vest, brown jacket, black hat, marked "Germany" **$75**

Owl, ceramic, Goebel, Germany (ILLUS., next page) **$50**

Parlor maid, ceramic, w/blue & white striped dress holding platter of food, marked "FOREIGN" **$65-85**

Parlor maid, ceramic, wearing blue dress w/white apron, marked "Japan" **$45-65**

Parlor maid with cat, ceramic, Japan **$35**

Peasant woman ceramic, w/black upswept hair carrying basket, marked "Germany" **$75-95**

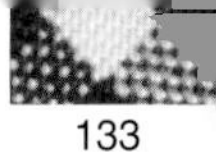

Goebel Owl Egg Timer

Penguin, glazed chalkware, standing on green & white base w/"Bagnor Regis" painted on front, marked "Manorware, England" **$35**

Pierrot, ceramic, sitting w/legs to side, marked "Germany" **$95-125**

Pixie, ceramic, Enesco, Japan, 5 1/2" h. **$15-25**

Prayer Lady Egg Timer

Prayer lady, ceramic, pink & white, Enesco (ILLUS.) **$50**

Rabbit with Carrot Egg Timer

Rabbit, ceramic, sitting, white w/red jacket, holding ear of corn that supports the timer, Germany (ILLUS.) **$50**

Rabbit, ceramic, wearing yellow pants w/blue suspenders, marked "Germany" **$65**

Rabbit, wood, brown rabbit standing by egg, marked "Germany" **$35**

Rabbit with floppy ears, ceramic, standing, tan, Germany **$50**

Rabbits, ceramic, double-type, various color combinations, Goebel, Germany, 4" h. **$50**

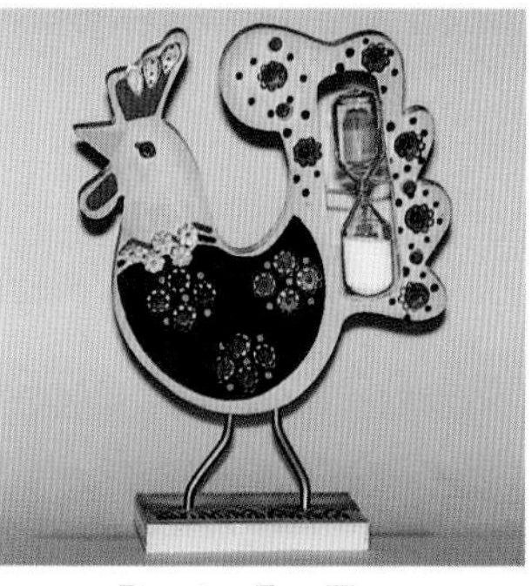

Rooster Egg Timer

Rooster, painted cut-out wood, w/sequins (ILLUS.) **$35**

Rooster, wood, multicolored, standing on thick base **$25**

Rooster Egg Timer

Rooster, wood, red wattle & comb, blue on tail, upturned head, Germany (ILLUS.) **$35**

Rooster on house, metal & wood, w/hole in roof for timer, marked "Gift Ideas, Philadelphia, Pennsylvania" **$15-20**

Roosters, ceramic, double-type, modeled by Horst Ashermann, timer marked w/3-, 4- & 5-minute intervals, Goebel, Germany, 1953 .... **$85-100**

Sailboat, ceramic, Manorware, England **$25**

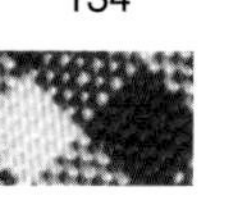

Sailboat with sailor, ceramic, lustreware, Germany **$50**

Santa Claus, ceramic, standing by wrapped gift, label reads "SONSCO," marked "Japan" **$50-75**

Santa Claus w/present, ceramic, Sonsco, Japan, 5 1/2" h. **$85**

Scotsman with bagpipes, plastic, England, 4 1/2" h. **$35**

Sea gull, ceramic, lustre, white w/brown-tipped spread wings & tail, purple base, Germany **$75**

Sea Gull Egg Timer with Bottle Opener

Sea gull, iron, white & tan bird w/red beak & legs, on black & white branch that is also a bottle opener (ILLUS.) **$20**

Squaw Egg Timer

Squaw, plastic, "For boilum egg, just turnum glass, Watchum sand go down, first class, when allum sand is onum bottom, Egg all done take out of potum" (ILLUS.).... **$35**

Swami, ceramic, dark skinned, w/butterfly & bird on hat, holding walking stick, marked "Germany" **$65-85**

Swami, ceramic, light skinned, marked "Japan" **$65-85**

Swami Egg Timer

Swami, ceramic, standing wearing turban, Germany (ILLUS.) **$110**

Swiss woman, ceramic, w/multicolored striped apron, marked "Germany" **$50**

Telephone, candlestick tube on base w/cup for timer, wooden, Cornwall Wood Products, South Paris, Maine **$25**

Telephone, black glaze on clay, Japan, 2" h. **$25**

Tillie Egg Timer

Tillie the Timer, iron, Amish lady on bench (ILLUS.) **$10**

"Timothy Timer," ceramic, w/upraised arms, label reads "Conley Lilley, Cape May, N.J., Chester, Pa.," turn onto head to activate sand (ILLUS., next page)...... **$45-65**

Vegetable person, ceramic, Japan **$95-125**

Victorian lady, ceramic, wearing green & pink gown, marked "Germany" **$50**

"Timothy Timer" Egg Timer

Waiter Egg Timer

Waiter, ceramic, standing next to ovoid holder for timer, black & white, Germany (ILLUS.)........ **$50**

Welsh woman, ceramic, Germany, 4 1/2" h........ **$35**

Welsh woman, ceramic, marked "Japan"....... **$35**

Welsh woman, plastic, wearing red cape **$25-35**

Windmill, ceramic, all green, goose sitting atop windmill, marked "Germany"........ **$50**

Windmill, ceramic, blue & white, marked "Japan"........ **$50**

Windmill, ceramic, blue & white, w/kissing Dutch couple, "Holland" on base........ **$50**

Windmill, ceramic, brown bird sitting atop yellow windmill, marked "Germany"........ **$35**

Windmill, ceramic, brown, black & yellow, w/dog standing on base, marked "Japan" **$100**

Windmill, ceramic, brown, black & yellow, w/two pink pigs standing on base, marked "Japan"........ **$85**

Windmill, ceramic, multicolored, marked "Germany"........ **$45**

Windmill, ceramic, white & blue, on base w/Dutch shoes & candleholder, unmarked........ **$35**

Windmill, ceramic, yellow & green, timer sits inside arm of windmill w/protruding end used as fourth arm, removable, Cardinal China Co., New Jersey........ **$25-45**

Windmill, metal, hanging-type, w/"USA, Keystone Coffee, Keystone Mills, Penbrook, PA" on base........ **$25-35**

Chapter 9

Napkin Dolls

Until the 1990s, napkin dolls were a rather obscure collectible, coveted by only a few savvy individuals who appreciated their charm and beauty. Today, however, these late 1940s and 1950s icons of postwar America are hot commodities.

Ranging from the individualistic pieces made in ceramics classes to jeweled Japanese models and the wide variety of wooden examples, these figures are no longer mistaken as planters or miniature dress forms. Of course, as their popularity has risen, so have prices, putting smiles on the faces of collectors who got in on the ground floor and stretching the pocketbooks of those looking to start their own collections.

Bobbie Zucker Bryson is co-author, with Deborah Gillham and Ellen Bercovici, of the pictorial price guide Collectibles For The Kitchen, Bath & Beyond - Second Edition, published by Krause Publications. It covers a broad range of collectibles including napkin dolls, stringholders, pie birds, figural egg timers, razor blade banks, whimsical whistle milk cups and laundry sprinkler bottles. Bryson can be contacted via e-mail at Napkindoll aol.com.

Ceramic, figure of a genie holding a lantern, marked "Genie at Your Service," by Enesco, 8" h. **$100-135**

Newer Napkin Lady Holding Tray

Ceramic, figure of a woman, black hair, wearing a long white dress w/red bodice & puffy sleeves, one hand on hip & the other holding up a blue tray, newer vintage, 9 1/4" h. (ILLUS.) **$30**

Ceramic, figure of a woman, blonde hair pulled back into a bun, pink dress w/a white collar, holding a white heart, marked on bottom "Brockmann," 6 1/2" h. **$65-85**

Napkin Doll-Candleholder Tall Lady

Ceramic, figure of a woman, her black hair pulled back into a bun & wearing a wide-brimmed red-trimmed hat forming a candleholder, her hands behind her back & wearing a long white jacket w/pale blue trim over a red bodice, the long white dress w/slits & hem trimmed w/thin red lines, 12 3/4" h. (ILLUS.) **$75-95**

Ceramic, figure of a woman on a base, black hair, molded pink lustre apron, one arm holding a toothpick holder bowl on her head, by Marcia of California, 13" h. **$125-150**

Green-dressed Lady with Candleholders

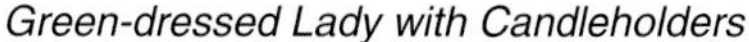

Ceramic, figure of a woman, red hair covered w/a green kerchief, wearing a long green dress w/a white blouse w/gold trim,

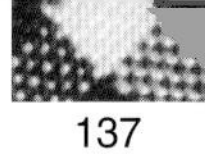
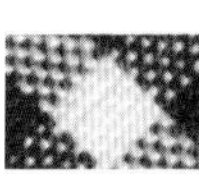

each arm supporting a tall square-based columnar white candlestick at the side, 10" h. (ILLUS.) **$115-135**

Newer Rosie Napkin Doll Lady

Ceramic, figure of a woman, red hair pulled back & parted in the middle w/a pink flower above each ear, wearing a long white dress w/a pink shawl collar, holding a pink rose in front, marked "Rosie," Holland Mold (H-132), newer vintage, 7 1/2" h. (ILLUS.) **$25-35**

Napkin Doll with Bowl on Her Head

Ceramic, figure of a woman, short brown hair, long blue dress w/puffy sleeves & h.p. flowers on the front, her arms up holding a wide, low gold-trimmed bowl on her head, marked "Japan," 9 1/4" h. (ILLUS.) **$50-65**

Ceramic, figure of a woman w/brown hair in a Colonial-style hairdo, wearing a long green off-the-shoulder dress, hands held up & clasped, marked "Frances - Edith King Originals, 1953," 11 1/2" h. **$75-95**

Ceramic, figure of a woman, wearing a green off-the-shoulder dress w/flowers on the front, her floppy-brimmed hat forming a candleholder, marked "Kreiss and Company," 10" h. **$65-85**

Ceramic, figure of a woman, wearing a long dress decorated w/maroon flowers & green leaves, also a blue hat, holding a blue toothpick holder bowl, signed "Helen Lewis, 1959," 9 1/2" h. **$95-135**

Ceramic, figure of a woman wearing a pink iridescent dress & black & pink wide-brimmed hat, white toothpick holder on each hip, marked "4059," 9 1/2" h.......... **$60-75**

Ceramic, figure of a woman, wearing a white dress w/yellow bodice & trim, holding out her skirt w/one hand, the other hand on her hip, marked "Tina," Mallory Studios, 9 1/2" h.................................... **$75-85**

Ceramic, figure of a woman, wearing a yellow & white dress, yellow pigtails, holding a white lily, Atlantic Mold, 11" h. **$65-75**

Ceramic, figure of a young girl, aqua & white dress w/a black bodice & black bows on front & back of skirt, large pockets for napkins, marked "3475" on bottom, 7 7/8" h.. **$75-95**

Ceramic, figure of a young girl, wearing a pink dress w/white ruffle trim, white picture hat w/pink rose & candleholder in the top, marked "Sunbonnet Miss - Holt Howard 1958," 5" h. **$125-150**

Ceramic, figure of an angel, pink & white & holding a bouquet, slits in shoulders for wings & in the rear, Japan paper sticker, 5 3/8" h... **$100-115**

Ceramic, figure of angel, blonde, wearing blue & white dress w/gold trim, holding maroon flowers w/green leaves, gold halo on head, two slits in shoulders for napkins to form "wings," 5 3/8" h. **$100-135**

Bartender/Waiter Napkin Doll & Shakers

Ceramic, figure of bartender/waiter, w/black mustache, red & white checked apron, black bow tie & shoes, holds a tray that

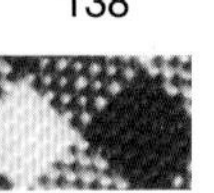

serves as candleholder, foil sticker w/"Viking Handmade, Made in Japan," w/matching salt & pepper shakers, 8 3/4" h. (ILLUS.) **$135-140**

Ceramic, figure of "Daisy," girl w/long brown braids wearing green dress, marked "Holland Mold," 7" h. **$75-100**

Ceramic, figure of genie, dressed in white robes trimmed in gold, jewel-decorated turban, holds a gold lantern, label reads "Genie at Your Service," Enesco, 8" h. **$100-135**

Byron Molds Napkin Doll

Ceramic, figure of girl holding flowers, red hair, yellow dress w/matching hair bow, arms clutch flowers to chest, marked "copyright Byron Molds," 8 1/2" h. (ILLUS.) **$55-75**

Atlantic Mold Napkin Doll

Ceramic, figure of girl holding lily, mouth open as if singing, brown bobbed hair w/yellow headband, bright yellow dress w/green leaf design, holds a blue lily in arms, Atlantic Mold, 11" h. (ILLUS.)....... **$50-65**

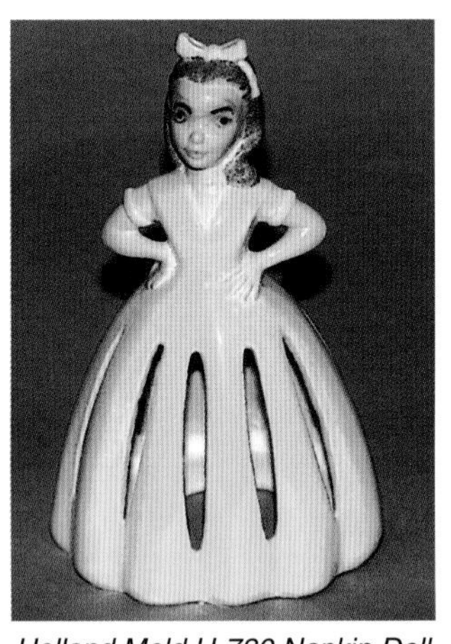

Holland Mold H-730 Napkin Doll

Ceramic, figure of girl w/red hair standing w/hands on hips wearing yellow dress & white bow in hair, Holland Mold H-730, 5" h. (ILLUS.) **$65-85**

Girl with Roses Napkin Doll

Ceramic, figure of girl w/reddish brown hair wearing white dress w/large bow at waist & ruffled hem, neckline & cuffs, holding pink roses, bending over slightly so that back of full skirt holds napkins, 8" h. (ILLUS.).. **$75-95**

Ceramic, figure of "Miss Versatility," woman in red & white dress w/red scallop trim & matching red picture hat that serves as candleholder, one hand held behind back, California Originals, 13" h............. **$60-75**

Ceramic, figure of Santa Claus, in red suit w/black belt & shoes, toothpick holes in hat, marked "Japan," w/a "Sage Store" label, 6 3/4" h... **$95-150**

Ceramic, figure of Santa Claus, wearing red & white suit & hat, white beard, slits in

rear for napkins, holes in hat for toothpicks, marked "Japan," 6 3/4" h. **$100-150**

Holt Howard Napkin Doll

Ceramic, figure of "Sunbonnet Miss," red-haired little girl in yellow dress w/white shoulder ruffle, matching yellow picture hat w/pink rose serves as candleholder, one hand pats hair, other arm is extended, marked "© Holt Howard 1958" (ILLUS.) **$135-165**

Uncle Sam Napkin Holder

Ceramic, figure of Uncle Sam, dressed in red, white & blue w/matching top hat, gold star buttons on vest, holding cloth American flag, Lillian Vernon Corporation, ca. 2003, 9" h. (ILLUS.).......... **$12**

Ceramic, figure of woman, black-haired Spanish dancer holding tambourine in one hand, the other holding skirt, wearing pink dress w/brown bodice, the skirt decorated w/yellow sunflowers, 17" h. (ILLUS., top next column) **$130-150**

Spanish Dancer Napkin Holder

Napkin Holder/Toothpick Holder

Ceramic, figure of woman holding tray, blonde, wearing black off-the-shoulder dress, one hand on hip, other holding pink covered tray, the lid w/holes to hold toothpicks, 8 1/2" h. (ILLUS.)................. **$75-95**

Woman in Hat Napkin Holder

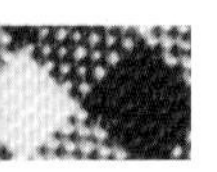

Ceramic, figure of woman in hat, in dress w/yellow drop waist & purple skirt, yellow & purple hat w/upturned brim, marked "Cal. Cer. Mold," 12 1/2" h. (ILLUS., previous page).. **$65-85**

Napkin Doll on Leafy Base

Ceramic, figure of woman w/black braids wearing light blue knee-length skirt & white top w/molded stays & blue cuffs, standing on leaf-covered base, one hand on hip, the other raised to head, 15" h. (ILLUS.)... **$125-150**

Napkin Doll from Puerto Rico

Ceramic, figure of woman w/black hair standing w/hands folded in front, wearing white dress w/pink bodice & hem, elbow-length gloves, front of skirt marked in gold "Arecibo Puerto Rico 1990," 12 1/2" h. (ILLUS.) **$45-65**

Woman with Umbrella Napkin Doll

Ceramic, figure of woman w/black hair wearing lavender skirt & purple blouse w/gilt buttons & collar, purple hat, holding green unfurled umbrella behind back, slits in skirt for napkins, 10 3/4" h. (ILLUS.) **$90-110**

Ceramic, figure of woman w/black hair wearing white dress w/red trim, balancing tray on head, 10" h................................. **$75-95**

Napkin Doll with Toothpick Holder

Ceramic, figure of woman w/brown hair in a bun, wearing brown dress w/white collar & cuffs, holding green heart w/holes for toothpicks, 6 1/2" h. (ILLUS.)................. **$65-85**

Ceramic, figure of woman w/brown hair in colonial style, wearing yellow dress trimmed in white & decorated in gold fur-like trim, w/matching hat forming candle-holder, gold-gloved hands in matching white & gold muff, marked "Kreiss and Company," 10 1/4" h. **$95-110**

Woman with Bowl Napkin Holder

Ceramic, figure of woman w/brown hair in pigtails wearing white dress w/blue flowers at hem, pink lace trim at neckline & cuffs, black bodice, standing w/one hand on hip, the other holding large bowl, 9" h. (ILLUS.) **$75-85**

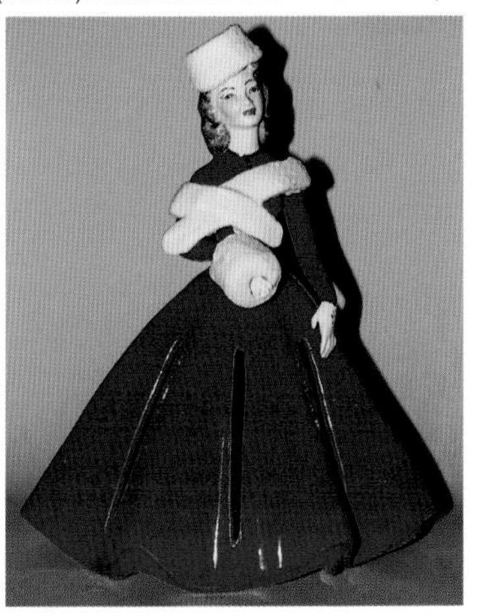

Red & White Napkin Doll

Ceramic, figure of woman w/brown hair wearing vivid red full-skirted coat w/white fur-like trim, hat & muff, white gloves, 11" h. (ILLUS.) **$80-95**

Ceramic, figure of woman w/colonial-style hairdo, wearing period dress & holding large picture hat at side, all pink, marked "USA" on bottom, 12" h. (ILLUS., top next column) **$50-60**

Ceramic, figure of woman w/colonial-style yellow hair, dressed in pink, white & yellow period dress trimmed in gold w/bell sleeves, ink mark reads "Japan," 9" h. (ILLUS., middle next column)................. **$75-85**

Pink Ceramic Napkin Doll

Colonial Woman Napkin Doll

Holland Mold Napkin Holder

Ceramic, figure of woman w/daisy, black hair w/bangs, dressed in blue & white dress & long white gloves, one hand fixes daisy behind ear, ca. 1958, marked "Holland Mold," 7 1/4" h. (ILLUS., previous page) **$75-95**

Napkin Doll Holding Fan

Ceramic, figure of woman w/fan, in 18th-c. white dress w/blue trim on bodice & sleeves & blue bows on front of dress & in her dark hair, one hand holds up white fan w/blue trim, marked "Jam. Calif. ©" (ILLUS.) **$55-65**

Napkin Doll with Glossy Finish

Ceramic, figure of woman w/long black hair wearing white dress w/gold neckline & cuffs & holding white & gold pitcher in both hands, applied lavender roses w/green leaves on one shoulder & on pitcher, glossy finish, handmade, 11" h. (ILLUS.) **$95-115**

Atlantic Mold Napkin Doll

Ceramic, figure of woman w/open mouth & brown hair, wearing vivid green & orange skirt & white blouse, holding yellow lily, Atlantic Mold, 11" h. (ILLUS.) **$65-75**

Handmade Atlantic Mold Napkin Doll

Ceramic, figure of woman w/open mouth & yellow bobbed hair, wearing full-skirted gown in shades of green & matching headband, holding orange lily, handmade from Atlantic Mold, 11" h. (ILLUS.) **$65-75**

Ceramic, figure of woman w/poodle, blonde, dressed in pink dress trimmed in black, matching hat serves as candleholder, blue jeweled eyes, crystal jeweled necklace & red jewel on finger, holds a white poodle, marked "Kreiss & Co.," 10 3/4" h. **$115-135**

Woman Napkin Doll/Toothpick Holder

Ceramic, figure of woman w/red hair, arms upraised to hold large bowl on head, wearing light & dark green puff-sleeved dress decorated on front w/flowers, jewel necklace, slits in skirt for napkins, bowl on head for toothpicks, marked "Japan," 9 1/4" h. (ILLUS.) **$60-75**

Napkin Doll Holding Bowl on Head

Ceramic, figure of woman w/short brown hair, wearing blue dress w/short puffy sleeves & black trim & decorated w/flowers on skirt, both hands raised to hold large bowl on head, marked "Japan," 9 1/4" h. (ILLUS.) **$50-65**

Ceramic, figure of woman w/toothpick tray, bobbed hair, white dress w/yellow scalloped trim, holds oblong toothpick tray attached at waist, 10 3/4" h. **$60-75**

Woman with Bird Napkin Doll

Ceramic, figure of woman w/toothpick tray, brown hair, green lustre dress decorated w/pink roses, one arm holds a toothpick tray w/similar decoration on her head, pink bird perches on other arm, 10 1/2" h. (ILLUS.).. **$75-95**

Napkin Doll/Toothpick Holder

Ceramic, figure of woman wearing pink dress & black & pink wide-brimmed hat, holding white toothpick holder at each side, marked "4059," 9 1/2" h. (ILLUS.) **$60-75**

Ceramic, figure of woman wearing white dress w/green decoration & gold necklace, a gold shoe peeking out from under skirt, 9 1/2" h. **$95-125**

Ceramic, figure of woman wearing white dress w/lavender flowers, hands holding large hat on head, iridescent finish, marked "Duncan Enterprises 1980," 6 1/2" h.. **$40-50**

Women with Fans Napkin Dolls

Ceramic, green figure of woman, fan masks candleholder, jewel-decorated, marked "Kreiss & Co.," 8 3/4" h. (ILLUS. right w/pink woman w/fan) **$65**

Davar Originals Napkin Doll

Ceramic, half doll, figure of milkmaid w/brown braids, wearing red dress w/white apron & polka dots, blue bow, blue & white cap, carrying buckets on yoke across her shoulders, on wire skirt-like base that holds napkins, marked "Davar Originals," 6" h. (ILLUS.) **$95-110**

Ceramic, half-doll, figural of Spanish lady w/black hair w/red & white flowers, wearing green dress w/white ruffled sleeves, holding red & white fan in one hand, other raised to her head, on wooden stand w/wires to hold napkins, 9 1/2" h. (ILLUS., top next column)... **$100-150**

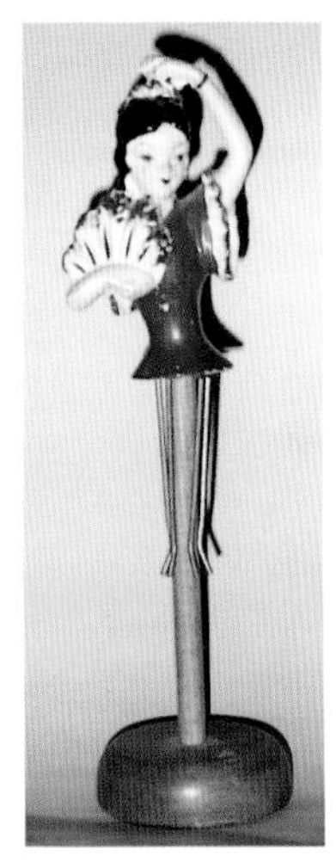

Spanish Lady Napkin Doll

Half-doll Napkin Holder

Ceramic, half-doll, figure of woman w/black hair wearing green off-the-shoulder dress, on wooden stand w/wires to hold napkins, Goebel X97, ca. 1957, 8 1/4" h. (ILLUS.)... **$225-250**

Ceramic, half-doll type, figure of woman w/red ponytail wearing pale shirt & yellow polka-dot scarf at neck, posing w/one hand at waist, the other behind head, on metal stand w/wires to hold napkins, Germany, 9 1/4" h. (ILLUS., next page)... **$150-175**

German Half-doll Napkin Holder

Ceramic, model of rooster, red, black & white w/yellow beak, slits in tail for napkins, w/egg-shaped salt & pepper shakers, 5 1/4" h. **$35-45**

Ceramic, pink figure of woman, fan masks candleholder, jewel-decorated, marked "Kreiss & Co.," 10 1/2" h. **$85**

Ceramic & metal, half-figure of a lady, red hair, wearing a pink & white off-the-shoulder dress, holding streamers to matching pink & white hat, on a brass stand w/wires to hold napkins, 8" h. **$135-175**

Ceramic & metal, half-figure of a Mexican lady, wearing a yellow dress w/white, red & blue scarf over her shoulder, one hand holding a matching yellow sombrero w/a red design, on a wooden stand w/wires to hold napkins, original box marked "Napkin Holder No. 405," 9" h. **$150-185**

Ceramic & metal, half-figure of a milk maid, light brown hair, wearing a red dress w/white dots, white apron w/blue trim, light blue bow at neck, w/matching blue & white cap, carrying buckets across shoulders, "Davar Originals" sticker, 6" h. **$95-110**

Ceramic & metal, half-figure of a milk maid, wearing a red dress w/white apron & polka dots, blue bow & a blue & white cap on her brown braids, carrying buckets across her shoulders, marked "Davar Originals," 6" h. **$95-110**

Ceramic & metal, model of a chicken & rooster, white w/gold trim, removable salt & pepper shaker heads, wire in tails to hold napkins, "Lefton" foil label, 4 3/8" h. **$25-35**

Chalkware, figure of a woman w/hands behind her back, light brown hair, wearing a green dress & matching hat w/candleholders, 13" h. **$95-125**

Umbrella-form Napkin Holder

Chrome, umbrella, wire holder forms umbrella when napkins are placed in it, on metallic red disk base, comes w/red, white & blue napkins, 9" h. (ILLUS.) **$15-35**

Metal, model of an umbrella, chrome w/metallic red base, fitted w/red & blue napkins, 9" h. **$15-35**

Metal, rear view figure of a dancer's legs w/upturned dress, marked "Can Can Serviette Holder," England, 4" h. **$95-135**

Metal Umbrella Napkin Holder

Metal, umbrella, wire holder forms umbrella when napkins are placed in it, comes w/original red napkins & box that reads "Porte Serviettes" & "Napkin Holder," Canada, 9 1/2" h. (ILLUS.)..................... **$30-40**

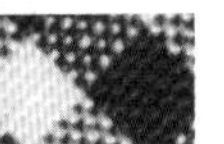

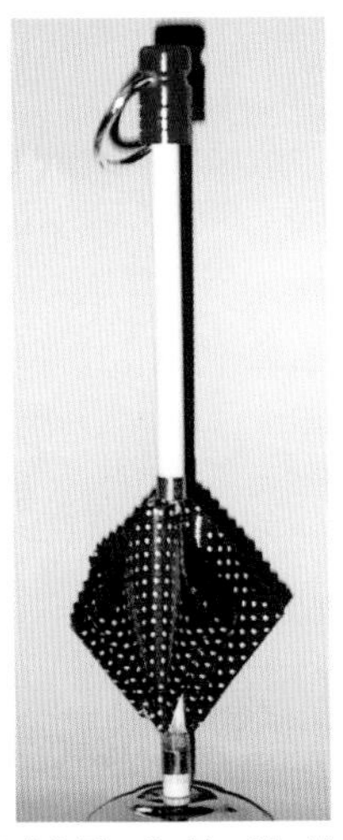

Metal & Plastic Napkin Holder

Metal & plastic, umbrella, red & white holder on silver-tone circular base w/white-dotted red plastic pouches near bottom that hold napkins to form umbrella, 11" h. (ILLUS.) **$15-20**

Sweetie Napkin Doll in Original Box

Plastic, half-figure of a young girl, synthetic black hair & open-close eyes, wearing a light blue & pink satin dress, plastic base for napkins, in original box marked "Sweetie Napkin Doll," ca. 1959, 11" h. (ILLUS.) **$40-60**

Wood, figure of a woman dressed in yellow, Finland, ca. 1949, 10 1/4" h. **$40-50**

Wood, figure of a woman, jointed arms, wearing a pink dress w/blue bodice trimmed in black, a strawberry w/toothpick holes on her head, 8" h. **$60-75**

Wood, figure of woman on wooden base, red, w/jointed arms, wearing picture hat & holding yellow wooden bucket, marked "G. Fried, Peplerhandlig Newer Market, Ges. Gesch.," 11 1/5" h. **$50-60**

Green Painted Wood Napkin Doll

Wood, figure of woman w/disproportionately short jointed arms wearing dark green dress w/narrow skirt & white vest, dark green brimmed hat, 10 1/2" h. (ILLUS.) **$40-50**

Painted Wood Napkin Doll

Wood, figure of woman w/jointed arms wearing dark pink dress w/white flowers & bodice & black hat, marked "Artefatos Catarinenses Ltda., Ave. Argalo, 80-Sao Bento do Sul, Santa Catarina, N-94, Industria, Bruseleira," 6 3/8" h. (ILLUS.) ... **$60-75**

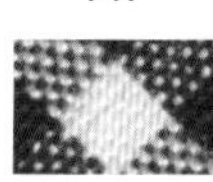

Wooden Napkin Doll Painted Yellow & Red

Wood, figure of woman w/stylized face, standing w/hands on hips, painted yellow w/red buttons, cuffs & hat, on red circular base, 11" h. (ILLUS.)............................. **$30-40**

Wood, half-figure of a woman w/yellow braids, red bodice, white Dutch hat, on a yellow & red base, 9 3/4" h. **$20-25**

Wood, model of dodo bird, w/slits in rear for napkins, 7" h. **$25-35**

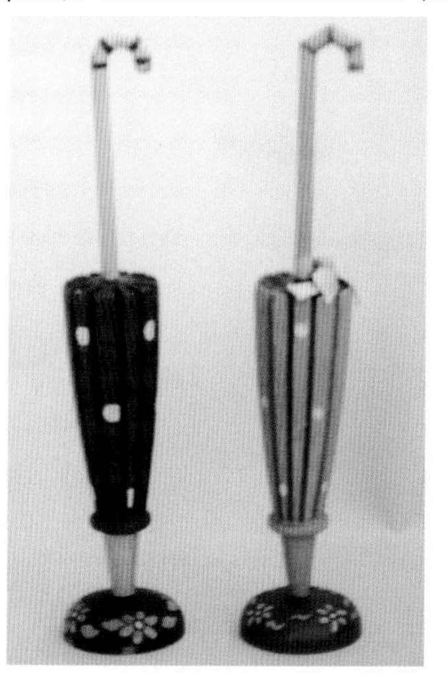

Umbrella Napkin Holders

Wood, model of umbrella, blue w/polka dots, tan cane-form handle, on circular base w/floral decoration, 8 1/2" h. (ILLUS. right w/red umbrella)....................................... **$25-35**

Wood, model of umbrella, red w/polka dots, tan cane-form handle, on circular base w/floral decoration, 8 1/2" h. (ILLUS. left w/blue umbrella).................................... **$25-35**

Half-figure Napkin Doll Marked "Napkins"

Wood, red half-figure, base marked "Napkins," ca. 1952, 11 1/2" h. (ILLUS.)..... **$35**

Wooden Dutch Girl Napkin Holder

Wood, two-dimensional half-figure of woman w/yellow braids in white Dutch-style hat, wearing red shirt w/white sleeves & yellow waist, on red & yellow circular base, 9 3/4" h. (ILLUS.) **$20-25**

Wood & glass, figure of a woman, jointed arms, wearing a green outfit w/white trim, matching picture hat, marked "Servy-Etta - USD Patent No. 159,005," a Woodnote Product, ca. 1951, 11" h. **$35-45**

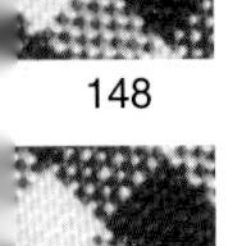

Chapter 10

Pie Birds

A pie bird can be described as a small, hollow device, usually between 3 1/2" to 6" long, glazed inside and vented from the top. Its function is to raise the crust of a pie to allow steam to escape, thus preventing juices from bubbling over onto the oven floor while providing a flaky, dry crust.

Originally, in the 1880s, pie birds were funnel-shaped vents used by the English for their meat pies. Not until the turn of the 20th century did figurals appear, first in the form of birds, followed by elephants, chefs, etc. By the 1930s, many shapes were found in America.

Today the market is flooded with many reproductions and newly created pie birds, usually in many whimsical shapes and subjects. It is best to purchase from knowledgeable dealers and fellow collectors.

Advertising, "Kirkbrights China Stores Stockton on Tees," ceramic, white, England **$95**

Advertising, "Lightning Pie Funnel England," ceramic, white, England **$75**

Advertising, "Paulden's Crockery Department Stretford Road," ceramic, white, England **$45**

Advertising, "Roe's Patent Rosebud," ceramic, England, 1910-30 .... **$95**

Advertising, "Rowland's Hygienic Patent," ceramic, England, 1910-30 .... **$95**

Advertising, "Sequel...Porcelain," ceramic, white, England **$85**

Advertising, "The Gourmet Crust Holder & Vent, Challis' Patent," ceramic, white, England **$95**

Advertising, "The Grimmage Purfection Pie Funnel," ceramic, England, 1910-30 ..... **$75**

Bird, ceramic, black on white base, yellow feet & beak, Nutbrown, England **$25**

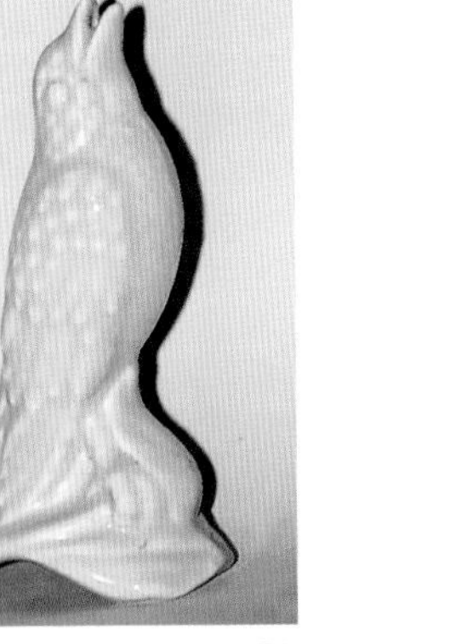

Camark Pottery Pie Bird in Blue

Bird, ceramic, Camark Pottery, Camden, Ark., ca. 1950s-60s, depending on color, 6 1/2" h. (ILLUS.) **$125-400**

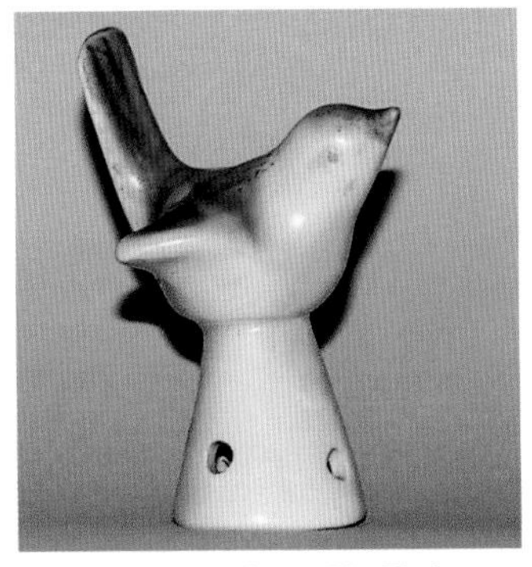

Half-doll Style Pie Bird

Bird, ceramic, half-doll style, blue & yellow on conical base, USA (ILLUS.) **$350**

Bird, ceramic, "Midwinter," black, England **$35**

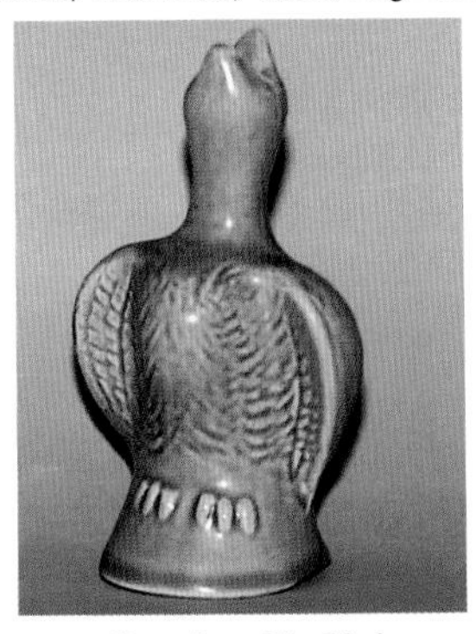

Sunglow Pie Bird

Bird, ceramic, tan glaze, Sunglow, England (ILLUS.) **$50**

Two-headed Pie Bird

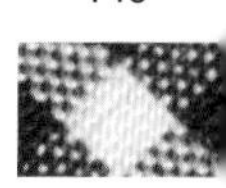

"Yankee Pie Bird"

Bird, ceramic, two-headed, Barn Pottery, Devon, England (ILLUS., previous page) **$50**

Bird, ceramic, two-piece, blue & white on white funnel, Royal Worcester, England **$50**

Rowe Pottery Pie Bird

Bird, ceramic, two-piece w/detachable base, 1992, Rowe Pottery (ILLUS.) **$25**

Bird, ceramic, w/flowers, Chic Pottery, ca. 1930s-60s, hard to find **$175**

Bird, ceramic, white w/wide mouth, England (ILLUS., top next column) **$50-60**

Bird, ceramic, white w/yellow beak, blue trim on tail & base, made in California, 1950s (ILLUS., bottom next column) **$300-500**

Bird, ceramic, "Yankee Pie Bird," black & brown, made in New England, 1960s (ILLUS., top of page) **$35**

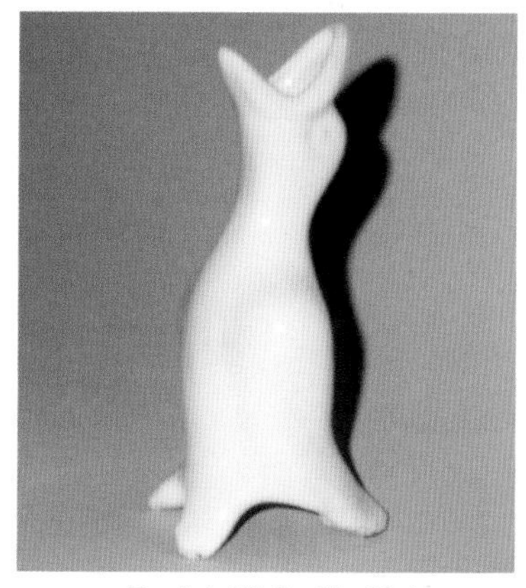

English White Pie Bird

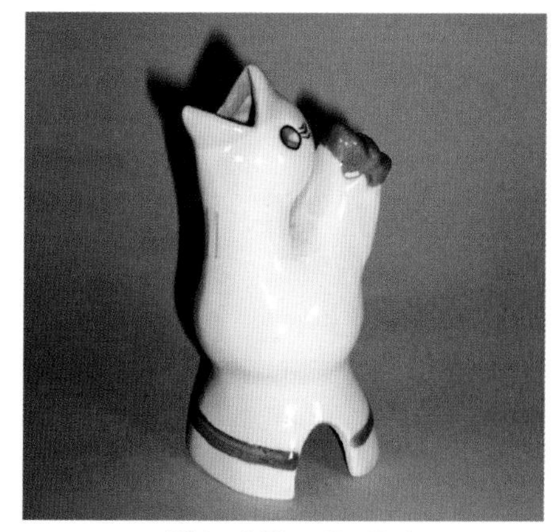

White & Blue Pie Bird

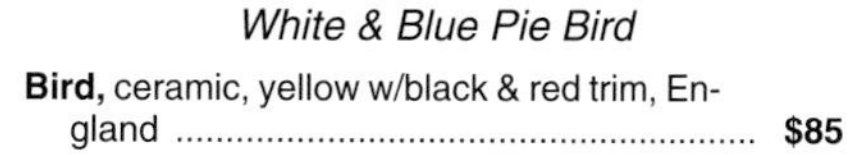

Bird, ceramic, yellow w/black & red trim, England **$85**

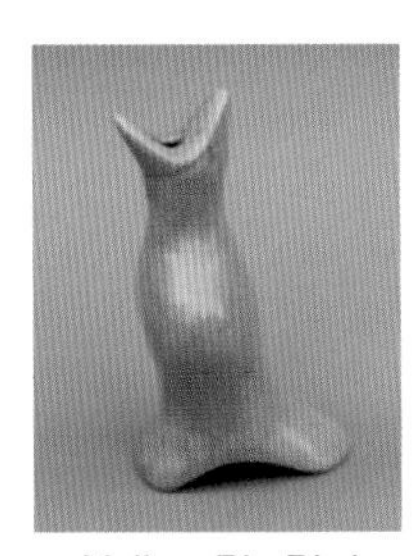

Yellow Pie Bird

Bird, ceramic, yellow w/wide mouth, England (ILLUS.) **$50-75**

Bird, glass, double-headed, marked "Scotland" **$125**

Bird, pointy beak **$65**

Bird, pottery, "Scipio Creek Pottery, Hannibal, MO" **$15**

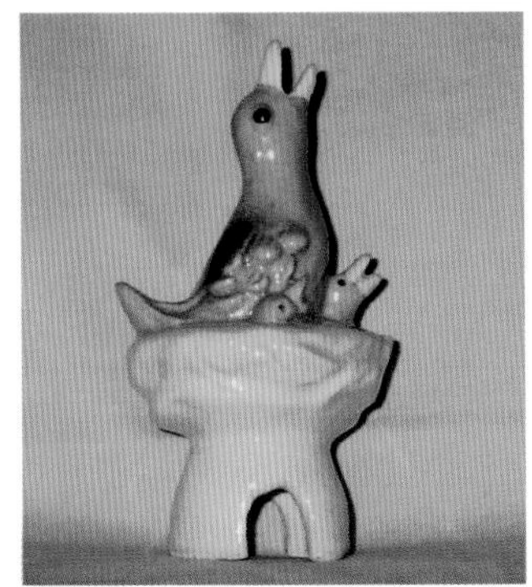

Rare Bird on Nest Pie Bird

Bird on nest w/babies, ceramic, Artisian Galleries, Fort Dodge, Iowa (ILLUS.) ...... **$500+**

Birds, ceramic, Pearl China, various colors, USA, each **$100-400**

Black Chef with Blue Smock

Black chef, ceramic, full-figured, blue smock, "Pie-Aire," USA, w/original tag (ILLUS.) **$150**

Black chef, ceramic, full-figured, green smock, "Pie-Aire," USA **$150**

Black Chef w/Gold Spoon Pie Bird

Black chef, ceramic, w/gold spoon, white w/red trim (ILLUS.) **$250**

Jackie Sammond Pie Bird & Owl

Blackbird, ceramic, 3" h., Jackie Sammond, early 1970s (ILLUS. right with owl) **$75**

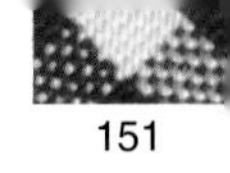

English Pie Bird

Blackbird, ceramic, black w/yellow beak & eyes, narrow, England (ILLUS.) **$125**

Blackbird, ceramic, England........................... **$25**

Blackbird, ceramic, for child's pie, 2 3/4" **$95**

Blackbird on Log Pie Bird

Blackbird, ceramic, perched on log, England (ILLUS.) **$50**

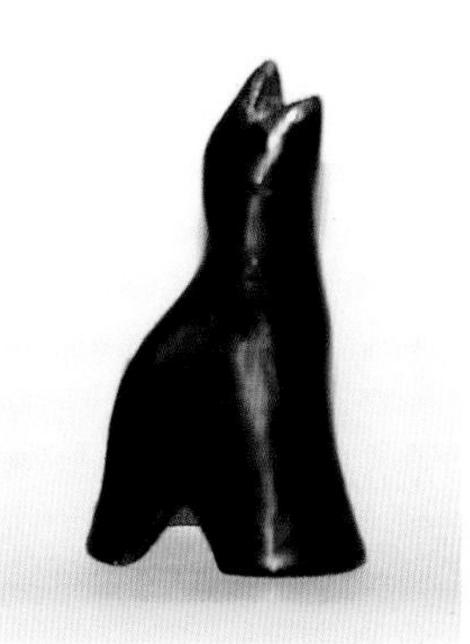

Stylized English Blackbird

Blackbird, ceramic, simple stylized shape w/brown beak, ca. 1930s-40s, English (ILLUS.)... **$125**

Very Large Black Pie Bird

Blackbird, ceramic, very large, 2 1/2" w x 5" h., English (ILLUS.) **$75**

Blackbird, ceramic, w/yellow trim on brown base **$65**

Wide-Mouth Blackbird Pie Bird

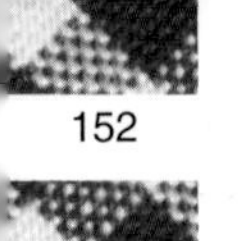

Blackbird, ceramic, wide mouth, yellow beak, fat, English (ILLUS., previous page) **$150**

Blackbird, clay w/black & yellow glaze, ca. 1960s-70s **$35**

Blackbird, red clay w/black glaze, ca. 1930s-40s **$35**

Bluebird, ceramic, Japan, post-1960 .... **$35**

Brown chef, ceramic, half-figure, England **$65**

Brown & white chef, ceramic, half-figure, England **$85**

Chef, ceramic, "A Lorrie Design, Japan," Josef Originals, 1980s **$85**

"Benny the Baker" Pie Bird

Chef, ceramic, "Benny the Baker," w/tools & box, Cardinal China Co., USA (ILLUS.) **$145**

"Pie-Aire" Chefs

Chef, ceramic, "Pie-Aire," solid color, green, red or yellow, each (ILLUS.) **$125**

Chef, ceramic, "Servex Oven China, Bohemia, Guaranteed Heatproof, RD 17494 Aus., RD 4098 N.Z.," Australia, 4 5/8" h. **$100**

Holland Servex Chef Pie Bird

Chef, ceramic, white w/black buttons, "The Servex Chef" in black letters on hat, marked "Holland" inside (ILLUS.) **$100**

Taunton Chefs Pie Birds

Chefs, ceramic, all-white, man & woman, Taunton, England, each (ILLUS.) **$95**

Cherry, apple & peach, ceramic, ca. 1950s, in original box, set of three **$150-300**

Chick, yellow w/pink lips, Josef Originals **$40**

Josef Originals Chick Pie Bird

Chick w/dust cap, "Pie Baker," by Josef Originals, ceramic (ILLUS., previous page) **$65**

Chicken, ceramic, "A Lorrie Design, Japan," Josef Originals, 1980s **$65**

Australian Pie Bird

Clown/Dopey, ceramic, white bust, Australian (ILLUS.) .... **$150+**

Dolphin, blue, marked "Bermuda" **$85**

Donald Duck, ceramic, "Walt Disney" marked on one side & "Donald Duck" on the other, rare (ILLUS., top next column) .... **$500+**

Dragon, ceramic, Creiciau Pottery, Wales, United Kingdom, each (ILLUS., second next column) .... **$85+**

Dragons, ceramic, various shapes & colors, 1980s-1990s, England, each (ILLUS. of three, bottom of page) **$50**

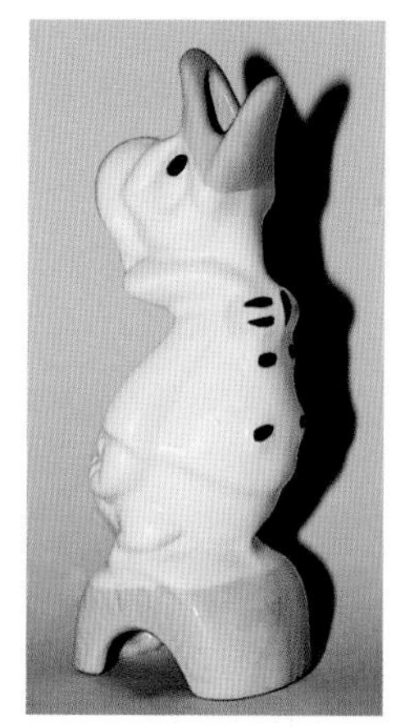

Rare Donald Duck Pie Bird

Welsh Dragon Pie Birds

English Dragon Pie Birds

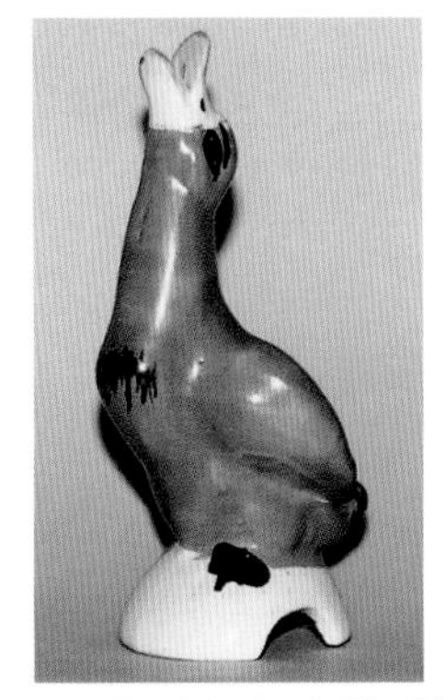

Brown English Duck Pie Bird

Duck, ceramic, brown w/white & yellow beak, black trim, white base, England (ILLUS.) **$95**

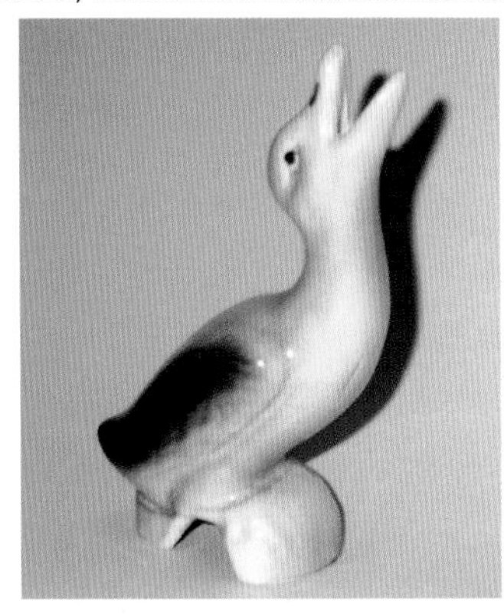

Blue Duck Pie Bird

Duck, ceramic, long neck, blue, USA (ILLUS.) **$45-65**

Duck, ceramic, pink, blue or yellow, full-bodied, USA, each **$45-65**

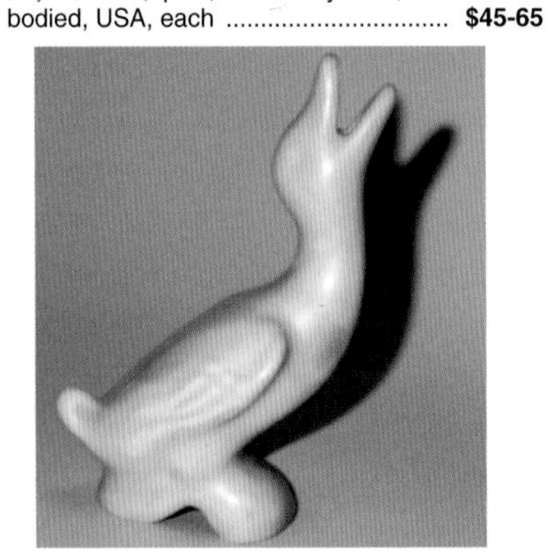

Solid-colored Duck Pie Bird

Duck, ceramic, solid-colored, USA, each (ILLUS.) .... **$125+**

Duck, ceramic, white, England **$95**

Duck, ceramic, yellow beak, white w/black detail, England **$95**

Duck, white w/black detail, yellow beak, England **$95**

Duck head, ceramic, beige w/black detail, England **$125**

Pink English Duck Head Pie Bird

Duck head, ceramic, pink, England (ILLUS.) **$95**

Duck head, tannish grey w/black eyes, England **$95**

Dutch Girl Multipurpose Pie Bird

Dutch girl, ceramic, doubles as pie vent, measuring spoon holder and/or receptacles for scouring pads & soap, Cardinal China, rare (ILLUS.) **$100-135**

Dwarf Dopey, ceramic, Disney **$300-450**

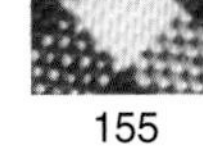

Grey Nutbrown, England Elephant

Elephant, all-grey w/trunk up, ca. 1930s, Nutbrown, England (ILLUS.) **$95**

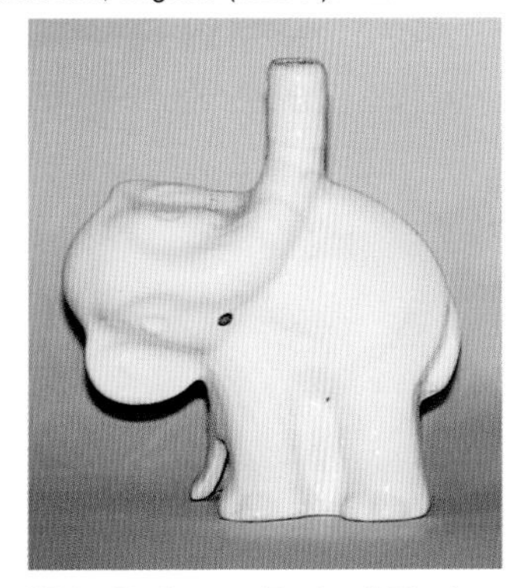

White Nutbrown England Elephant

Elephant, all-white w/trunk up, Nutbrown, England (ILLUS.)... **$50**

Standing Elephant Pie Bird

Elephant, ceramic, all-white, standing on back legs, trunk over head, England (ILLUS.)... **$100**

Elephant, ceramic, dark grey w/yellow glaze inside, England................................ **$100**

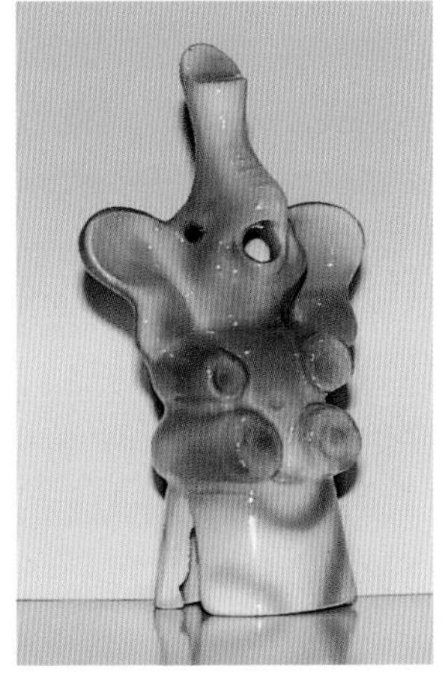

Cardinal China Elephant Pie Bird

Elephant, ceramic, grey & pink w/swirled pink base, Cardinal China Co. incised "CCC" on back, USA (ILLUS.) **$175**

Elephant, ceramic, white, ca. 1930s **$125**

"Fred the Flour Grader" Pie Bird

"Fred the Flour Grader," ceramic, black & white, from Homepride Flour, ca. 1978 (ILLUS.).. **$65-100**

Funnel, ceramic, brown on white base, Royal Worcester, England **$125**

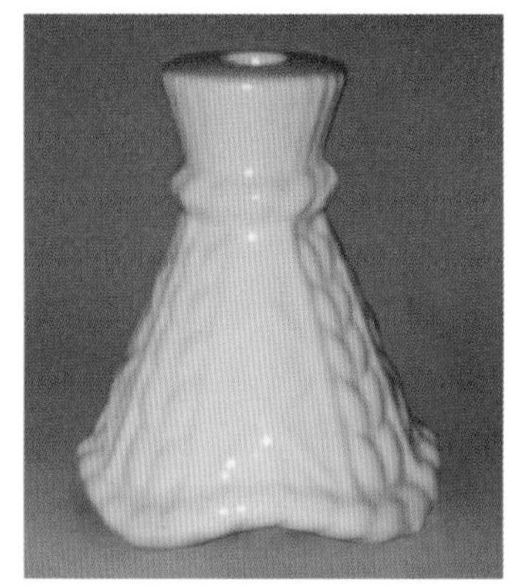

Wheat Stalk Funnel Pie Bird

Funnel, ceramic, model of wheat stalk, cream & white, England, ea. (ILLUS.).. **$75-100**

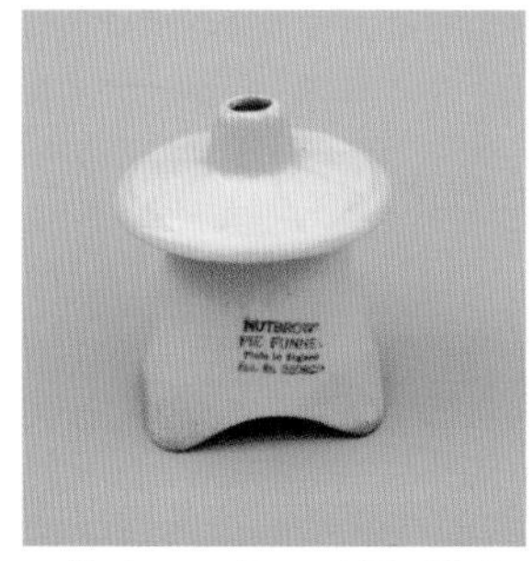

Nutbrown Funnel Pie Bird

Funnel, ceramic, Nutbrown w/unusual top lip, England (ILLUS.) **$75-95**

Funnel, ceramic, plain white, England **$22**

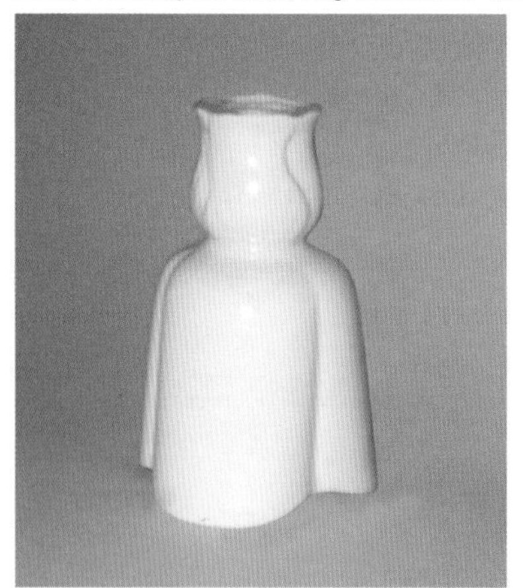

Rosebud Funnel Pie Bird

Funnel, ceramic, rosebud, white, England (ILLUS.)... **$150-175**

Funnel, cylindrical, England **$50-75**

Funnel Pie Bird with Handle

Funnel w/handle, ceramic, England (ILLUS.) **$125-150**

Charles & Diana Funnel-shaped Pie Bird

Funnel-shaped, ceramic, white w/blue transfer-printed image of Prince Charles & Princess Diana above “Charles and Diana 1981” (ILLUS.) **$45**

Gourmet Pie Cup

Gourmet pie cup, ceramic, England (ILLUS.).. **$75-95**

Granny Pie Baker

Granny, ceramic, "Pie Baker," figure of woman holding bowl, Josef Originals (ILLUS.) **$65-95**

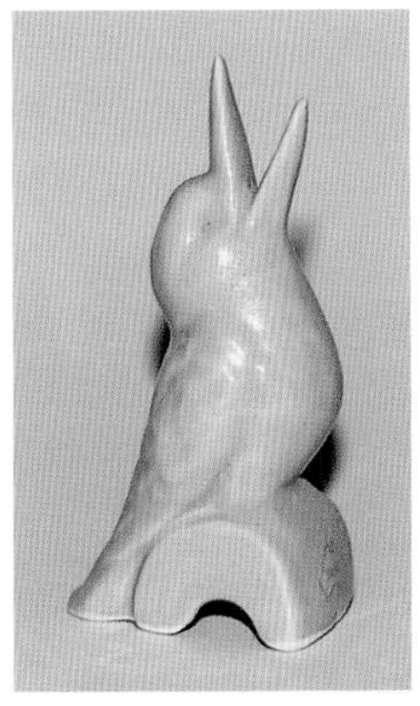

Kookaburra Pie Bird

Kookaburra, ceramic, light blue, Australia (ILLUS.) .... **$125+**

Luzianne Mammy Pie Baker

Luzianne Mammy, ceramic, black woman dressed in yellow shirt & green skirt, carrying a red tray w/coffee service, white turban on head (ILLUS.) **$65**

Clarice Cliff Mushroom Pie Bird

Mushroom, ceramic, white w/brown & green trim, designed by Clarice Cliff, ca. 1930s, England (ILLUS.).......................... **$85+**

Josef Originals Owl

Owl, ceramic, "A Lorrie Design, Japan," Josef Originals, 1980s (ILLUS.)............. **$175-295**

Owl, ceramic, Jackie Sammond, USA. ca. 1970s (ILLUS. left with blackbird, page 150).. **$125**

"Patches" pie bird, Morton Pottery, USA **$35**

Peasant Woman Pie Baker

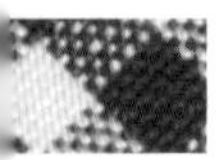

Peasant woman, ceramic, brown glaze, 1960s-70s (ILLUS., previous page) **$75**

Pie Baker Pie Bird

"Pie Baker," figure of a lady holding a bowl, by Josef Originals, ceramic (ILLUS.)........... **$95**

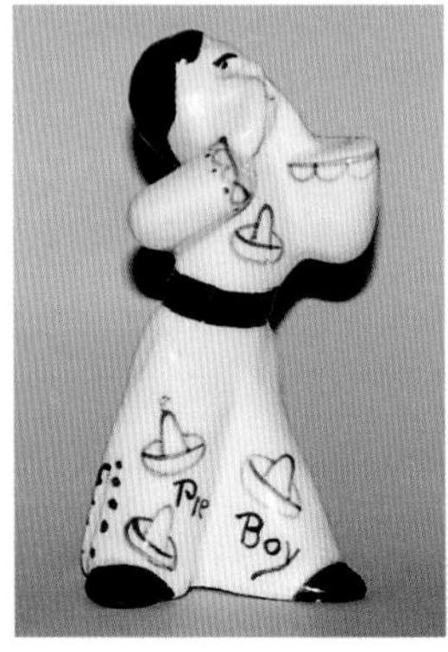

Rare Pie Boy Pie Bird

"Pie Boy," ceramic, white w/black & green trim, Squire Pottery of California, USA, rare (ILLUS.) **$350-500**

"Pie-Chic," ceramic, given as premium in Pillsbury Flour, USA............................... **$35-65**

Marion Drake Rooster Pie Bird

Rooster, ceramic, Marion Drake, white w/black, red & yellow trim on brown base (ILLUS.)... **$50**

Rooster, ceramic, white & black w/red comb, brown base, Marion Drake.......... **$65-85**

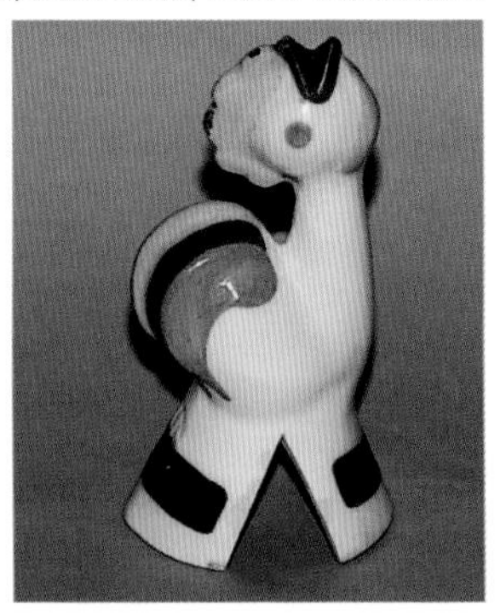

Rooster "Patrick" Pie Bird

Rooster "Patrick," ceramic, many color variations, California Cleminsons, USA, each (ILLUS.)... **$35-75**

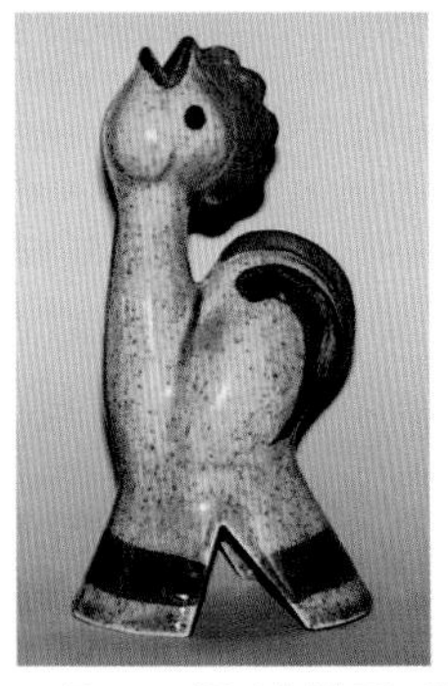

Rare Brown "Patrick" Pie Bird

Rooster "Patrick," ceramic, tan w/brown trim, California Cleminsons, USA, rare (ILLUS.)... **$175**

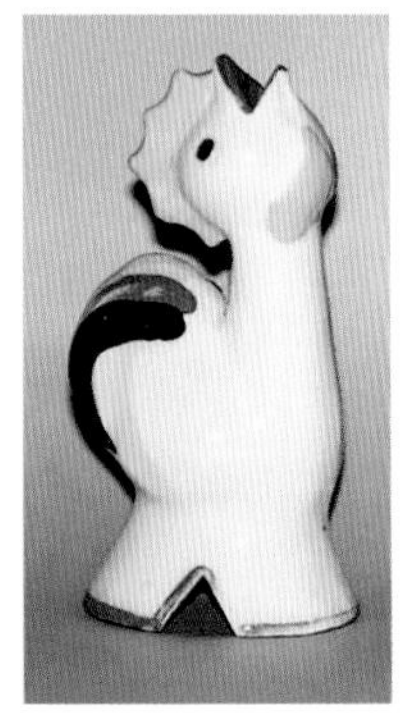

Cleminsons Rooster Pie Bird

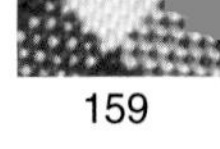
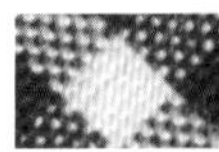

Rooster "Patrick," ceramic, white w/pink & burgundy trim, thin line around base, California Cleminsons, rare (ILLUS., previous page) **$85**

Seal, black, ceramic, Japan........................... **$125**

Green Songbird Pie Bird

Songbird, ceramic, beige, green, blue & pink variations, USA, each (ILLUS.)............ **$50**

Chic Pottery Black Songbird

Songbird, ceramic, black w/gold beak, feet & trim, Chic Pottery (ILLUS.).............. **$100-125**

American Pottery Pie Bird

Songbird, ceramic, blue & yellow, American Pottery Company, 1940-50 (ILLUS.) **$40-50**

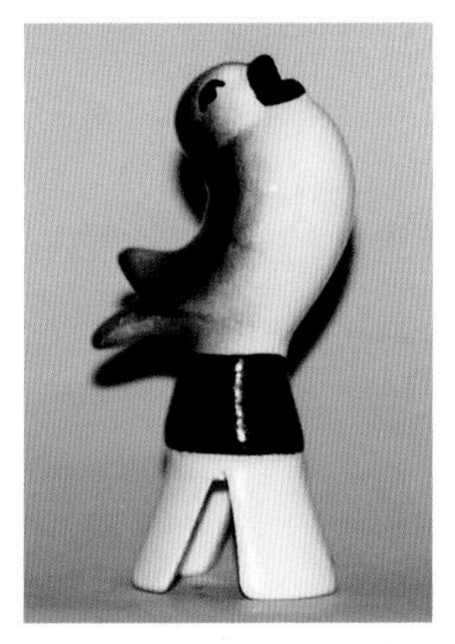

Puff-chested Songbird Pie Bird

Songbird, ceramic, lavender & brown trim, puff-chested, ca. 1940s (ILLUS.)....... **$300-400**

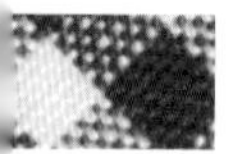

"Patch" Pie Bird

Songbird, ceramic, "Patch," white, yellow, green & pink, Morton Pottery (ILLUS.) **$35-50**

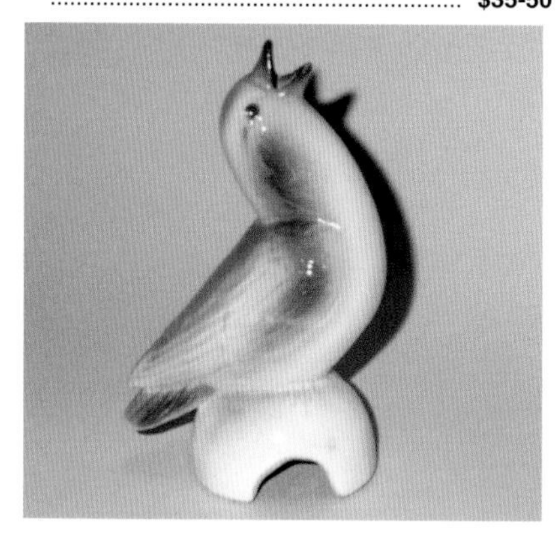

Sweet Songbird Pie Bird

Songbird, ceramic, Sweet Songbird, American, white, yellow, grey & green (ILLUS.) **$400+**

Songbird, ceramic, yellow, USA **$125**

Thistle-shaped Pie Bird

Thistle-shaped, ceramic, blue, England (ILLUS.) **$125**

Unusual pie vent, ceramic, "The Bleriot Pie Divider," white, 1910-20 ..... **$450**

Welsh Woman Pie Bird

Welsh woman, ceramic, brown w/large black hat, 1969, commemorating investiture of Prince Charles (ILLUS.) ..... **$200+**

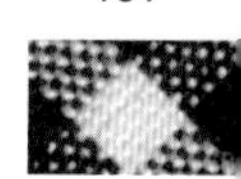

Chapter 11

Reamers

Reamers are a European invention dating back to the 18th century. Devised to extract citrus juice as a remedy for scurvy, by the 1920s they became a must in every well-equipped American kitchen. Although one can still purchase inexpensive glass, wood, metal and plastic squeezers in today's kitchen and variety stores, it is the pre-1950s models that are so highly sought after today. Whether it's a primitive wood example from the late 1800s or a whimsical figural piece from post-World War II Japan, the reamer is one of the hottest kitchen collectibles in today's marketplace - Bobbie Zucker Bryson

Ceramic, boat-shaped, pale green w/pink, blue & white flowers, cream reamer cone, handle & inside bowl, Shelley - England, 7" h. **$225-250**

Boat-shaped Leaf-decorated Reamer

Ceramic, boat-shaped, white w/gilt line trim, decorated w/rust-colored leaves & navy blue, small loop handle, 3 1/2" h. (ILLUS.) **$45-65**

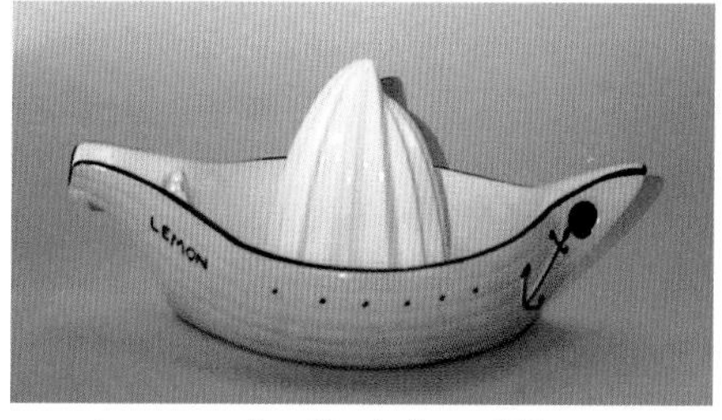

Lemon-yellow Boat-shaped Reamer

Ceramic, boat-shaped, yellow w/black trim & white interior & cone, side w/image of anchor & word "Lemon" in black, 3" h. (ILLUS.) **$75-100**

Ceramic, bowl-shaped on ribbed pedestal base, yellow, Red Wing USA, 6 3/4" h. (ILLUS., top next column) **$115-125**

Ceramic, bucket-style, two-piece, tan w/embossed cherub, flowers & decorative panels, green trim, rattan handle, marked "Made In Japan, Pat. 49541," 7 3/4" h. (ILLUS., middle next column) **$60-85**

Red Wing Reamer

Bucket-style Handled Reamer

Reamer with Caricature of a Woman

Ceramic, caricature of woman w/brown face, two-piece, crossed eyes & oversize red lips, wearing yellow bandana & gold hoop earrings, yellow & white cone forming hat, marked "Made in Germany," 2 3/4" h. (ILLUS.) **$175-200**

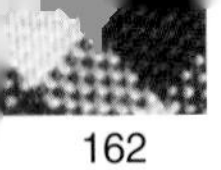

Ceramic, creamer-shaped, two-piece, low round body in white w/multi-colored flowers & gold trim, gold handle, marked "Nippon" **$160**

Manx Cat Creamer-Style Reamer

Ceramic, creamer-style, two-piece, beige w/image of black cat & "Manx Cat From The Isle of Man," reamer on lid, marked "Crown Devon, Made in England," 3 1/2" h. (ILLUS.) **$75-85**

Reamer with Kitten Decoration

Ceramic, creamer-style, two-piece, green w/molded white kitten in yellow pajamas on front, yellow, green, pink & white top, marked "Made in Japan 429," 4" h. (ILLUS.) **$50-75**

"Sourpuss" Clown Ceramic Reamer

Ceramic, figural clown head reamer in saucer base,white w/black & pink & marked "Sourpuss," 4 3/4" d. (ILLUS.) **$90-125**

Lemon & Clown Head Ceramic Reamer

Ceramic, figural clown head reamer top on a yellow lemon-shaped pitcher-style base, two-piece, "Florida" printed around rim, marked "Made In Japan," 5" h. (ILLUS.) **$150**

Oriental Man's Head Reamer

Ceramic, figural Oriental man's head, two-piece, w/collar as base, hat as lid/reamer, light blue w/dark grey highlights, incised "9496," 5 3/4" h. (ILLUS.).................. **$125-150**

Ceramic, figural smiling face, two-piece, ruffled top, yellow w/orange & black trim, marked "Carltonware," 3 3/4" h........... **$95-125**

Clown Reamer in Aqua & Maroon

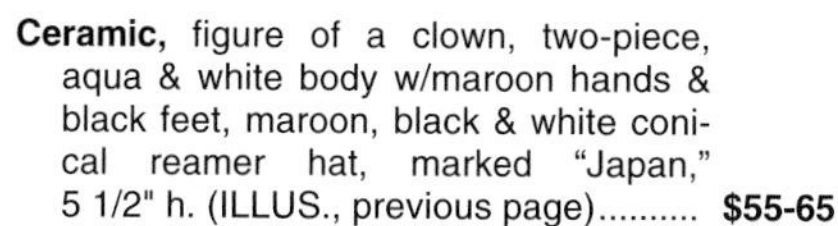

Ceramic, figure of a clown, two-piece, aqua & white body w/maroon hands & black feet, maroon, black & white conical reamer hat, marked "Japan," 5 1/2" h. (ILLUS., previous page).......... **$55-65**

Ceramic, figure of a native woman, two-piece, w/brown face & wide red lips, wearing gold hoop earrings & a bandana on her head, yellow & white conical reamer hat, marked "Made in Germany" on the base, 2 3/4" h. **$175-200**

Reamer in the Form of Amish Man

Ceramic, figure of Amish man, three-piece, black pants, green shirt, yellow cone top & hat, marked "JCC, NRCA, PA-1996," 5 1/2" h. (ILLUS.) **$40-50**

Chef Reamer

Ceramic, figure of black chef lying on his back, white w/blue trim, 2 3/4" h. (ILLUS.) **$200-275**

Ceramic, figure of boy sitting cross-legged, two-piece, wearing lavender outfit w/black trim, white cone hat w/lavender trim, 5" h. (ILLUS., top next column) .. **$285-400**

Ceramic, figure of chef lying on his back, two-piece, white w/blue, black shoes, yellow pants, white cone, turquoise & black trim, 2 1/2" h. **$175-200**

Ceramic Boy in Lavender Outfit Reamer

Colorful Ceramic Clown Reamer

Ceramic, figure of clown, cream & mulitcolored w/a yellow & green hat, stamped "Made in Japan" & "Japan," ca. 1930s-40s, 8" h. (ILLUS.) **$75**

Ceramic, figure of clown, cups in green & white w/yellow & orange trim to match reamer, marked "Hand Painted Made in Japan," 3 1/8", each (ILLUS. w/reamer, next page) **$10-25**

Figure of a Clown Head Reamer

Ceramic, figure of clown head in saucer, white w/orange trim, hearts on cheeks &

red lips, Goebel, Germany, 5" d. (ILLUS.) **$235-285**

Bulbous Brown Clown Reamer

Ceramic, figure of clown, light brown bulbous body & cone hat, blue buttons & collar, 6" h. (ILLUS.) **$50-65**

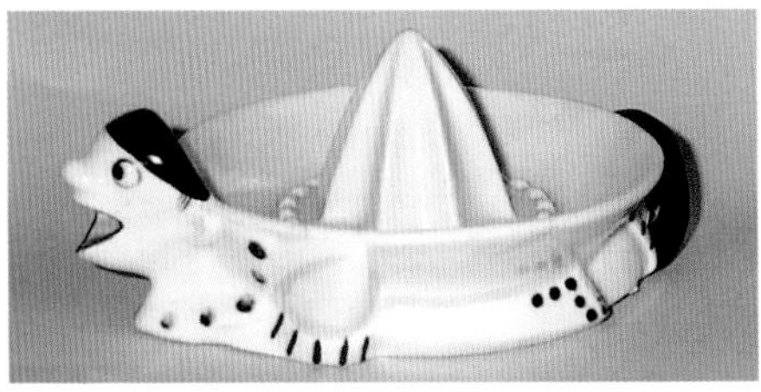

Prone Clown Figural Reamer

Ceramic, figure of clown lying prone, the open mouth forming the spout, white w/yellow, red, blue & black trim, incised "6358," 4" d. (ILLUS.) **$135-175**

Figural Clown Reamer w/Matching Cups

Ceramic, figure of clown, reamer w/green & white body w/yellow & orange trim, marked "Hand Painted Made in Japan," 8 3/4" (ILLUS. center) **$85-125**

Reamer Clown Salt & Pepper Shakers

Ceramic, figure of clown, reamer/salt & pepper shakers, white w/red trim & red & blue dots, 3 1/4" h., pr. (ILLUS.) **$20-35**

1960s Sigma Ceramic Clown Reamer

Ceramic, figure of clown, red w/black & orange on white, marked "SIGMA," ca. 1960s, 6 1/2" h. (ILLUS.) **$60-75**

Blue & Yellow Clown Reamer

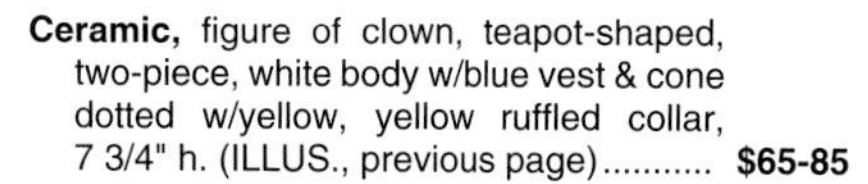

Ceramic, figure of clown, teapot-shaped, two-piece, white body w/blue vest & cone dotted w/yellow, yellow ruffled collar, 7 3/4" h. (ILLUS., previous page) **$65-85**

Green & White Clown Reamer

Ceramic, figure of clown, two-piece, green body w/green & white cone hat, small loop handle, marked "Made in Japan," 4 1/2" h. (ILLUS.) **$50-65**

Maroon, Green & White Clown Reamer

Ceramic, figure of clown, two-piece, maroon & white w/maroon & green cone, marked "Made in Japan," 5 1/2" h. (ILLUS.) **$65-95**

Ceramic, figure of clown, two-piece, sitting cross-legged & wearing a dark orange suit w/white ruffled collar & cone, Germany, 5" h. (ILLUS., top next column) **$250-300**

Ceramic, figure of clown, two-piece, white pitcher bottom w/black & orange stripes, orange collar, orange & black cone hat, 6 1/2" h. **$75-95**

Ceramic, figure of clown, two-piece, white w/green polka-dot body, green & black collar, black feet, brown hands, blue & white cone hat, loop handle, marked "Made In Japan," 7" h. **$85-95**

Ceramic, figure of clown, two-piece, yellow body w/maroon buttons & collar, cone hat, 6" h. **$75-100**

Ceramic, figure of clown w/pig head top, tan & light green body, yellow hat cone, marked "Hand Painted Made in Japan," 5" h. **$175-250**

Seated Cross-Legged Clown Reamer

Ceramic, figure of clown, white & black w/red hearts and black & white cone, red hair, two-piece, marked "Sigma," 6 1/2" h. **$115**

Ceramic, figure of clown, white, blue, green & yellow striped outfit, white cone top w/thin blue line, marked "Made in Japan," 8" h. (ILLUS. left, below) **$50-65**

Two Colorful Cearmic Clown Reamers

Ceramic, figure of clown, white, blue, green & yellow, w/blue & white top, marked "Made in Japan," 6" h. (ILLUS. right) **$50-65**

Ceramic, figure of clowns, reamer/salt & pepper shakers, yellow & orange w/black trim, 2 3/4" h., pr. **$20-35**

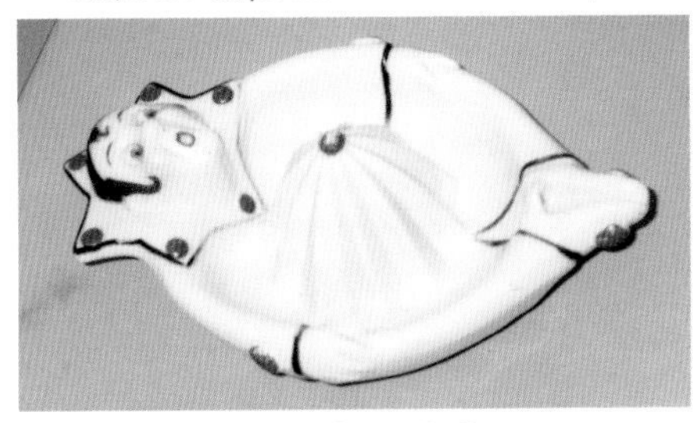

Court Jester Ceramic Reamer

Ceramic, figure of court jester lying on his back, saucer-shaped, white w/black & red trim, 4" d. (ILLUS.) **$325**

Cross-legged Boy Ceramic Reamer

Ceramic, figure of cross-legged boy, two-piece, dressed in a red outfit w/white collar & black tie & shoes, wide reamer hat in white w/red trim, 5 1/2" h. (ILLUS.)...... **$275-350**

Ceramic Crouching Man Reamer

Ceramic, figure of crouching man, two-piece, white w/detailed face & black trim, Germany, first half 20th c., 3 1/2" h. (ILLUS.) **$175-200**

Ceramic, figure of man's face, two-piece, red w/white top, 3 1/2" h. **$45-60**

Rounded Man's Head Reamer

Ceramic, figure of man's head, two-piece, rounded w/side-glancing blue eyes & smiling mouth, yellow w/red dots ruffled collar, blue lustre reamer top, brown hair tuft forms small spout at side, 4" h. (ILLUS.) **$125-150**

Ceramic Mexican Man Reamer

Ceramic, figure of Mexican man, teapot-shaped, two-piece, wearing bright orange jacket, yellow, orange, green & black serape & black pants, the yellow & orange cone forming his sombrero, one hand on hip forming handle, sitting next to green cactus that forms spout, 5 1/2" h. (ILLUS.) **$250-300**

Ceramic, figure of roly-poly man, two-piece, holding a top hat that acts as the spout, white w/black & yellow trim, 4 3/4" h. (ILLUS., next page) **$275-300**

Figural Roly-poly Man Reamer

Toby Face Cermic Reamer

Ceramic, figure of Toby face, probably base on Royal Doulton Sairey Gamp character jug design, brown hair, green shirt, light green bow tie, white w/touch of blue cone top, marked "Japan," 4 1/4" h. (ILLUS.) . **$175-225**

Ceramic, figure of white face, two-piece, w/expressive black eyes, rosy cheeks & red lips, Japan, 4 1/2" h. **$65-85**

Woman's Head Reamer

Ceramic, figure of woman's head w/black hair, sitting in round ruffled white lustre saucer base w/ring handle & small rim spout, 3 1/4" h. (ILLUS.) **$325-400**

Ceramic, figures of clowns, reamer/salt & pepper shakers, 2 1/2" - 3 3/4", marked "Japan," pr.. **$20-35**

Ceramic Chick Juice Reamer

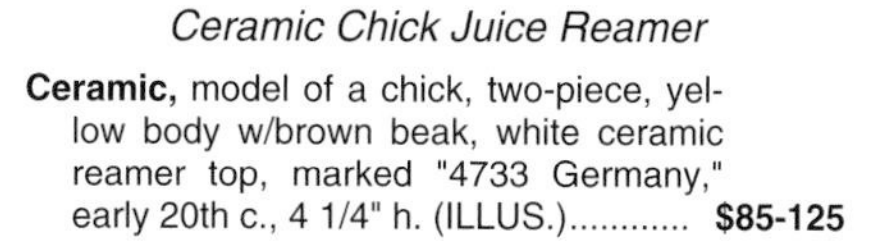

Ceramic, model of a chick, two-piece, yellow body w/brown beak, white ceramic reamer top, marked "4733 Germany," early 20th c., 4 1/4" h. (ILLUS.)............ **$85-125**

Ceramic Duck Juice Reamer

Ceramic, model of a duck, two-piece, green head & yellow bill on a white body w/brown wings, ceramic white reamer top, marked "4732 Germany," early 20th c., 4 1/4" h. (ILLUS.) **$85-125**

Swan-shaped Two-piece Reamer

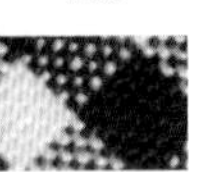

Ceramic, model of a swan, two-piece, off-white w/pink rose designs & green trim, 4 1/4" h. (ILLUS., previous page) **$75-85**

Bear Reamer

Ceramic, model of bear, seated, orange body & rim on white reamer top, marked "Foreign," 4 1/2" h. (ILLUS.) **$225-275**

Ceramic, model of bear, two-piece, yellow, marked "Foreign," 4 1/2" h. **$325-400**

Figural Red Bird Reamer

Ceramic, model of bird, red head w/grey beak forms reamer, red body w/green wings, 4 3/4" h. (ILLUS.) **$400-500**

Ceramic, model of camel, kneeling, beige lustre w/light green top, 4 1/4" h......... **$225-250**

Ceramic, model of cat head, two-piece, stylized blue & white face w/side-glancing eyes, pink bow tie, yellow & white reamer top, side handle w/finger grips, 5 1/4" h. (ILLUS., top next column) **$60-75**

Figural Cat Head Ceramic Reamer

Figural Chick & Elephant German Reamers

Ceramic, model of chick, two-piece, yellow w/maroon crown & wings, Germany, 3 1/2" h. (ILLUS. right with yellow elephant reamer) **$225-250**

Two-piece Figural Chick Reamer

Ceramic, model of chick, two-piece, yellow w/orange crown, bill & feet, green tail & wings, white cone, marked "Sarsasparilla, W.N.Y. © 1984, Deco Designs, #970," 3 1/2" h. (ILLUS.) **$50-60**

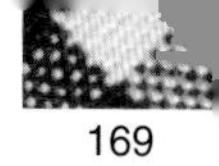

Figural Laughing Dog Head Reamer

Ceramic, model of dog head, laughing, white, pink, orange & black, marked "Made in Japan," 4 3/4" h. (ILLUS.) ... **$175-225**

Ceramic, model of dog, yellow w/red & black trim, marked "Made in Japan," 8" h. **$250-325**

Ceramic, model of duck, two-piece, California Classics, ca. 1989, 3 1/4" h............. **$20-25**

Ceramic, model of duck, two-piece, w/white lustre body, blue head, orange beak, yellow top knot, marked "Made In Japan," 2 3/4" h.. **$35-50**

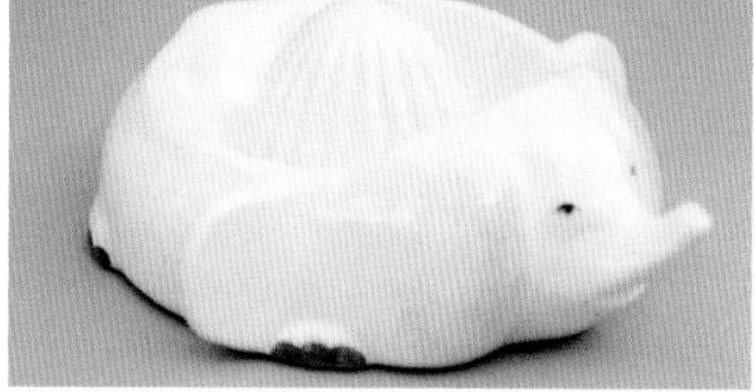

Portuguese Elephant Reamer

Ceramic, model of elephant, low saucer-form, white w/pink tint, marked "Mideramica Made in Portugal," 4" d. (ILLUS.) **$25-35**

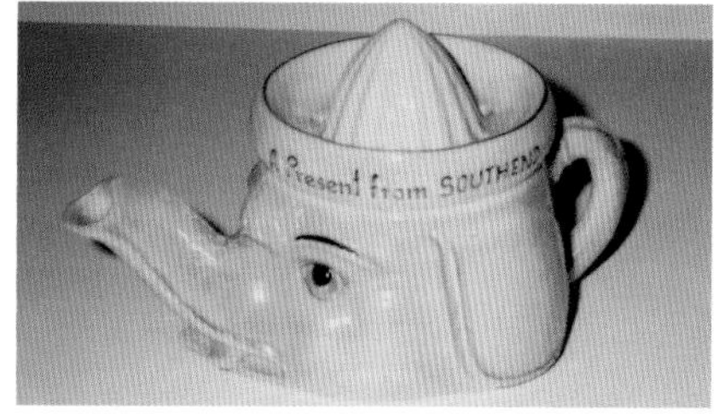

Ceramic Figure of Elephant Reamer

Ceramic, model of elephant, orange luster w/green trim & white cone, marked "A Present from Southend-on-Sea" on rim top "Made in Czechslovakia", 3 1/2" h. (ILLUS.)... **$225-250**

Elephant with Colorful Blanket Reamer

Ceramic, model of elephant, standing, white w/back covered w/multicolored blanket, w/sticker that says "Souvenir of Montreal," 6" h. (ILLUS.).................... **$100-150**

Ceramic, model of elephant, three-piece, w/trunk raised, large ears w/yellow, green & brown design, cane handle, 7" h. **$250-300**

Ceramic, model of elephant, two-piece, yellow w/black trim & white cone, Goebel, Germany, 4 1/8" h. (ILLUS. left with chick, previous page)......................... **$250-275**

Figural Fish Reamer

Ceramic, model of fish, saucer-shaped, yellow, 5 1/2" d. (ILLUS.)........................... **$50-75**

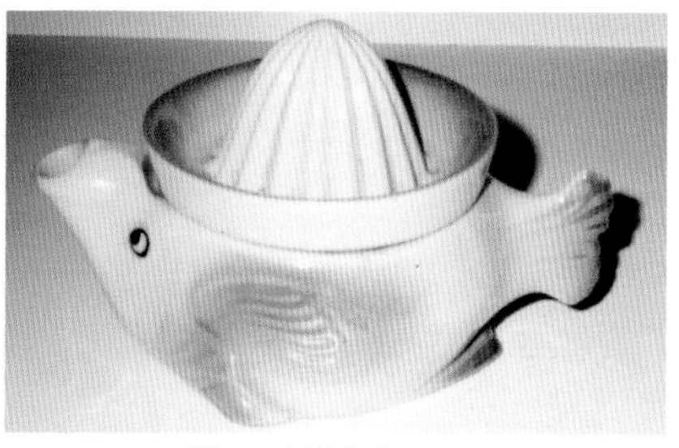

Figural Fish Reamer

House Reamer with Matching Tumbler

Ceramic, model of fish, two-piece, orange & white, marked "Jager," 3 1/4" h. (ILLUS., previous page) **$175-200**

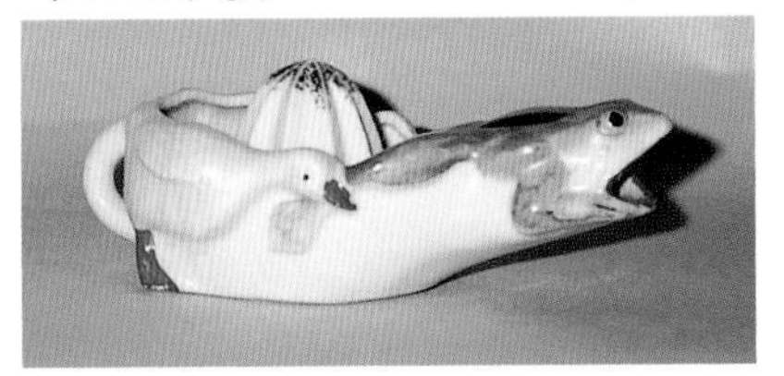

Goose Chasing Frog Reamer

Ceramic, model of green frog chased by white goose, the open-mouthed frog forming the spout, the goose forming the side of the saucer, embossed "Made in Japan," 1 3/4" h. (ILLUS.) **$110-150**

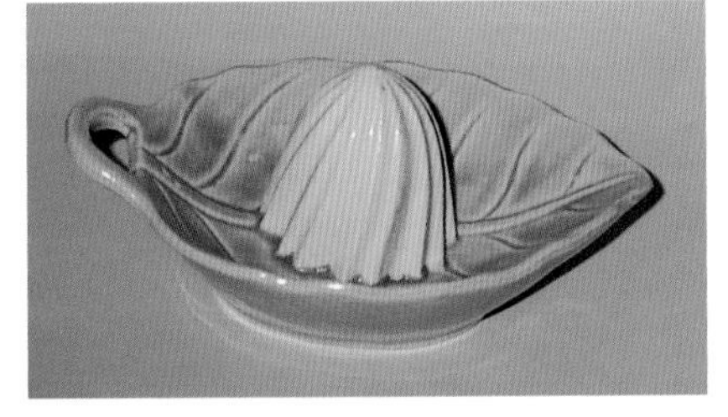

Leaf-form Ceramic Reamer

Ceramic, model of green leaf holding the yellow cone, saucer-shaped, 4" d. (ILLUS.) **$30-35**

Ceramic, model of house, tan w/green & red trees, green trim & blue windows, marked "Made in Japan," w/six 3 1/4" matching cups, 5 1/2" h., the set **$90-125**

Ceramic, model of house, two-piece, white w/brown roof & handle, blue windows, green grass & cherry trees in front, marked "Made in Japan," 5 1/2" h., w/matching juice tumbler (ILLUS., top of page) **$95-125**

House w/Windmill Reamer

Ceramic, model of house w/windmill, beige w/multi-colored trim & yellow cone, marked "Martutomoware, Handpainted Japan," 4 1/2" h. (ILLUS.) **$90-125**

Ceramic, model of lemon slice, two-piece, yellow w/green handle, marked "Japan," 6 3/4" h.. **$35-45**

Ceramic, model of lemon, two-piece, yellow w/green leaves, brown stem, white cone, marked "House of Speyer," 4 1/2" h... **$50-60**

Ceramic, model of lime, two-handled, marked "Orange For Baby" on front & "Handpainted" on bottom, 4 3/8" h......... **$50-75**

Figural Monkey Reamer

Ceramic, model of monkey, sitting cross-legged, brown & tan w/white top, marked "Germany," 4 1/4" h. (ILLUS., previous page) **$175-225**

Figural Ceramic Mouse Reamer

Ceramic, model of mouse, two-piece, grey body w/pink ears & stylized smiling face, cone hat in dark blue & white, limited edition, 4 1/2" h. (ILLUS.)............................ **$45-55**

Goebel Orange-shaped Reamer

Ceramic, model of orange, two-piece, realistic w/green leaf spout & brown branch handle, white top & reamer cone, marked "Goebel," Germany, 4 1/2" h. (ILLUS.) **$65-75**

Figural Orange Two-Piece Reamer

Ceramic, model of orange, two-piece, w/a green loop handle, marked "Japan" on the base, 3 3/4" h. (ILLUS.) **$45-55**

"Orange for Baby" Reamer

Ceramic, model of orange, two-piece, yellow w/pebbled surface resembling orange peel, white & yellow cone top, front reads "Orange for Baby," marked "Registered Germany," 4" h. (ILLUS.) **$60-75**

Ceramic, model of orange w/white top & cone, painted smiling face, marked "Florida" on the front, 3 1/2" h. **$45-55**

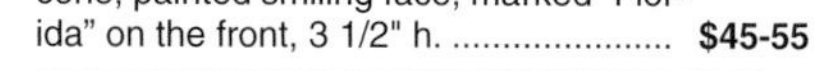

Figural Orange Reamer

Ceramic, model of orange w/yellow & blue flowers & green leaves, "Kiddies Orange Juice," two-piece, marked "Germany," 4" h. (ILLUS.) **$50-75**

Ceramic, model of orange w/yellow & blue flowers & green leaves, "Orange For Baby," two-piece, marked "Goebel GW Co., Germany," 3 1/2" h.............................. **$75-100**

Orchid-form Reamer

Ceramic, model of orchid, two-piece, pink & white w/green handle & bottom, 3" h. (ILLUS., previous page) **$100-115**

Ceramic, model of pansy blossom, two-piece, decorated w/a yellow & purple pansy, white top w/ruffled rim, 4" h. **$60-75**

Ceramic, model of pear, three-piece, orange w/gold trim & green stem, marked “Handpainted Made in Japan,” 4" h. **$45-55**

White Pear Ceramic Reamer

Ceramic, model of pear, three-piece, white w/black & gold trim, marked “Handpainted Made in Japan,” 5" h. (ILLUS.).......... **$45-55**

California Classics Pig Reamer

Ceramic, model of pig, two-piece, all-white, California Classics, ca. 1989, 3 1/4" h. (ILLUS.).. **$20-25**

Ceramic, model of red strawberry w/green leaves, marked “401 Beswick England,” 4" h. **$50-75**

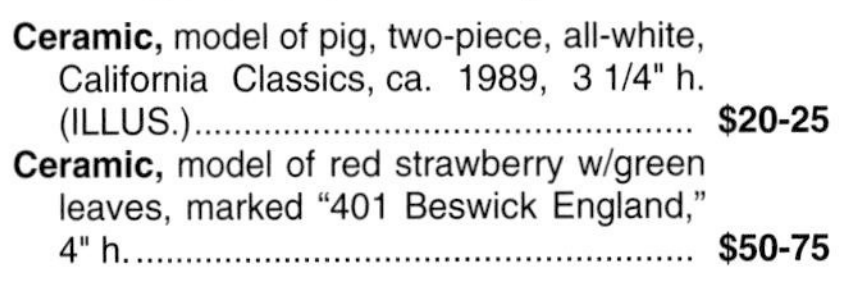

Reamer in the Form of a Rose

Ceramic, model of rose, pink flower on green leaves, stem forming handle, a rosebud forming the spout, marked “Erphila Germany,” 1 3/4" h. (ILLUS.) **$200-250**

Figural Ceramic Snail Reamer

Ceramic, model of snail, two-piece, beige shell w/rust-colored dots, green body & cone, open-mouthed head forms spout, 4 1/2" h. (ILLUS.) **$35-45**

Two-piece Pitcher Reamer with Clown Head

Ceramic, pitcher-shaped, figural clown head reamer top w/green cone, two-piece w/colorful stylized orange & yellow flowers on the base, 6" h. (ILLUS) **$55-65**

Flowered Universal Cambridge Reamer

Ceramic, pitcher-shaped, two-piece, cream w/yellow & purple flowers & green leaves, marked “Universal Cambridge, Ovenproof, Made in USA,” 9 1/2" h. (ILLUS.).............................. **$150-175**

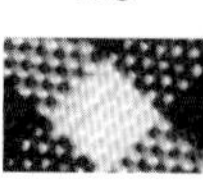

Universal Potteries Pitcher Reamer

Ceramic, pitcher-shaped, two-piece, off-white decorated w/scene of blue & green garden gate & flowerpots on steps, marked "Universal Potteries Oven Proof," 9" h. (ILLUS.) **$135-165**

Squat Pitcher-form Reamer

Ceramic, pitcher-shaped, two-piece, squat form w/lip & circular handle, white ground w/maroon & yellow flower design, gold trim, marked "Hand Painted Japan," 3 3/4" h. (ILLUS.) **$75-95**

Ceramic Two-piece Pitcher Reamer

Ceramic, pitcher-shaped, two-piece, tall footed light pink body w/green trim, colorful pink, yellow & blue flower sprig, marked "Pantry BAK-IN by Ware, Crooksville," 8 1/4" h. (ILLUS.) **$100-125**

Tall Pitcher-form Reamer

Ceramic, pitcher-shaped, two-piece, tall form w/lip, C-form handle & short outcurved base, pale pink ground w/painted floral decoration in pinks, blues, yellows & greens, thin green rim decoration, marked "Pantry Bak-In Ware by Crooksville," 8 1/4" h. (ILLUS.) **$125-175**

Japanese Ceramic Pitcher-style Reamer

Ceramic, pitcher-shaped, two-piece, tapering cylindrical body in beige w/red & yellow flowers & black trim, reamer lid, bottom marked "Japan," 8 1/2" h., the set (ILLUS.) **$45-60**

Reamer with Basketweave Design

Ceramic, pitcher-shaped, two-piece, w/C-form handle, basketweave design in dark

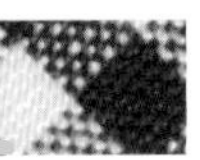

green w/orange & maroon flowers & light green leaves, yellow top & cone, black trim, marked "Maramotoware Hand Painted Japan," 4" h. (ILLUS.) **$40-50**

Ceramic, pitcher-shaped, two-piece, white w/yellow plaid design, marked "Japan" on bottom, 7" h. **$55-65**

Ceramic, pitcher-shaped, white w/multi-colored flowers & green trim, three-piece, marked "Made in Japan," w/lid & six cups, 7" h. **$75**

Pitcher-style Clown Head Reamer

Ceramic, pitcher-style, figural clown head yellow reamer top, base decorated w/yellow & purple flowers, yellow cone & lustre trim, marked "Made in Japan," 6" h. (ILLUS.) **$75-95**

Ceramic Pitcher Reamer & Juice Cup

Ceramic, pitcher-style, light bluish green tall tapering cylindrical pitcher w/long pointed handle, h.p. w/blue & green flowers & light brown trim, w/six matching juice cups, marked "Hand Painted Japan," 8 1/2" h., the set (ILLUS. of part) **$45-60**

Ceramic, pitcher-style, one-piece, green, Art Deco design, w/spring-loaded cone, Ade-O-Matic, Genuine Coorsite Porcelain, 9" h. (ILLUS., next column) **$150-175**

Ceramic, pitcher-style, two-piece, cream w/yellow & purple flowers & green leaves, marked "Universal Cambridge, Ovenproof, Made In USA," 9 1/2" **$175-195**

Ceramic, pitcher-style, two-piece, w/blue & green garden gate & multi-colored flowers, marked "Universal Cambridge, Ovenproof Made in USA," 9" h. **$150-175**

Green One-Piece Ceramic Reamer

Ceramic, pitcher-style, two-piece, w/multicolored floral design, marked "Universal Cambridge Ovenproof Made in USA," 9" h. **$135-165**

Ceramic, pitcher-style, two-piece, w/red & black cattail design, marked "Universal Cambridge, Ovenproof Made in USA," 9" h. **$135-165**

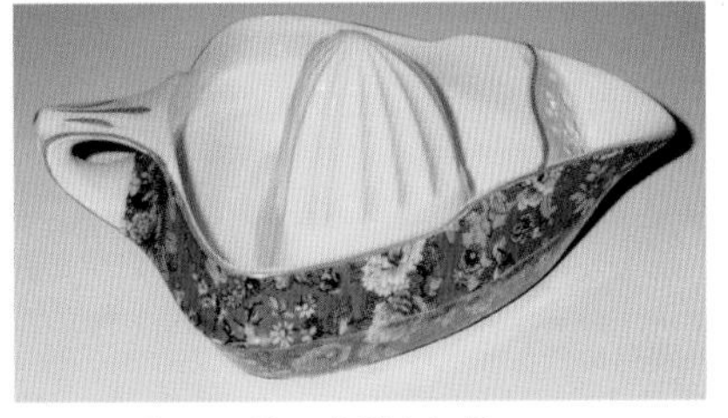

Crown Ducal Chintz Reamer

Ceramic, sauceboat shaped, blue Chintz/multicolored flowers, marked "Crown Ducal, Made in England," 3 1/2" h., 8" l. (ILLUS.) **$350-400**

Sauceboat-shaped Pedestal Reamer

Ceramic, sauceboat-shaped, beige decorated w/orange fruit & green leaves,

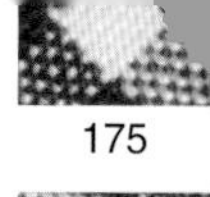

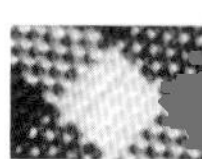

blue & white pedestal base, black handle & trim, marked "Made in Japan," 3" h. (ILLUS.) **$60-75**

Ceramic Saucer Reamer with Flowers

Ceramic, saucer-shaped, cream ground w/a brown rim band & tab handle, exterior h.p. w/blue & purple flowers w/yellow centers & green leaves, ca. 1930s (ILLUS.) **$20-25**

Ceramic, saucer-shaped, cream, tan & maroon w/blue trim, England, 3 1/4" d. **$75-95**

Ceramic, saucer-shaped, cream & tan w/maroon & blue trim, marked "A Present From Framington," "Made In England," 3 1/4" d. **$125-150**

Ceramic, saucer-shaped, cream & tan with maroon & blue trim, marked "A Present From Framington, Made in England," 3 1/4" d. **$125**

Ceramic, saucer-shaped, figural clown head reamer in saucer, maroon & white cone hat w/maroon trim, loop handle, Germany, 5" d. **$225-275**

Ceramic, saucer-shaped, figural clown head reamer in saucer, orange & white, Germany, 5" d. **$225-275**

Green Hall "Medallion" Reamer

Ceramic, saucer-shaped, green exterior w/finely ribbed band, cream interior, tab/loop handle, "Medallion" shape, Hall China Co., marked "Hall," 6" d. (ILLUS.) **$400**

Ceramic, saucer-shaped, green, marked "U.S.A. Zippy Trademark Patent Applied For Wolverine Products Inc., Detroit, Mich.," 6 1/2" d. x 3 1/4" h. **$90-110**

Ceramic, saucer-shaped, green & yellow w/red & tan trim, Dutch boy on one side & windmill on other, marked "A Present from Newport IOW, Made in England," 5 1/4" d. **$100-135**

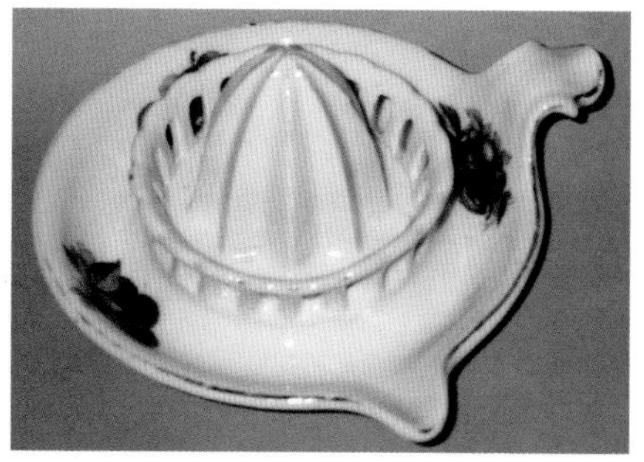

Reamer w/Lattice Edging & Cherries

Ceramic, saucer-shaped, lattice edging around the cone, white w/red cherries, green leaves & gold trim, 5 1/2" d. (ILLUS.) **$75-95**

French Scenic Gold-trimmed Reamer

Ceramic, saucer-shaped, one-piece, white w/gold trim, w/figures of tree, swan, butterfly & flowerpot, marked "Made In France - Limoges France," 3 1/2" d. (ILLUS.) **$75-95**

Ceramic, saucer-shaped, red & cream, Hall China, 6" h. **$500-600**

Ceramic, saucer-shaped, rough orange finish, white interior, green handle, Czechoslovakia, 2 1/4" h. **$30-35**

Ceramic, saucer-shaped, strainer cap on front, green, table handle w/hanging hole, Japan **$40-45**

Ceramic, saucer-shaped, turquoise, marked "U.S.A. Zippy Trademark Patent Applied For Wolverine Products Inc., Detroit, Mich.," 3 1/4" h., 6 1/2" d. **$85-115**

Quimper Pottery Reamer

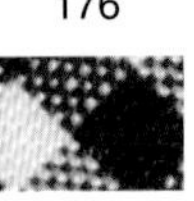

Ceramic, saucer-shaped, two-piece, beige w/red, yellow, blue & tan trim, "Quimper Ivoire Corbell" patt., marked "Henriot Quimper France 1166," 2 3/4" h. (ILLUS., previous page) **$200-250**

Ceramic, saucer-shaped, white w/dark blue & gold trim, marked "Germany," 3 1/2" h. **$100-135**

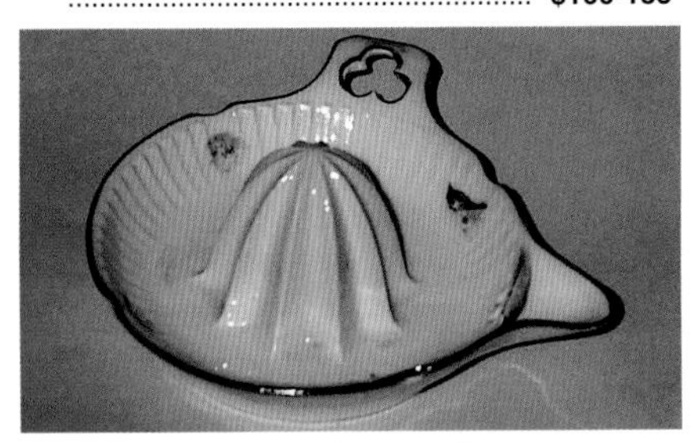

Saucer-style Ceramic Reamer

Ceramic, saucer-shaped, white w/gold trim, decorated w/images of sewing implements, the handle w/cloverleaf cutout, 5 1/4" d. (ILLUS.) **$40-50**

Ceramic, saucer-shaped, white w/gold trim & designs, petal-style tab handle, Japan, 3" h. **$145-150**

Floral Decorated Saucer-shaped Reamer

Ceramic, saucer-shaped, white w/light & dark pink roses, green leaves & gold & dark cobalt blue trim, 4 1/2" d. (ILLUS.) **$100-135**

Flowered Reamer with Gold Trim

Ceramic, saucer-shaped, white w/multicolored flowers & gold trim, tab handle (ILLUS.) **$185**

Simple Reamer with Autumn Leaves

Ceramic, simple round shape w/spout, beige w/autumn leaf design on sides & tab handle, gold foil sticker reads "Limited Edition Produced Exclusively by China Specialties," 6" h. (ILLUS.)............ **$125-175**

French Tapering Cylindrical 3-Piece Reamer

Ceramic, tapering cylindrical sides w/reamer top, white w/multicolored flowers & sterling silver trim, marked "France," w/underplate, 5 3/8" h., 3 pcs. (ILLUS.) **$175-200**

Maroon Teapot-Style Jiffy Juicer

Ceramic, teapot-shaped, maroon, marked "Jiffy Juicer U.S. Pat 2, 755 Sept. 20, 1938" 5 1/4" h. (ILLUS.) **$75-90**

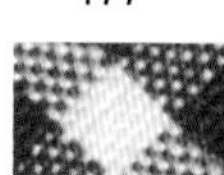

Two Miniature Teapot-shaped Reamers

Ceramic, teapot-shaped, miniature, two-piece, tan lustre w/red & yellow flowers in pots, 2 1/4" h. (ILLUS. left with other miniature teapot reamer).......................... **$100-125**

Ceramic, teapot-shaped, miniature, two-piece, tan lustre w/red & yellow flowers in pot flanked by blue fence, 2" h. (ILLUS. right with other miniature teapot-shaped reamer)... **$100-125**

Pink Ceramic Teapot-style Reamer

Ceramic, teapot-shaped, pink, marked "Jiffy Juicer, US Pat. 2,130,755, Sept. 2, 1938," 5 1/4" h. (ILLUS.) **$75-90**

Ceramic, teapot-shaped, three-piece, orange & white w/gold trim, cone sits under gold-handled lid, 3 1/2" h. **$50-60**

Petal-form Ceramic Reamer

Ceramic, teapot-shaped, two-piece, bright orange petal bottom w/bright yellow top, loop handle, marked "Made in Japan," 3 3/4" h. (ILLUS.) **$55-65**

LaVerne Hemmers Reamer

Ceramic, teapot-shaped, two-piece, decorated w/lavender & purple flowers on pink ground, marked "1990 LaVerne Hemmers," 5" h. (ILLUS.) **$20-30**

Teapot-shaped Floral-decorated Reamer

Ceramic, teapot-shaped, two-piece, decorated w/pink, blue & orange flowers & black leaves on white ground, deep orange lustre rim band & handle, black line trim, orange lustre & white top, marked "Japan," 4 3/4" h. (ILLUS.) **$45-60**

Teapot-shaped Painted Ceramic Reamer

Ceramic, teapot-shaped, two-piece, earth-tones & purple pansy-type flowers on white ground, green lustre trim on handle & rim of body, lid & spout, ribbed lid w/holes for liquid to pass through, reamer

in the form of a head with yellow ribbed cone hat, marked "Made in Japan," 6" h. (ILLUS.) **$75-125**

Ceramic Reamer with Pebble Finish

Ceramic, teapot-shaped, two-piece, figural clown head cone reamer in green & white, white pebble finish decorated w/maroon & blue flowers & green leaves, dark blue/green trim, 6" h. (ILLUS.) **$45-60**

Ceramic Reamer with Baby Sleeping on Moon

Ceramic, two-piece, tapering cylindrical two-handled yellow base w/a molded scene of a baby sleeping on a crescent moon, blue and orange cone, marked "Made in Japan," 4" h. (ILLUS.) **$60**

Ceramic, two-piece, white & cobalt blue w/gold trim, ruffled top, 3 1/2" h. **$150-160**

Ceramic, two-piece, wide cylindrical two-handled base in yellow molded w/two dogs under a red umbrella, yellow, green, red & white cone, marked "75/476 Made in Japan," 4 1/4" h. (ILLUS., top next column) **$60-75**

Ceramic, two-piece, wide tapering cylindrical base w/angled handles, off-white ground molded in relief w/three small yellow chicks jumping rope, blue & red thin border bands, marked "Japan," 4" h. (ILLUS., middle next column) **$55-65**

Two-Handled Reamer with Dogs

Two-handled Reamer with Chicks Scene

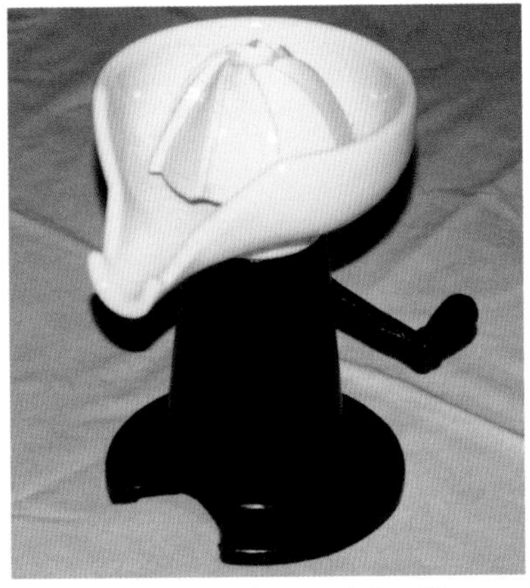

Handy Equipment Lemon Juicer/Reamer

Ceramic & metal, cast iron & porcelain, lemon-type, crank handle on metal base, "Handy Equipment Corp. Bridgeport Conn," 7 3/4" h. (ILLUS.) **$300**

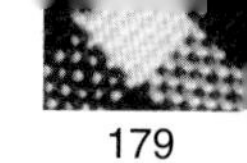
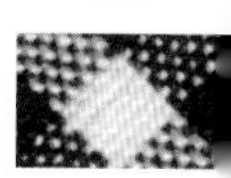

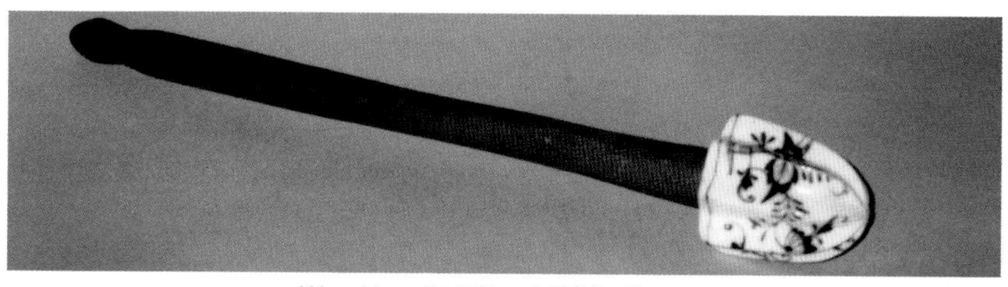

Wood-handled Blue & White Reamer

Ceramic & Metal Presto Juicer

Ceramic & metal, white bowl on green base, Presto Juicer National Electric Appliance Corp. Bridgeport, Conn., 7 5/8" h. (ILLUS.) **$60-75**

Ceramic w/sterling silver trim, three-piece w/tray, white ground w/orange flowers, green leaves, rust trim, marked "France," 5" h. **$225-250**

Ceramic & wood, blue & white cone w/wood handle, 10 1/8" l. (ILLUS., top of page) **$150-175**

Ceramic & wood, blue & white cone, 8 3/4" wooden handle, Germany **$275**

Federal Fluted Amber Orange Reamer

Glass, amber transparent, fluted sides & loop handle, orange reamer, Federal, 6 1/2" d. (ILLUS.) **$45**

Federal Glass Amber Reamer

Glass, amber transparent, ribbed panels w/loop handle, Federal Glass Co., 6 1/4" d. (ILLUS.) .... **$**

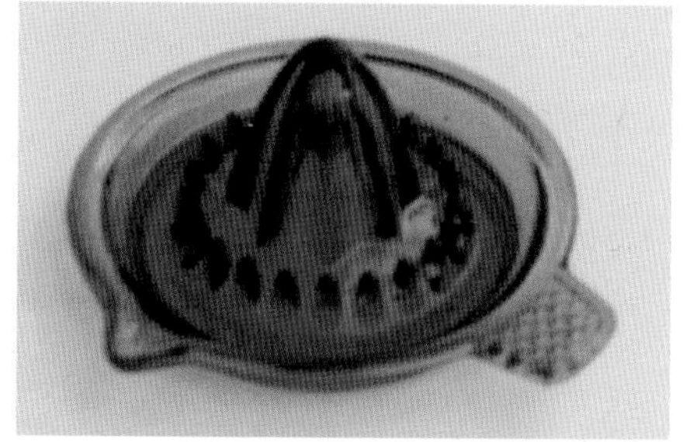

Amber Tab-handled Glass Reamer

Glass, amber transparent, saucer-shaped w/diamond-patterned side tab handle, inner seed dam knobs (ILLUS.) **$30-40**

Federal Glass Reamer with Tab Handle

Glass, amber transparent, saucer-shaped w/tab handle, one-piece,

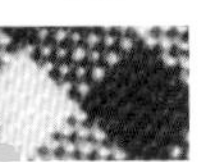

ribbed sides, Federal Glass Company, 5 1/4" d. (ILLUS.) **$20-25**

Saunders Black Glass Reamer

Glass, black opaque, round shape w/pointed cone, angled handle, marked "Saunders Reamer Pat. Appl'd For," 6 1/8" d. (ILLUS.) **$1,750-2,000**

Glass, black opaque, round w/square loop handle, embossed "Sunkist," marked "Pat. No. 18764 Made in USA," McKee Glass Co., 6" d. **$700-750**

Glass, black opaque, round w/square loop handle & large, flat grapefruit reamer cone, McKee Glass Co., 6" d. **$1,250-1,350**

Blue Delphite Jenny Ware Glass Reamer

Glass, blue Delphite, Jenny Ware, lemon squeeze, Jeanette Glass Co., 5 1/8" d. (ILLUS.) **$75-90**

Fenton Blue Opaque Reamer

Glass, blue opaque, footed rounded body w/tiny spout, loop handle, reamer cone in cover, Fenton Art Glass Co., 6 3/8" h. (ILLUS.) **$3,000-3,800**

Glass, blue opaque, saucer-shaped, ruffled edge & tab handle, 5" d. **$110-120**

Glass, blue opaque, saucer-type, Fenton Art Glass Co., 6 3/8" h. **$3,000-3,800**

Butterscotch Glass Reamer

Glass, butterscotch, embossed "SUNKIST," marked "Pat. No. 18764 Made in USA," McKee Glass Co., 6" d. (ILLUS.) **$700-850**

Glass, Chalaine Blue, embossed "Sunkist," orange reamer, marked "Pat. No. 18764 Made in USA," McKee Glass Co., 6" d....... **$350**

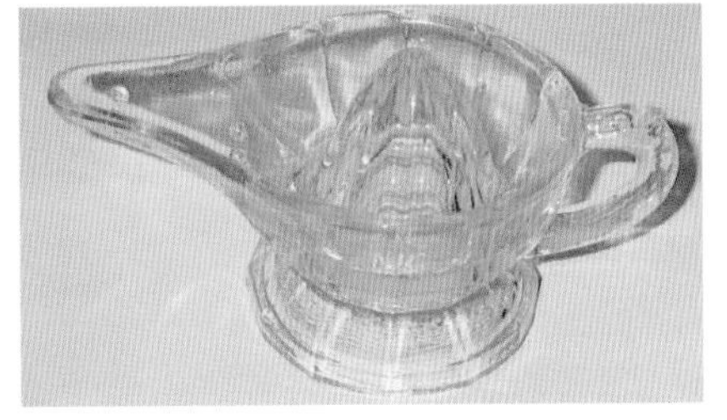

Spouted Glass Reamer on Pedestal Base

Glass, clear, boat-shaped, long spout, C-form handle, on short pedestal base, 3 1/4" h. (ILLUS.) **$40-55**

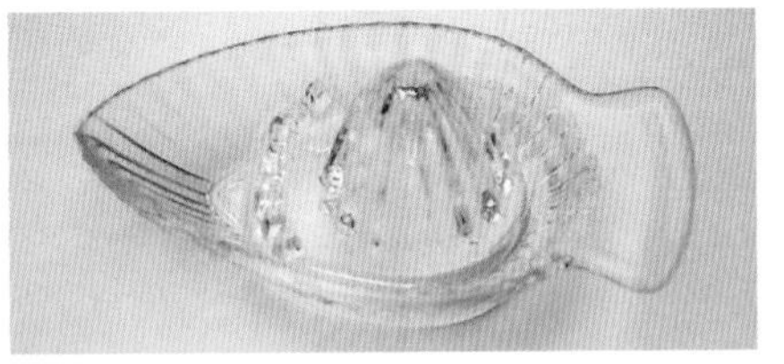

Clear Glass Boat-shaped Reamer

Glass, clear, boat-shaped, w/long spout & tab handle, ridged sides, seed dam, 3 7/8" w. (ILLUS.).................................. **$45-60**

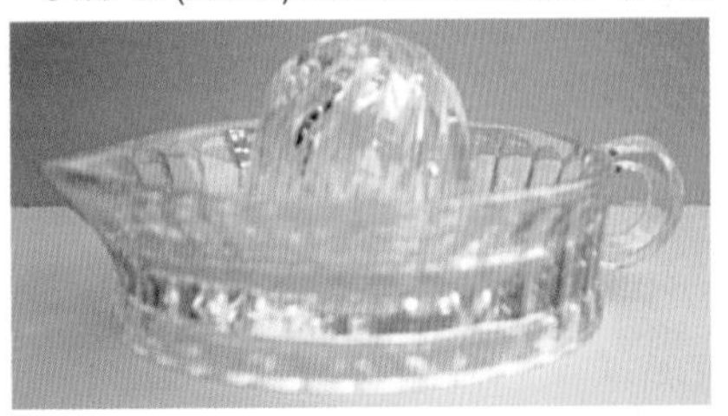

Clear Ribbed "Monster" Reamer

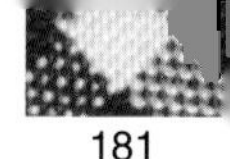

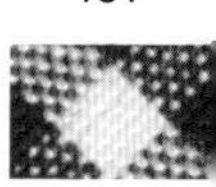

Glass, clear, deep ribbed sides, swirled cone, called the "monster," 6 3/4" d. (ILLUS., previous page) **$35-45**

Glass, clear, Jenny Ware, loop handle, Jeannette Glass co., 5 1/2" d. **$90-125**

Glass Lemon Squeezer - Reamer

Glass, clear, "Little Handy Lemon Squeezer," marked "Silver & Co., New York Pat. APD For", 6 1/2" l. (ILLUS.)................ **$100-125**

Pacific Coast Glass Works Reamer

Glass, clear, round shape w/fluted sides, loop handle, marked "Sunkist Oranges Lemons," Pacific Coast Glass Works, 6" d. (ILLUS.) **$40-50**

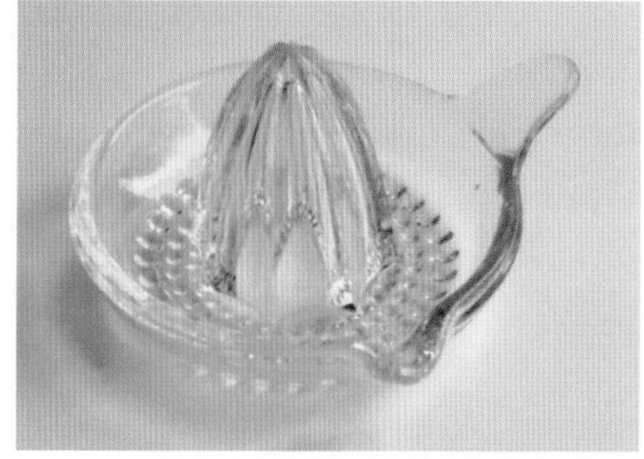

Clear Nickel Plate Glass Hobnail Reamer

Glass, clear, saucer-style, oblong tab handle & Hobnail pattern on bottom, Nickel Plate Glass Co., 4" d. (ILLUS.) **$30-40**

Glass, clear, saucer-type w/small loop handle, Cambridge Glass Company, 4 1/8" d.. **$15-20**

Glass, clear, two-piece w/removable reamer cone, square loop handle, marked "Jerrie Juicer - Avoid Hot Water"........ **$550-600**

Glass, clear, two-piece, Westmoreland Glass Company, 4 5/8" h. **$60-70**

Glass, clear, w/square loop handle, embossed "Valencia" on front, 6" d......... **$185-225**

Rare Blue Criss Cross Orange Reamer

Glass, cobalt blue, Criss Cross patt., orange reamer, Hazel Atlas Glass Co., 6 1/8" d. (ILLUS.) **$250-300**

Glass, Crown Tuscan pink (pink opaque), embossed "SUNKIST" & marked "Pat. No. 18764 Made in USA," McKee Glass Co., 6" d. **$300-400**

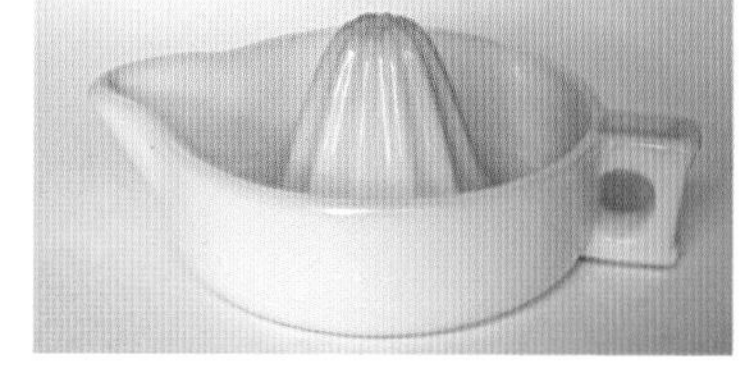

Custard McKee Sunkist Orange Reamer

Glass, custard, embossed "Sunkist," orange reamer, McKee Glass, 6" d. (ILLUS.)........... **$85**

McKee Custard Grapefruit Reamer

Glass, custard, grapefruit reamer, McKee Glass, 6" d. (ILLUS.)................................ **$245**

Edna Barnes Red Glass Reamer

Glass, dark transparent red, two-piece, paneled base & round reamer top, limited edition by Edna Barnes, marked on the bottom w/a "B" in a circle, 3 1/2" h. (ILLUS., previous page) **$35-40**

Glass, deep orangish Amberina, saucer-shaped, limited edition by Edna Barnes, marked on the bottom w/a "B" in a circle, 2 1/2" d. (ILLUS. right with pale blue opaque reamer, top of page 184)........... **$15-20**

Glass, French Ivory, footed saucer-shaped w/loop handle, McKee Glass Company, 5 1/2" d. **$30-35**

Glass, frosted clear, two-piece, decorated w/"Baby's Orange," 4 1/4" h. **$45-60**

Glass, green opaque, long pointed cone, embossed "Saunders," 6 1/8" d. **$1,400-1,600**

Pale Green Tuf-Glass Oranger Reamer

Glass, green pale transparent w/deep straight sides w/a wide spout & side tapering tab handle, oranger reamer w/unusual pointed cone, Tuf-Glass (ILLUS.) **$175**

Green Glass Ribbed Fry Reamer

Glass, green transparent, double-ribbed w/loop tab handle, Fry, 6 1/4" d. (ILLUS.) **$65**

Glass, green transparent, ribbed w/loop handle, Anchor Hocking Glass Company, 6" d. **$20-25**

Green Hazel Atlas Criss Cross Reamer

Glass, green transparent, saucer-shaped, raised ringed foot w/Criss Cross patt. saucer & a swirled rib reamer cone, Hazel Atlas Co., 6 1/8" d. (ILLUS.) **$25-35**

Glass, green transparent, saucer-shaped w/loop handle, embossed "Valencia" on the front, 6" d. **$190-250**

Glass, green transparent, saucer-shaped, w/ridges & tab handle, Anchor Hocking Glass Co., 5 3/8" d. **$20-25**

Green Measuring Cup Reamer

Glass, green transparent, two-cup measuring cup base w/peg handle, two-piece, 5 1/8" h. (ILLUS.) **$50-65**

Glass, green transparent, two-cup measuring pitcher base & reamer top, Hazel Atlas Glass Co., 5 3/4" **$30**

Glass, greenish yellow slag, loop handle, fleur-de-lis embossed on side, 6 1/4" d. **$425-500**

McKee Jade Green Lemon Reamer

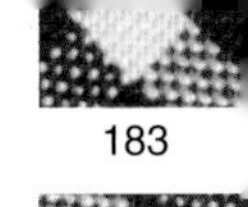

Glass, Jade green, saucer-shaped lemon reamer, McKee Glass Co., 6" d. (ILLUS., previous page) **$25-35**

Fenton Jade Green Pitcher-Reamer

Glass, Jade green, two-piece measuring pitcher base, footed bulbous body w/reamer cover, Fenton Art Glass Co., 6 3/8" h. (ILLUS.) **$1,000-1,200**

Jennyware Jadite Lemon Reamer

Glass, Jadite, Jenny Ware, saucer-shaped lemon-type, Jeannette Glass Co., 6" d. (ILLUS.).. **$25-35**

Jeannette Jadite Orange Reamer

Glass, Jadite, saucer-shaped w/loop handle, orange reamer, smaller of two sizes made, Jeannette, 5" d. (ILLUS.).................. **$65**

Jeannette Reamer with Measuring Cup

Glass, Jadite, two-cup measuring cup base, two-piece, Jeannette Glass Co., 6 1/4" h. (ILLUS.)... **$55-65**

Blue Glass Reamer

Glass, light blue transparent, saucer-shaped w/seed dam & tab handle, 4 3/4" d. (ILLUS.) **$100-120**

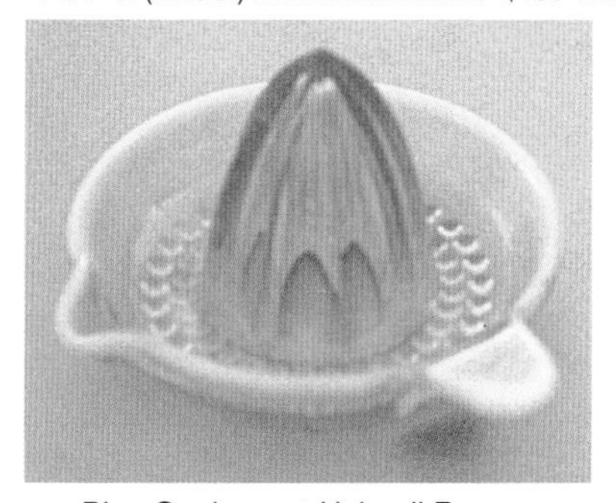

Blue Opalescent Hobnail Reamer

Glass, light blue & white opalescent, saucer-shaped w/tab handle & Hobnail patt. in bottom, 4" d. (ILLUS.) **$150-165**

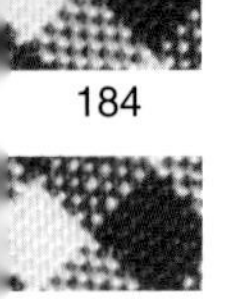

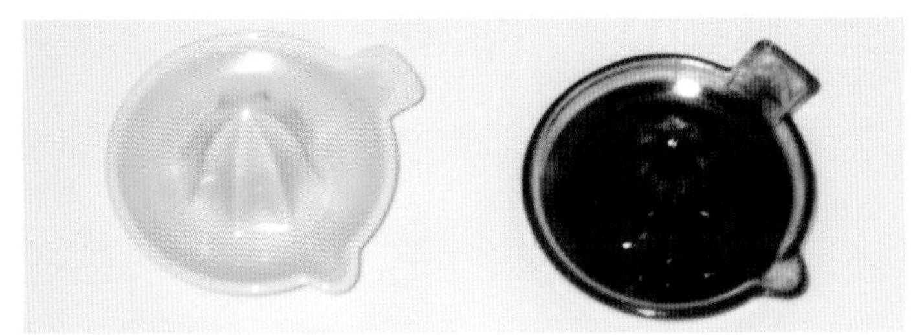

A Pale Blue & Amberina-colored Reamer by Edna Barnes

Glass, milk glass, embossed "SUNKIST," " McKee Glass Co., 6" d. ... **$15**

Glass, milk glass, embossed Valencia, 6 1/4" d. ... **$100**

Glass, milk glass, one-piece, deep sides w/swirled ribs, twin-spout, side handle, 3 1/4" h. ... **$35-50**

Glass, milk glass, saucer-shaped w/loop handle, w/embossed fleur-de-lis emblem on the front, 6 1/4" d. ... **$85-115**

Glass, milk glass, two-cup measuring pitcher base w/a thin red & black stripe, reamer top w/red stripe trim, two-piece, Hazel Atlas Glass, 5 3/8" h. ... **$65**

Glass, milk glass, two-piece w/two handles, printed color images of Jack & Jill on the side, 4 1/2" h. ... **$60-70**

Glass, off-green transparent, Tuf-Glass, "slick" handle, 6 1/2" d. ... **$85-115**

Glass, opalescent Crown Tuscan pink, embossed "SUNKIST" & marked "Pat. No. 18764 Made in USA," McKee Glass Co., 6" d. ... **$375**

Opalescent Ribbed Fry Reamer

Glass, opalescent, one-piece, ribbed sides & tab/loop handle, Fry Heat Resisting Glass, 6 1/4" d. (ILLUS.) ... **$20-30**

Glass, opalescent white, embossed "SUNKIST" & marked "Pat. No. 18764 Made in USA," McKee Glass Co., 6" d. ... **$95-135**

Glass, pale blue opaque, saucer-shaped, limited edition by Edna Barnes, marked on the bottom w/a "B" in a circle, 2 1/2" d. (ILLUS. left with Amberina-colored reamer, top of page) ... **$15-20**

Glass, pink transparent, embossed on the side "SUNKIST," orange reamder, marked "Pat. No. 18764 Made in USA - McKee Glass Co.," 6" d. ... **$95**

Hex Optic Pitcher-Ice Bucket-Reamer

Glass, pink transparent, pitcher-style, two-piece, Hex Optic patt. pitcher-ice bucket base w/reamer top, 5" d., 9" h. (ILLUS.) ... **$95**

Paden City Party Line Pitcher-Reamer

Glass, pink transparent, pitcher-style, two-piece, "Party Line Measuring Set," four-cup measure on one side, etched flowers on other, Paden City Glass Co., 8 3/4" h. (ILLUS., previous page) **$150-175**

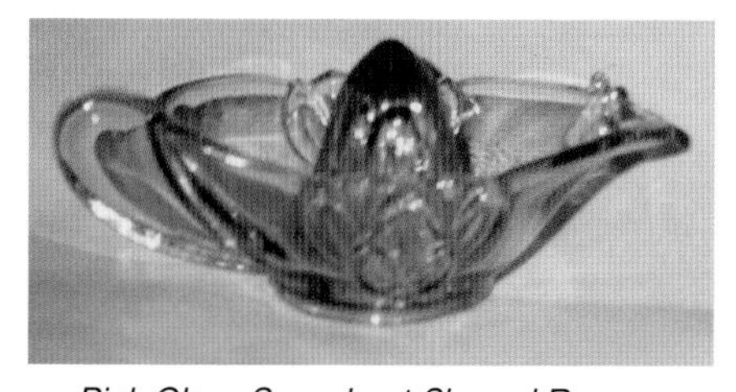

Pink Glass Sauceboat-Shaped Reamer

Glass, pink transparent, sauceboat-shaped w/scallop design, 3 1/4" d. (ILLUS.) **$100-125**

Pink Glass Jeannette Reamer

Glass, pink transparent, saucer-shaped, concentric rings forming the base w/a tab side handle, orange reamer, Jeannette Glass Co., 5 7/8" d. (ILLUS.).................. **$40-50**

Glass, pink transparent, saucer-shaped, one-piece w/tab handle, Jeannette Glass Company, 5 7/8" d. **$40-50**

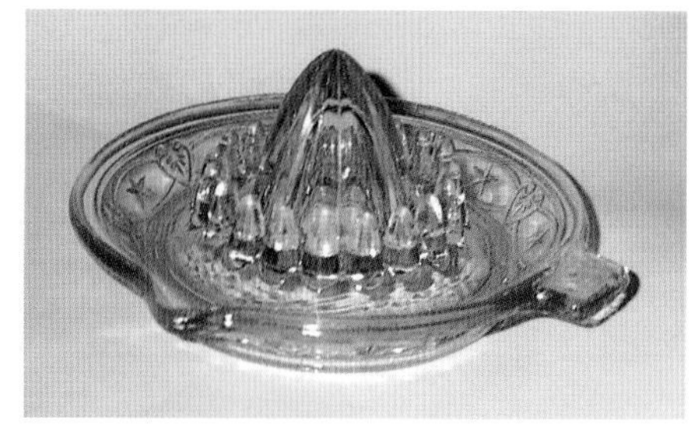

Pink Stars & Hearts Glass Reamer

Glass, pink transparent, saucer-shaped w/molded stars & hearts design around the sides, tab handle, 4 7/8" d. (ILLUS.) **$60-75**

Hazel Atlas Pink Ribbed Reamer

Glass, pink transparent, saucer-shaped w/ribbed sides & squared loop rim handle, Hazel Atlas Glass Co., 5 5/8" d. (ILLUS.) **$50-65**

Glass, pink transparent, two-cup measuring cup base & reamer top, two-piece, Hazel Atlas Glass Company, 5 3/8" h. **$140-160**

Glass, pink transparent, two-cup measuring pitcher base & reamer top, two-piece, U.S. Glass Company, 5" h. **$50-65**

Glass, red transparent, saucer-shaped, Fenton Art Glass Co., 6 3/8" h. **$1,300-1,500**

Glass, ruby red, two-piece measuring pitcher-style, bulbous pitcher w/reamer top, Fenton Art Glass Co., 6 3/8" h. **$1,300-1,500**

Yellow Milk Glass Grapefruit Reamer

Glass, Seville Yellow, one-piece, grapefruit-type, McKee Glass Company, 6" d. (ILLUS.)... **$225-275**

Glass, Skokie Green, embossed "SUNKIST," " McKee Glass Co., 6" d.................... **$85**

Ultramarine Jenny Ware Glass Reamer

Glass, Ultramarine, Jenny Ware, Jeannette Glass Co., 5 1/4" d. (ILLUS.) **$100-135**

Glass & metal, amber glass tall tapering base w/metal reamer top, "Party Line - Speakeasy Cocktail Shaker," No. 156, Paden City Glass Co., 9 1/4" h. **$95-125**

Glass & metal, green metal base w/milk glass bowl, ceramic cone, marked "Sunkist Jucit Refined," electric, 8 3/4" h. **$45-55**

Glass & Metal Servmor Juice Extractor

Glass & metal, green transparent glass measuring cup base w/hinged metal handled top, marked "Servmor Juice Extractor Patented" U.S. Glass Co., ca. 1930s, 5" h. (ILLUS.) **$75**

Glass & metal, green transparent glass tall tapering base w/metal reamer top, "Party Line - Speakeasy Cocktail Shaker," No. 156, Paden City Glass Co., 9 1/4" h. (ILLUS., top next column) **$75-85**

Glass & silver, clear pressed glass w/embossed silver trim on base, loop handle, France, 3 1/4" d. (ILLUS., middle next column) **$85-100**

Paden City "Speakeasy Cocktail Shaker"

Silver-trimmed Clear Glass Reamer

Goldplate Footed Boat-shaped Reamer

Goldplate, boat-shaped on wide low pedestal foot, wide arched end spout, long loop handle, tall reamer on interior, mark of Lynn Silversmith, 4" l. (ILLUS.) **$90-100**

Goldplate, three-piece cocktail shaker, marked "Made in Italy," 9" h. **$75-100**

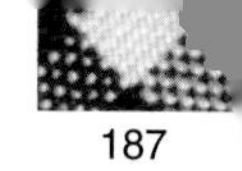

Cast Aluminum Saucer-shaped Reamer

Metal, cast aluminum, saucer-shaped w/seed barriers & two spouts, long handle w/hanging hole, 6" w. (ILLUS.) **$45**

Metal, countertop tilting screw-on type, marked "Seald Sweet Juice Extractor," 13" h. **$55-65**

Metal, hand-held, marked "Lemon Squeezer," 6 3/4" l. **$8-10**

Metal, hand-held model, Foley, 8 1/4" l. **$2-4**

Metal & Wood Kwik Way Reamer

Metal, one-piece w/hinged top & green wooden handle, marked "Kwik Way Products Inc., Pat No. 1743661," 7 1/2" l. (ILLUS.) **$10-15**

Metal, red enamel base, Juice-O-Mat Single Action model, 8 1/2" h. **$12-18**

Metal, sauceboat-shaped, gold plate outside, silver plate inside, Lyn-Silversmith, 4" d. **$95-125**

Metal, white enamel base w/chrome body, top & handle, marked "Juice-O-Mat Tilt Top," 7" h. **$12-18**

Metal, hinged back handle to plunger-type mechanism painted cream, above reamer fitted on cylindrical metal container, Super Juicer, Household Products Mfg. Co., ca. 1940s, 6" h. (ILLUS., top next column) **$25**

Metal & glass, green metal cylindrical base on a chrome band, milk glass bowl w/long side spout & ceramic cone, marked "Sunkist Juicit Refined," electric, 8 3/4" h. (ILLUS., middle next column) **$40-45**

All-Metal Super Juicer Reamer

Metal & Glass Sunkist "Juicit" Reamer

Metal & glass, hinged black metal w/clear glass insert, marked "Williams," 7 3/4" l. **$50-75**

Metal & glass, green transparent glass bowl & cone, green metal frame w/crank handle & table clamp, "Mount Joy, 11" h. **$165-185**

Metal & plastic, metal top w/bottom cranks, gold plastic base, marked "L.E. Mason Co., Boston, Mass. - Mason Seald Sweet Juicer," 7 1/2" h. **$15-25**

Dur-X Fruit Juice Extractor & Corer

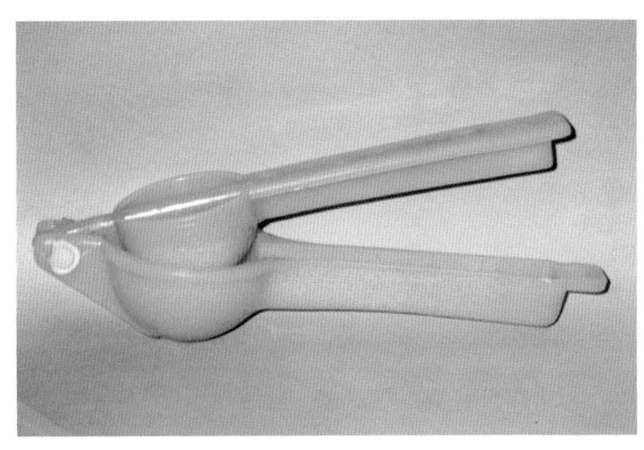

Plastic Long-Handled Yellow Reamer

Plastic, Dur-X Fruit Juice Extractor & Corer, w/original box, marked "Kwiki-P1 Juicer Pat. Pend.," 2 3/4" h. (ILLUS., previous page) **$6-8**

Plastic, model of fish, yellow w/red eye, marked "SQUEEZEIT CORP., Morris Heights 53, N.Y.C., Pat. Pend.," 4" l. ... **$8-12**

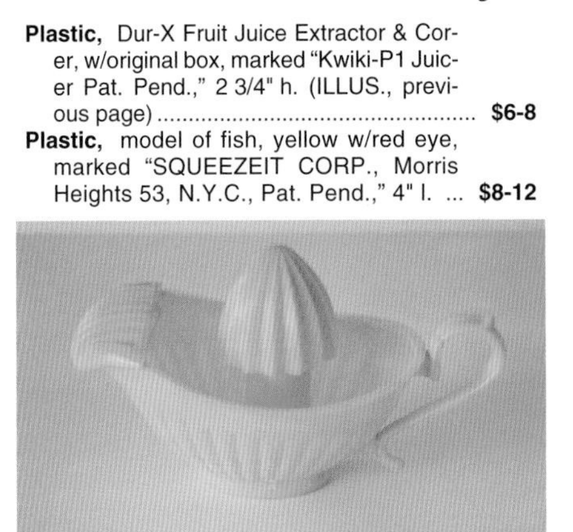

Boat-Shaped Plastic Reamer

Plastic, one-piece, boat-shaped (ILLUS.)...... **$5-8**

Plastic, yellow, hinged w/long handles, 8" l. (ILLUS., top of page).................................. **$4-6**

Plastic & Bakelite Reamer

Plastic & Bakelite, saucer-type, green base w/tab handle, metal strainer & Bakelite cone, marked "Pressitor, Brev. Dep." on handle & "Brev Suisse" on base, 5 3/4" d. (ILLUS.) **$40-50**

Enameled Cocktail Shaker/Reamer

Silver plate, cocktail shaker/reamer, tapering cylindrical sides w/black & red enamel stripes, metal reamer on top, marked "Germany," 5" h. (ILLUS.) **$85-100**

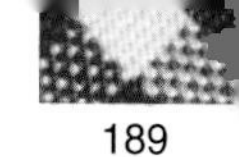

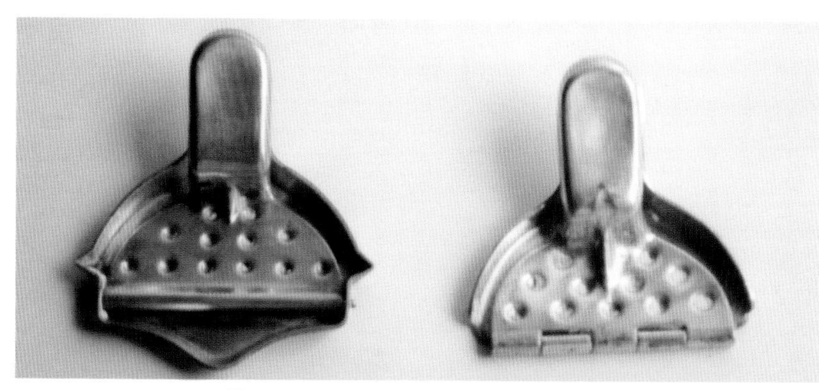

Silver Plate & Stainless Steel Lemon Slices

Silver plate, half-round scoop-style lemon slice w/tab handle, 3" l. (ILLUS. left with stainless steel lemon slice) **$15**

Silver Plate Nutcracker-style Reamer

Silver plate, hinged nutcracker-style w/long spiral-twist handles, 10" l. (ILLUS.) **$55-75**

Silver Plate Reamer with Hammered Finish

Silver plate, low cylindrical saucer-style, hammered finish, wide rim spout & squared loop handle, marked "T&T, NS, 30 66, Hand Hammered," 5 1/8" d. (ILLUS.) **$100-125**

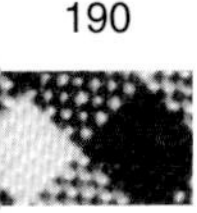

Silver Plate CS Co. 20 Reamer

Silver plate, low cylindrical saucer-style, marked "CS Co 20," 6 5/8" h. (ILLUS.).. **$75-100**

Embossed Silver Plate Reamer

Silver plate, low saucer-style, engraved design on sides, hammered finish on interior, marked "Apollo, E.P.N.S., Made in USA By Bernard Rice's Sons, Inc., 4492, Etchardt, Design Pat'd. Apr 22, '24," 4 3/4" d. (ILLUS.) **$125-150**

Silver Plate Figural Bird Reamer

Silver plate, model of bird, Muss Bach, 4 1/2" l. (ILLUS.)..................................... **$15-20**

Silver plate, sauceboat-shaped, gold-plated exterior, silver plate interior, Lyn-Silversmith, 4" d. **$95-125**

Meriden Silver Plate Teapot Reamer

Silver plate, teapot-style, two-piece, marked "Meriden S.P. Co. International S. Co.," 5 1/8" h. (ILLUS.) **$100-125**

Silver plate, teapot-style, two-piece, marked "T&T - Hand Hammered," 4" h. **$125-150**

Bernard Rice Silver Plate Reamer

Silver plate, two-piece, simple round shape base w/leaf-form tab handle, marked "Apollo EPNS, Made By Bernard Rice's Sons, Inc., 5230," 2 3/4" h. (ILLUS.) **$125-150**

Shallow Silver Plate Reamer

Silver plate, shallow saucer-style w/pointed spout & thin ring handle, 4" d. (ILLUS.) **$125-135**

Silver Plate Gravy Boat "Meriden" Reamer

Silver plate, gravy boat-style, marked "Meriden S.P. Co. International Silver Co." 4 5/8" d. (ILLUS.) **$85-100**

Silver plate & wood, a round wood platform base centered by a silver plate drip pan, supporting reamer raised on curved slender legs, hinged long-handled top, England, 7 3/4" h. (ILLUS., top next page) **$175-200**

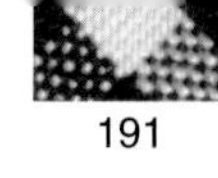

English Silver Plate & Wood Reamer

Stainless steel, half-round scoop-style lemon slice w/tab handle, 3" l. **$8-10**

Stainless steel, model of a bird, 4" l. **$8-12**

Stainless Steel Lemon Slice Squeezer

Stainless steel, shallow long boat-form w/hinged lemon slice squeezer, 5" l. (ILLUS.) **$6-8**

Gorham Sterling Silver Reamer

Sterling silver, saucer-shaped, open tab handle, marked “Black Starr - Gorham Sterling 909,” 4 1/4" d. (ILLUS.) **$225-275**

Wood, hand-held, hinged back w/small hole strainer, 12" l. **$35-50**

Wood, hand-held w/ribbed reamer cone, ca. 1850, 5 3/4" l. **$35-45**

Wood, hinged, hand-held, 10" l. **$40-50**

Wood & ceramic, hand-held type w/ceramic bowl & hinged wood top w/reamer cone, 9 1/2" l. **$35-45**

Chapter 12

Three Cartoon Character Shaker Sets

Salt & Pepper Shakers - Novelty Figurals

All are ceramic unless otherwise noted.

Astro Boy & Astro Girl, cartoon character-type, Japan, 1980s, pr. (ILLUS. right with Popeye & Olive Oyl and Pixie & Dixie sets, top of page) **$150**

Babies Salt & Pepper Shakers

Babies, one sitting w/nodder head, other reclining on back, 4" h., pr. (ILLUS.) **$38**

Black bartender condiment set, bartender holds a tray in each hand w/a foaming mug of beer forming the shakers, his head lifts off to form condiment dish, 4 1/4" h., the set (ILLUS., top next page) **$365**

Black chefs advertising "The Royal, Boise, Idaho," marked on their hats "Smokquee," 3 1/2" h., pr. (ILLUS., top next column)... **$200+**

Advertising Black Chef Shakers

Black Children Baseball Players

Black children baseball players, chalkware, 3" h. (ILLUS.) **$65**

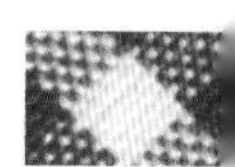

Black Bartender Condiment Set

Bottle of pop & box of popcorn, miniature, 2" h., pr. **$15**

Miniature Bowling Pin & Ball Shakers

Bowling pin & ball, miniature, 1 1/2" h., pr. (ILLUS.) **$28**

Boy & girl kissing, plastic, one-piece, Hong Kong, each (ILLUS. of two, top next column) **$5**

Bunny "Snuggle-Hugs," yellow, Regal China by Van Tellingen, pr. **$40**

Carpet sweepers, metal, one black, one white, 2" h., pr. **$20**

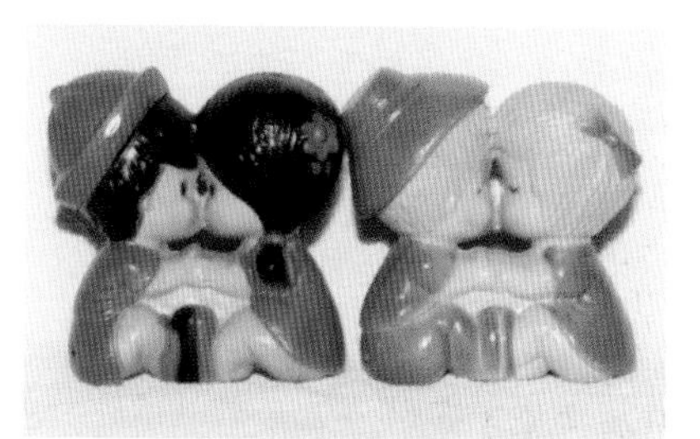

Plastic One-piece Shaker Sets

Cash Register & Coins Shakers

Cash register & stack of coins, 2 1/4" h., pr. (ILLUS.) **$20**

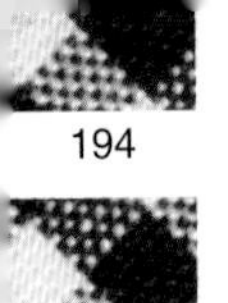

Cat Holding Fish Shakers

Cat holding fish, one of a series set of animals w/hearts on their faces, 5" h. (ILLUS.) **$35**

Cat with Fireplace Condiment Set

Cat w/fireplace condiment set. cat divides in two to form shakers, fireplace form condiment holder, 5" h., the set (ILLUS.) **$35**

Clowns on circus balls, nodder-type, 4" h., pr. **$300**

Miniature Coca-Cola Bottle & Hot Dog

Coca-Cola bottle & hot dog, miniature, 1 1/2" h., pr. (ILLUS.) **$38**

Croquet set, plastic, USA, the set (ILLUS. right with plastic flowerpot and old fashioned sewing machine, bottom of page) **$40**

Three Figural Plastic Shaker Sets

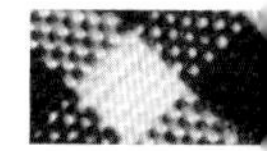

Anthropomorphic Style Figural Shaker Sets

Dust Pan Head ladies, anthropomorphic-style, PY Japan, pr. (ILLUS. left with Idaho "Spud" heads & tomato head kids, top of page) **$85**

Dutch Boy & Dutch Girl "Snuggle-Hugs," Regal China by Van Tellingen, pr. **$65**

Elf, Twin Winton, 6 1/2" h., pr. **$60**

Fair Trylon & Perisphere, Bakelite, souvenir of the New York 1939 World's Fair, 3" h., pr. **$35**

Flowers & flowerpot, plastic, USA, the set (ILLUS. center with croquet set & old fashioned sewing machine, previous page) **$18-20**

Garfield & Arlene, w/original paper tag, 3 1/4" h., pr. **$70**

Girl Exiting Cake Salt & Pepper Set

Girl exiting cake, Clay Art, 4" h., the set (ILLUS.) **$23**

Golliwog Driving Car Shaker Set

Golliwog driving car, England, 4" h., the set (ILLUS.) **$95**

Guitar & accordian, miniature, 1" h., pr. **$25**

"Happy Homer," advertising-type, for Staggs-Bilt Homes, Phoenix, Arizona, 1,000 sets made, Japan, 1950s, pr. (ILLUS. far left with Heintz Ketchup & Pillsbury sets, top next page) .... **$225+**

Staggs-Bilt, Heinz & Pillsbury Advertising Shakers

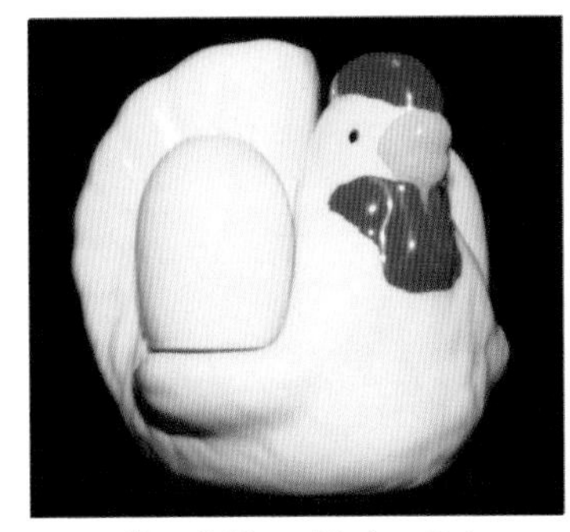

Hen & Eggs Shaker Set

Hen & eggs, white egg shakers sit on wings of white hen w/red comb & wattle, yellow beak, black eyes, tail acts as napkin holder, China, the set (ILLUS.) **$8**

Hen on nest & rooster, by Metlox, pr. **$45**

Hitchhiker & brown bag, 3 1/2" h., pr. **$15**

Santa & Mrs. Claus Human Beans

Human Beans, dressed like Santa & Mrs. Claus, Enesco, 3 1/2" h., pr. (ILLUS.) **$19**

Humpty Dumpty, nursery rhyme theme, eggs sit on low wall, Japan, pr. (ILLUS. left with Rub-A-Dub-Dub and Jonah and the Whale sets, top next page) **$20**

Idaho "Spud" Heads, anthropomorphic-style, Japan (ILLUS. center with Dust Pan Head ladies and tomato head kids, top of page 195) **$65**

Indian couple in round drum, nodder-type, 4" h. **$35**

John F. Kennedy in rocking chair, black trousers, 4" h., the set **$50**

Jonah & the Whale, story theme, small figure of Johan inside the whale, Japan, pr. (ILLUS. right with Humpty Dumpty & Three Men in a Tub sets, top next page) **$25**

Katzenjammer Kids, one-piece, by Goebel, Germany, 3" h. **$500**

Ketchup bottles, plastic, advertising-type, "Heinz Tomato Ketchup," red w/yellow cap & black & white label, Hong Kong, pr. (ILLUS. center back with Staggs-Bilt & Pillsbury sets, top of page) **$10**

Las Vegas Showgirl with Dice Shakers

Las Vegas showgirl w/dice, England, 5" h., the set (ILLUS.) **$75**

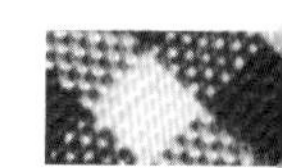

Nursery Rhyme & Story Salt & Pepper Sets

Loch Ness Monster Condiment Set

Little Bo Peep, Relco nursery rhyme series, Japan, pr. **$35**

Little Red Riding Hood, Relco nursery rhyme series, Japan, pr. **$40**

Loch Ness Monster condiment set, head & tail form condiment holders, two humps form the salt & pepper shakers, Sylvac, England, 4" h., the set (ILLUS., second from top of page) **$95**

Love Bug "Snuggle-Hugs," grey, 3 5/8" h., Regal China by Van Tellingen, pr. **$50**

Man & hat, stacker-type, 3 1/2" h. (ILLUS., next column) **$25**

Margaret Thatcher & Neil Kinnock, 4" h., pr. **$55**

Mary & Little Lamb, 4" h., pr. **$55**

Matador & bull condiment set, nodder-type, 4" h., the set **$95**

Man & Hat Stacker Shakers

Fitz & Floyd Mice in Cheese Shakers

Mice in cheese, nodder-type, "Say Cheese," by Fitz & Floyd, Japan, 1980, pr. (ILLUS.) **$300-350**

Mother Goose, figure of Mother Goose flanked by white goose salt & pepper shakers, on a narrow rockwork base, three-piece set, 3" h. **$55**

Niagara Falls, souvenir-type, boat shaker on stand, removable falls forms second shaker, the set.. **$45**

Old fashioned sewing machine, plastic, w/movable parts, the set (ILLUS. left with croquet set and flowerpot, bottom of page 194)... **$25**

Padlock & keys, miniature, 1/2" h., pr. **$25**

Miniature Pancakes & Syrup Pitcher Set

Pancakes & syrup pitcher, miniature, 1" h., pr. (ILLUS.) **$29**

Perfume atomizer & powder dish, miniature, 1 1/2" h., pr. (ILLUS., top next column).. **$33**

Pillsbury Doughboy & cupcake, advertising-type, "Funfettie," pr. (ILLUS. front right with Staggs-Bilt & Heinz sets, top of page 196).. **$35**

Pixie and Dixie, cartoon character-type, Japan (ILLUS. center with Astro Boy & Girl and Popeye & Olive Oyl, top of page 192) ... **$50**

Mini Perfume Atomizer & Powder Dish

Popeye & Olive Oyl, cartoon character-type, Vandor, pr. (ILLUS. left with Astro Boy & Girl and Pixie & Dixie sets, top of page 192).. **$125**

Bone China Rabbit Shakers

Rabbits, miniature, bone china, white w/pink trim, original red & gold stickers, 2" h., pr. (ILLUS.) **$14**

Miniature Rosemeade Raccoon Shakers

Raccoons, miniature, Rosemeade Pottery, 2" h., pr. (ILLUS.) **$100**

Raggedy Ann & Andy, 4" h. **$23**

Sailor & mermaid, Van Telligen, 4" h., pr. ... **$100**

Shakespeare Bust Salt & Pepper Shakers

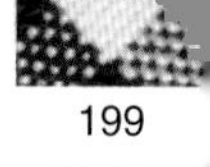

Shakespeare busts, 3 1/2" h., pr. (ILLUS., previous page) **$23**

Shoeshine boxes, metal, miniature, one black, one white, 1" h., pr. **$20**

Twin Winton Squirrel Shakers

Squirrels, Twin Winton, USA, pr. (ILLUS.) **$25**

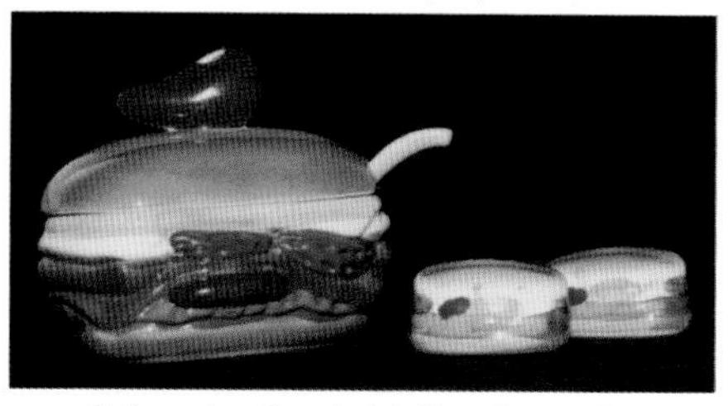

Submarine Sandwich Condiment Set

Submarine sandwiches condiment set, large sandwich w/applied red pepper forming handle of lid holds condiments, smaller sandwiches are salt & pepper shakers, Japan, the set (ILLUS.) **$22**

Swordfish, miniature, black-striped w/pink fins, marked "PY Japan," 2" h., pr. **$20**

Three Men in a Tub condiment set, nursery rhyme theme, figural shakers on a tub-shaped sugar bowl, nursery rhyme printed along the side, the set (ILLUS. center with Humpty Dumpty & Jonah and the Whale sets, top of page 197) **$65**

Tomato Head Kids, anthropomorphic-style, Japan, pr. (ILLUS. right with Dust Pan Head ladies and Idaho "Spud" Heads, top of page 195) **$20-25**

Tomato & Strawberry couple, wearing formal dress, 4" h., pr. **$50**

Turkey nodder condiment set, souvenir-type, the nodding turkey shakers atop a long rectangular base w/a center lid & ladle for condiments, base printed in color w/castle scene & "Souvenir of Casa Loma," 5" h., the set (ILLUS., bottom of page) **$95**

Two peas in a pod, Fitz & Floyd, 2" h., the set **$40**

Wee Dutch Boy & Girl Shakers

Wee Dutch Boy & Girl, Ceramic Arts Studio of Madison, Wisconsin, 3" h. & 2 3/4" h., pr. (ILLUS.) **$30-40**

Yosemite Sam, 4" h., pr. **$130**

Casa Loma Souvenir Turkey Nodder Condiment Set

Chapter 13

String Holders

String holders were standard equipment for general stores, bakeries and homes before the use of paper bags, tape and staples became prevalent. Decorative string holders, mostly chalkware, first became popular during the late 1930s and 1940s. They were mass-produced and sold in five-and-dime stores like Woolworth's and Kresge's. Ceramic string holders became available in the late 1940s through the 1950s. It is much more difficult to find a chalkware string holder in excellent condition, while the sturdier ceramics maintain a higher quality over time.

Apple, ceramic, handmade, 1947 .... **$45**
Apple, chalkware.. **$35**
Apple, chalkware, elongated shape........... **$35-55**
Apple w/face, ceramic, "PY"......................... **$125**
Apple with berries, chalkware, common........ **$30**

Apple with Worm String Holder

Apple with worm, chalkware, "Willie the Worm," ca. 1948, Miller Studio (ILLUS.) **$45**

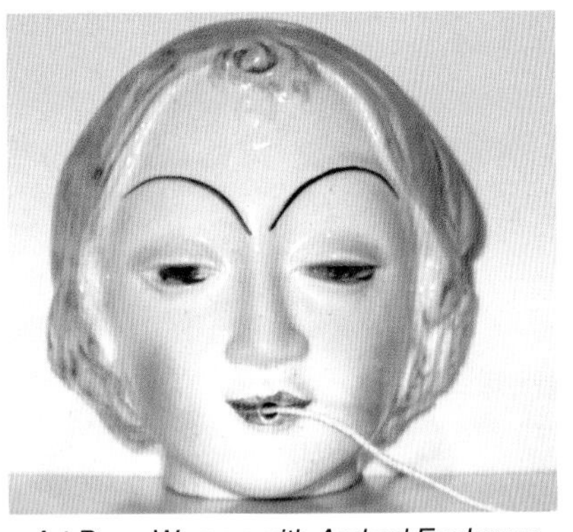

Art Deco Woman with Arched Eyebrows

Art Deco woman, arched eyebrows, blonde bobbed hair (ILLUS.).................................. **$85**

Art Deco Woman String Holder

Art Deco woman, chalkware, green beret & scarf (ILLUS.)... **$120**

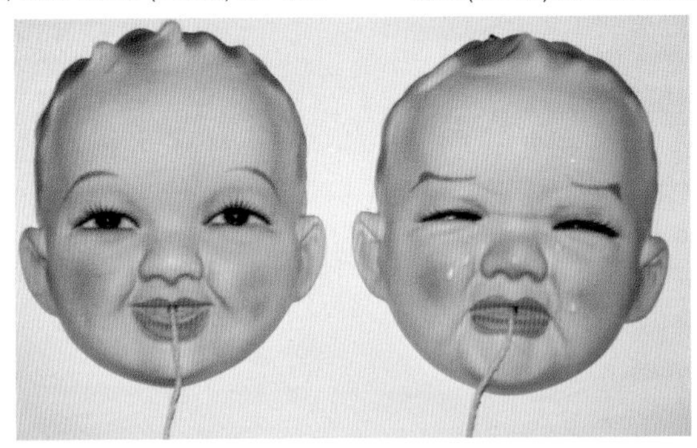

Baby Face String Holders

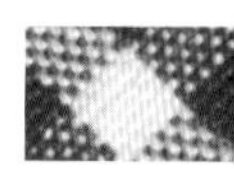

Babies, ceramic, heads only, one crying, one happy, Lefton, pr. (ILLUS., bottom previous page) **$175**
Baby, chalkware, frowning **$95**
Balloon, ceramic, variety of colors, each **$25**
Bananas, chalkware, ca. 1980s-present **$25**

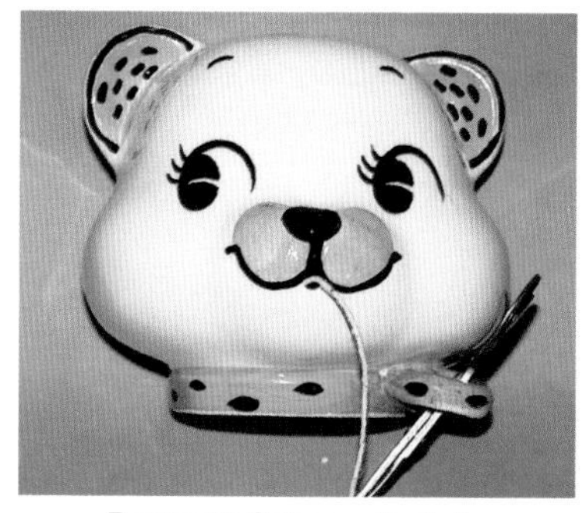

Bear with Scissors In Collar

Bear, w/scissors in collar, ceramic, Japan (ILLUS.) **$35**

Goebel Bears Egg Timer

Bears, ceramic, brown & tan, white base, Goebel (ILLUS.) **$135**
Betty Boop, chalkware, original **$400**
Bird, ceramic, green, "Arthur Wood, England," also found in blue & brown **$15**
Bird, ceramic, green, scissors fit in tail, Japan **$30**
Bird, ceramic, in birdhouse, "String Swallow" (ILLUS., top next column) **$45**
Bird, ceramic, yellow bird on green nest, embossed "String Nest Pull," Cardinal China, U.S.A. **$45**
Bird, chalkware, peeking out of birdhouse **$150**
Bird, heavy pottery, brown **$25**
Bird & birdhouse, wood & metal **$35**
Bird in birdcage, chalkware (ILLUS., middle next column) **$75**
Bird on birdhouse, chalkware, cardboard, "Early Bird," bobs up & down when string is pulled, handmade **$25**
Bird on branch, ceramic, Royal Copley **$45**

"String Swallow" Bird String Holder

Bird in Birdcage String Holder

Bird on branch, wooden, w/birdhouse **$25-45**
Bird on nest, ceramic, countertop-type, Josef Originals **$35**
Birds in a cage, chalkware, two birds **$95-125**

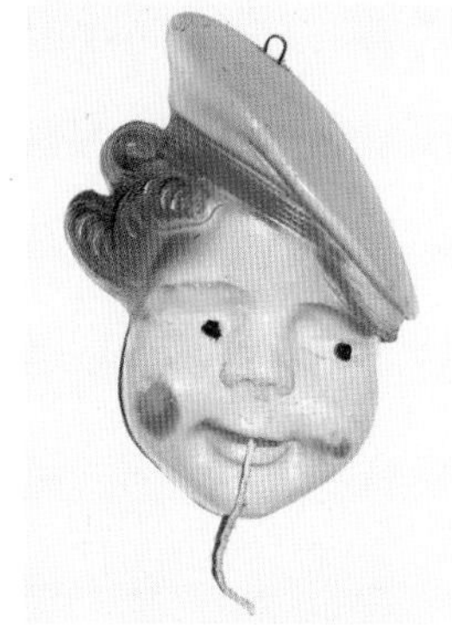

Boy with Tilted Cap

Boy, w/tilted cap, chalkware (ILLUS.) **$95**

Boy, w/top hat and pipe, eyes to side, chalkware $45
Brother Jacob and Sister Isabel, chalkware, newer vintage, each $55

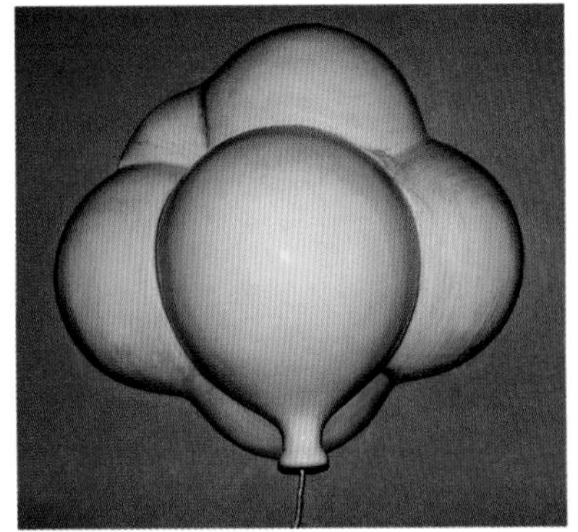

Bunch of Balloons String Holder

Bunch of balloons, ceramic, green, pink & blue, ca. 1983, Fitz & Floyd (ILLUS.) $35

Bunch of Fruit String Holder

Bunch of fruit, chalkware (ILLUS.) $150
Butler, ceramic, black man w/white lips & eyebrows, Japan, hard to find $150

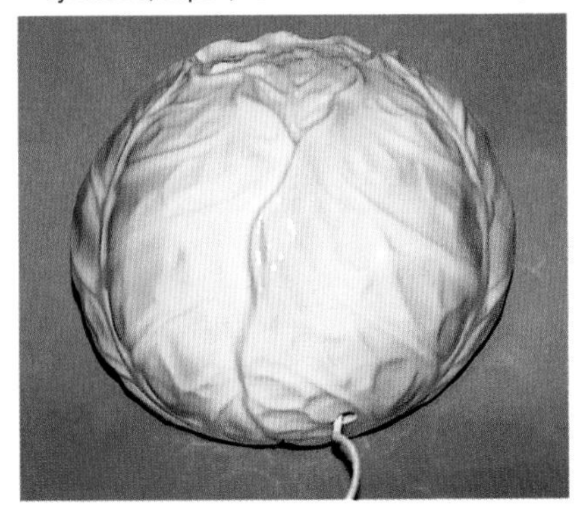

Cabbage String Holder

Cabbage, ceramic, Japan (ILLUS.) $95
Campbell Soup boy, chalkware, face only .. $150

Black Cat with Gold Bow

Cat, ceramic, black w/gold bow, handmade (ILLUS.) $35
Cat, ceramic, black w/yellow bow $25
Cat, ceramic, brown $25
Cat, ceramic, climbing a ball of string $50

Holt Howard String Holder

Cat, ceramic, climbing ball of string, Holt Howard (ILLUS.) $85
Cat, ceramic, full-figured, "Horton Ceramics" $25
Cat, ceramic, full-figured w/flowers & scissors $35
Cat, ceramic, head only, black w/green eyes (ILLUS., next page) $45

Cat Face Ceramic String Holder

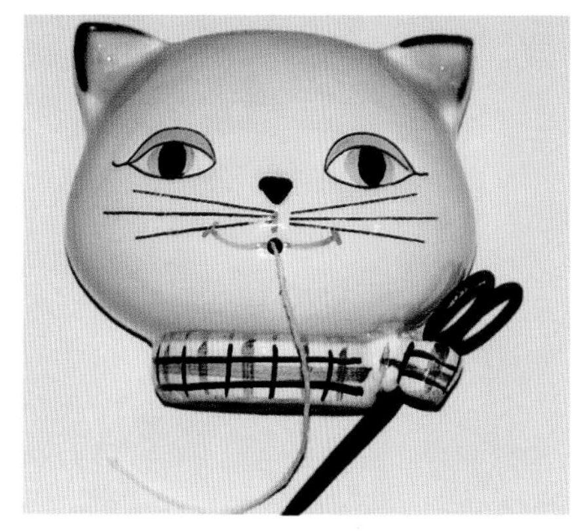

Holt Howard Cat String Holder

Cat, ceramic, head w/scissors held in plaid neck ribbon, Holt Howard (ILLUS.) **$30-50**

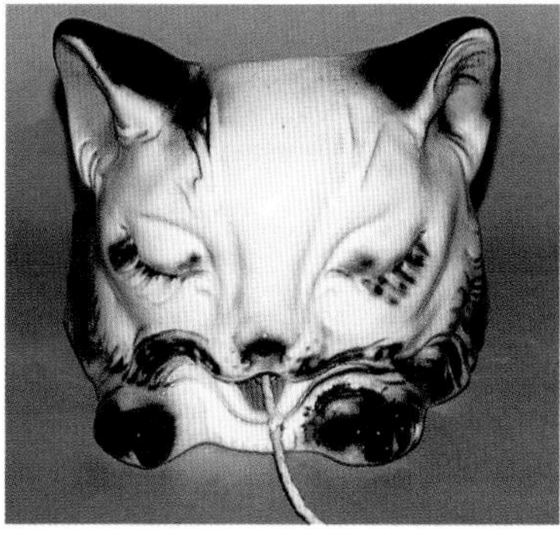

"Knitter's Pal" String Holder

Cat, ceramic, "Knitter's Pal" (ILLUS.) **$25**
Cat, ceramic, sleeping, spatterware **$25**

Cat, ceramic, w/crossed paws, white, handmade **$25-45**
Cat, ceramic, w/matching wall pocket **$50**

Cat with Plaid Collar String Holder

Cat, ceramic, w/plaid collar, space for scissors, Japan (ILLUS.) **$35**
Cat, ceramic, w/scissors in collar, "Babbacombe Pottery, England" **$20**
Cat, ceramic, w/string coming out extended paw, pearlized white glaze **$35**
Cat, ceramic, white face w/pink & black polka dot collar bow **$55**

Cat with Ball of String Holder

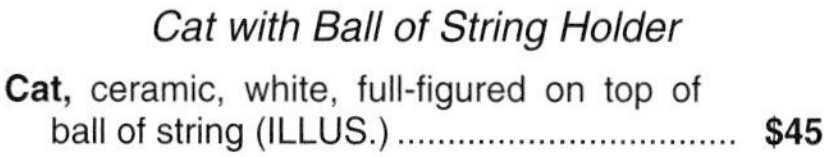

Cat, ceramic, white, full-figured on top of ball of string (ILLUS.) **$45**

Cat Face String Holder

Cat, ceramic, white, w/large green eyes, scissors hang on bow (ILLUS.) **$35**

Cat on Ball of String String Holder

Cat, chalkware, grinning, on a ball of string, Miller Studio, 1952 (ILLUS.) **$35**

Cat, chalkware, head only, black & white **$95**

Cat, chalkware, on ball of string, Miller Studio, 1948 .... **$35**

Cat, chalkware, w/bow, holding ball of string ... **$35**

Composition Cat String Holder

Cat, composition, sitting yellow cat w/red ball of string, marked "Lorrie Design, Japan" (ILLUS.)... **$35**

Cat face, ceramic, holding ball of string, found in many color combinations, handmade, some newer than others **$25**

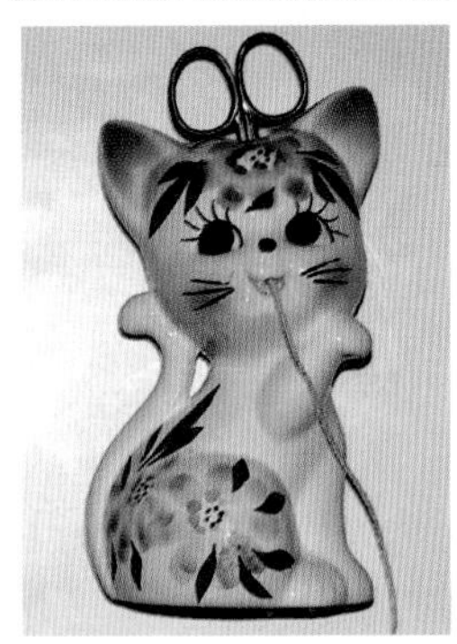

Cat with Flowers String Holder

Cat w/flowers, ceramic, scissors in head (ILLUS.)... **$35**

Cat w/paws up, ceramic, string comes out of tummy **$35**

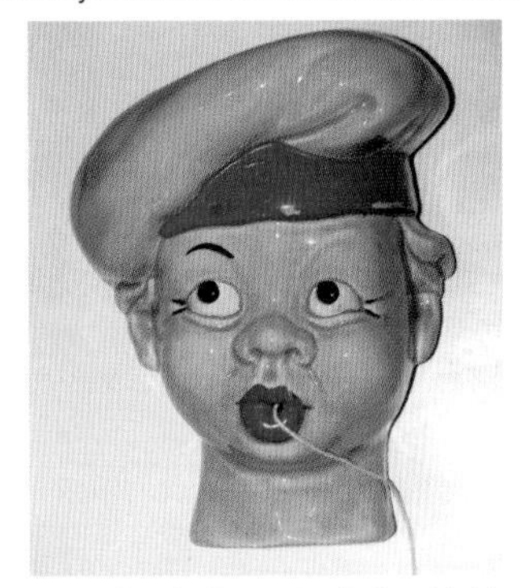

Black Chef Ceramic String Holder

Chef, ceramic, black (ILLUS.) **$175**

Light-skinned Chef String Holder

Chef, ceramic, full-figured, light-skinned, Japan, hard to find (ILLUS.)...................... **$125**

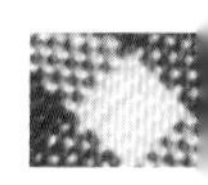

Chef, ceramic, "Gift Ideas Creation, Phila., Pa.," w/scissors in head **$25**

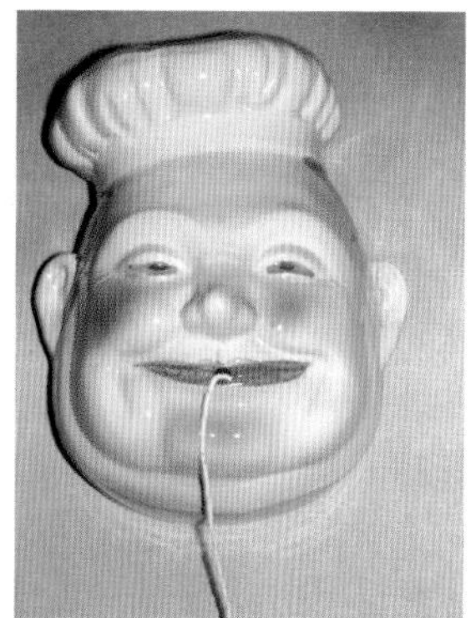

Ceramic Chef Head String Holder

Chef, ceramic (ILLUS.) **$125**

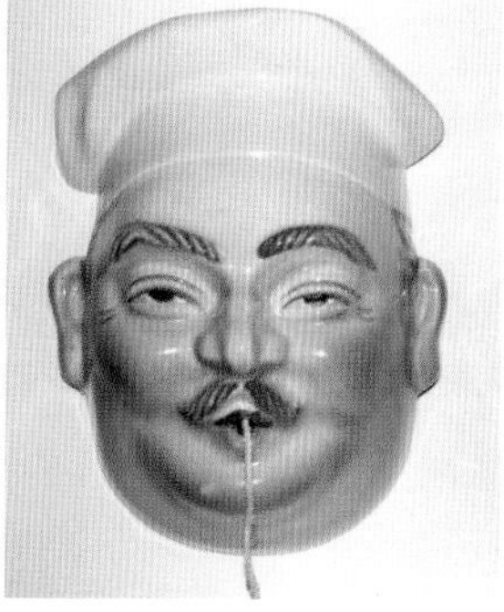

Japanese Chef String Holder

Chef, ceramic, Japan (ILLUS.) **$125**

Chef with Rosy Cheeks

Chef, ceramic, w/rosy cheeks, marked "Japan" (ILLUS.) **$28**

Chef, chalkware **$65**

Chef, chalkware, baby face w/chef's hat....... **$135**

Chef with Black Face

Chef, chalkware, black face, white hat (ILLUS.) **$125**

Chef, chalkware, chubby-faced, "By Bello, 1949," rare **$350**

Common Chef Head String Holder

Chef, chalkware, common (ILLUS.) **$35**

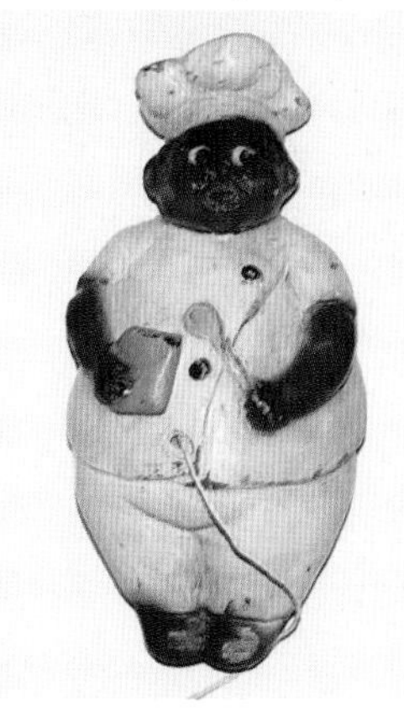

Chef with Spoon & Box String Holder

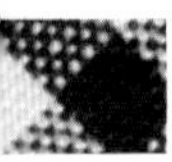

Chef, chalkware, full-figured black chef w/spoon & blue box (ILLUS., previous page) **$95**

Chef, chalkware, "Little Chef," Miller Studio, 1950s **$125**

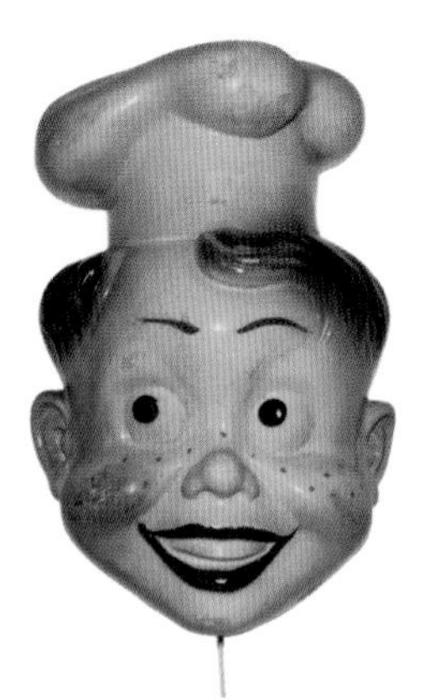

Chef with Bushy Eyebrows

Chef, chalkware, Rice Crispies (ILLUS.) **$125**

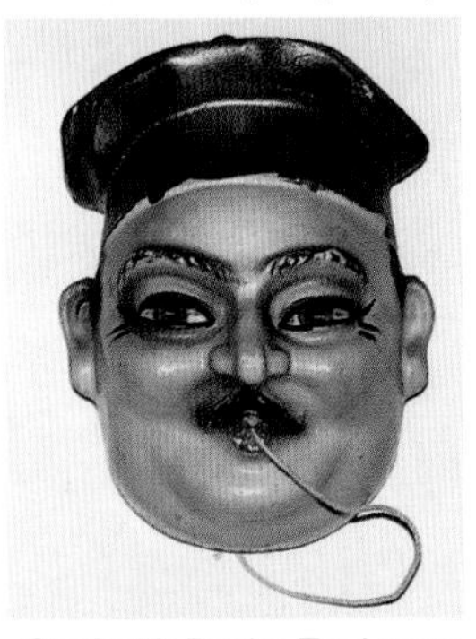

Chef with Bushy Eyebrows

Chef, chalkware, unusual version of chef w/bushy eyebrows (ILLUS.) **$75**

Chef with Large Hat

Chef, chalkware, w/large hat facing left (ILLUS.) **$95**

Chef with a Bottle

Chef w/bottle & glass, ceramic, full-figured, Japan (ILLUS.) **$95**

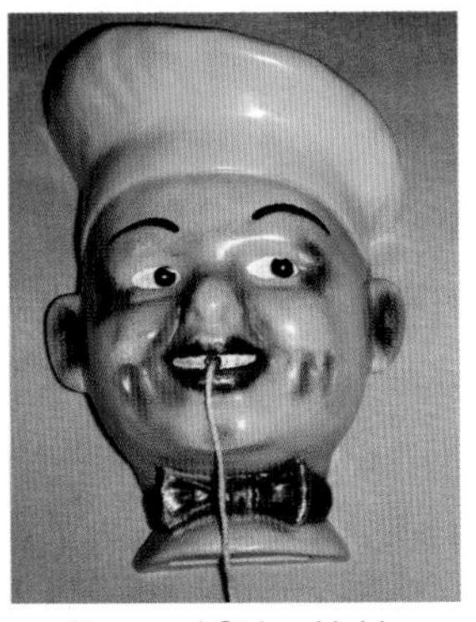

Norwood String Holder

Chef w/red bow tie, chalkware, The Norwood Co., Cincinnati, Ohio (ILLUS.) **$85**

Bunch of Cherries String Holder

Cherries, chalkware, bunch on leafy stem (ILLUS.) **$125**

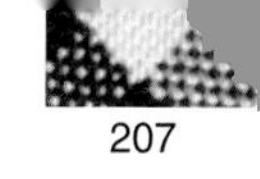
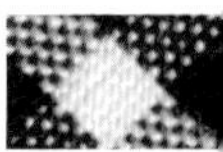

Chicken, ceramic, "Quimper of France," found in several patterns, still in production **$75**
Chicken, ceramic, unmarked **$35**
Chicken, ceramic, yellow & green w/red trim, scissors in tail, France **$65**

Chipmunk String Holder

Chipmunk's head, ceramic, white & brown, red & white striped hat & bow, bow holds scissors, Japan (ILLUS.) **$35**

Chipmunk String Holder

Christmas chipmunk, ceramic (ILLUS.) **$35**
Clown, ceramic, full-figured, "Pierrot," hand holds scissors **$65**
Clown, chalkware, "Jo-Jo," ca. 1948, Miller Studio (ILLUS., top next column) **$125**
Cow head, chalkware, Elsie the Cow (ILLUS., middle next column) **$300**
Crock, ceramic, "Kitchen String," by Burleigh Ironstone, Staffordshire, England, w/scissors in top **$45**
Darned String Caddy (The)," ceramic, marked "Fitz & Floyd, MCMLXXVI" (ILLUS., bottom next column) **$20**

Jo-Jo the Clown String Holder

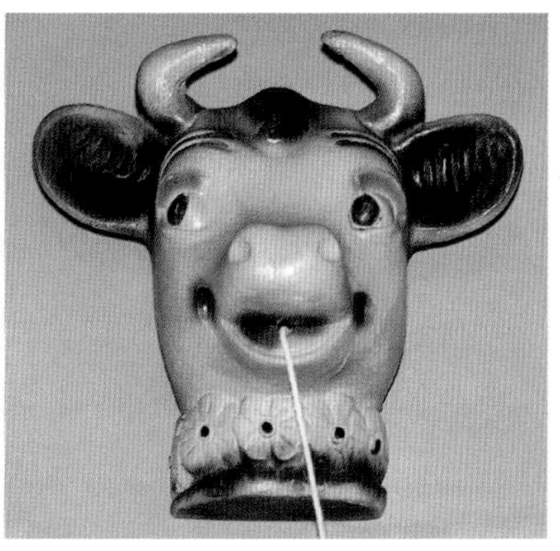

Elsie the Cow String Holder

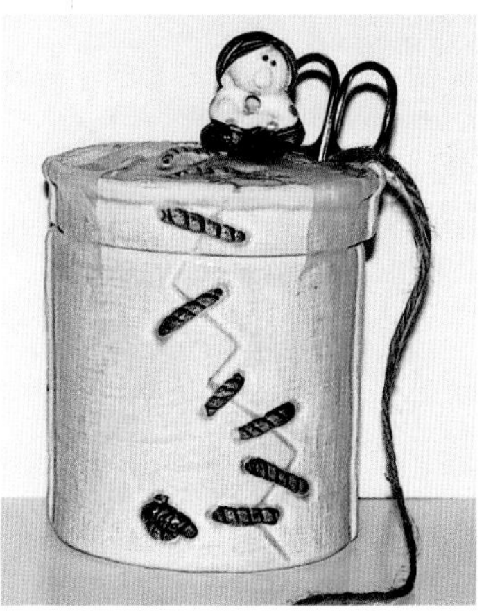

"The Darned String Caddy"

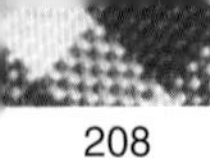

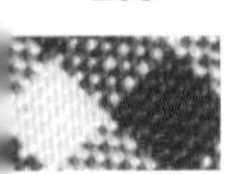

Dog, ceramic, "Bonzo," comic character dog w/bee on chest **$75**

Bonzo Face String Holder

Dog, ceramic, Bonzo face,comic character dog, marked "Japan," rare (ILLUS.) **$350**

Ceramic Boxer String Holder

Dog, ceramic, Boxer (ILLUS.) **$55**
Dog, ceramic, Collie, "Royal Trico," Japan...... **$55**
Dog, ceramic, full-figured Shaggy Dog, w/scissors as glasses, marked "Babbacombe Pottery, England" **$20**
Dog, ceramic, German Shepherd, "Royal Trico, Japan" **$55**

Dog String Holder

Dog, ceramic (ILLUS.)..................................... **$50**
Dog, ceramic, Schnauzer................................ **$95**

Scottie String Holder

Dog, ceramic, Scottie, marked "Royal Trico, Japan" (ILLUS.)... **$55**
Dog, ceramic, w/diamond-shaped eyes **$65**
Dog, ceramic, w/puffed cheeks **$25**

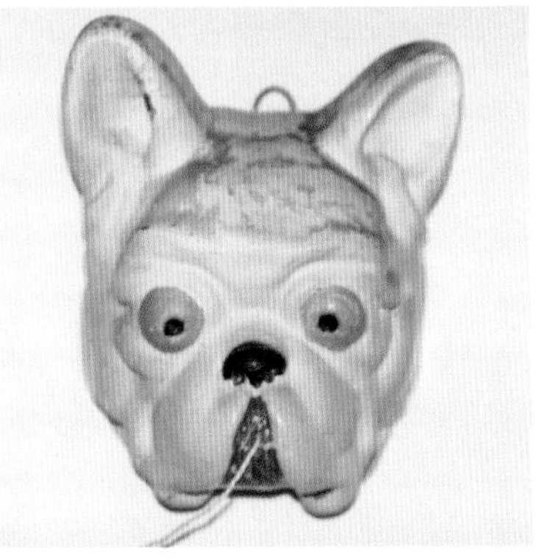

Bulldog String Holder

Dog, chalkware, bulldog w/studded collar, ca. 1933 (ILLUS.) **$95**

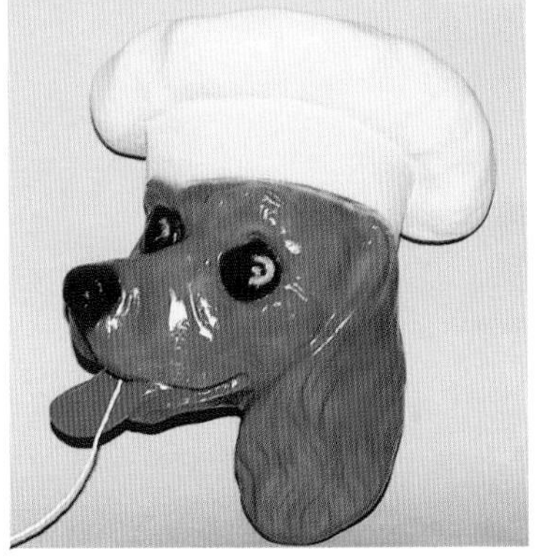

Dog with Chef's Hat String Holder

Dog, chalkware, w/chef's hat, "Conovers Original" (ILLUS., previous page).............. **$175**

Westie with Bow String Holder

Dog, chalkware, Westie, bow at neck (ILLUS.) ... **$85**

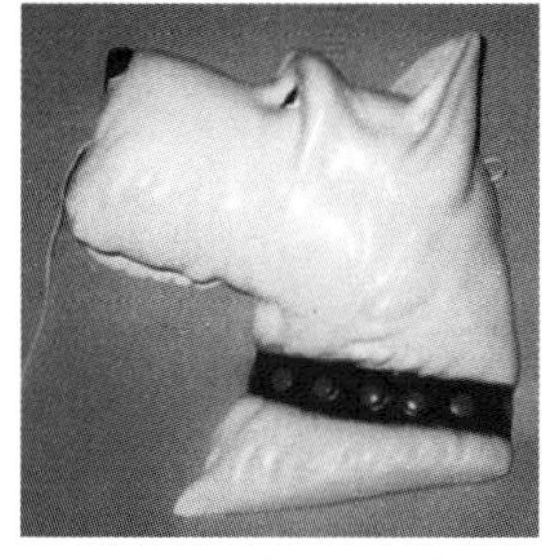

Westie with Studded Collar

Dog, chalkware, Westie, white w/studded color (ILLUS.)... **$75**

Dog, wood, "Sandy Twine Holder," body is ball of string.. **$20**

Dog with Black Eye

Dog w/black eye, ceramic, w/scissors holder in collar, right eye only circled in black, England (ILLUS.).. **$25**

Dove, ceramic, Japan **$25**

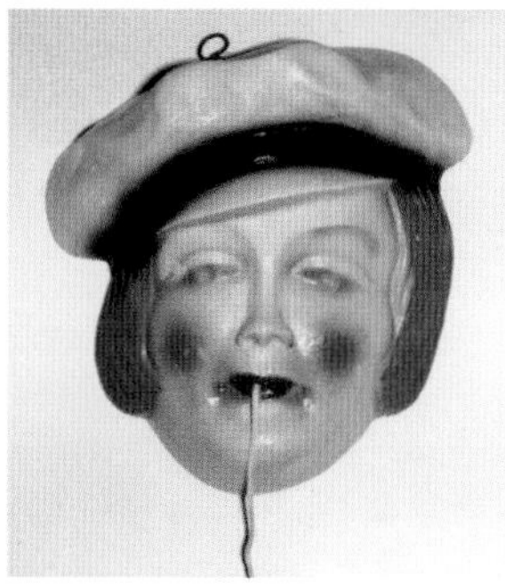

Dutch Boy String Holder

Dutch Boy, chalkware (ILLUS.)................... **$135**

Dutch Boy, chalkware, w/cap........................ **$75**

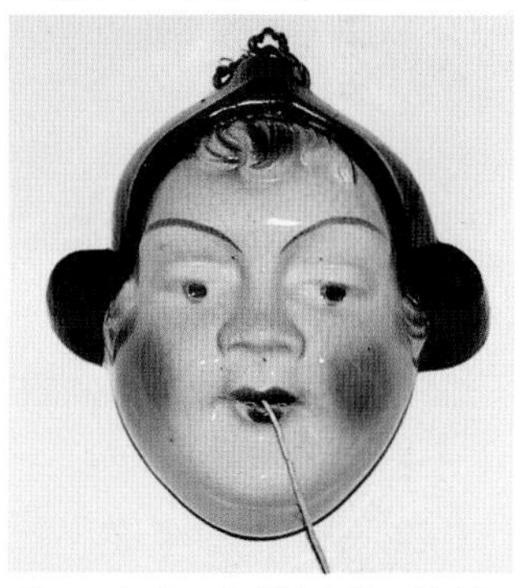

Ceramic Dutch Girl String Holder

Dutch Girl, ceramic, head only, Japan (ILLUS.) **$25**

Dutch Girl with Flowers String Holder

Dutch Girl, ceramic, w/flowers, full-figured, Japan (ILLUS.).. **$125**

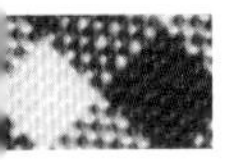

Dutch Girl, chalkware, face only, common **$35-50**

Elephant, ceramic, "Hoffritz, England" **$20**

Elephant, ceramic, marked "Babbacombe Pottery, England," scissors as glasses **$20**

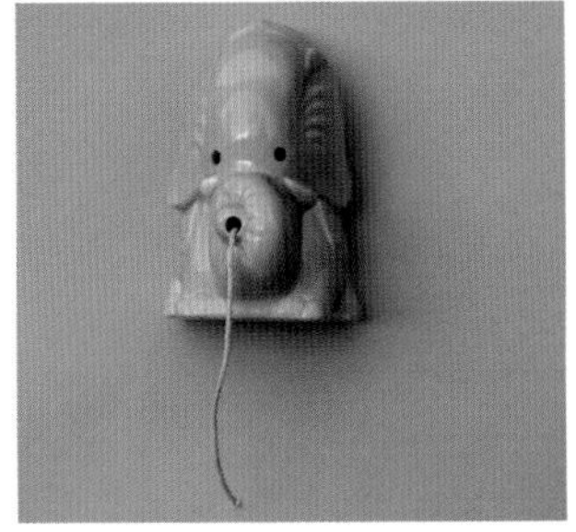

Elephant String Holder

Elephant, ceramic, white, trunk cruls holding string (ILLUS., middle next column) **$30-40**

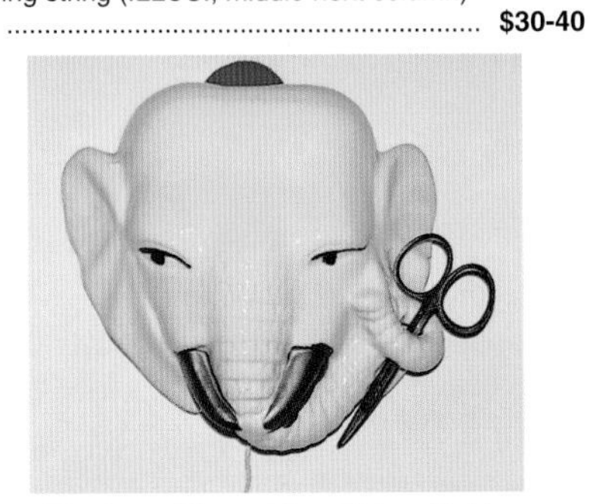

Elephant Pincushion-String Holder

Elephant, ceramic, white w/gold tusks, pincushion on head, Japan (ILLUS.)................ **$35**

Elephant, ceramic, yellow, England................ **$35**

Father Christmas String Holder

Father Christmas, ceramic, Japan (ILLUS.) ... **$95**

Flowerpot, ceramic, yellow, w/measuring spoon holder **$75**

Fox without mane, ceramic, scissors as glasses, marked "Babbacombe Pottery, England".. **$25**

French Chef String Holder

French chef, ceramic, scissors fit into hat, newer vintage (ILLUS.) **$35-40**

Chalkware Chef String Holder

French chef, chalkware, w/scarf around neck (ILLUS.) **$85**

Frog String Holder

Frog, ceramic, countertop-type, Babbacombe Pottery, England (ILLUS.) **$35**

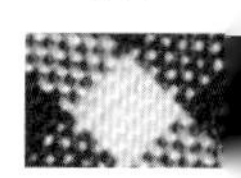

Funnel-shaped, w/thistle or cat & ball, ceramic **$35**
Girl in bonnet, chalkware, eyes to side.......... **$65**
Gollywog, bisque, England.......... **$165**
Gourd, chalkware.......... **$50**
Granny, ceramic, full-figured, top of nose holds scissors that look like glasses **$25**

Granny in Rocking Chair String Holder

Granny in rocking chair, ceramic, marked "PY," Japan (ILLUS.).......... **$65**

Grapes String Holder

Grapes, chalkware, bunch (ILLUS.) **$50**
Green pepper, ceramic, Lego sticker **$35-45**
Heart, ceramic, puffed, heart reads "You'll always have a 'pull' with me!" California Cleminsons (ILLUS., top next column).......... **$35**

Puffed Heart String Holder

Humpty Dumpty String Holder

Humpty Dumpty, ceramic, sitting on wall, white & yellow (ILLUS.).......... **$35**

Indian in Headdress String Holder

Indian w/headdress, chalkware, brightly colored (ILLUS., previous page) **$150**
Indian with headband, chalkware.............. **$175**
Iron w/flowers, ceramic................................ **$35**

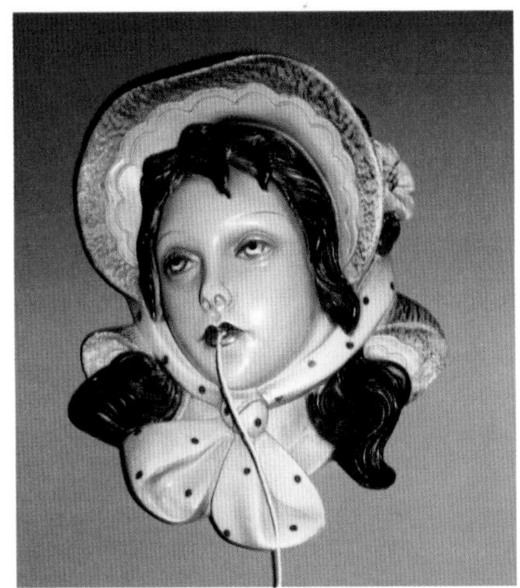

Lady in Bonnet String Holder

Lady in bonnet w/bow, chalkware (ILLUS.) **$95**
Ladybug, chalkware.. **$35**

Cleminsons House String Holder

Latchstring house, ceramic, California Cleminsons (ILLUS.).................................. **$85**

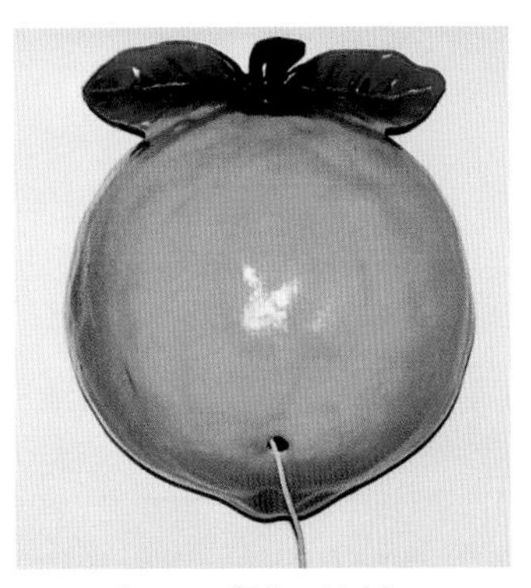

Lemon String Holder

Lemon, ceramic, Japan (ILLUS.).................... **$75**

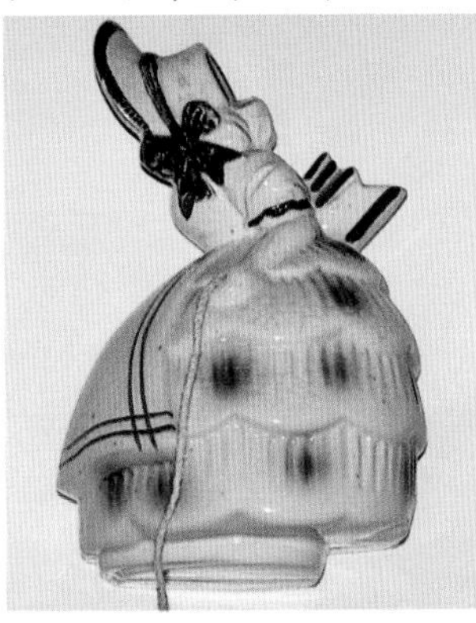

Little Bo Peep String Holder

Little Bo Peep, ceramic, white w/red & blue trim, marked "Japan" (ILLUS.) **$85**
Little Red Riding Hood, chalkware, head wearing hood **$150**

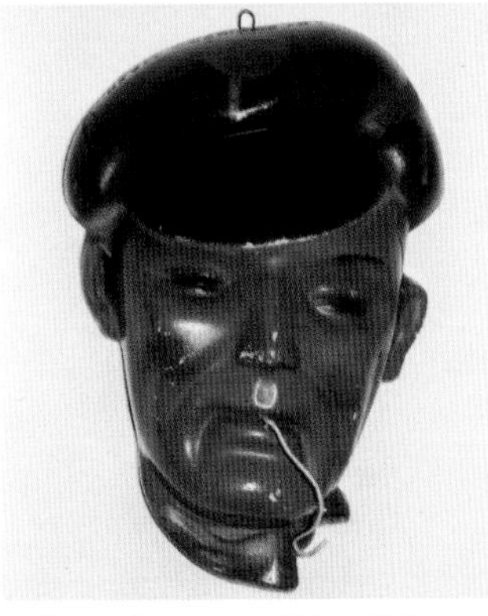

Longshoreman String Holder

Longshoreman, chalkware, marked "By Dughesne, 1940" (ILLUS.)........................ **$175**

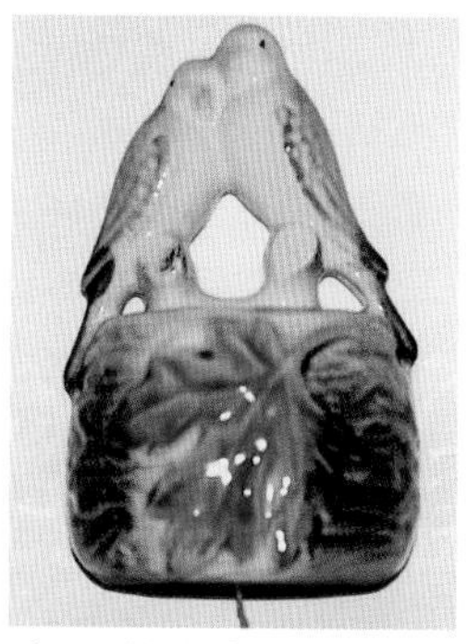

Loverbirds String Holder

Lovebirds, ceramic, Morton Pottery (ILLUS.) **$35**

Maid, ceramic, Sarsaparilla, 1984 .... **$35**

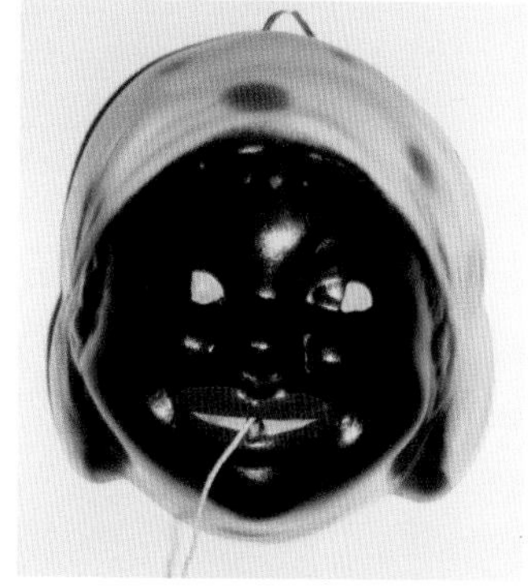

Mammy Face String Holder

Mammy, bisque, head only (ILLUS.)............. **$150**

Mammy, ceramic, full-figured, plaid & polka dot dress, Japan **$75**

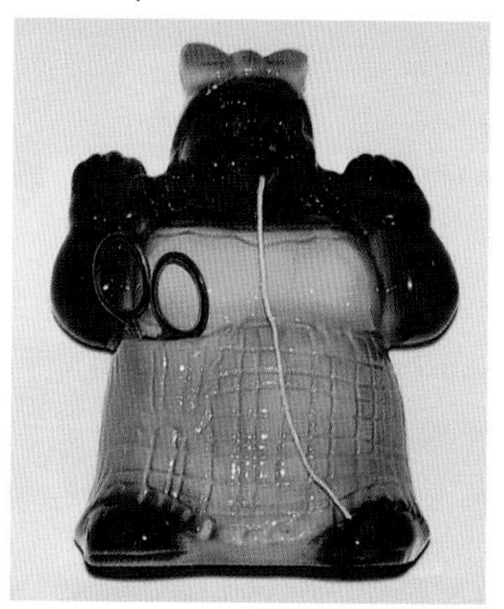

Mammy String Holder

Mammy, ceramic, full-figured, w/arms up & scissors in pocket (ILLUS.) **$100**

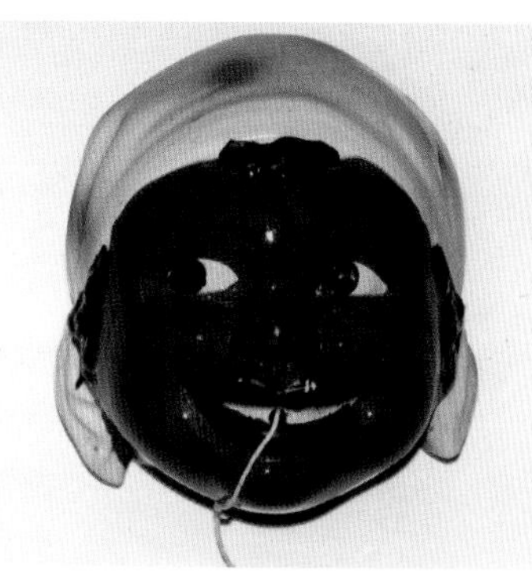

Mammy Face String Holder

Mammy, ceramic, head only, Japan (ILLUS.) . **$250**

Mammy Holding Flowers

Mammy, chalkware, full-figured, holding flowers, marked "MAPCO" (ILLUS.)............ **$95**

Mammy, chalkware, head only, many variations .... **$125+**

Mammy, chalkware, head only, marked "Ty-Me" on neck .... **$150+**

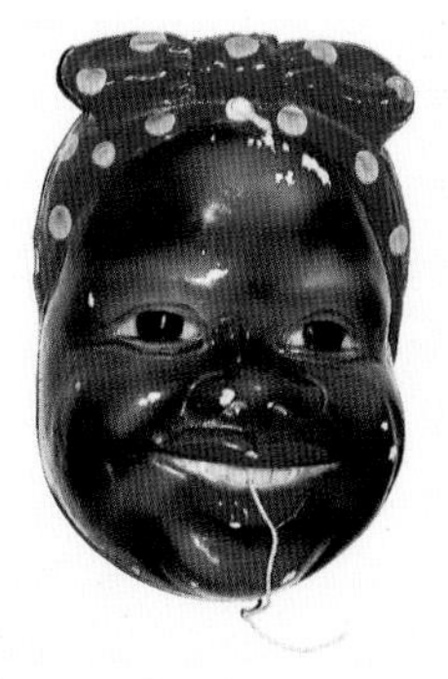

"Genuine Rockalite" Mammy

Mammy, chalkware, head only, w/polka-dot bandana, marked "Genuine Rockalite," made in Canada (ILLUS., previous page) ... **$125**

Mammy String Holder

Mammy, cloth & wood (ILLUS.) **$50**

Mammy, cloth-faced, "Simone," includes card that reads "I'm smiling Jane, so glad I came to tie your things, with nice white strings," rare **$95**

Coconut Mammy

Mammy, coconut, w/red and blue floral scarf (ILLUS.) **$20**

Mammy, felt, head only, w/plastic rolling eyes.. **$35**

Man, ceramic, head only, drunk, designed by & marked "Elsa" on back, Pfaltzgraff, York, Pennsylvania **$50**

Man, chalkware, head only, marked across collar "Just a Gigolo" (ILLUS., top next column) **$85**

Man in the Moon face, chalkware (ILLUS., middle next column)................................. **$200**

Mexican man, chalkware, head only, common **$30**

Mexican man, chalkware, head only, flower-trimmed hat (ILLUS., bottom next column)... **$60**

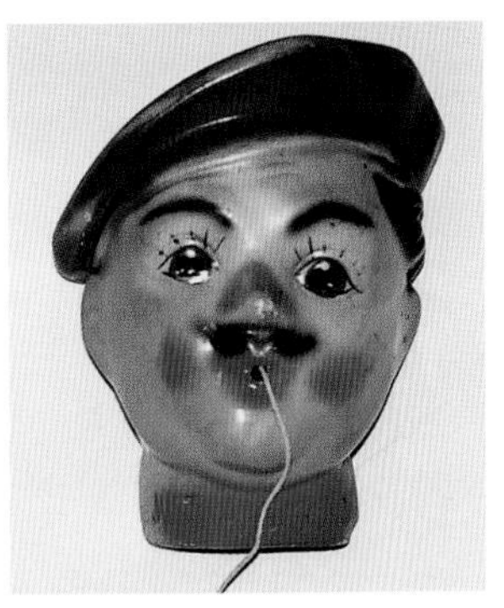

Gigolo Man String Holder

Man in the Moon String Holder

Mexican Man with Flowered Hat

Mexican woman, chalkware, head only, w/braids & sombrero **$95**

Monkey, chalkware, sitting on ball of string, found in various colors **$95**

Mouse, ceramic, countertop-type, Josef Originals sticker **$25**

Mouse, ceramic, England **$20**

Oriental man, ceramic, w/coolie hat, Abingdon Pottery .... **$250+**

Owl, Babbacombe Pottery, England **$20**

Owl, ceramic, full-figured, Josef Originals **$20**

Pancho Villa String Holder

Pancho Villa, chalkware (ILLUS.)................. **$125**
Parrot, chalkware, brightly colored.................. **$85**
Peach, ceramic.. **$25**

Chalk Peach String Holder

Peach, chalkware (ILLUS.)............................ **$35**
Pear, chalkware.. **$30**

Peasant Woman Knitting String Holder

Peasant woman, ceramic, full-figured, knitting sock, sticker reads "Wayne of Hollywood" (ILLUS.).. **$85**

Penguin, ceramic, full-figured w/scissors holder in beak, marked "Arthur Wood, England"... **$35**

Pink Pig String Holder

Pig, ceramic, hanging or countertop-type, pink (ILLUS.).. **$50**

Pig String Holder

Pig, ceramic, Holt Howard (ILLUS.)................ **$75**

Floral Decorated Pig String Holder

Pig, ceramic, white w/red & yellow flowers & green leaves decoration, scissors holder on back near tail, Arthur Wood, England (ILLUS.)... **$35**
Pig w/flowers, ceramic.................................. **$65**
Pineapple, chalkware, "Prince Pineapple," by Miller Studio **$125**
Pirate & gypsy, wood fiber, pr....................... **$95**
Porter, clay, without teeth, marked "Fredericksburg Art Pottery, U.S.A." (ILLUS., next page).. **$95**
Prayer lady, ceramic, by Enesco................. **$125**
Pumpkin Cottage, Manorware, England, ceramic **$45**

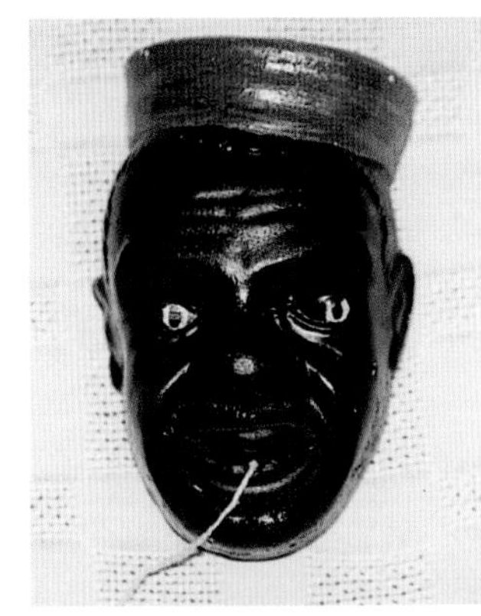

Porter String Holder

R2D2 String Holder

Robot R2D2, ceramic, countertop, newer vintage, marked "Sigma" (ILLUS.)............... **$65**

Rooster, black w/yellow & white trim, red comb & wattle, yellow beak & feet, paper label w/"Made in Japan," 10 1/4" h......... **$35-45**

Rooster, porcelain, head only, Royal Bayreuth.. **$225**

Rooster head, chalkware, red **$50**

Chalkware Rose String Holder

Rose, chalkware (ILLUS.) **$65**

Sailor Boy, chalkware.................................... **$85**

Sailor Girl (Rosie the Riveter) Holder

Sailor Girl (Rosie the Riveter), chalkware (ILLUS.)... **$145**

Santa Claus, ceramic, sitting, unmarked........ **$50**

Scottish woman, chalkware, head only, w/plaid scarf.. **$250+**

Snail String Holder

Snail, ceramic, dark brown (ILLUS.)............... **$20**

Soldier, chalkware, head only, w/hat.............. **$30**

Southern Belle String Holder

Southern Belle, ceramic, w/very full skirt, Japan (ILLUS.)... **$65**

Southern gentleman with ladies, ceramic $65

Spanish Ladies String Holders

Spanish ladies, chalkware, each (ILLUS.) $95
Strawberry, chalkware, w/white flower, green leaves & no stem $45
Susie Sunfish, chalkware, Miller Studio, 1948, many reproductions of this one - be cautious $95
Teapot, ceramic, w/parakeet, Japan $35
Teddy bear, ceramic, brown, hole for scissors in bow at neck, marked "Babbacombe Pottery, England" $20
Thatched-roof cottage, ceramic $25
Tom cat, ceramic, "Takahashi, San Francisco," Japan $25

Tomato String Holder

Tomato, ceramic (ILLUS.) $35
Tomato, chalkware $35
Tomato chef, ceramic, eyes closed, "Japan" $50
Witch in pumpkin, ceramic, winking $95

Woman in Flowered Dress String Holder

Woman, ceramic, full-figured, blue dress w/white & red flowers, Japan (ILLUS.) $50
Woman w/turban, chalkware $85

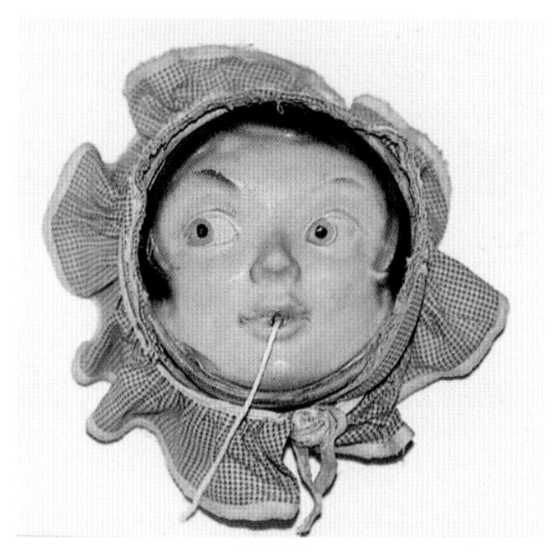

Chalkware, Cardboard & Cloth String Holder

Woman's face, chalkware on cardboard box w/cloth bonnet (ILLUS.) $50
Young black girl, ceramic, w/surprised look, Japan $135

Chapter 14

Kitchen Glassware

Federal Leaf-decorated Batter Bowl, Leftover Jar & Mixing Bowls

Glasbake Crab-shaped Baking Dishes

Baking dishes, crab-shaped, Glasbake by McKee, manufactured in the 1920s, boxed set of six (ILLUS.)........................ **$20-24**

Batter bowl, decorated post-production w/green, gold & brown leaves, Federal Glass Company, perhaps a grocery or department store promotion, batter bowl (ILLUS. far right w/leftover jar & mixing bowls, top of page)................................ **$15-25**

Fire-King Jadeite Batter Bowl

Batter bowl, Jadeite, w/spout & angled handle, 3/4" w. rim band, Fire King (ILLUS.) **$40-45**

Batter mixing bowl, milk glass w/turquoise Pennsylvania Dutch scenes, two-spout rim, Pyrex, 9" d. **$20**

Androck Beater Jar with Metal Mixer

Beater jar, clear deep ringed & ribbed bowl fitted w/a low domed metal cover w/an arched arm supporting the beater mechanism w/a red wood handle, Androck, 1930s, 6" h. (ILLUS.) **$55**

Butter dish, cov., one-pound, custard w/pressed flower on the cover, McKee Glass, 4 x 8 1/4".. **$145**

Butter dish, cov., one-pound, green transparent Criss Cross patt., domed cover, Hazel Atlans, 3 1/4 x 7 1/4"......................... **$85**

Federal Ribbed Amber Butter Dish

Butter dish, cov., one-pound size, amber rectangular low base w/tab handles &

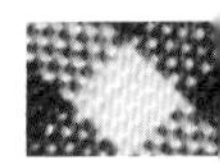

high matching cover, impressed "BOTTOM" on the base, Federal Glass Co., 3 1/4 x 5 1/2" (ILLUS.) **$45**

Butter dish, cov., quarter-pound, Jade-ite base & clear glass domed cover, Fire King **$95**

One-Pound Block Optic Butter Dish Cover

Butter dish cover, lid for one-pound butter dish, green transparent Block Optic pattern, by Hocking Glass Co., cover alone (ILLUS.) **$20-25**

Cake pan, clear, "Flamex," from Sears, Roebuck & Co., maker unknown **$10-12**

McKee Chalaine Blue Canister

Canister, Chalaine Blue, wide cylindrical base & flat fitted cover, McKee, 4 1/2" d., 2 1/2" h. (ILLUS.) **$75**

Clambroth Hoosier-style Flour Canister

Canister, clambroth Hoosier-style flour canister, wide cyindrical shaped w/heavy molded rings, flat metal lift-off cover, 7" d., 7 1/2" h. (ILLUS.) **$125**

Clear Hoosier-style Flour Canister

Canister, clear Hoosier-style flour canister, tilted rounded design w/stippled ribbing & a fitted metal cover, rests on a metal ring stand, 6" d., 9" h. (ILLUS.) **$255**

Two Clear Hoosier-type Tea Canisters

Canister, clear Hoosier-type, upright paneled design embossed "TEA," screw-on metal lid, 5" h. (ILLUS. left with Napanee square canister) **$45**

Two Clear Hoosier-type Coffee Canisters

Canister, clear Hoosier-type, upright paneled design embossed w/"Coffee," screw-on metal lid, 8" h. (ILLUS. right with Triple Skip pattern coffee canister)...... **$60**

Canister, clear Hoosier-type, upright ribbed pattern embossed w/"Coffee," screw-on metal lid, 8" h. **$55**

Canister, clear Hoosier-type, upright square Napanee-style ribbed design embossed "TEA," screw-on metal lid, 5" h. (ILLUS. right with paneled tea canister)...... **$55**

Canister, clear Hoosier-type, upright Triple Skip ribbed pattern embossed w/"Coffee," screw-on metal lid, 8" h. (ILLUS. left with paneled coffee canister) **$70**

Canister, clear Hoosier-type, upright zipper pattern embossed w/"Coffee," screw-on metal lid, 8" h. **$75**

Hocking Canister with Silhouette Scene

Canister, clear w/green silhouette decoration of old men at a table, square w/green metal screw-on cover, Hocking, 4 1/2" w., 6 3/4" h. (ILLUS.) **$65**

McKee Custard Cereal Canister

Canister, custard w/"Cereal" in black block letters, wide cylindrical shape w/flat fitted glass cover, McKee, 6 1/4" d., 6" h. (ILLUS.) **$135**

McKee Custard "Sugar" Canister

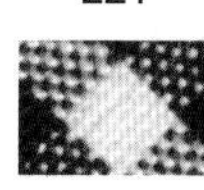

Canister, custard w/ red script "Sugar," wide cylindrical body w/fitted flat glass cover, McKee, 6 1/4" d., 6" h. (ILLUS., previous page) **$135**

Rare McKee Red Dots Tea Canister

Canister, custard w/Red Dots decoration & "Tea," square shaped w/screw-on metal cover, McKee, 28 oz., rare, 6 1/4" h. (ILLUS.) **$245**

Two Green Diagonal Rib Canisters

Canister, forest green transparent, square w/a diagonal rib design & large rectangular label panel, screw-on metal lid, Owens Glass, 20 oz., 6" h. (ILLUS. right with 40 0z. diagonal rib canister)................. **$35**

Canister, forest green transparent, square w/a diagonal rib design & large rectangular label panel, screw-on metal lid, Owens Glass, 20 oz. rice or tea size, 6" h., each **$45**

Canister, forest green transparent, square w/a diagonal rib design & narrow rectangular label panel, screw-on metal lid, Owens Glass, 40 oz., 7 1/4" h. (ILLUS. left with 20 0z. diagonal rib canister)........... **$55**

Owens Forest Green Flour Canister

Canister, forest green transparent, upright oval cylindrical shape w/fine ribbing, "Flour" in a vertical panel up the front, screw-on metal lid, Owens Glass, 8" h. (ILLUS.)... **$65**

Canister, forest green transparent, upright oval cylindrical shape w/fine ribbing, "Tea" or "Rice" in a vertical panel up the front, screw-on metal lid, Owens Glass, medium size, 6" h., each............................. **$65**

Canister, green transparent, upright flat panel shape w/scew-on metal lid, Hocking, 10 oz., 5" h. **$40**

Rare Hazel-Atlas Green Glass Canister

Canister, green transparent, upright paneled cylindrical shaped w/flat glass cover w/inset handle, Hazel-Atlas, rare, 4" w., 6" h. (ILLUS.) **$145**

Hazel-Atlas Green Art Deco Tea Canister

Canister, Jadite green fired-on color w/a stylzed floral Art Deco decoration & "Tea" in black, black screw-on cover, Hazel-Atlas, 5" h. (ILLUS.) **$95**

Canister, Jadite w/"Coffee" in black letters, cylindrical ringed shape w/screw-on metal cover, Jeannette, 40 oz. **$325**

Canister, Jadite w/"Coffee" "Tea," "Sugar," or "Cereal" in black, square w/flat cover w/inset handle, Jeannette, 48 oz., 5 1/2" h., each **$295-365**

Jeannette Jadite Tea Canister

Canister, Jadite w/"Tea" in black letters, cylindrical ringed shape w/screw-on metal cover, Jeannette, 16 oz., 4 3/4" h. (ILLUS.) **$195**

Canister, light green transparent wide squared shaped w/rounded corners & fluted panels, angled panel on the front w/the label "COOKIES," screw-on metal lid, originally sold w/5 lbs. of coffee & included a label so it could be converted to a cookie jar, Hocking Glass, 6 1/2" w., 8" h. (ILLUS., top next column) **$110**

Canister, milk glass w/Blue Circle decoration & "Cereal," fitted ringed blue cover w/knob handle, Vitrock line by Hocking, rare, 5 1/4" h. (ILLUS. right with Vitrock Flour & Sugar canisters, top next page) **$75-85**

Canister Converted to a Cookie Jar

Canister, milk glass w/Blue Circle decoration & "Flour," fitted ringed blue cover w/knob handle, Vitrock line by Hocking, 5 1/4" h. (ILLUS. left with Vitrock Cereal & Sugar canisters, top next page)............... **$65**

Canister, milk glass w/Blue Circle decoration & "Sugar," fitted ringed blue cover w/knob handle, Vitrock line by Hocking, rare, 5 1/4" h. **$85**

Canister, milk glass w/Blue Circle decoration & "Sugar," fitted ringed white cover w/knob handle, Vitrock line by Hocking, 5 1/4" h. (ILLUS. center with Vitrock Flour & Cereal canisters, top next page) **$65**

Red Ships Canister and Refrigerator Jar

Canister, milk glass w/Red Ships patt., cylindrical w/flat milk glass cover, McKee, 24 oz., 5" d., 3 1/2" h. (ILLUS. top with Red Ships refrigerator jar)........................... **$55**

Group of Three Hocking Vitrock Canisters and Covers

Canister, Skokie Green w/"Coffee" in black block letters, wide cylindrical shape w/flat fitted glass cover, McKee, 6 1/4" d., 6" h. **$235**

Canister, Skokie Green w/"Coffee" in black, square w/screw-on metal top, McKee, 48 oz. **$325**

Canister, Skokie Green w/"Tea" in black, square w/screw-on metal top, McKee, 28 oz., 6 1/4" h. **$255**

Hocking 20 oz. & 40 oz. Paneled Canisters

Canister, green transparent, upright flat panel shape w/scew-on metal lid, Hocking, 20 oz., 6" h. (ILLUS. right with Hocking 40 oz. flat panel canister) **$50**

Hocking Ribbed & Paneled Canisters

Canister, green transparent, upright ribbed & paneled shape w/scew-on metal lid, Hocking, 20 oz., 6" h. (ILLUS. left with Hocking 40 oz. ribbed & paneled canister) **$85**

Canister, green transparent, upright flat panel shape w/scew-on metal lid, Hocking, 40 oz., 8" h. (ILLUS. left with Hocking 20 oz. flat panel canister) **$65**

Canister, green transparent, upright ribbed & paneled shape w/fitted glass lid w/knob handle, Hocking, 40 oz., 9" h. (ILLUS. right with Hocking 20 oz. ribbed & paneled canister) **$100**

Vitrock Blue Circle Sugar Canister

Canister w/original screw-on metal lid, milk glass w/Blue Circle decoration & "Sugar," Vitrock line by Hocking, rare, 5 1/4" h. (ILLUS.) **$115**

Two Jeannette Jadite Canisters

Canisters, Jadite, upright square shape w/flat fitted cover w/inset handle, no label, no sunflower design on the cover, Jeannette, each (ILLUS. of two)................. **$65**

Clear Glass Canning Funnel

Canning funnel, clear, unknown production dates or manufacturer, 4 3/8" across the top & 2" across the bottom, 3" h. (ILLUS.) **$15-20**

Casserole, cov., milk glass w/Gay Fad "Peach Blossom" decoration, clear cover, 1 qt... **$25**

Fire King Gay Fad Fruits Casserole

Casserole, cov., milk glass w/h.p. Gay Fad Fruits design, clear domed cover, Fire King, 8 1/4" d. (ILLUS.)............................. **$28**

Fire King Sapphire Blue Philbe Casserole & Trivet

Casserole, cov., Philbe patt., sapphire blue, Fire King, 8" d. (ILLUS. with matching trivet).. **$20-30**

McKee Glasbake Covered Casserole

Casserole, cov., clear, part of an embossed set from Glasbake, by McKee Glass Company, two-cup capacity, 6" d. across the top, not counting the tab handles (ILLUS.) **$10-12**

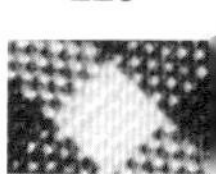

Pyrex "Arsenic" Yellow Casserole

Casserole, cov., oval, "Arsenic" yellow, Pyrex by Corning Glass (ILLUS.) **$12-18**

Fire King Philbe Cereal Bowl/Pie Baker

Cereal bowl or deep pie baker, sapphire blue, Philbe patt., Fire King, 5 3/8" d. (ILLUS.) **$22**

SILEX "Dripolator" Coffeepot

Coffeepot, cov., drip-type, SILEX "2 Cup Dripolator," sapphire, complete with hard-to-find insert, attributed to Anchor Hocking because of sapphire color, but no documentation, 3 piece set (ILLUS.) **$30-45**

Fire King Tulips Cottage Cheese Bowl

Cottage cheese bowl, footed, milk glass w/green Tulips patt., came in four different colors, stackable, Fire King (ILLUS.) **$12-18**

Small Cobalt Blue Chevron Creamer

Cream pitcher, cobalt blue, Chevron patt., rectangular top, Hazel-Atlas, gas station giveaway w/matching sugar bowl, small size, 3 " h. (ILLUS.)................................ **$20-25**

Cream pitcher, cobalt blue, Chevron patt., rectangular top, Hazel-Atlas, large size **$25-30**

Clear Chevron Cream Pitcher

Cream pitcher, clear, Chevron patt., more commonly seen in cobalt, rectangular top 2 1/2 x 4 1/2", to the tip of the spout, Hazel-Atlas, 3 7/8" h. (ILLUS.) **$10-15**

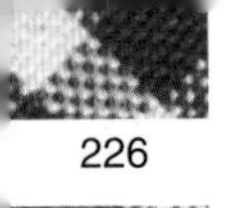

Fire King "Flared" Custard Cup

Custard cup, sapphire blue, Philbe patt. "flared" design, Fire King by Anchor Hocking, w/original label (ILLUS.) **$8-10**

Pyrex Custard Cups w/Original Box

Custard cups, crystal, PYREX, in original box, set of 6 (ILLUS.) **$25-35**

Hazel-Atlas Milk Glass Drippings Jar

Drippings jar, cov., cylindrical milk glass base w/flanged rim, wide flat cover w/a black oval enclosing "DRIPPINGS" in black, uncommon, Hazel-Atlas, 4" d. (ILLUS.) **$95**

Jeannette Delphite Blue Drippings Jar

Drippings jar, cov., Delphite blue, flattened cover w/inset handle, no lettering, Jeannette, 5 1/2" d. (ILLUS.) **$65**

McKee Chalaine Blue Double Egg Cup

Egg cup, double, Chalaine Blue, McKee Glass, 4 1/2" h. (ILLUS.) **$40**

Egg cup, double, clear, Old English Threading design, 1930s, 4 1/4" h. (ILLUS., next page) **$18**

Old English Threading Clear Egg Cup

Fire King Jade-ite Double Egg Cup

Egg cup, double, Jade-ite, Fire King, 4" h. (ILLUS.) **$45**

Egg cup, single, footed, pale green transparent, Hocking, 3 3/8" h. **$25**

Pale Yellow Hocking Egg Cup

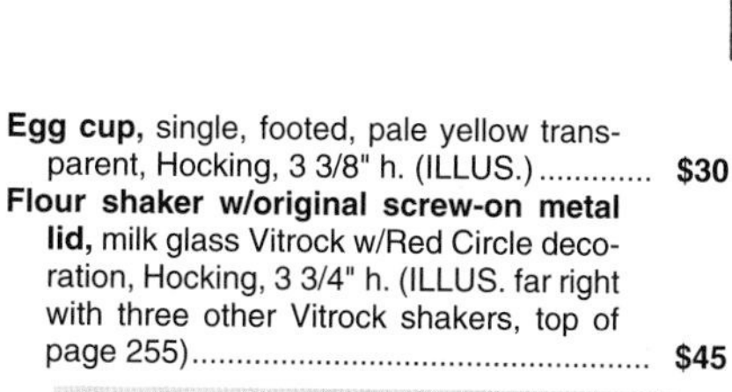

Egg cup, single, footed, pale yellow transparent, Hocking, 3 3/8" h. (ILLUS.) **$30**

Flour shaker w/original screw-on metal lid, milk glass Vitrock w/Red Circle decoration, Hocking, 3 3/4" h. (ILLUS. far right with three other Vitrock shakers, top of page 255) **$45**

Jeannette Jadite Ring Flour Shaker

Flour shaker w/original screw-on metal lid, range-size, cylindrical Jadite ringed shaker w/black block lettering, Jeannette, 5" h. (ILLUS.) **$75**

Evenflo Formula Measuring Pitcher

Fire King Jade-ite Three-Piece Range Set

Formula measuring pitcher, clear w/red enameled name & measurements, Even-flo-made baby feeding accessories, similar shaped & poorly pictured pitchers are advertised in most catalogs of the 1940s, the measurements on the other side are in ounces, up to 32 ounces (ILLUS., previous page) **$18-25**

Grease jar, cov., ivory w/deep flaring sides, decorated in the Apples patt., Fire King, 5 3/4" d. **$75**

Grease jar, cov., ivory w/deep flaring sides, decorated in the Modern Tulips patt., Fire King, 5 3/4" d. **$65**

Grease jar, cov., ivory w/deep flaring sides, decorated in the Pastel Stripes patt., Fire King, 5 3/4" d. **$65**

Grease jar, cov., ivory w/deep flaring sides, decorated in the Red Dots or Black Dots patt., Fire King, 5 3/4" d., each **$75**

Fire King Tulips Pattern Grease Jar

Grease jar, cov., ivory w/deep flaring sides, decorated in the Tulips patt., Fire King, 5 3/4" d. (ILLUS.) **$60**

Fire King Ivory Ringed Grease Jar

Grease jar, cov., ivory wide cylindrical container w/molded rings, scew-on metal cover decorated w/a colorful tulips on flowerpots design, Fire King, 4 1/2" h. (ILLUS.) **$45**

Grease jar, cov., Jade-ite wide cylindrical container w/molded rings, scew-on metal cover decorated w/a colorful tulips on flowerpots design, Fire King, 4 1/2" h. (ILLUS. center with matching range-size salt & pepper shakers, top of page) **$65**

Grease jar, cov., milk glass Vitrock w/the Blue Circle patt., blue or white glass cover, Hocking Glass, 1950s, 6" h. **$75**

Grease jar, cov., milk glass Vitrock w/the green Flowerpots design, domed glass cover, Hocking Glass, 1950s, 6" h. **$95**

Hocking Vitrock Red Circle Grease Jar

Grease jar, cov., milk glass Vitrock w/the Red Circle patt., ringed & domed red glass cover w/large knob, Hocking, 1950s, 6" h. (ILLUS.) **$55**

Hocking Vitrock Red Circle Grease Jar

Grease jar, cov., milk glass Vitrock w/the Red Circle & stylized flower design, screw-on metal cover, Hocking Glass, 1950s, 5 1/2" h. (ILLUS.)............................ **$65**

Hocking Vitrock Flowerpots Grease Jar

Grease jar, cov., milk glass Vitrock w/the red Flowerpots design, domed glass cover w/black & red banding, Hocking Glass, 1950s, 6" h. (ILLUS.) **$45**

Hocking Vitrock Red Tulips Grease Jar

Grease jar, cov., milk glass Vitrock w/the Red Tulips patt., ringed & domed red glass cover w/large knob, Hocking, 1950s, 6" h. (ILLUS.) **$55**

Labeled Green Hocking Drippings Jar

Grease or drippings jar, cov., green transparent, round ribbed base w/paper label reading "Drippings," slightly domed cover w/round inset handle, Hocking Glass, 1930s, 6" d. (ILLUS.) **$75**

Hocking Green Grease/Drippings Jar

Clear Star Pattern Vitex-Glas Knife & Box

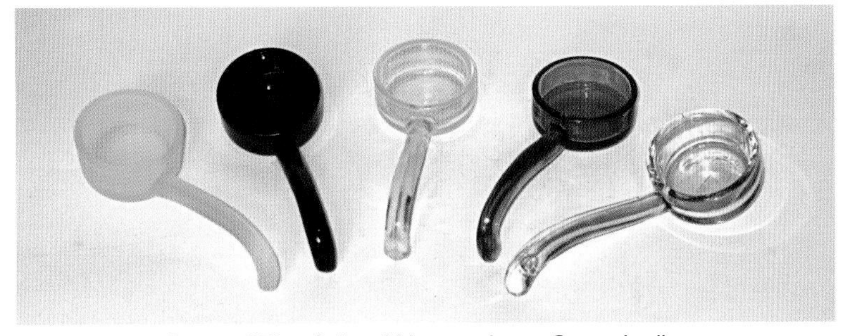

Group of Five Colored Mayonnaise or Sauce Ladles

Grease or drippings jar, cov., green transparent, wide rounded shape w/slightly domed cover centered by a three-part handle, Hocking Glass, 1930s, 5 1/2" d. (ILLUS., previous page) **$55**

Knife, clear Buffalo-type, block handle w/or without h.p. decoration, 9 1/4" l. **$28**

Knife, clear, Star patt., in original Vitex-Glas Knife box marked "Pat Pend - Made in USA," 9" l. (ILLUS., top of page) **$35**

Knife, clear, three leaves & flower patt., Dur-X, 8 1/2" l. **$30**

Knife, green transparent, Areo-Flo, 7 1/2" l. ... **$65**

Knife, pink transparent, three leaves & flower patt., Dur-X, 8 1/2" l. **$45**

Clambroth & Clear Canning Ladles

Ladle, jam or canning-type, clambroth w/round hole in the center of the bowl to allow slow dispensing, 9 1/2" l. (ILLUS. bottom with clear jam or canning ladle) **$35**

Ladle, jam or canning-type, clear w/round hole in the center of the bowl to allow slow dispensing, 9 1/2" l. (ILLUS. top with clambroth jam or canning ladle) **$28**

Ladle, mayonnaise or sauce, amber, 5" l. (ILLUS. second from right with four other ladles, second from top of page) **$25**

Ladle, mayonnaise or sauce, clear, braided handle, Duncan & Miller, 5" l. **$22**

Ladle, mayonnaise or sauce, clear, elongated bowl, Fostoria, 5" l. **$26**

Ladle, mayonnaise or sauce, clear, round flat bowl, 5" l. **$18**

Ladle, mayonnaise or sauce, clear, round flat bowl w/floral cutting, 5" l. **$22**

Ladle, mayonnaise or sauce, clear, shell-shaped bowl, Cambridge, 5" l. **$24**

Ladle, mayonnaise or sauce, ebony, 5" l. (ILLUS. second from left with four other ladles, second from top of page) **$30**

Ladle, mayonnaise or sauce, green frosted, 5" l. (ILLUS. far left with four other ladles, second from top of page) **$45**

Ladle, mayonnaise or sauce, green transparent, 5" l. (ILLUS. third from left with four other ladles, second from top of page) **$26**

Ladle, mayonnaise or sauce, green transparent, elongated bowl, Fostoria, 5" l. **$45**

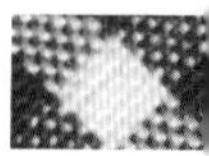

Fire King Philbe Pattern Sapphire Blue Loaf Pan

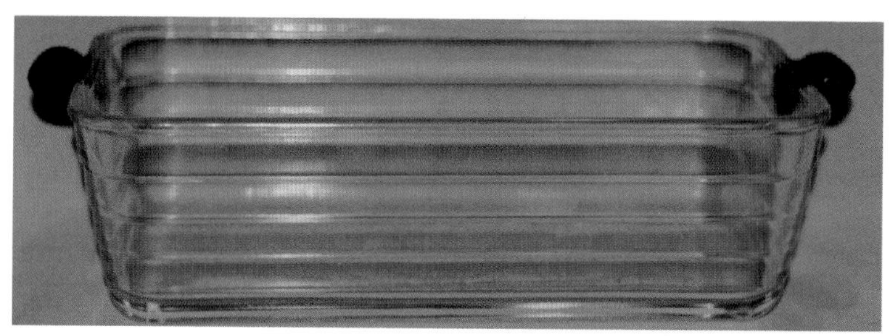

McKee Glasbake Loaf Pan with Red Handles

Ladle, mayonnaise or sauce, milk glass, round bowl, either Westmoreland or Fenton, 5" l. **$25**

Ladle, mayonnaise or sauce, Moonlight blue, shell-shaped bowl, Cambridge, 5" l. **$50**

Ladle, mayonnaise or sauce, pink transparent, 5" l. (ILLUS. far right with four other ladles, second from top previous page) **$26**

Leftover dish, cov., round, Ultramarine, Jenny Ware, flat cover, Jeannette, 32 oz. **$85**

Leftover jar, w/clear lid, decorated post-production w/green, gold & brown leaves, Fire King by Anchor Hocking, perhaps a grocery or department store promotion **$10-15**

Leftover jar, without clear lid, decorated post-production w/green, gold & brown leaves, Fire King by Anchor Hocking, perhaps a grocery or department store promotion (ILLUS. center front w/batter bowl & mixing bowls, top of page 218)....... **$5-8**

Loaf or bread baking pan, sapphire blue, Philbe patt., Fire King, 5 x 9" (ILLUS., top of page) **$18**

Loaf pan, old "Arsenic" yellow, Pyrex by Corning Glass (ILLUS., top next column) **$6-8**

Loaf pan, clear, rectangular ringed sides w/red-painted handles, Glasbake by McKee Glass Co., 5 x 9" (ILLUS., second from top of page) **$8-10**

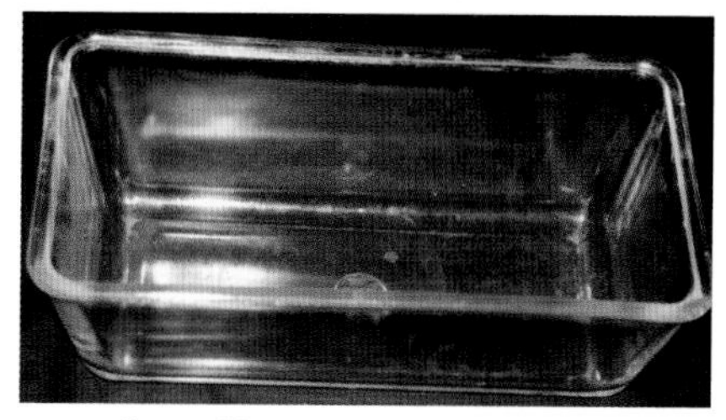

Pyrex "Arsenic" Yellow Loaf Pan

Green Paneled Cylindrical Match Holder

Match holder, cov., light green transparent, cylindrical paneled shape w/domed

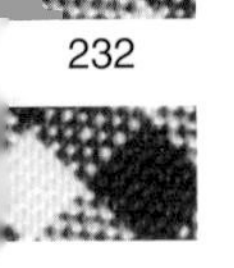

green-painted metal cover, 3 1/2" h. (ILLUS.) **$65**

Match holder, cov., light pink transparent, cylindrical paneled shape w/chrome cover w/cut-out for removing matches, 3 1/2" h. **$55**

Match holder, Delphite blue, cylindrical , no cover, black lettering, Jeannette **$125**

Federal Amber 2-Cup Measuring Cup

Measuring cup, amber, triple-spout, tapering cylindrical sides w/measurements, no handle, two-cup, Federal Glass, 4 3/8" h. (ILLUS.) **$50**

Measuring cup, clear, footed, measurements on the sides & "Measuring and Mixing" pressed into the bottom, two-cup, Hocking Glass, 3 3/4" h. **$25**

Measuring cup, clear, Jenny Ware, ounces marked on tab handle, Jeannette, 1 cup..... **$35**

Measuring cup, clear, triple-spout, tapering cylindrical sides w/measurements, no handle, two-cup, Federal Glass, 4 3/8" h. ... **$35**

Fire-King Commemorative Measuring Cup

Measuring cup, commemorative, clear w/red wording, "Commemorating 50 Years - Fire-King," 1992, 2 cup (ILLUS.) **$15-18**

McKee Custard Two-Cup Measure

Measuring cup, custard, two-cup, McKee, 1930s, 3 1/2" h. (ILLUS.) **$50**

McKee Custard & Red Dots Measuring Cup

Measuring cup, custard w/the Red Dots decoration, two-cup, McKee, 1930s, 3 3/4" h. (ILLUS.) **$165**

Measuring cup, Delphite blue, 1/2 cup, Jeannette, from a set **$55**

Hocking Green Measuring Cup

Measuring cup, green transparent, footed, measurements on the sides & "Measuring and Mixing" pressed into the bottom, two-cup, Hocking Glass, 3 3/4" h. (ILLUS.) **$55**

Hocking Green 1-Cup Measuring Cup

Measuring cup, green transparent, single spout, measurement marking to the rim, arched spout, one cup, Hocking, 3" h. (ILLUS.) **$48**

Hazel-Atlas Green Spouted Measuring Cup

Measuring cup, green transparent, triple-spout, measurements around the sides, one-cup, Hazel-Atlas, 3 3/4" h. (ILLUS.) **$55**

Measuring cup, green transparent, triple-spout, measurements around the sides, marked "Kellogg's" on the bottom, one-cup, Hazel-Atlas, 3 3/4" h. **$58**

Measuring cup, Jade-ite, impressed sunflower in the bottom, two-cup, Jeannette, 3 3/4" h. **$65**

Measuring cup, pink transparent, Jenny Ware, ounces marked on tab handle, Jeannette, 1/2 cup **$60**

Measuring cup, pink transparent, triple-spout, measurements around the sides, marked "Kellogg's" on the bottom, one-cup, Hazel-Atlas, 3 3/4" h. **$65**

Fire King Sapphire Blue 1-Cup Measure

Measuring cup, sapphire blue, single spout, measurements on the sides, one-cup, Fire King (ILLUS.) **$30**

Measuring cup, sapphire blue, triple-spout, measurements on the sides, one-cup, Fire King **$45**

Measuring cup, Skokie Green, two-cup, McKee, 3 3/4" h. **$65**

Jenny Ware Ultramarine Measuring Cup Set

Fire King Jade-ite Measuring Cup Set

Measuring cup set: 1/4, 1/3, 1/2 & 1 cup measures; Jenny Ware, round deep fluted sides w/rim tab handle, ounces marked on the handle, Ultramarine, Jeannette Glass, the nested set (ILLUS., bottom previous page) **$255**

Measuring cup set: 1/4, 1/3, 1/2 & 1 cup size; Jade-ite, marked on the tab handle, Fire King, 1950s, the nested set (ILLUS., top of page) **$225**

Measuring pitcher, footed, clear, wet measures on one side, dry on the other, McKee, four-cup, 1930s, 6" h. **$135**

McKee Seville Yellow Measuring Pitcher

Measuring pitcher, footed, Seville Yellow, wet measures on one side, dry on the other, McKee, four-cup, 1930s, 6" h. (ILLUS.) **$145**

Measuring pitcher, footed, Skokie Green, wet measures on one side, dry on the other, McKee, four-cup, 1930s, 6" h. **$195**

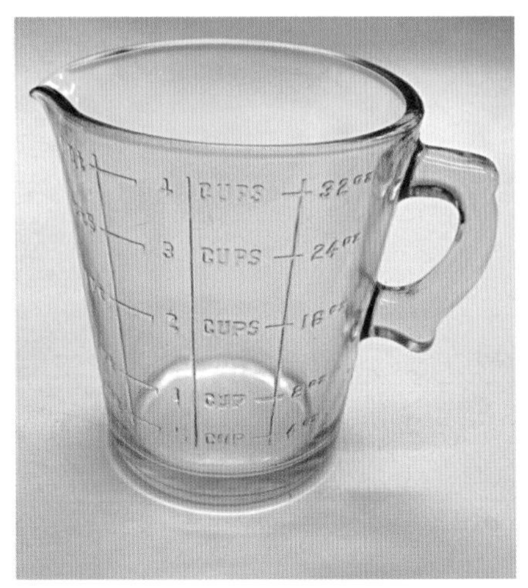

Hocking Green 4-Cup Measuring Pitcher

Measuring pitcher, green transparent, tapering cylindrical sides w/measurement markings, four-cup, Hocking, 6" h. (ILLUS.) ... **$95**

Fire King Chanticleer Spouted Mixing Bowl

Mixing bowl, milk glass w/colorful Chanticleer patt., double-spout rim, Fire King, 2 1/2 qt., 8 3/4" w. (ILLUS.)......................... **$35**

Fire King Red Dots Mixing Bowl

Mixing bowl, milk glass w/the Red Dots patt., Splashproof design w/tapering sides, Fire King, 8 1/2" d. (ILLUS.).............. **$65**

Mixing bowl, part of three-piece set in sapphire blue Philbe patt., referred to as "Utility Bowls" by the company, Fire King by Anchor Hocking, 1942-1948, innovative rolled rim to decrease or prevent rim chips, 6 7/8" d. bowl **$28-30**

Group of Three Decorated Milk Glass Mixing Bowls

Mixing bowl, milk glass w/brown Polka Dots decoration, Hazel-Atlas, 4 3/4" d. (ILLUS. center two larger Pyrex mixing bowls)... **$15**

Jade-ite Swedish Modern Mixing Bowl

Mixing bowl, Jade-ite, Swedish Modern shape by Fire King, smallest size, 5" w. (ILLUS.).. **$65**

Mixing bowl, Jade-ite, Swirl shape, Fire King, 5" d.. **$250**

Mixing bowl, milk glass w/orange Dots decoration, Pyrex, 5 3/4" d. (ILLUS. right with small Hazel-Atlas & larger Pyrex bowls).. **$16**

Two McKee Glass Custard Mixing Bowls in the Red Dots Pattern

Mixing bowl, custard w/the Red Dots patt., McKee Glass Co., 6 1/2" d. (ILLUS. right with larger Red Dots bowl).......................... **$85**

Mixing bowl, green transparent, Rest Well shape w/wide fluted panels around the lower half, wide rolled rim, Hazel -Atlas, 6 1/2" d. **$24**

Mixing bowl, milk glass w/black Gooseberry patt., Pyrex, 6 3/4" d. **$12**

McKee Chalaine Blue Mixing Bowl

Mixing bowl, Chalaine Blue, McKee Glass Co., 7" d. (ILLUS.)....................................... **$75**

Fire King Ivory Bead Edge Mixing Bowl

Mixing bowl, Ivory, Bead Edge shape, Fire King, 7 1/8" d. (ILLUS.).............................. **$35**

Mixing bowl, green transparent, Criss Cross patt., Hazel-Atlas, 7 1/2" d................ **$45**

Fire King Kitchen Aides Pattern Bowl

Mixing bowl, milk glass w/the red Kitchen Aides patt., Splashproof design, shows various kitchen utensils, Fire King, 7 1/2" d. (ILLUS.) **$100**

Fire King Turquoise Splash Proof Bowl

Mixing bowl, turquoise, Splash Proof style, Fire King, 7 1/2" d. (ILLUS.) **$30**

Mixing bowl, custard, bell-shaped, McKee, marked, 8" d. **$40**

Mixing bowl, custard w/Jade green stripes, bell-shaped, McKee, marked, 8" d. **$60**

Fire King Jade-ite Swirl Mixing Bowl

Mixing bowl, Jade-ite, Swirl shape, Fire King, 8" d. (ILLUS.) **$28**

Mixing bowl, milk glass w/the Red Ships patt., bell-shaped, McKee Glass Co., 8" d. **$50**

Federal Amber Ribbed Mixing Bowl

Mixing bowl, amber, deep ribbed sides w/a wide rolled rim, Federal Glass, 8 1/2" d. (ILLUS.)... **$30**

Fire King Modern Tulips Mixing Bowl

Mixing bowl, ivory w/the Modern Tulips patt. in black & red, Splashproof design, Fire King, 8 1/2" d. (ILLUS.) **$55**

Hocking Fluted Green Mixing Bowl

Mixing bowl, light green transparent, deep sides w/fluted panels & a wide rolled rim, Hocking Glass, 8 1/2" d. (ILLUS.) **$35**

Mixing bowl, milk glass w/the Tulips patt., Splashproof design, 8 1/2" d. **$65**

Mixing bowl, turquoise, Splash Proof style, Fire King, 8 1/2" d. **$35**

Mixing bowl, custard w/the Red Dots patt., McKee Glass Co., 9" d. (ILLUS. left with smaller Red Dots bowl, previous page) **$65**

McKee Red Bow Pattern Bowl

Mixing bowl, milk glass w/Red Bow decoration, bell-shaped, McKee, 9" d. (ILLUS.)..... **$65**

Mixing bowl, milk glass w/royal blue Dots decoration, Pyrex, 9" d. (ILLUS. left with small Hazel-Atlas & smaller Pyrex bowls, page 235)... **$18**

Hazel Atlas Black Flowers Mixing Bowl

Mixing bowl, milk glass w/the Black Flowers patt., accented w/thin red orange & yellow rings, Hazel Atlas, 9" d. (ILLUS.) **$50**

Mixing bowl, milk glass w/the Red Ships patt., bell-shaped, McKee Glass Co., 9" d.. **$45**

Mixing bowl, cobalt blue, Criss Cross patt., Hazel-Atlas, 9 1/2" d. **$125**

Mixing bowl, green transparent, deep sides w/convex ribbing, Hazel-Atlas, 9 1/2" d. **$35**

Fire King Tulips Pattern Mixing Bowl

Mixing bowl, ivory w/the Tulips patt., Splashproof design, Fire King, 9 1/2" d. (ILLUS.)... **$65**

Mixing bowl, turquoise, Splash Proof style, Fire King, 9 1/2" d. **$55**

U.S. Glass Pink "Slick Handle" Bowl

Mixing bowl, pink transparent, "slick handle" style, U.S. Glass Co., 10" w. (ILLUS.).......... **$55**

Mixing bowl, part of three-piece set in Sapphire blue Philbe patt., referred to as "Utility Bowls" by the company, Fire King by Anchor Hocking, 1942-1948, innovative rolled rim, to decrease or prevent rim chips, 10 1/8" d. bowl **$32-38**

Mixing bowl, pink transparent, deep sides w/convex ribbing, Hazel-Atlas, 10 1/2" d. ... **$55**

Large Pink Rest Well Mixing Bowl

Mixing bowl, pink transparent, Rest Well shape w/wide fluted panels around the lower half, wide rolled rim, Hazel -Atlas, 10 3/4" d. (ILLUS.) **$55**

Mixing bowl set: cobalt blue, deep sides w/convex ribbing, Hazel-Atlas, 6 1/2" d., 7 1/2" d., 8 1/2" d., 9 1/2" d. & 10 1/2" d., the set **$225**

Mixing bowl set, Jade-ite, Swedish Modern shape by Fire King, 5" w., 6" w., 7 1/4" w. & 8 3/8" w., the set................................... **$325**

Mixing bowl set, milk glass w/brown designs, American Hertiage line, features eagles, cats, weathervanes, corn & more, Pyrex, 5 3/4" d., 7" d. & 9" d., the set **$30**

Mixing bowl set, milk glass w/flaring sides & abstract dot & scroll designs in red, blue, green & yellow, by Federal, mark is an "F" in a shield, the bowls measure 5" d., 6" d., 7" d., 8" d., & 9" d., five-piece set (ILLUS., top next page).................... **$65-75**

Mixing bowl set, yellow on milk glass, green on milk glass, blue on milk glass & red on milk glass, Pyrex, 6 1/2" d., 7 1/2" d., 8 1/2" d. & 10" d., the set............ **$75**

Federal Five-Piece Mixing Bowl Set

Mixing bowls, amber, deep ribbed sides w/a wide rolled rim, Federal Glass, 6 1/2" d., 7 1/2" d., 8 1/2" d. & 9 1/2" d., each **$25-40**

Mixing bowls, decorated post-production w/green, gold & brown leaves, Federal Glass Company, depending on size, each (ILLUS. back left & center w/batter pitcher & leafover jar, top of page 218).. **$10-25**

Mixing bowls, four graduated sizes, four different fired-on colors, 1 pt., 1 qt., 1 1/2 qt. & 2 1/2 qt., Fire King, boxed set **$65-85**

Mixing bowls, Ivory, Swirl shape, Fire King, 6" d., 7" d., 8" d. & 9" d., each................ **$15-25**

Mixing bowls, ivory w/the Modern Tulips patt. in black & red, Splashproof design, Fire King, 6 1/2" d., 7 1/2" d., 8 1/2" d. & 9 1/2" d., each.. **$45-60**

Mixing bowls, ivory w/the Tulips patt., Splashproof design, Fire King, 6 1/2" d., 7 1/2" d., 8 1/2" d. & 9 1/2" d., each....... **$45-65**

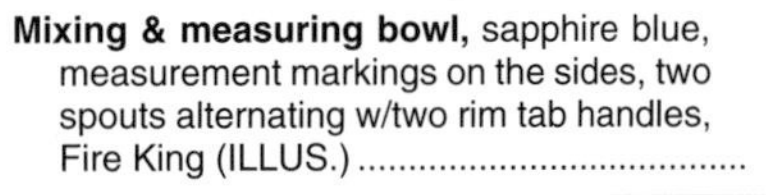

Nested Set of Fire King Jade-ite Swedish Modern Mixing Bowls

Mixing bowls, Jade-ite, Swedish Modern shape by Fire King, graduated set of 4 (ILLUS.)... **$365-400**

Mixing bowls, Jade-ite, Swirl shape, Fire King, 6" d., 7" d., 8" d. & 9" d., each....... **$24-30**

Mixing bowls, light green transparent, deep sides w/fluted panels & a wide rolled rim, Hocking Glass, 6 1/2" d., 7 1/2" d., 8 1/2" d., 9 1/2" d., 10 1/2" d. & 11 1/2" d., each..................................... **$25-45**

Mixing bowls, milk glass w/the Red Dots patt., Splashproof design, Fire King, 6 1/2" d., 7 1/2" d., 8 1/2" d. & 9 1/2" d., each... **$65-75**

Mixing bowls, milk glass w/the red Kitchen Aides patt., Fire King, 6 1/2" d., 7 1/2" d., 8 1/2" d. & 9 1/2" d., each.................... **$75-150**

Mixing bowls, pink transparent, deep ribbed sides w/a wide rolled rim, Federal Glass, 6 1/2" d., 7 1/2" d., 8 1/2" d. & 9 1/2" d., each....................................... **$30-55**

Fire King Sapphire Blue Mixing & Measuring Bowl

Mixing & measuring bowl, sapphire blue, measurement markings on the sides, two spouts alternating w/two rim tab handles, Fire King (ILLUS.)....................................... **$45**

McKee Ivory Mug with Angled Handle

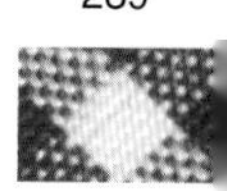

Mug, custard, fancy angled handle, McKee, 3 1/2" h. (ILLUS., previous page)................ **$35**

Rare Green Imperial Paneled Mug

Mug, green transparent, footed flaring & paneled design, Imperial Glass, rare, 5 1/2" h. (ILLUS.) **$65**

Mug, ivory or milk glass, D-style, Fire King, each **$10**

Fire King Jade-ite Mug with D-style Handle

Mug, Jade-ite, D-style, Fire King (ILLUS.)....... **$18**

Mug, Jade-ite, thick restaurant ware, Fire King (ILLUS., top next column) **$28**

Mug, milk glass, tankard-style w/fluted sides, rare, 6 3/4" h. (ILLUS., middle next column) **$55**

Mug, milk glass w/Davy Crocket decoration in brown or red, 1950s, Hazel-Atlas............ **$30**

Mug, milk glass w/decoration of Snoopy (from Peanuts) & "Life is a Joy," Fire King **$45**

Mug, milk glass w/Esso tiger logo decoration, Fire King.. **$13**

Fire King Jade-ite Restaurant Ware Mug

Milk Glass Fluted Tankard-style Mug

Mug, milk glass w/red circus characters decoration, Hazel-Atlas............................... **$24**

Mug, milk glass w/Strawberry Shortcake decoration, Fire King.................................. **$22**

Mug, sapphire blue, Philbe patt., Fire King by Anchor Hocking, "thick" style, perhaps a shaving mug, no rim on the base (ILLUS. left with thin style mug, top next page).. **$35-40**

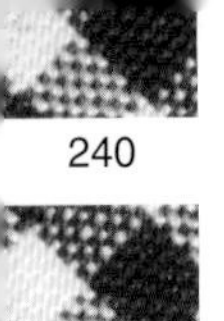

Fire King Thin and Thick Philbe Mugs

Two McKee Skokie Green "Tom & Jerry" Mugs

Mug, sapphire blue, Philbe patt., Fire King by Anchor Hocking, "thin" style coffee mug, pronounced rim on the base (ILLUS. right with thick style mug, top of page)............ **$30-35**

Mug, Skokie Green, marked in black "Tom & Jerry," McKee Glass Co., each (ILLUS. of two, second from top of page)............ **$20-25**

Fire King D-Style Turquoise Mug

Mug, turquoise, D-style, Fire King (ILLUS.) **$30**

Unusual Milk Glass Napkin Holder

Napkin holder, milk glass, upright rectangular shape w/arched end panels, molded on the front w/a circle divided by a bar reading "Nap-O-Fold," 2 1/4 x 4", 4" h. (ILLUS.)... **$125**

Three Milk Glass Pepper Shakers

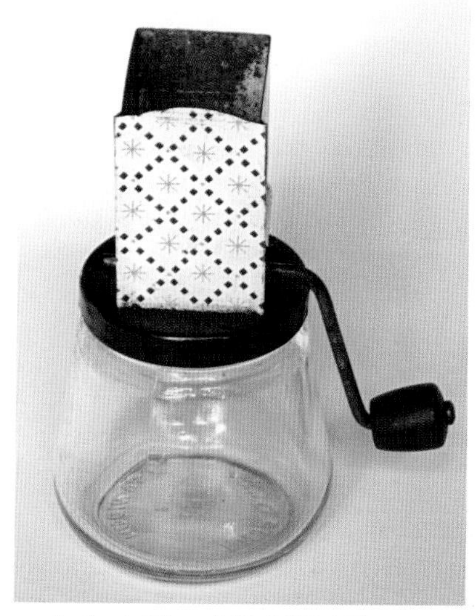

Androck Glass & Metal Nut Chopper

Nut chopper, clear tapering cylindrical jar base w/a scew-on metal top fitted w/a tall square feeder tube decorated w/a blue & ylleow lattice design, side crank handle turns grinders, Androck, 6" h. (ILLUS.) **$35**

Pepper shaker w/original metal lid, range-size, milk glass, square, black scroll design & "White Pepper" on front, 3 1/4" h. (ILLUS. center with two Dutch girl & windmill shakers, top of page) **$12-15**

Tipp City Pepper Shaker with Lady Decor

Pepper shaker w/original scew-on metal lid, range-size, square milk glass decorated on each side w/the black silhouetted figure of a Victorian lady watering flowers & the word "Pepper" in black script, green lid, Tipp City, 4" h. (ILLUS.).... **$45**

Pepper shaker w/original screw-on aluminum lid, range-size, milk glass, square, black Dutch girl & windmill design, (ILLUS. right with two other pepper shakers, top of page) **$18-22**

Pepper shaker w/original screw-on aluminum lid, range-size, milk glass, square, blue Dutch girl & windmill design, 3 1/8" h. (ILLUS. left with two other pepper shakers, top of page) **$20-25**

Two Different Pepper Shakers

Pepper shaker w/original screw-on metal cap, range-size, fired-on green, metal cap, Hocking Glass Company, 4 7/8" h. (ILLUS. left with Scottie pepper shaker, top of page) **$40-45**

Pepper shaker w/original screw-on metal lid, milk glass Vitrock w/Red Circle decoration, Hocking, 3 3/4" h. (ILLUS. second from left with three other Vitrock shakers, top of page 255) **$40**

Jeannette Delphite Blue Pepper Shaker

Pepper shaker w/original screw-on metal lid, range-size, cylindrical Delphite blue ringed shaker w/black block lettering, Jeannette, 5" h. (ILLUS.) **$85**

Pepper shaker w/original screw-on metal lid, range-size, pale pink transparent square shape w/molded looped front panel enclosing "Pepper," Hazel-Atlas, 4 3/4" h. (ILLUS., top next column) **$65**

Pepper shaker w/original screw-on metal lid, range-size, square milk glass decorated w/three small black Scottie dogs w/red bows, red lettering, Hazel-Atlas, 4 3/4" h. (ILLUS., bottom next column) **$50**

Pepper shaker w/original screw-on yellow metal lid, milk glass, black & red Scottie dog design, 3 1/4" h. (ILLUS. right fire-on green pepper shaker, top of page) **$35**

Hazel-Atlas Pink Square Pepper Shaker

Hazel-Atlas Scottie Dog Pepper Shaker

Pie plate, Jade-ite, Philbe patt., juice saver style, Fire King, 10 3/8" d. **$425**

Pie plate, sapphire blue, Philbe patt., Fire King, 9" d. **$15**

Clear Beads & Bars Milk Pitcher

Pitcher, clear, milk size, Beads & Bars patt., part of breakfast set, Hocking Glass, 20 oz. (ILLUS.) **$25**

Jeannette Jadite Pitcher

Pitcher, Jadite, wide spout, angled handle, impressed sunflower in the bottom, Jeannette, 5 1/2" h. (ILLUS.) **$65-75**

Jade-ite Beads & Bars Pattern Pitcher

Pitcher, Jade-ite, milk size, Beads & Bars patt., Fire King by Anchor Hocking, 20 oz. (ILLUS.) **$125-175**

Pink Glass Pudding or Gelatin Mold

Pudding or gelatin mold, pink transparent, deep flaring lobed sides, rare, 5 3/4" d., 3" h. (ILLUS.) **$100**

Tipp City Flower Basket Three-Piece Range Set on Tray

Range set: rectangular milk glass grease jar w/flat red metal cover & matching square salt & pepper shakers, all on a long red metal rectangular tray w/an upright center handle, each piece decorated w/the red & black Flower Basket patt., Tipp City, shakers 2 3/4" h., the set (ILLUS.) **$175**

Fire King Ivory Range Set

Range set: salt & pepper shakers & grease jar; ivory, ringed cylindrical shape w/"Tulip" lids, Fire King by Anchor Hocking, note corrosion of salt lid (difficult to find good condition), the set (ILLUS.)............ **$85-95**

Tipp City Range Set with Rooster Decoration

Range set: salt & pepper shakers & larger sugar & flour shakers; square milk glass decorated w/a Rooster design in black, red & green w/black lettering, Tipp City, salt & pepper 2 3/4" h., flour & sugar 4" h., the set (ILLUS.).. **$135**

Owens Forest Green Diagonally Ribbed Range Set

Range set: salt & pepper, sugar & flour; forest green square shakers w/diagonal ribbing & small printed label for each, original screw-on metal lids, Owens, 4 1/4" h., the set (ILLUS.) **$100**

Tipp City Four-Shaker Range Set with Red, Yellow & Black Flowers

Range set: salt & peppers shakers & flour & sugar shakers all in a metal tray; square milk glass decorated w/a sprig of flowers in red, yellow & black, original metal lids, in a shallow rectangular metal tray w/arched center handle, Tipp City, salt & pepper 2 3/4" h., flour & sugar 4" h., the set (ILLUS.)................................... **$155**

Milk Glass Shaker Set w/Cherry Design

Range set: salt & peppers shakers & flour & sugar shakers w/original screw-on metal lids in fitted black metal latticework holder; square milk glass w/red cherry design, red metal caps, marked "Tipp USA," 3 3/4" h., the set (ILLUS.).. **$95**

Range Shaker Set with Scroll Design

Milk Glass Hazel-Atlas Five-Piece Range Set

Range set: salt & peppers shakers & flour & sugar shakers w/original screw-on metal lids, cylindrical milk glass w/green scroll design above & below "Sugar," "Salt," "Pepper" & "Flour," black metal caps, 3 3/4 to 4 1/2" h., the set (ILLUS., bottom previous page) **$95**

Range set: salt & pepper shakers, sugar shaker & flour shaker, all w/original screw-on metal lids, & a cov. grease jar; square milk glass shakers, each piece w/a black oval enclosing the name, Hazel-Atlas Glass Company, shakers w/"High Hat" tops, 4 1/2" h., the set (ILLUS., top of page) **$250-275**

Two Hocking Green Range Shakers

Range shaker or jar w/original screw-on metal lid, pale green transparent, square w/ribbed sides & a diagonal space for the printed label reading "Flour," Hocking, 10 oz., 5" h. (ILLUS. left with square smooth panel shaker) **$45**

Range shaker or jar w/original screw-on metal lid, pale green transparent, square w/smooth sides, Hocking, 10 oz., 5" h. (ILLUS. right w/ribbed panel shaker)........... **$45**

Fire King Tulips or Apples Range Shakers

Range shakers w/original screw-on metal lids, milk glass, cylindrical shape w/colorful Tulips or Apples decoration, Fire King, 5" h., each (ILLUS.) **$40-45**

Range shakers w/original screw-on metal lids, square milk glass, each printed w/a black oval reserve around name salt, pepper, sugar or flour, Hazel-Atlas, 4 3/4" h., each (ILLUS. of four, top next page).. **$35-45**

Range shakers w/original screw-on metal lids, square milk glass, each printed w/a green oval reserve around name salt, pepper, sugar or flour, Hazel-Atlas, 4 3/4" h., each **$40-48**

Clear & Ultramarine Jenny Ware Shakers

Grouping of Hazel-Atlas Range Shakers with Black Lettering

Ranger shaker w/original screw-on metal lid, clear, Jenny Ware, footed paneled shaped w/silver & black label reading "Pepper," Jeannette, 4 1/4" h. (ILLUS. right with Ultramarine shaker, previous page) **$35**

Ranger shaker w/original screw-on metal lid, Ultramarine, Jenny Ware, footed paneled shaped w/panel for label, Jeannette, 4 1/4" h. (ILLUS. left with clear shaker) **$45**

Clear Criss Cross Water Bottle

Refigerator water bottle, clear, Criss Cross patt. by Hazel Atlas, screw-on metal cap, one-quart capacity (ILLUS.)........ **$35-45**

Refrigerator dish, cov., clear, Criss Cross patt., square, Hazel-Atlas, 8" w. **$45**

Refrigerator dish, cov., clear, design of fruits pressed into the cover, 4" w. **$8**

Refrigerator dish, cov., clear, rectangular, design of vegetables pressed into the cover, 4 x 8" **$14**

Refrigerator dish, cov., cobalt blue, Criss Cross patt., square, Hazel-Atlas, 4" w. **$65**

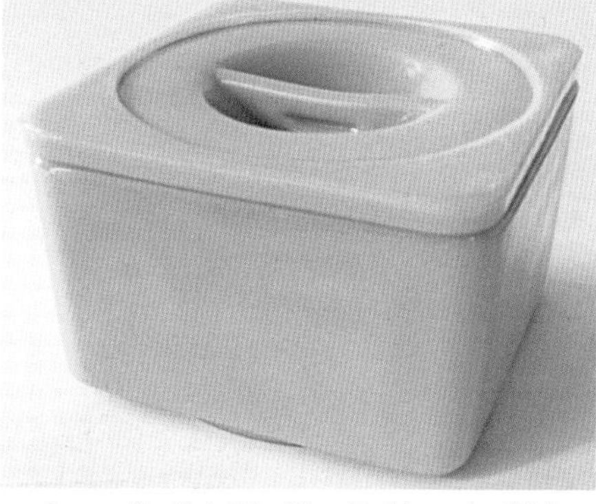

Jeannette Delphite Blue Refrigerator Dish

Refrigerator dish, cov., Delphite blue, square w/flat cover w/inset handle, Jeannette, 4 1/2" w., 2 3/4" h. (ILLUS.) **$55**

Refrigerator dish, cov., green transparent, Criss Cross patt., rectangular, Hazel-Atlas, 4 x 8" **$65**

Hocking Green Refrigerator Dish

Refrigerator dish, cov., green transparent, cylindrical w/flat cover w/inset handle, Hocking, 6 1/4" d., 4" h. (ILLUS., previous page) $65

Refrigerator dish, cov., Jade-ite, Philbe patt., rectangular, Fire King, 4 1/2 x 9"........ $65

Refrigerator dish, cov., Jade-ite, Philbe patt., square, Fire King, 4 1/2 x 5" $45

Refrigerator dish, cov., Jadite, rectangular w/flat cover w/inset handle, Jeannette, 5 x 9" $65

Pink Criss Cross Refrigerator Dish

Refrigerator dish, cov., pink transparent, Criss Cross patt., square, Hazel-Atlas, 4" w. (ILLUS.) $55

Refrigerator dish, cov., rectangular, blue over milk glass base & clear cover, Pyrex, 3 1/2 x 4 3/4" $18

Hazel-Atlas Banded Refrigerator Dish

Refrigerator dish, cov., round, milk glass w/the base & domed cover decorated w/narrow bands in gold, red & black, Hazel-Atlas (ILLUS.) $45

Refrigerator dish, cov., sapphire blue, Philbe patt., square, Fire King, 4 1/2 x 5" ... $35

Clear Criss Cross Refrigerator Jar

Refrigerator jar, cov., clear, Criss Cross patt., Hazel Atlas, 4 x 4" (ILLUS.) $25-35

Refrigerator jar, cov., rectangular milk glass w/blue-printed decoration & clear cover, Pyrex, manufactured by Corning Glass Company, beginning in 1940 & only recently discontinued, 1 1/2 pint (ILLUS. center with 1 1/2 cup jars, top next page) $12-15

Pyrex "Bluebelle" Refrigerator Jar

Refrigerator jar, cov., squared shape, "Bluebelle" line in Canadian blue, Pyrex by Corning, scarce, 3 1/2 x 4 3/4" (ILLUS.)........... $20-25

Refrigerator jar, milk glass w/clear cover, Gay Fad hand-painted patt., decorated w/peach blossoms, Fire King by Anchor Hocking, bought by Gay Fad Studios of Lancaster, Ohio & hand-painted for resale, late 1950s & 1960s, large size, 4 x 8" (ILLUS. bottom with two small fruit-decorated jars, bottom next page) $25-35

Grouping of Pyrex Refrigerator Jars

Fire King Hand-painted Gay Fad Refrigerator Jars

Refrigerator jar, milk glass w/Red Ships patt., rectangular w/flat milk glass cover, 4 x 8" (ILLUS. bottom with Red Ships canister, page 222) **$45**

Refrigerator jar, cov., sapphire blue, Philbe patt., Fire King by Anchor Hocking, 1942-1948, large size, 4 x 8" (ILLUS. bottom with two smaller jars, top next page) **$25-30**

Refrigerator jars, cov., square w/clear glass lids, each in milk glass w/fired-on exterior colors including yellow, maroon, blue & red, Pyrex, manufactured by Corning Glass Company, beginning in 1940 & only recently discontinued, 1 1/2 cup size, each (ILLUS. left & right with 1 1/2 pt. jar, top of page) **$10-12**

Refrigerator jars, milk glass w/clear covers, Gay Fad hand-painted patt., decorated w/fruits, Fire King by Anchor Hocking, bought by Gay Fad Studios of Lancaster, Ohio & hand-painted for resale, late 1950s & 1960s, small size, 4 x 4" each (ILLUS. top with long Gay Fad peach blossom jar, second from top of page)... **$20**

Refrigerator jars, cov., sapphire blue, Philbe patt., Fire King by Anchor Hocking, 1942-1948, small size 4 x 4", each (ILLUS. top with long refrigerator jar, top next page).. **$20-25**

Refrigerator or leftover jar, milk glass base w/clear cover, newer thinner jar w/plain sides, Fire King, Anchor Hocking, ca. 1950s, small 4 x 4" (ILLUS. top left with other Jade-ite jar and larger Jade-ite jar, center next page) **$15-20**

Refrigerator or leftover jar, cov., Jadeite, rectangular w/flat cover & inset handle, Jeannette Glass Company, large, 4 x 8", 3 3/8" h. (ILLUS. bottom with two smaller jars, bottom next page) **$55-65**

Group of Three Sapphire blue Philbe Pattern Refrigerator Jars

White & Jade-ite Fire King Refrigerator Jars

Refrigerator or leftover jar, Jade-ite base w/clear cover, newer thinner jar w/plain sides, Fire King, Anchor Hocking, ca. 1950s, small 4 x 4" (ILLUS. top right with milk glass and larger Jade-ite jar) **$15-20**

Refrigerator or leftover jar, Jade-ite w/clear cover, newer thinner jar w/plain sides, Fire King, Anchor Hocking, ca. 1950s, large 4 x 8" (ILLUS. bottom with smaller Jade-ite & milk glass jars) **$65**

Refrigerator or leftover jars, Jadeite, squre w/flat covers & inset handles, Jeannette Glass Company, small, 4 x 4", 2 1/2" h., each (ILLUS. top with long jar, bottom of page) **$40-45**

Roaster pan, cov., Philbe patt., sapphire blue, lid & bottom are same piece, Fire King, 8 3/4" d. **$55**

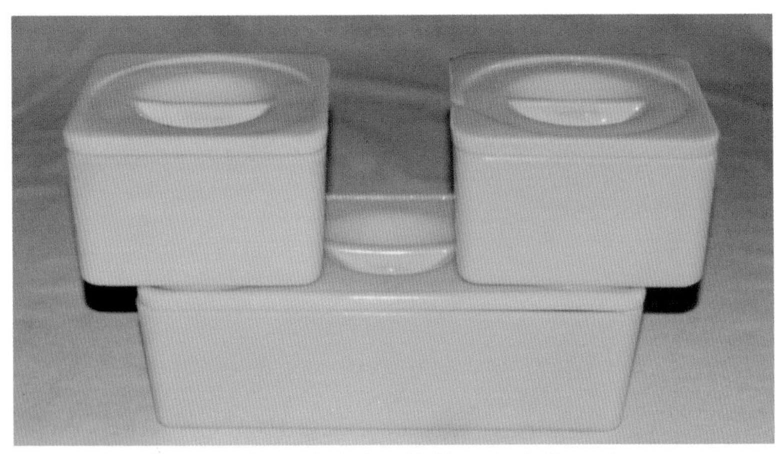
Group og Jeannette Jadeite Refrigerator-Leftover Jars

Fire King Large Philbe Pattern Sapphire Roaster Pan

Roaster pan, cov., Philbe patt., sapphire blue, deep lid version, Fire King, 10 3/4" d. (ILLUS.) **$95**

Rare Green U.S. Glass Salt Box

Salt box, cov., green transparent, footed round & paneled base w/a center-hinged flat chrome cover, larger of two sizes made, U.S. Glass Co., 5 1/2" d., 3 3/4" h. (ILLUS.)... **$285**

Salt box, cov., hanging-type, milk glass half-round shape w/hinged wooden cover, raised back panel w/hanging hole, molded word "SALT" on front, 6 3/4" w., 5" h. **$225**

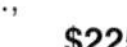

Hoosier-type Clear Rectangular Salt Box

Salt box, Hoosier-type, clear, open rectangular, ribbed sides, 3 1/2 x 6" (ILLUS.) **$45**

Hoosier-style Clear Triple Skip Salt Box

Salt box, Hoosier-type, clear, open round, Triple Skip patt., 4 3/8" d., 3 1/4" h. (ILLUS.) **$65**

Fire King Black Dots Pepper Shaker

Salt or pepper shaker w/original screw-on metal lid, range-size, cylindrical milk glass w/the Black Dots decoration, lid decorated in color w/tulips & the word "Salt" or "Pepper," Fire King, 4 1/2' h., each (ILLUS. of pepper shaker).................. **$45**

Range Size Shakers with Dutch Kids

Salt & pepper shakers w/original metal lids, range-size, square milk glass w/red Dutch Kids skating decoration, Hazel-Atlas, 5" h., pr. (ILLUS.) **$60**

McKee Milk Glass Roman Arches Shakers

Salt & pepper shakers w/original scew-on metal lids, range-size, milk glass Roman Arches shape w/wording in black script, McKee, 4 1/4" h., pr. (ILLUS.) **$65**

Shakers with Gate & Tree Design

Salt & pepper shakers w/original screw-on aluminum lids, range-size, milk glass, square, black gate w/red & black tree & flower design, 3 1/8" h., each (ILLUS.) **$30-35**

Shakers with Blue Circle Design

Salt & pepper shakers w/original screw-on aluminum lids, range-size, milk glass, square, decorated w/blue circles, 3 5/8" h., pr. (ILLUS.) **$45**

Shakers with Apples

Salt & pepper shakers w/original screw-on black metal lids, range-size, milk glass, square, decorated w/red apple & green leaves, 3 1/4" h., each (ILLUS.)... **$20-25**

Tappan Chef Salt & Pepper Shakers

Salt & pepper shakers w/original screw-on black plastic lids, range-size, milk glass, square w/fired-on blue & yellow,

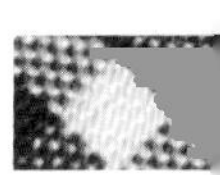

printed black figure of Tappan chef on front, 3 3/4" h., each (ILLUS.) **$25**

McKee Roman Arches Red Sailboats Shakers

Salt & pepper shakers w/original screw-on lids, range-size, milk glass Roman Arches shape w/Red Sailboats decoration, pepper w/original metal lid, salt w/original red plastic lid, McKee, 3 3/4" h., each (ILLUS.).......................... **$30-45**

McKee Black Roman Arches Shakers

Salt & pepper shakers w/original screw-on metal lids, range-size, black Roman Arches shape w/wording in white script, McKee, 4 1/4" h., pr. (ILLUS.) **$75**

Salt & pepper shakers w/original screw-on metal lids, range-size, custard, Roman Arches shape, Red Dots decoration, McKee, rare, 4 1/4" h., the set **$165**

Salt & pepper shakers w/original screw-on metal lids, range-size, cylindrical ivory w/the Modern Tulips decoration, the metal covers painted w/"S" for salt & "P" for pepper, Fire King, pr. **$80**

Salt & pepper shakers w/original screw-on metal lids, range-size, cylindrical milk glass decorated in the Pastel Bands design, repainted lids, Fire King, 4 1/2" h., pr. **$75**

Fire King Tulips Salt & Pepper Shakers

Salt & pepper shakers w/original screw-on metal lids, range-size, cylindrical milk glass w/Tulips decoration, color decoration of tulips on the metal lids, Fire King, the set (ILLUS.)... **$90**

Orange Range-Size Hocking Shakers

Salt & pepper shakers w/original screw-on metal lids, range-size, fired-on orange w/metal caps, round w/ribbed design, black lettering, Hocking Glass Company, 4 3/4" h., each (ILLUS.)................ **$30-35**

Green Salt & Pepper Shakers

Salt & pepper shakers w/original screw-on metal lids, range-size, green trans-

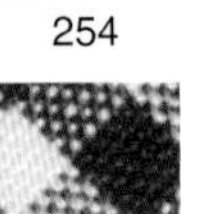

parent glass, square, embossed panel w/ "Salt" & "Pepper," each (ILLUS.) **$65**

Salt & pepper shakers w/original screw-on metal lids, range-size, Jade-ite, cylindrical w/molded rings, metal lids decorated in color w/tulips & the word "Salt" or "Pepper," no wording on the sides, Fire King, pr. (ILLUS. left & right with matching grease jar, page 228) **$85-95**

Jeannette Jadite Ringed Shaker Set

Salt & pepper shakers w/original screw-on metal lids, range-size, Jadite cylindrical ringed shape w/letters in black block letters, Jeannette, 5" h., pr. (ILLUS.)......... **$120**

Hazel-Atlas Blue Windmills Range Set

Salt & pepper shakers w/original screw-on metal lids, range-size, milk glass, square, decorated w/blue windmills & red lettering, red metal lids, Hazel-Atlas, 5" h., pr. (ILLUS.) **$60**

Salt & pepper shakers w/original screw-on metal lids, range-size, milk glass, square printed w/a blue or red Sailboats design & the lettering in red or blue,2 3/4" h., pr. (ILLUS., top next column) **$45**

Milk Glass Salt & Peppers with Sailboats

Shakers with Hat Decoration

Salt & pepper shakers w/original screw-on metal lids, range-size, milk glass, square, red & blue design of "Uncle Sam" hats, 3 1/8" h., pr. (ILLUS.) **$45-55**

McKee Skokie Green Salt & Pepper Shakers

Salt & pepper shakers w/original screw-on metal lids, range-size, Skokie Green Roman Arches shape w/wording in black script, McKee, 4 1/4" h., pr. (ILLUS.) **$145-165**

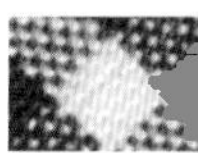
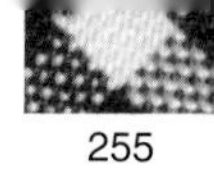

Group of Four Hocking Vitrock Circle Decoration Shakers

Milk Glass Shakers with Tulips

Salt & pepper shakers w/original screw-on white plastic lids, range-size, milk glass, square w/beveled corners, printed w/red & yellow tulip design on front, marked "Made in USA," 3 3/8" h., pr. (ILLUS.) **$30-35**

Salt shaker w/original screw-on metal lid, milk glass Vitrock w/Blue Circle decoration, Hocking, 3 3/4" h. (ILLUS. far left with three other Vitrock shakers, top of page) **$45**

Rare Fire King Kitchen Aides Salt Shaker

Salt shaker w/original screw-on metal lid, range-size, cylindrical milk glass decorated w/the red Kitchen Aides design, features an egg beater, sifter & other utensils, ivory-painted lid w/"S" for salt, rare, Fire King, 4 1/2 h. (ILLUS.) **$150**

Hazel-Atlas Square Green Salt Shaker

Salt shaker w/original screw-on metal lid, range-size, green transparent, square w/a looped front panel framing "SALT," Hazel-Atlas, 4 3/8" h. (ILLUS.) **$60**

Salt shaker w/original screw-on metal lid, range-size, square custard w/a small black rectangle & black lettering, McKee, 5" h. **$45**

Skokie Green McKee Salt Shaker

Group of Four McKee Roman Arches Range-Size Shakers

Hazel-Atlas Ringed Milk Glass Salt or Sugar Shakers

Salt shaker w/original screw-on metal lid, range-size, square Skokie Green w/a small black rectangle & black lettering, McKee, 5" h. (ILLUS., previous page)......... **$75**

Shaker w/original screw-on metal lids, range-size, square Skokie Green w/a small black rectangle & the wording "Pepper," "Flour" or "Sugar," McKee, 5" h., each **$65-85**

Shakers w/original screw-on metal lids, range-size, custard, Roman Arches shape, Red Dots or Green Dots decoration, marked Salt, Pepper, Sugar & Flour, McKee, 4 1/4" h., each (ILLUS. of four, top of page) **$75-95**

Shakers w/original screw-on metal lids, range-size, ringed cylindrical milk glass, each printed in block letters in green, red or black w/either "Salt" or "Sugar," Hazel-Atlas, 4 3/4" h., each (ILLUS. of three, second from top of page) **$40-45**

Scarce Fire King Jade-ite Skillet Dish

Skillet dish, Jade-ite, single spout & side handle, not for stove top use, Fire King by Anchor Hocking, 6 1/4" d. at top, not counting the spout or handle (ILLUS.) **$100-125**

Jeannette Jadite Spice Set

Group of Three Clear Hoosier-style Spice Shakers

Spice set: cinnamon, ginger, pepper, cloves, red pepper & nutmeg; cylindrical ringed Jadite w/a domed metal lid, each w/a gold colored paper label on the front, a red label on the back, Jeannette Glass Co., they contained "Bit Hit" spices from the Euclid Coffee Company, Cleveland, Ohio, 4 1/2" h., each (ILLUS. of the set, bottom previous page) **$35-45**

Spice shaker w/original screw-on metal lid, clear Hoosier-style, cylindrical paneled style w/shield-shaped paper label & middle ring for hanging in a Hoosier cabinet, 3 1/4" h. (ILLUS. left with two other Hoosier-style spice shakers, top of page) ... **$20**

Spice shaker w/original screw-on metal lid, clear Hoosier-style, cylindrical w/no center ring, 3 1/4" h. (ILLUS. right with two other Hoosier-style spice shakers, top of page).. **$18**

Spice shaker w/original screw-on metal lid, clear Hoosier-style, cylindrical w/Triple Skip ribbed patt., 3 1/4" h. (ILLUS. center with two other Hoosier-style spice shakers, top of page) **$22**

Spice shaker w/original screw-on metal lid, clear Hoosier-style, cylindrical w/zipper patt., 3 1/4" h. **$25**

Spice shakers w/original screw-on metal lids, milk glass, square, printed w/Red Cherries decoration & green leaves, printed in red w/the name of the spice such as "Nutmeg," "Paprika," "Ginger" or others, red metal lid, Tipp City, 2 3/4" h., each (ILLUS. of three, bottom of page) **$20-35**

Three Tipp City Red Cherries Spice Shakers

Spice Shakers with Dutch Scenes

Spice shakers w/original screw-on red metal lids, milk glass, square w/beveled corners, each printed w/various blue Dutch scenes on front, paper labels on reverse, red star & name of spice in red letters above scene, 3 1/4" h., each (ILLUS.) **$12-20**

"The Herb Chest" Spice Shakers

Spice shakers w/original screw-on red metal lids, milk glass, square w/beveled corners, each w/printed blue herb designs on front, marked "The Herb Chest" & "Sage," "Rosemary," "Savory," "Bay Leaves," "Marjoram," "Oregano" & "Thyme," 3 3/16" h., each (ILLUS.) **$12-20**

Cobalt Chevron Open Sugar Bowl

Sugar bowl, open, cobalt blue, Chevron patt., Hazel-Atlas, gas station give-away w/the matching creamer, large size, 3 1/2" h. (ILLUS.) **$24-28**

Sugar bowl, open, cobalt blue, Chevron patt., Hazel-Atlas, gas station give-away w/the matching creamer, small size, 3" h. **$20-25**

Clear Hoosier-style Zipper Sugar Shaker

Sugar shaker or muffineer w/original screw-on metal lid, clear Hoosier-style, tapering cylindrical shape w/Zipper patt., shaker top, 4 1/2" h. (ILLUS.)...................... **$45**

Clear Crackle & Ribbed Sugar Shaker

Sugar shaker w/original metal pour top, clear Hoosier-style, cylindrical w/crackle pattern background & clear ribbing, Topping Mfg. Co., New York, New York, 6" h. (ILLUS.).. **$75**

Clear Pear-shaped Ribbed Sugar Shaker

Sugar shaker w/original metal screw-on pour top, clear pear shape w/wide panels & thin ribs, chrome top w/pouring flap, Dripcut Starling Corp., Santa Barbara, California, 5 1/2" h. (ILLUS.) **$35**

Rare Hazel-Atlas Dots Sugar Shaker

Sugar shaker w/original scew-on metal lid, range-size, square milk glass w/blue & black Dots decoration of oval panel w/"Sugar" in black, Hazel-Atlas, rare, 4 3/4" h. (ILLUS.) **$175**

A Variety of Sugar Shakers

Sugar shaker w/original screw-on lid, milk glass w/red metal cap, square, image of black Scottie dog w/red bow sitting on red blanket, 3 1/4" h. (ILLUS. center w/two other sugar shakers, top of page) **$30-35**

Rare Light Green Bullet Sugar Shaker

Sugar shaker w/original screw-on metal base, light green transparent, cylindrical ribbed bullet-shape w/center round pouring opening in the domed top, a screw-on metal bottom, rare, 6" h. (ILLUS.) **$265**

Sugar shaker w/original screw-on metal lid, forest green transparent glass w/domed metal cap, square w/angled ribbing, Owens Illinois, 4" h. (ILLUS. left with Scottie dog & cornucopia shakers, top of page) **$20-25**

Sugar shaker w/original screw-on metal lid, green transparent, cylindrical fluted "rocket" shape w/unusual conical metal dispenser top, marked "Tilt A Spoon Pour - Measuring Device Corp., NY - Pat 1-18-26," rare, 7 1/2" h. (ILLUS., top next column) **$295**

Rare Green Rocket-shaped Sugar Shaker

Green Jeannette Paneled Sugar Shaker

Sugar shaker w/original screw-on metal lid, green transparent, tapering cylindrical paneled body w/a metal shaker top, Jeannette, 4 1/2" h. (ILLUS.) **$145**

Sugar shaker w/original screw-on metal lid, Jadite, tapering cylindrical paneled body w/a metal shaker top, Jeannette, 4 1/2" h. **$195**

Sugar shaker w/original screw-on metal lid, milk glass Vitrock w/Black Circle decoration, Hocking, 3 3/4" h. (ILLUS. second from right with three other Vitrock shakers, page 255) **$45**

Jeannete Jadite Square Sugar Shaker

Sugar shaker w/original screw-on metal lid, range-size, square Jadite shaker w/black block lettering, Jeannette, 5" h. (ILLUS.).. **$65**

Sugar shaker w/original screw-on red metal lid, milk glass, square, multicolored horn of plenty decal, 4 3/8" h. (ILLUS. right w/two other sugar shakers, top previous page) **$15**

Fostoria Mayfair Green Syrup Pitcher

Syrup pitcher & cover, green transparent, Mayfair patt., cylindrical body w/rim spout & shaped loop handle, flat cover w/angled loop handle, Fostoria Glass, 6" h. (ILLUS.)... **$125**

Fine Green Imperial Hand-etched Syrup

Syrup pitcher & cover, green transparent, slightly tapering cylindrical body w/cupped rim w/spout, fancy hand-etched design of flowers & leaves, applied green threaded handle, inset glass cover w/knob finial, Imperial Glass, 6" h. (ILLUS.)... **$195**

Hocking Green Fluted Syrup Pitcher

Syrup pitcher w/clip-on metal cover, green transparent, slightly tapering cylindrical fluted body w/D-form loop handle, spring-hinged top, Hocking, 4 1/4" h. (ILLUS.)....................................... **$65**

Hazel-Atlas Green Tapering Syrup Pitcher

Syrup pitcher w/clip-on metal cover, green transparent, tapering cylindrical body w/optic ribbing & neck ring, small angled handle, spring-hinged top, Hazel-Atlas, 6" h. (ILLUS.) **$68**

Hocking Green Fluted Syrup Pitcher

Syrup pitcher w/clip-on metal cover, green transparent, tapering cylindrical fluted body w/angled handle, spring-hinged top, Hocking, 5 3/4" h. (ILLUS.)....... **$75**

Hazel-Atlas & Cambridge Pink Syrup Pitchers

Syrup pitcher w/clip-on metal cover, pink transparent, bulbous body & cylindrical ringed neck w/small loop handle, tab-hinged metal lid, Hazel-Atlas, 6" h. (ILLUS. left with pink Cambridge syrup)..................... **$95**

Syrup pitcher w/clip-on metal cover, pink transparent, tapering cylindrical body w/applied loop handle, metal lid w/hinged flap over spout, Cambridge, 4 1/4" h. (ILLUS. right with pink Hazel-Atlas syrup) **$115**

Pyrex Teapot w/Blue Handle

Teapot, cov., clear w/blue plastic handle, Pyrex by Corning Glass (ILLUS.)........... **$20-30**

Green Glass "Protecto" Trivet

Trivet, green transparent, round w/a wide ring of thick ribs around the top, indented center impressed "Protecto," for hot pans, 5" d. (ILLUS.) **$25**

Trivet or hot plate, clear, Philbe patt., arched tab handles, Fire King, 8 1/2" d. **$20**

Fire King Sapphire Blue Philbe Pattern Trivet

Trivet or hot plate, sapphire blue, Philbe patt., arched tab handles, Fire King, 8 1/2" d. (ILLUS.) **$30**

Chapter 15

Kitchen Utensils

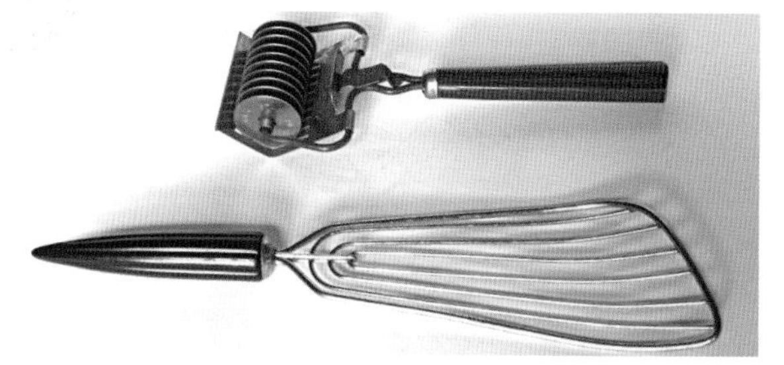

Batter Beater and Noodle Cutter

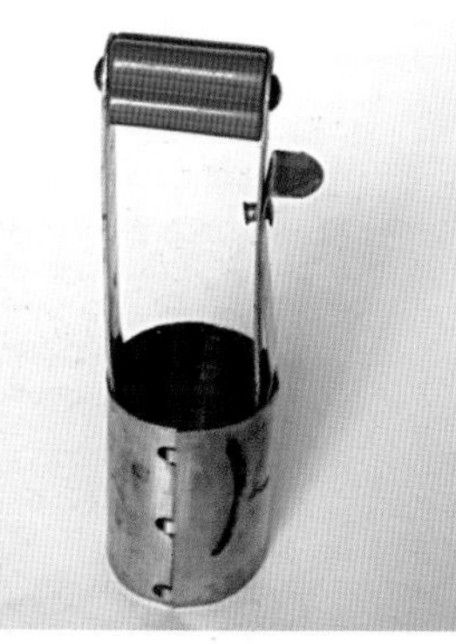

Apple Corer with Bakelite Handle

Apple corer, metal cylindrical plunger blade w/side lever to eject core, ribbed red Bakelite handle, 4 1/4" h. (ILLUS.) **$15**

Baster, long pointed clear glass tube & squeeze rubbe bulb, "Artbeck," Pyrex glass tube, w/original container (ILLUS., top next column) **$15-20**

Batter beater, long flaring wire blade & ribbed black Bakelite handle, 8" l. (ILLUS. bottom with noodle cutter, top of page) **$18**

Cake turner (now called a spatula), wide flat arched stainless steel blade w/window pane cut-outs, wooden handle painted red w/a gold stripe, 12" l. (ILLUS. top with other cake turner, bottom of page) **$13**

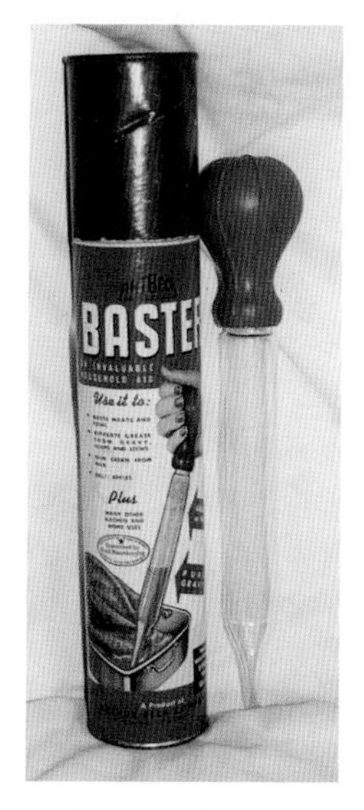

"Artbeck" Baster & Original Container

Cake turner (now called a spatula), wide rectangular metal blade w/crow's foot design of circular cut-outs, slender green swirl Bakelite handle, 12 3/4" l. (ILLUS. bottom with other cake turned, bottom of page) **$18**

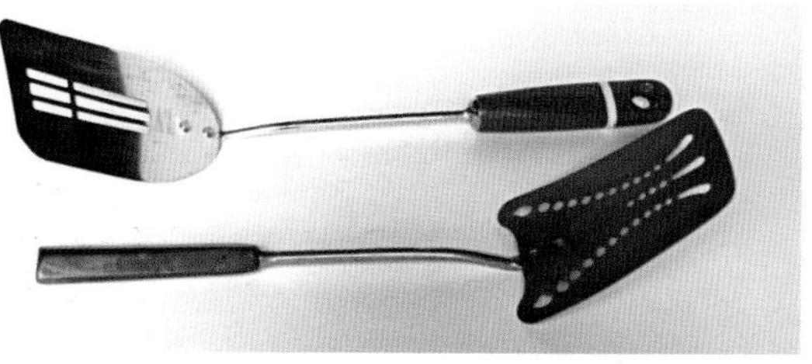

Two Old Cake Turners/Spatulas

Chopper with Four-part Blade

Chopper, four-part flaring metal chopping blade w/a hexagonal red Bakelite handle, 6" l. (ILLUS.) **$16**

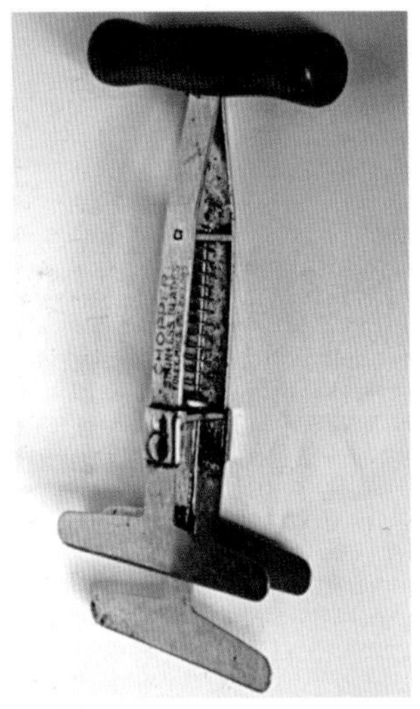

Wood-handled Three-Blade Chopper

Chopper, three narrow metal blades operated by a spring-action mechanism w/a turned red-painted wood handle, 7 1/2" l. (ILLUS.) **$22**

Early Metal Doughnut Cutter

Doughnut cutter, round cylindrical metal w/crimped top edge & center cylindrical tube to form hole, loop wide handle at the side, early 20th c., 2 3/4" l. (ILLUS.) **$25**

Egg beater, hand-held w/push-down action to turn the looped beater, green wood knob handle, 12 1/2" l. (ILLUS., bottom of page) **$25**

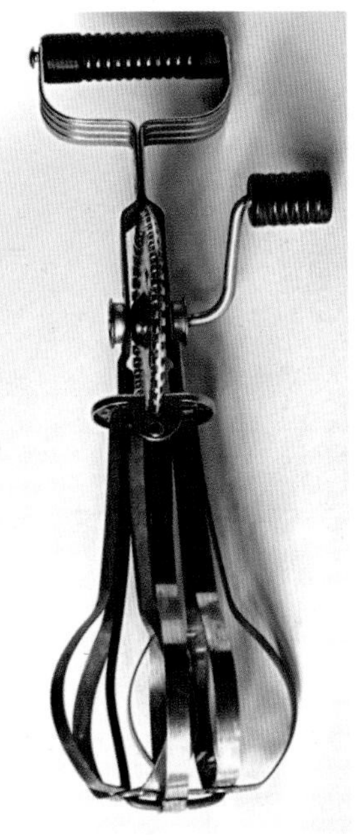

Egg Beater with Red Bakelite Handles

Egg beater, metal blade & crank handle w/ringed red Bakelite knob, ringed red Bakelite hand grip at the top, 12 1/2" l. (ILLUS.) **$25**

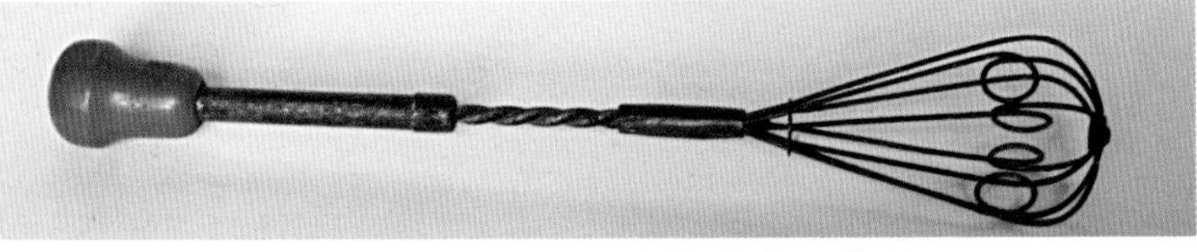

Hand-held Egg Beater with Push-down Action

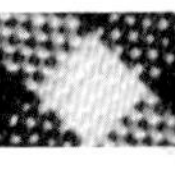

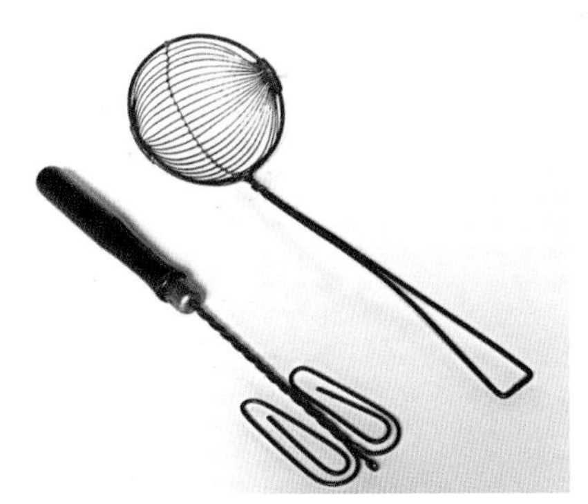

Egg Beater/Drink Mixer and Vegetable Skimmer

Egg beater or drink mixer, Archimedian drill style w/two looped wire blades & twisted wire stem attached to a long turned wood handle, 12 1/2" l. (ILLUS. left with vegetable skimmer)........................ **$35**

All-metal Painted Egg Scale

Egg scale, all-metal, the base painted cream & the weighing mechanism painted jade green, weighs & grades eggs, 8 1/2" l., 6" h. (ILLUS.) **$50**

Old Metal Egg Separator

Egg separator, metal, flanged rim embossed "Mitchell & Co. Kitchen Dept. Haverhill, MA," tab handle w/hole, 3 1/2" w. (ILLUS.).. **$28**

1940s Flour Sifter with Nasturiums

Flour sifter, metal, colorful decoration of orange & yellow nasturiums & green leaves, red plastic handle grip, squeeze-handle operation w/moving screens, 1940s, 6 1/4" h. (ILLUS.) **$28**

Flour Sifter Decorated with Apples

Flour sifter, metal, decorated w/scattered red apples on a white ground, strap handle at back, wire crank handle w/wooden knob turns to move the sifting screens, 1930s-40s, 5 3/4" h. (ILLUS.) **$25**

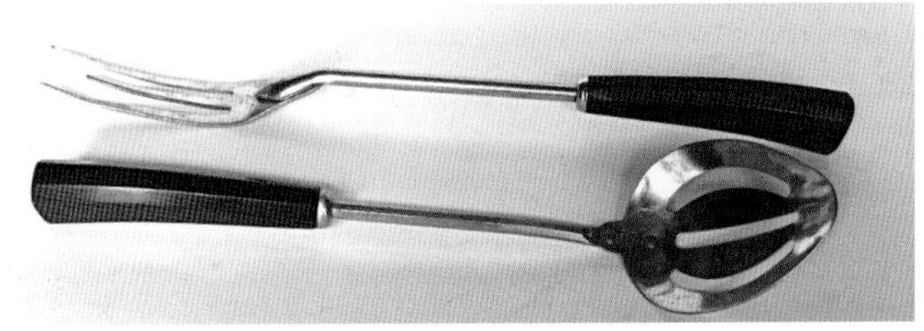

Meat Fork and Slotted Spoon with Bakelite Handles

Four Utensils with Bakelite "Rocket" Design Handles

Meat fork, three-tine w/shorter center tine, red Bakelite faceted handle, 13" l. (ILLUS. top with slotted spoon, bottom previous page) **$16**

Meat fork, two-tine, butterscotch Bakelite handle in the "rocket" design, Androck, 10" l. (ILLUS. bottom with "rocket" spatula and spoons, top of page)......................... **$14**

Sunbeam Mixmaster & Matching Bowl

Mixer & glass bowl, electric, Sunbeam Mixmaster, Chicago Flexible Shaft Co., cream colored metal body, folding handle on stand, came in pink, yellow or blue, matching bowl by McKee Glass, ca. 1960s, the set (ILLUS.) **$45-55**

Noodle cutter, cylinder w/ten round blade in a metal framework, red paneled Bakelite handle (ILLUS. top with batter beater, top of page 263)............................. **$25**

Olive tongs, long slender metal retactable prongs w/a two-color Bakelite olive knob grip, 10 1/4" l. (ILLUS. top with vegetable parer, top next page).................................. **$25**

Pastry blender, arched multiple wire blender attached to a red Bakelite handle w/horizontal ribbing, 5 1/2" w. (ILLUS. bottom with potato masher) **$18**

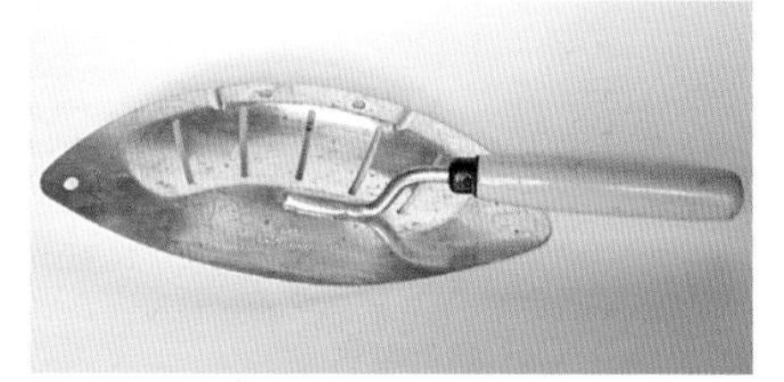

Aluminum and Wood Early Pot Drainer

Pot drainer, curved wedge-shaped aluminum blade w/yellow wood handle, held against side of pot to allow water to drain off, Foley, 11 1/2" l. (ILLUS.)....................... **$25**

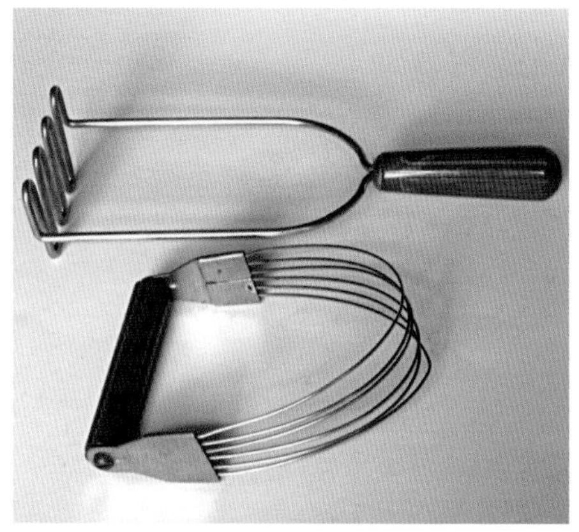

Metal & Plastic Potato Masher and Pastry Blender

Potato masher, tightly undulating metal band attached to long arched metal handles w/a red Bakelite ribbed grip, 10" h. (ILLUS. with pastry blender) **$16**

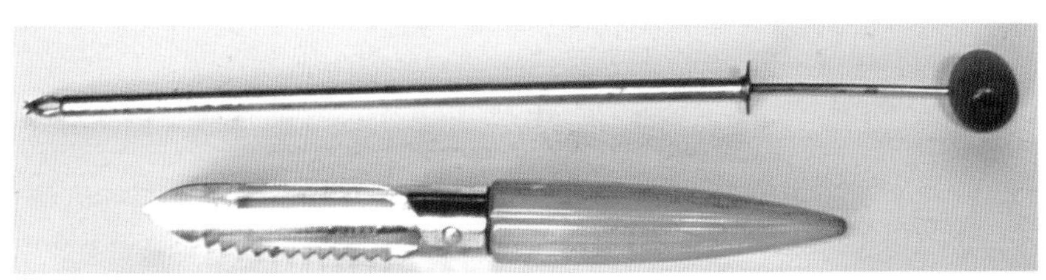

Olive Tongs and Vegetable Parer

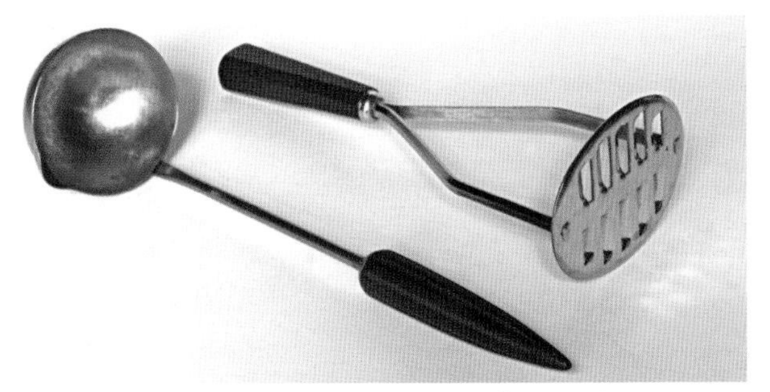

Old Potato-Vegetable Masher and Soup Ladle

Potato or vegetable masher, oval metal slotted plate attached to long slender metal arms joined at the six-sided red Bakelite handle, 9 1/2" l. (ILLUS. top with soup ladle, second from top of page).......... **$17**

Rolling pin, aluminum w/a brushed finish, pink plastic handles, 1960s......................... **$25**

Rolling pin, aluminum w/screw-on aluminum cap at each end, 1950s.................. **$10-20**

Portmeirian China Botanic Gardern Pattern Rolling Pin

Rolling pin, ceramic, closed handles, Botanic Garden decoration, Portmeirian China, 13 1/2" l. (ILLUS.)............................ **$95**

Rolling pin, ceramic, Dainty Flower patt., Harker Pottery Cameoware, blue or pink, each **$60-75**

Rolling pin, ceramic, ivory glaze printed in black w/"Kelvinator," given w/the purchase of a refrigerator, 1940s **$65-95**

Rolling pin, ceramic, ivory glaze w/color decal decoration of cactus & Mexican pots, one handle w/cork closure for adding ice water, other handle w/cut-out for hanging on the wall, Harker China..... **$125-150**

Rolling pin, ceramic, ivory glaze w/color Petit Point decal decoration, one handle w/cork closure for adding ice water, other handle w/cut-out for hanging on the wall, Harker China...................................... **$100-125**

Rolling pin, ceramic, Modern Age/ Modern Tulip patt., Bakerite - HotOven Ware, Harker Pottery, 14 3/4" l. (ILLUS., bottom of page).. **$50-75**

Ceramic Silhouette Pattern Rolling Pin

Rolling pin, ceramic, overall white glass w/black printed Silhouette or Tavern Scene decoration, silver trim on handles, one handle w/cork closure for filling w/ice water, other handle w/cut-out for hanging on the wall, unknown maker but designed to match the Hall China Silhouette patt. (ILLUS.).. **$100-125**

Harker Modern Tulip Rolling Pin

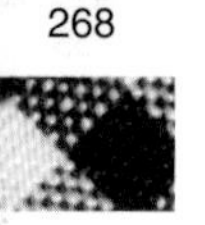

Rolling pin, ceramic, Red Apple I patt., Bakerite/HotOven Ware, Harker Pottery, 14 3/4" l. **$70-90**

Rolling pin, Chalaine Blue glass, one handle w/screw-off metal lid to add ice water, McKee **$500-800**

Rolling pin, clambroth translucent glass, screw-on wooden handles **$150**

Rolling pin, clear glass, hollow w/metal screw-off lid at end of one handle, lid in black w/gold lettering reading "Century of Progress - 1933," souvenir of the Chicago Century of Progress exposition **$55**

Rolling pin, clear glass, hollow w/metal screw-off lid at one end of handle **$15-25**

Rolling pin, Jadite glass, circular bands on handles, one handle w/metal screw-off lid to add ice water, McKee, rare **$1,500**

Rolling pin, milk glass, screw-on metal handles, maker unknown **$100**

Rolling pin, milk glass, wooden handles, mark of the Imperial Mfg. Co., Cambridge, Ohio, 15" l. **$95**

Rolling pin, solid wood, narrow w/no handles, tapering at both ends, designed to work w/fine pastry, ca. 1920, 17" l. **$30-45**

Rolling pin, wooden w/green-painted handles, 1930s **$20**

Rolling pin, wooden w/red-painted handles w/an ivory stripe, 1930s **$25**

Slotted spoon, oblong metal bowl w/curved cut-outs, faceted red Bakelite handle, 12 1/2" l. (ILLUS. bottom with three-tine meat fork, top of page 265) **$14**

Slotted spoon or cake beater, large oblong slotted spoon, butterscotch Bakelite "rocket" design handle, Androck, 1930s-40s, 11" l. (ILLUS. second from top with "rocket" handled meat fork, spatula and other spoon, top of page 266) **$18**

Soup ladle, round metal bowl w/single spout, thin metal handle to the red Bakelite "rocket" form grip, Androck, 11" l. (ILLUS. bottom with the potato or vegetable masher, top of page 267) **$20**

Spatula, narrow long metal blade, butterscotch Bakelite "rocket" design handle, Androck, 1930s-40s, 11" l. (ILLUS. top with "rocket" handled meat fork and spoons, top of page 266) **$14**

Spoon, cooking-type, large oblong solid bowl, butterscotch Bakelite "rocket" design handle, Androck, 1930s-40s, 11" l. (ILLUS. second from bottom with "rocket" handled meat fork, spatula and other spoon, top of page 266) **$16**

Aunt Jemima Plastic Syrup Pitcher

Syrup pitcher, molded plastic, figural Aunt Jemima in red, white & black, F&F Mold & Die Works, Dayton, Ohio, 6" h. (ILLUS.) **$65**

Rare Blue Willow Porcelain Toaster

Toaster, electric, porcelain case in the Blue Willow patt., by Toastrite, central heating panel, on four feet, used only as exhibition piece at its introduction in 1928 (ILLUS.) **$2,300**

Vegetable parer, half-round serrated metal blade w/a butterscotch Bakelite "rocket" form handle, Androck, 7" l. (ILLUS. bottom with olive tongs, top page 267) **$20**

Vegetable skimmer, all-wire w/a round bowl of fine wire attached to a slender wire stem w/angular loop handle, 13" l. (ILLUS. right with eggbeater/drink mixer, page 265) **$28**

Chapter 16

Tea Serving Accessories

People around the world have been drinking tea for centuries, and the brewing of the perfect cup has long been considered an art form. Tea balls, or infusers as they're sometimes called, were used to hold loose tea and hung into the pot or cup to properly steep. Most of the pieces came with a bottom or tray to catch the residual drips of water and tea. When tea bags came into common use and the potential of tea stains persisted, the decorative tea strainer was put into service as an acceptable receptacle even at the most elegant tables.

Tea Strainer with Roses & Heavy Gold

Ceramic, two-part tea strainer, white w/large deep rose red & pink h.p. roses & green leaves w/heavy bands of gold trim, 5" l., 1 1/2" h. (ILLUS.) **$40-55**

Tea Strainer with Blue Flowers

Ceramic, two-part tea strainer, white w/small dark blue flowers & blue border, 5" l., 1 1/2" h. (ILLUS.) **$25-30**

Celadon Green Tea Strainer

Ceramic, two-piece tea strainer, celadon green glaze, marked "Made in Japan," 6" l., 1 1/2" h. (ILLUS.) **$40-50**

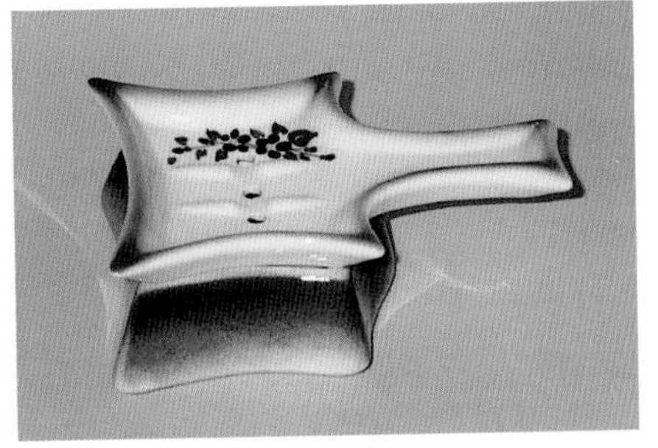

California-made Painted Tea Strainer

Ceramic, two-piece tea strainer, the squared top w/pointed corners & a rectangular tab handle resting on a conforming flaring base, dark blue trim, small h.p. red blossoms & green leaves on the top, marked "Decora Ceramics Handpainted California," 4" l., 1 1/2" h. (ILLUS.)......... **$15-20**

Pansy-shaped Ceramic Tea Strainer

Ceramic, two-piece tea strainer, the top molded as a pansy blossom in purple, yellow & pink w/a green leaf handle, white base, marked "Made in Japan," 4" l., 1 1/4" h. (ILLUS.) **$15-20**

Cobalt-trimmed Tea Strainer

Ceramic, two-piece tea strainer, white w/cobalt blue scalloped border trim & h.p. small blue flowers & green leaves,

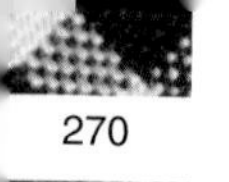

marked "Made in Japan," 6 1/8" l., 2" h. (ILLUS.) **$40-55**

Made in Japan Painted Tea Strainer

Ceramic, two-piece tea strainer, white w/h.p. purple & pink flowers & green leaves w/gold trim, marked "Made in Japan," 5 7/8" l., 1 1/2" h. (ILLUS.) **$35-45**

Rose-decorated Tea Strainer

Ceramic, two-piece tea strainer, white w/printed dark pink roses & green leaves, gold trim, marked "T-103," 3 5/8" l., 1 1/4" h. (ILLUS.) **$15-20**

Nippon Two-piece Tea Strainer

Porcelain, two-piece tea strainer, deep yellow & dark brown h.p. decoration of red trees & gold trim, marked "Hand Painted Nippon," early 20th c., 4 7/8" l., 1 1/4" h. (ILLUS.) **$25-35**

Geisha Girl Porcelain Tea Strainer

Porcelain, two-piece tea strainer, Geisha Girl porcelain decorated w/a central landscape w/Geishas, trimmed w/panels of dark red w/green, pink & blue highlights & ornate gold trim, ca. 1920s, 6" l., 1 1/2" h. (ILLUS.) **$95-125**

Fancy Painted Nippon Tea Strainer

Porcelain, two-piece tea strainer, pale green, pink & yellow ground w/ornate overlaid gold flowers & beading, marked "Nippon Hand Painted," 6" l., 1 5/8" h. (ILLUS.) **$95-125**